Mapping Subaltern Studies and the Postcolonial

MAPPING

This series of readers, published in association with *New Left Review*, aims to illuminate key topics in a changing world.

OTHER TITLES IN THE SERIES:

Mapping Ideology
Edited and introduced by Slavoj Žižek

Mapping the Nation
Edited by Gopal Balakrishnan and introduced by Benedict Anderson

Mapping the West European Left
Edited by Perry Anderson and Patrick Camiller and introduced by Perry Anderson

Mapping the Women's Movement
Edited by Monica Threlfall and introduced by Sheila Rowbotham

Mapping Subaltern Studies and the Postcolonial

Edited and introduced by
Vinayak Chaturvedi

VERSO
London • New York

First published by Verso 2000

Verso
UK: 6 Meard Street, London W1V 3HR
USA: 180 Varick Street, New York NY 10014–4606

Verso is the imprint of New Left Books

ISBN 1–85984–723–4
ISBN 1–85984–214–3 (pbk)

British Library Cataloguing in Publication Data
A catalogue record for this book is available from the British Library

Library of Congress Cataloging-in-Publication Data
A catalog record for this book is available from the Library of Congress

Typeset in 10/12pt ITC New Baskerville by SetSystems Ltd, Saffron Walden, Essex
Printed and bound in Great Britain by Biddles Ltd, Guildford and King's Lynn

Contents

Introduction

This book 'maps the terrain' of the Subaltern Studies project of writings on South Asian history and society. Subaltern Studies was initially conceived as a three-volume series to revise the 'elitism' of colonialists and bourgeois-nationalists in the historiography of Indian nationalism.[1] Today, after the publication of ten volumes, the project has achieved the status of a global academic institution. Whereas the research agenda of Subaltern Studies during the early 1980s was primarily limited to the history of colonial India, later contributions transcend both regional and disciplinary boundaries: by the end of the 1980s, Subaltern Studies was the most dynamic sector within the emerging disciplines of postcolonial theory and cultural studies in the Anglo-American academy. The founding of the Latin American Subaltern Studies Group in 1993,[2] and the proliferation of essays and monographs on 'subalternity' in Africa, China, Ireland, Latin America and Palestine exemplify the spectacular expansion of this originally subcontinental enterprise.[3] However, as the Subaltern Studies project became increasingly influential, its relationship to the heterodox Gramscian Marxism which had informed its founding theoretical charter became increasingly distant. This collection of essays traces the trajectory of Subaltern Studies from the Marxism of its inception, to its current post-Marxist contours, and it critically tracks the history of this transformation.

At the end of the 1970s, Ranajit Guha – the founding editor of *Subaltern Studies* – and a group of young historians based in Britain embarked on a series of discussions about the contemporary state of South Asian historiography.[4] From the onset, the underlying principle which united the group – Shahid Amin, David Arnold, Partha Chatterjee, David Hardiman and Gyanendra Pandey[5] – was a general dissatisfaction with historical interpretations of the 'Freedom Movement' in India which celebrated elite contributions in the making of the Indian nation while denying the 'politics of the people'.[6] At one level, the idea for Subaltern Studies was conceived as a historiographical 'negation' of both a rigidly formulaic 'orthodox' Marxism and the 'Namierism' of the Cambridge School in Britain, both of which failed to account for the dynamic and improvisational modes of peasant political agency.[7] Guha sought to situate the subalternist critique of historiography within a tradition reaching back to the nineteenth century, when Indian intellectuals began publicly debating the relationship of politics to scholarship.[8] Subaltern Studies began as an attempt to transform the writing of colonial Indian history by drawing on the fluid concepts of class and State articulated in the *Prison Notebooks* of Antonio Gramsci.[9] The very name of the project, and title of the series, demonstrated a commitment to further developing the political agenda of this Italian revolutionary socialist. The six-point methodological programme on the history of the subaltern classes in Gramsci's 'Notes on Italian History' was taken up as a framework for writing about and, more distantly, shaping an authentic 'politics of the people'.[10] This was a theoretically self-conscious break from the economic determinism of 'orthodox' Marxist scholarship, and a promise to write histories from 'below' where subaltern classes were the subjects in the making of their own history.

There are three important factors to consider in examining the intellectual origins of Subaltern Studies whose interplay is reflective of the dialectic between Western Marxism and Indian political culture. First is the intellectual influence of Susobhan Sarkar, the eminent Bengali historian who taught Ranajit Guha as a student at Presidency College in Calcutta.[11] Sarkar, to whom Guha dedicated his first book, *A Rule of Property for Bengal*,[12] provided the first comprehensive reception to Gramsci's writings in India.[13] During the late 1950s, at a time when most Marxists in the West were unfamiliar with Gramsci, Sarkar began discussing Gramsci's work with his students.[14] In this same period (1958–59), Guha became Sarkar's colleague in the History Department of Jadavpur University. Sarkar's interest in Gramsci continued through the next decade, as demonstrated by the publication of 'The Thought of Gramsci' in 1968.[15] The availability of English translations of *The Modern Prince and Other Essays* in 1957[16] had generated a small Gramsci-literate public which could read Sarkar's work with critical understanding. Second, the idea for Subaltern Studies took shape in Britain when Gramsci's writings were radically transforming the culture of English Marxism. Already by 1960, Eric Hobsbawm had published *Primitive Rebels*[17] and 'For a History of Subaltern Classes' in the Italian journal *Società*,[18] both works employing Gramscian concepts to analyse peasant societies. Hobsbawm freed the study of 'primitive rebellions' from the categories of crime and backwardness, and this would have a major influence on Guha's seminal *Elementary Aspects of Peasant Insurgency in Colonial India.*[19] From the early 1960s, the writings of Perry Anderson and Tom Nairn in the pages of the *New Left Review* provided the most comprehensive development and critique of Gramscian thought outside Italy.[20] In the 1970s,[21] the reception of Gramsci in Britain extended deep into the intellectual projects of Raymond Williams[22] and Stuart Hall.[23] There was great diversity in the appropriation of Gramsci's often ambivalent conceptual apparatus: Anderson and Nairn were primarily interested in the combined and uneven development of the European State form, while Hall and Williams focused on the authoritarian valences of popular culture and questions of hegemony. Both of these thematic concerns, addressed within the context of colonial India, were central to the project at its inception, and to varying degrees remain so even now. Other similarly oriented influences mingled with Gramsci's and were explicitly registered within the pages of the *Subaltern Studies* series. E. P. Thompson, Christopher Hill and Rodney Hilton belonged to that cluster of British historians whose reconstructions of the historical experiences of workers, peasants and 'common people' revolutionized the study of history the world over.[24] The concern with writing 'histories from below' – part of a self-conscious effort to correct social history's traditional bias for the perspective of the elite classes[25] – was taken up by the subalternists and addressed to the colonial context. Ranajit Guha explicitly made this point in the Preface to the first volume of the series:

> The aim of the present collection of essays, the first of a series, is to promote a systematic and informed discussion of subaltern themes in the field of South Asian studies, and thus help to rectify the elitist bias characteristic of much research and academic work in this particular area . . . The dominant groups will therefore receive in these volumes the consideration they deserve without, however, being endowed with that spurious primacy assigned to them by the long-standing tradition of elitism in South Asian studies. Indeed, it will be very much a part of our endeavour to make sure that our emphasis on the subaltern functions both as a measure of objective assessment of the role of the elite and as a critique of elitist interpretations of that role.[26]

In addition, even if less decisive than the populist agenda of history from 'below', was Robert Brenner's contribution to the long-standing debate on the transition from feudalism to capitalism.[27] Brenner's critique of techno-economic determinism that characterized much Marxist history and theory, placed the struggle at the centre of historical analysis. His emphasis, often referred to as political Marxism, became a central focus of Partha Chatterjee's theoretical opus – 'More on Modes of Power and the Peasantry' – and a defining moment for the project.[28] Chatterjee's contribution to the Brenner Debate, linking Marxian social theory to Foucauldian notions of power within nineteenth- and twentieth-century India, became the primary model for writing about 'community' as the organizing principle for subaltern politics.[29] Third, political developments closer to home mediated and rearticulated these intellectual influences stemming from Britain. Subaltern Studies emerged in the aftermath of a period of Maoist peasant insurgency of Naxalbari and Indira Gandhi's turn towards authoritarianism during the 'Emergency' years of 1975–77.[30] At its origins, the project, while reflecting the 'disillusionment' of the 1970s, was meant to explore the relationship between revolutionary theory and mass struggle in India.[31] This point is clearly exemplified in Ranajit Guha's writings in the early 1980s, as well as in his political associations: not only was he actively involved with Maoist student organizations, but his theorization of the violent nature of subaltern ideology and consciousness reflected the political landscape of the period. For Guha, a new epistemology was required to understand the antinomian dimensions of subaltern politics. Meticulous thick descriptions of insurgency could disclose the otherwise concealed political character of peasant consciousness by reconstructing the vantage point, the spontaneous ideology of the peasant rebel.

In 1982 the project was launched with the publication of *Subaltern Studies I* by Oxford University Press in Delhi. The following three years witnessed the publication of *Subaltern Studies II* (1983), *Subaltern Studies III* (1984) and *Subaltern Studies IV* (1985), as well as Guha's seminal monograph associated with the series – the previously mentioned *Elementary Aspects of Peasant Insurgency in Colonial India* (1983). The first four volumes of the series, under the editorship of Guha, mainly adhered to the programme of writing history from 'below' about nineteenth- and twentieth-century India. Fragmentary episodes illustrating the autonomous politics of the people demonstrated the utility of Gramsci's prescriptions: 'Every trace of independent initiative on the part of subaltern groups should therefore be of incalculable value for the integral historian. Consequently, this kind of history can only be dealt with monographically, and each monograph requires an immense quantity of material which is often hard to collect.'[32] While the general trends of scholarship remained largely in line with Guha's manifesto and sixteen-point critique of historiography, a modest secondary literature developed in India which questioned the consistency of contributors' applications of Gramscian concepts to Indian history. Similarly, criticisms also emerged of the project's claims to writing new, revisionist histories from 'below'. While the early volumes of *Subaltern Studies* had employed the analytical tools of history writing inherited from British Marxist historians, they had signally failed to engage with a long tradition of historical scholarship dating back to the 1940s on themes of peasant rebellion.[33] The first critical reaction to Subaltern Studies thus became known as 'arguments within Indian Marxism',[34] with the most comprehensive discussions being published between 1982–88 in *Social Scientist,* a New Delhi-based journal with links to the Communist Party of India (Marxist).[35] The Indian response focused on the emergence of dividing lines between Subaltern Studies and Marxism. Whereas in the first four volumes primacy was given to the peasant rebel as an autonomous political subject in the making of his own history, by the end of *Subaltern Studies IV* signs of a shift were already present.[36]

By 1986, the Subaltern Studies project was confronted with internal debates about its future development: the tradition of historical materialism had come to be seen by many as a significant, and yet limited, resource for a project which now claimed to contest Eurocentric, metropolitan and bureaucratic systems of knowledge. In addition, what had been an integral part of the project – the search for an essential structure of peasant consciousness – was now no longer acknowledged as valid. The repudiation of that search was, in a sense, a 'post-structuralist moment'.[37] Foucault would from here on loom even larger in subaltern critiques of all traditions which appeared to adhere uncritically to the 'Enlightenment project'.[38] The arrival of Foucauldian and post-structuralist critiques of Marxism resulted in an intellectual bifurcation within the project, with some members continuing to write histories from 'below', and others moving towards various post-Marxist stances.[39] These internal debates within Subaltern Studies reflected the general intellectual climate facing the left: the problem of conceiving an agenda of how to reimagine Marxism within the cultural logic of late capitalism.[40] In a register symptomatic of the political problem at stake here, the Subaltern collective publicly maintained that the presence of ideological differences and 'the lack of any clear "subaltern theory" was a strength rather than a weakness'.[41] *Subaltern Studies V* (1987) and *Subaltern Studies VI* (1989) – also edited by Guha – instantiate the beginnings of the formal shift in the project.[42]

Subaltern Studies, while receiving critical acclaim in India throughout the 1980s, was largely overlooked in North America, and even in a Britain of multiple Marxisms.[43] Meanwhile, the focus of the debates within Indian Marxism continued to address concerns raised from the onset of the dialogues in India. However, by March 1988 the editors of *Social Scientist*, while acknowledging the historiographical contributions of the project, argued that '[s]ome may feel that . . . by now so much has been written on the "subaltern school" that the topic itself has become somewhat stale'.[44] In the same year, Subaltern Studies formally arrived in the Anglo-American academic world with the publication of *Selected Subaltern Studies*[45] – a collection of seminal essays from volumes I–V – and with the first serious discussions of its agendas in British-based journals such as *Modern Asian Studies* and *The Journal of Peasant Studies*.[46] The most systematic engagement with the project came from scholars with ties to the University of Cambridge.[47] Like the reception in India, these scholars, albeit from a variety of intellectual and political positions, posited trenchant critiques which sought to reveal the internal discontinuities between the original manifesto and the practice of writing history. The response in the US, however, was strikingly different. Subaltern Studies became hugely influential in the US academy – something which can be explained, in part, by the ways in which it coincided with the emergence of identity politics and multi-culturalism. In fact, one of the earliest published statements about the project acclaimed it not for its historiographical contributions or political commitments, but celebrated it as 'Indians . . . perhaps for the first time since colonization, showing sustained signs of reappropriating the capacity to represent themselves'.[48] In addition, Edward Said's patronage of the project, in his Foreword to *Selected Subaltern Studies*, coincided with the internal bifurcation of the project as well as with the genesis of the body of literature commonly known as postcolonial theory.[49] It was here that, for the first time since its beginnings, Subaltern Studies was articulated as a postcolonial project.[50] With its arrival in the USA, there was a substantial increase in the influence of literary criticism and postcolonial theory on the subsequent development of the project.[51] Since then, most of the contributions to the *Subaltern Studies* series have moved towards culture, conceived in terms of textual and discourse analysis, and away from the economic base as the central zone of power and contestation.[52] Subaltern Studies, as practised in volumes VII–X (1992–99), has assumed increasingly pronounced post-Marxist forms, as it has accommodated itself to the culturalist atmosphere of US humanities departments.

There is more than a little irony in all this. Whereas Subaltern Studies began as a critical engagement with Marxism in the early 1980s, much of the writing from the collective in the following decade, having shifted methodologically and theoretically, could best be identified with what may be called 'a certain spirit of Marx'.[53] What was initially a project of uncovering subaltern agency and consciousness as a means of revising political histories of the Indian nationalist movement, underwent a shift towards critical theories of discourse which challenged the foundations of Enlightenment thought while attempting to maintain vestiges of a negotiated Marxist past.[54] Where does the project stand today? As a globalized academic institution, its impact has been felt far beyond the reaches of the Anglo-American academy, and is evidenced by its presence in the intellectual cultures of nations such as Bolivia, Japan and Senegal.[55] Subaltern Studies continues its strong ties with India, which remains the sole place of publication for the series. In addition, the project is no longer a solely English-language endeavour and publications are accompanied by translations of essays from the series into regional languages such as Bengali, Hindi and Tamil. The growing dimensions of the project have raised the question of the direction of Subaltern Studies in the context of a world-capitalist economy undergoing globalization and opened up a new series of possible futures. The exigencies of contemporary politics, as seen in the issues of caste, gender and secularism, would have a central role in defining new agendas.[56] Another possibility involves the construction of a critical theory of subalternity which goes beyond the context of colonial India and the nationalist movement, addressing concerns of late-twentieth-century imperialism and the future of new international social movements.[57] It is testimony to the perennial importance of the issues made central by the original Subaltern Studies collective that the problems of agency, subject positions and hegemony constitute to the ontological resistance of all varieties of historical determinism, techno-economic or cultural.

The texts included in this volume represent a balance sheet of the Subaltern Studies project. They provide a panoramic view of the seminal writings emerging from the key theorists of Subaltern Studies between 1982 and 1999. Also included in the collection are selections from distinguished intellectuals specializing in Indian history and politics, whose writings provide a comprehensive assessment of the origins and formal shifts in the project. As a caveat, it may be important to say something about the necessary omissions from the collection. Due to the large secondary literature emerging around the project in recent years, it has been difficult to include all relevant essays which would have made this volume complete. Readers will find that there are no inclusions of essays from the first reception of the project in India, although two later essays are included; it would be otiose to reproduce essays here which comprise a central focus of a forthcoming volume on the histories of dialogue around Subaltern Studies.[58] In making the selections, an attempt has been made not to repeat essays and discussions from the original series. There are two important reasons for such a choice: first, as the members of the collective emphasize their own 'autonomous voices' within the project, it was pertinent to select essays which were published independently of the series and reflected theoretical shifts in the 1980s and 1990s; second, by presuming an audience which was already familiar with the original essays found in the pages of *Subaltern Studies*, this volume was designed to be a companion collection of texts. The essays are organized according to the intellectual trajectory of the project. Theoretical statements from the members of the Subaltern Studies collective are followed in sequence with critiques, thereby providing a historical framework for the discussions and debates centring on the project. With the exception of the first essay by Ranajit Guha from *Subaltern Studies I* and a new interview with Gayatri Chakravorty Spivak, the initial pieces were published in academic journals and edited volumes in India, Britain and the USA. However, it should be emphasized that the essays selected for this volume do not presume a specialized knowledge of Indian history or politics, and can be read independently of the series. The aim is to provide sources for addressing the relationship of Subaltern Studies to contemporary social theory, while also contributing to the ongoing debates in the social sciences and humanities.

The idea for this collection originally emerged in a conversation with Gopal Balakrishnan: as an appreciative postscript, I would like to thank him for his encouragement and meticulous suggestions throughout this venture. The additional two members of the intellectual triumvirate – Robin Blackburn and Sebastian Budgen – have provided fraternal patience and thoughtful guidance in helping bring the book to its final form. I am extremely grateful to Chris Bayly, Casiano Hacker-Cordón, Rosalind O'Hanlon and Shabnum Tejani, whose discussions and detailed comments have helped to improve the overall quality of the text.

Notes

1. Ranajit Guha, 'Preface', *Subaltern Studies IV* (Delhi, 1985), p. vii.

2. Latin American Subaltern Studies Group, 'Founding Statement', *boundary 2*, 20 (Fall, 1993), pp. 110–21.

3. For example, see Daniel Nugent, ed., *Rural Revolt in Mexico. U.S. Intervention and the Domain of Subaltern Politics* (Durham: Duke University Press, 1998); Vincent C. Peloso, *Peasants on Plantations. Subaltern Strategies of Labor and Resistance in the Pisco Valley, Peru* (Durham: Duke University Press, 1998); John Beverley, *Subalternity and Representation: Arguments in Cultural Theory* (Durham: Duke University Press, forthcoming; Walter Mignolo, *Local Histories/Global Designs: Coloniality, Subaltern Knowledge and Border Thinking*

(Princeton: Princeton University Press, forthcoming; J. Rabasa, J. Sanjines, R. Carr, eds, 'Subaltern Studies in the Americas', *disposito/n* 46, XIX (1996); Frederick Cooper, 'Conflict and Connection: Rethinking African History', *American Historical Review* 99 (December 1994), pp. 1516–45; Terence Ranger, 'Subaltern Studies and "Social History"', *South African Review of Books* (February/May 1990), pp. 8–10; Terence Ranger, 'Power, Religion and Community: The Matobo Case', in Partha Chatterjee and Gyanendra Pandey, eds, *Subaltern Studies VII* (Delhi: Oxford University Press, 1992), pp. 221–46; David Lloyd, 'Outside History: Irish Histories and the "Subalternity Effect"', in Dipesh Chakrabarty and Shahid Amin, eds, *Subaltern Studies IX* (Delhi: Oxford University Press, 1996), pp. 260–77; Rosemary Sayigh, 'Gendering the "Nationalist Subject": Palestinian Camp Women's Life Stories', in Gautam Bhadra, Gyan Prakash and Susie Tharu, eds, *Subaltern Studies X* (Delhi: Oxford University Press, 1999), pp. 234–52. For more detailed bibliographic references on Latin American Subaltern Studies, see Florencia Mallon, 'The Promise and Dilemma of Subaltern Studies: Perspectives from Latin American History', *American Historical Review* 99 (December 1994), pp. 1491–515, especially p. 1492, fn. 1, and p. 1500, fn. 20. Also see the Select Bibliography for additional references.

4. Shahid Amin and Gautam Bhadra, 'Ranajit Guha: A Biographical Sketch', in David Arnold and David Hardiman, eds, *Subaltern Studies VIII* (Delhi: Oxford University Press, 1994), p. 224.

5. In addition to Ranajit Guha, these scholars constituted the first editorial collective of *Subaltern Studies. Subaltern Studies I* included only essays from the collective; however, all subsequent volumes also have contributions from scholars working on subaltern themes, but who are not directly associated with the project. By the time *Subaltern Studies II* was published (1983), Dipesh Chakrabarty and Gautam Bhadra were added to the collective. Sumit Sarkar joined by 1984, but departed from the collective by 1994 to become one of its critics. There were no additions until *Subaltern Studies IX* (1996), when Sudipta Kaviraj, Shail Mayaram, M. S. S. Pandian, Gyan Prakash, Ajay Skaria, Gayatri Chakravorty Spivak and Susie Tharu became editorial members. The first six volumes of the series were edited by Ranajit Guha, while the others have been co-edited by two or three members: volume VII by Partha Chatterjee and Gyanendra Pandey, volume VIII by David Arnold and David Hardiman, volume IX by Shahid Amin and Dipesh Chakrabarty, and volume X by Gautam Bhadra, Gyan Prakash and Susie Tharu.

6. See Ranajit Guha, 'On Some Aspects of the Historiography of Colonial India', in Vinayak Chaturvedi, ed., *Mapping Subaltern Studies and the Postcolonial* (London: Verso, 2000).

7. See Dipesh Chakrabarty, 'An Invitation to a Dialogue', in Ranajit Guha, ed., *Subaltern Studies IV* (Delhi: Oxford University Press, 1985), pp. 364–76; David Hardiman, 'The Indian "Faction": A Political Theory Examined', in Ranajit Guha, ed., *Subaltern Studies I* (Delhi: Oxford University Press, 1982), pp. 198–231.

8. Ranajit Guha, 'Preface', *Dominance without Hegemony. History and Power in Colonial India* (Cambridge: Harvard University Press, 1997), pp. ix.

9. See David Arnold, 'Gramsci and Peasant Subalternity in India', in Vinayak Chaturvedi, ed., *Mapping Subaltern Studies and the Postcolonial* (London: Verso, 2000).

10. See Ranajit Guha, 'Preface,' in Ranajit Guha, ed., *Subaltern Studies I* (Delhi: Oxford University Press, 1982), p. vii.

11. For full biographical details, see Shahid Amin and Gautam Bhadra, 'Ranajit Guha: A Biographical Sketch', in David Arnold and David Hardiman, eds, *Subaltern Studies VIII. Essays in Honour of Ranajit Guha* (Delhi, 1994), pp. 222–5.

12. Ranajit Guha, *A Rule of Property for Bengal: An Essay on the Idea of Permanent Settlement* (Paris: École Pratique des Hautes Études, 1963).

13. See Barun De, 'Susobhan Chandra Sarkar', in *Essays in Honour of Professor S. C. Sarkar* (New Delhi: People's Publishing House, 1976), pp. xvii–1; Barun De, 'Susobhan Sarkar (1900–1982) – A Personal Memoir', *Social Scientist*, 11, 2 (1983), pp. 3–15.

14. Henry Schwartz, *Writing Cultural History in Colonial and Postcolonial India* (Philadelphia: University of Pennsylvania Press, 1997), p. 130.

15. Susobhan Sarkar, 'The Thought of Gramsci', *Mainstream* (November 2, 1968). Also see Susobhan Sarkar, 'General President's Address', *Indian History Congress. Proceedings of the Thirty Third Session. Muzaffarpur, 1972* (New Delhi: Sudha Publications), pp. 1–18.

16. Antonio Gramsci, *The Modern Prince and Other Essays*, trans. Louis Marks (London: Lawrence and Wishart, 1957).

17. Eric Hobsbawm, *Primitive Rebels* (originally 1959; Manchester: Manchester University Press, 1971).

18. Eric Hobsbawm, 'Por lo studio delle classi subalterne', *Società* 16 (1960).

19. In this period, Hobsbawm's interpretations of Gramsci's writings were also influential in Italy, especially in the work of Carlo Ginzburg. Although there were important intellectual parallels, especially relating to Gramsci, it should be emphasized that Ginzburg's focus on writing subaltern histories differed from that of Ranajit Guha. See Carlo Ginzburg, 'Witches and Shamans', *New Left Review* 200 (July/August 1993), p. 79; also, Carlo Ginzburg, *The Cheese and the Worms. The Cosmos of a Sixteenth-Century Miller* (Penguin edition, 1987), pp. 129–30, n. 2.

20. For a brief history, see Perry Anderson, 'Forward', *English Questions* (London: Verso, 1992).

21. For a comprehensive listing of publications related to the 1970s writings of Antonio Gramsci, see Aijaz Ahmad, 'Fascism and National Culture: Reading Gramsci in the Days of *Hindutva*', in *Lineages of the Present. Political Essays* (New Delhi: Tulika, 1996), p. 232.

22. Raymond Williams, *Marxism and Literature* (Oxford: Oxford University Press, 1977).

23. Stuart Hall's contributions were originally published in the journal *Marxism Today*. These essays are also reproduced in Stuart Hall, *The Hard Road to Renewal. Thatcherism and the Crisis of the Left* (London: Verso, 1988).

24. See Rajnarayan Chandavarkar, 'The Making of the Working Class: E. P. Thompson and Indian History', in Vinayak Chaturvedi, ed., *Mapping Subaltern Studies and the Postcolonial* (London: Verso, 2000). Except for the influence of E. P. Thompson, the impact of the British Marxist Historians on the origins of the project has never been assessed, especially as the project has moved away from its social history origins.

25. Harvey J. Kaye, *The British Marxist Historians. An Introductory Analysis* (London: Macmillan, 1995), p. 6.

26. Ranajit Guha, 'Preface', *Subaltern Studies I* (Delhi: Oxford University Press, 1982), p. vii.

27. Robert Brenner, 'Agrarian Class Structure and Economic Development in Pre-Industrial Europe', *Past & Present*, 70 (February 1976), pp. 30–75; Robert Brenner, 'The Origins of Capitalist Development: A Critique of Neo-Smithian Marxism', *New Left Review* 104 (July/August 1977), pp. 25–92; Robert Brenner, 'Dobb on the Transition From Feudalism to Capitalism', *Cambridge Journal of Economics*, 2, 2 (June 1978), pp. 121–40. Also, T. H. Aston and C. H. E. Philpin, *The Brenner Debate. Agrarian Class Structure and Economic Development in Pre-Industrial Europe* (Cambridge: Cambridge University Press, 1985).

28. Partha Chatterjee, 'More on Modes of Power and the Peasantry', in Ranajit Guha, ed., *Subaltern Studies II* (Delhi: Oxford University Press, 1983), pp. 311–49.

29. Partha Chatterjee, 'The Nation and Its Peasants', in Vinayak Chaturvedi, ed., *Mapping Subaltern Studies and the Postcolonial* (London: Verso, 2000).

30. For a comment on this point, see Ranajit Guha, 'Introduction', *A Subaltern Studies Reader 1986–1995* (Minneapolis: Minnesota University Press, 1997), p. xi.

31. A critical assessment of this point is raised in Tom Brass, 'Moral Economists, Subalterns, New Social Movements and the (Re-) Emergence of a (Post-) Modernized (Middle) Peasant', in Vinayak Chaturvedi, ed., *Mapping Subaltern Studies and the Postcolonial* (London: Verso, 2000).

32. Antonio Gramsci, *Selections from the Prison Notebooks*, in Quintin Hoare and Geoffrey Nowell Smith, eds and trans. (New York: International Publishers, 1971), p. 52.

33. D. N. Dhanagare, 'Subaltern Consciousness and Populism: Two Approaches in the Study of Social Movements', *Social Scientist*, 16, 11 (1988), pp. 18–35.

34. This point was articulated by Dipesh Chakrabarty, 'Marx after Marxism: A Subaltern Historian's Perspective', *Economic and Political Weekly*, 28, 22 (May 29, 1993), pp. 1094–6. Many of the same debates over questions of structure and agency in the writing of history in the context of English Marxism were taken up around the time Subaltern Studies was conceived. See E. P. Thompson, *The Poverty of Theory and Other Essays* (London: Merlin, 1978); and Perry Anderson, *Arguments within English Marxism* (London: New Left Books, 1979).

35. Suneet Chopra, 'Missing Correct Perspective', *Social Scientist*, 10, 8 (1982), pp. 55–63; Javeed Alam, 'Peasantry, Politics and Historiography: Critique of New Trend in Relation to Marxism', *Social Scientist*, 11, 2 (1983), pp. 43–54; Partha Chatterjee, 'Peasants, Politics and Historiography: A Response', *Social Scientist*, 11, 5 (1983), pp. 58–65; Sangeeta Singh, *et al.*, 'Subaltern Studies II: A Review Article', *Social Scientist*, 12, 8 (1984) pp. 3–41; Partha Chatterjee, 'Modes of Power: Some Clarifications', *Social Scientist*, 13, 2 (1985), pp. 53–60; Kapil Kumar *et al.*, 'Subaltern Studies III & IV: A Review Article', *Social Scientist*, 16, 3 (1988), pp. 3–40; Partha Chatterjee, 'For an Indian History of Peasant Struggle', *Social Scientist*, 16, 11 (1988), pp. 3–17. Also, see Dipesh Chakrabarty, 'Invitation to a Dialogue', in Ranajit Guha, ed., *Subaltern Studies IV* (Delhi: Oxford University Press, 1985), pp. 364–76. For a complete bibliography of the Indian reception, see Select Bibliography.

36. See Bernard Cohn, 'The Command of Language and the Language of Command', and Gayatri Chakravotry Spivak, 'Subaltern Studies: Deconstructing Historiography', in Ranajit Guha, ed., *Subaltern Studies IV* (Delhi: Oxford University Press, 1985), pp. 276–329, 330–63.

37. Partha Chatterjee, 'In Conversation with Anuradha Dingwaney Needham', *Interventions*, 1, 3 (1999), p. 416.

38. Foucault had already exercised considerable influence on at least two prominent Subalternists – Partha Chatterjee and David Arnold. The first concern with Foucault began with a reformulation of the Brenner Debate. Later, Foucault was influential in Subaltern Studies' reception of the post-structuralist critique of Enlightenment reason. One lacuna in the assessment of the project to date is a systematic analysis examining its relationship to Foucault's writings.

39. See Dipesh Chakrabarty, 'Radical Histories and Question of Enlightenment Rationalism: Some Recent Critiques of *Subaltern Studies*', in Vinayak Chaturvedi, ed., *Mapping Subaltern Studies and the Postcolonial* (London: Verso, 2000). Although published in the aftermath of the shift, the following essays demonstrate this point: Dipesh Chakrabarty, 'Marx after Marxism: A Subaltern Historian's Perspective', *Economic and Political Weekly*, 28, 22 (May 29, 1993), pp. 1094–6; and Dipesh Chakrabarty, 'Postcoloniality and the Artifice of History: Who Speaks for "Indian" Pasts?', *Representations* 37 (Winter 1992), pp. 1–26.

40. See Fredric Jameson, *The Cultural Turn. Selected Writings on the Postmodern, 1983–1998* (London: Verso, 1998), especially 'Marxism and Postmodernism', pp. 33–49. Also Fredric Jameson, *Postmodernism or, The Cultural Logic of Late Capitalism* (London: Verso, 1991).

41. David Hardiman, '"Subaltern Studies" at Crossroads', *Economic and Political Weekly* (February 15, 1986), p. 290. This point is also repeated in Ranajit Guha, 'Introduction', *A Subaltern Studies Reader 1986–1995* (Minnesota: Minneapolis, 1997), p. ix.

42. The intellectual trajectory of Subaltern Studies has distant echoes of another twentieth-century school of thought, the Frankfurt School, which also posited critiques of determinist and positivist interpretations of Marxism, and attempted to establish the grounds for a theory of culture on a radical questioning of Enlightenment canons of reason. A comparative study of the Frankfurt School and the Subaltern Studies project, yet to be executed, will contribute to ongoing debates on the nature of Marxism.

43. Exceptions include the following book reviews: Sandria Freitag, *Journal of Asian Studies* 43, 4 (August 1984), pp. 779–80; Lance Brennan, *Pacific Affairs* 57, 3 (Fall 1984),

pp. 509–11; Walter Hauser, *Journal of Asian Studies* 45, 1 (November 1985), pp. 174–7; Anand Yang, *Journal of Asian Studies* 45, 1 (November 1985), pp. 177–8. Scholars examining the international reception of Gramsci's writings were unaware of the project's origins in Britain and development of debates in India. For example, see David Forgacs, 'Gramsci and Marxism in Britain', *New Left Review* 176 (July–August 1989), pp. 70–88.

44. Editorial Note, *Social Scientist* 16, 3 (March 1988), p. 1.

45. Ranajit Guha and Gayatri Chakravorty Spivak, eds, *Selected Subaltern Studies* (New York and Oxford: Oxford University Press, 1988).

46. Rosalind O'Hanlon, 'Recovering the Subject: Subaltern Studies and Histories of Resistance in Colonial South Asia', *Modern Asian Studies* 22, 1 (1988), pp. 189–224; C. A. Bayly, 'Rallying Around the Subaltern', *Journal of Peasant Studies* 16, 1 (1988), pp. 110–20. David Arnold's important statement in the 1984 issue of the *Journal of Peasant Studies* about the subalternist use of Gramscian concepts appears to be an exception in this instance: see 'Gramsci and Peasant Subalternity in India', *Journal of Peasant Studies* 11, 4 (1984), pp. 155–77. All three essays are included in this collection.

Indeed, 1988 was also the publication year of Gayatri Chakravorty Spivak's 'Can the Subaltern Speak?', in Gary Nelson and Lawrence Grossberg, eds, *Marxism and the Interpretation of Culture* (Urbana: University of Illinois Press, 1988), pp. 271–313, an essay which brought issues of gender to the forefront of Subaltern Studies. Gayatri Chakravorty Spivak's 'Subaltern Studies: Deconstructing Historiography', in Ranajit Guha, ed., *Subaltern Studies IV* (Delhi, 1985), pp. 330–63 (also revised for the introduction to *Selected Subaltern Studies*, pp. 3–32), predated 'Can the Subaltern Speak?'; however, it is fair to say that the impact of the latter piece brought forward a major lacuna in the project. In a related development, the publication of *Subaltern Studies IX* (1996) witnessed a methodological shift towards oral history and anthropology, as 'orality', 'voices', and 'speech', in addition to gender issues, became the dominant themes of the volume: see Ranajit Guha's 'The Small Voice of History', Ajay Skaria's 'Writing, Orality and Power in the Dangs, Western India, 1800s–1920s', Kamala Visweswaran's 'Small Speeches, Subaltern Gender: Nationalist Ideology and Its Historiography', Shail Mayaram's 'Speech, Silence and the Making of Partition Violence in Mewat', and Susie Tharu and Tejaswini Niranjana's 'Problems for a Contemporary Theory of Gender'. Spivak's 'Can the Subaltern Speak?' may have provided a major impetus for this shift. From a different vantage point, C. A. Bayly's 'Rallying Around the Subaltern' and Terence Ranger's 'Subaltern Studies and "Social History"', *South African Review of Books* (February/May 1990), pp. 8–10, also raised concerns about methodological limitations of the project.

Included in this book are Gyan Pandey's statement addressing questions of methodology in the project in 'Voices from the Edge: The Struggle to Write Subaltern Histories', and Spivak's comments on the relationship of Subaltern Studies to Marxism and feminism and the project's future in 'The New Subaltern: A Silent Interview'.

47. The most significant of whom include C. A. Bayly, Tom Brass, Rajnarayan Chandavarkar, Rosalind O'Hanlon and David Washbrook.

48. Ronald Inden, 'Orientalist Constructions of India', *Modern Asian Studies*, 20, 3 (1986), p. 445.

49. Edward W. Said, 'Foreword', *Selected Subaltern Studies*, pp. v–x. For example, Said states: 'All in all the first appearance of a selection from *Subaltern Studies* before a general Anglo-American audience is a noteworthy event . . . So in reading this selection from *Subaltern Studies* one becomes aware that this group of scholars is a self-conscious part of the vast post-colonial cultural and critical effort.'

50. For more explicit articulations of this point, see Dipesh Chakrabarty, 'Postcoloniality and the Artifice of History: Who Speaks for "Indian" Pasts?', *Representations* 37 (1992), pp. 1–26; Gyan Prakash, 'Postcolonial Criticism and Indian Historiography', *Social Text*, 31/32 (1992), pp. 8–19; Gyan Prakash, 'Subaltern Studies as Postcolonial Criticism', *American Historical Review*, 99, 5 (1994), pp. 1475–90. Also, see Perry Anderson, *The Origins of Postmodernity* (London: Verso, 1998), pp. 118–20, for a comment on the relationship between the development of postcolonial theory and identity politics.

51. See Sumit Sarkar, 'Orientalism Revisited: Saidian Frameworks in the Writing of Modern Indian History', in Vinayak Chaturvedi, ed., *Mapping Subaltern Studies and the Postcolonial* (London: Verso, 2000).

52. This is not to say that individual members of the collective, or non-members who contribute to the volumes, do not address questions of political economy or global capitalism – implicitly or explicitly – in writings elsewhere. The Sixth Subaltern Studies Conference (Lucknow, 1999) addressed these exact concerns, demonstrating how the recent projects of Chatterjee, Prakash and Spivak are situated within debates on globalization. (See Hiranmay Dhar and Roop Rekha Verma, 'Fractured Societies, Fractured Histories', *Economic and Political Weekly* [May 8, 1999], pp. 1094–7.) It is important, however, to trace the metamorphoses and transferences which have taken place since the emergence of the project, when such issues were addressed in the pages of *Subaltern Studies*. For example, it is worth speculating on the following question: if the emergence of Subaltern Studies and its early volumes reflected the political climate of the 1970s, what then explains the logic of its transformation in the following decades? See Sumit Sarkar, 'The Decline of the Subaltern in *Subaltern Studies*', in Vinayak Chaturvedi, ed., *Mapping Subaltern Studies and the Postcolonial* (London: Verso, 2000).

Perry Anderson's essay on the writings of Carlo Ginzburg illustrates important connections with politics and intellectual discourses, which, rather strikingly, have parallels with the transformations in the Subaltern Studies project. He states: 'Ginzburg's early work reflected the insurgency of the late sixties, whose mass character was more pronounced in Italy than any other European society. It spoke of class culture and repressive tolerance, peasant war and social utopia. With the subsidence of the eighties, the tone has changed.' See Perry Anderson, 'Nocturnal Enquiry: Carlo Ginzburg', in *A Zone of Engagement* (London: Verso, 1992), p. 228.

53. Jacques Derrida, 'Specters of Marx', *New Left Review* 205 (1993), pp. 31–58. Also Jacques Derrida, *Specters of Marx: The State of the Debt, the Work of Mourning, and the New International*, trans. Peggy Kamuf (London: Routledge, 1994).

54. See Gyan Prakash, 'Writing Post-Orientalist Histories of the Third World: Perspectives from Indian Historiography', Rosalind O'Hanlon and David Washbrook, 'After Orientalism: Culture, Criticism and Politics in the Third World', Gyan Prakash, 'Can the "Subaltern" Ride? A Reply to O'Hanlon and Washbook,' in Vinayak Chaturvedi, ed., *Mapping Subaltern Studies and the Postcolonial* (London: Verso, 2000). The essays in this debate focus on the consistency of a coeval application of Marxist theory with post-structuralist-deconstructionist theory by the Subalternists. In a polemical riposte, Prakash attributes O'Hanlon and Washbrook's image of a two-horse rider (one Marxist and the other post-structuralist-deconstructionist) to their propensity towards colonialist interpretations of the inability of the 'Western-educated Indians to ride horses' (Prakash, p. 221). It may be useful to quote M. K. Gandhi to provide an alternative interpretation to the two-horse rider. He states, in a letter written to Purnima Banerjee discussing political strategies: 'What I mean to say is that neither you nor anyone else can ride two horses at the same time' (*Collected Works of Mahatma Gandhi*, Vol. 82, pp. 331–2; originally cited in Partha Chatterjee, *Nationalist Thought and the Colonial World. A Derivative Discourse* [Minneapolis: University of Minnesota Press, 1993], p. 113). Also, see David Washbrook, 'Orients and Occidents: Colonial Discourse Theory and the Historiography of the British Empire', in Robin Winks, ed., *Oxford History of the British Empire, Volume V: Historiography* (Oxford: Oxford University Press, 1999).

55. Dipesh Chakrabarty, 'Reconstructing Liberalism? Notes toward a Conversation between Area Studies and Diasporic Studies', *Public Culture*, 10, 3 (1998), p. 465.

56. Partha Chatterjee, 'In Conversation with Anuradha Dingwaney Needham', *Interventions*, 1, 3 (1999), p. 417. See also Gayatri Chakravorty Spivak, *A Critique of Postcolonial Reason* (Cambridge: Harvard University Press, 1999).

57. These questions are addressed in my paper 'Antinomies of Subalternity and Globalization'.

58. David Ludden, ed., *Reading Subaltern Studies: Perspectives on History, Society, and Culture in South Asia* (Delhi: Oxford University Press, forthcoming).

1

On Some Aspects of the Historiography of Colonial India[1]

Ranajit Guha

1. The historiography of Indian nationalism has for a long time been dominated by elitism – colonialist elitism and bourgeois-nationalist elitism.[2] Both originated as the ideological product of British rule in India, but have survived the transfer of power and been assimilated to neo-colonialist and neo-nationalist forms of discourse in Britain and India respectively. Elitist historiography of the colonialist or neo-colonialist type counts British writers and institutions among its principal protagonists, but has its imitators in India and other countries too. Elitist historiography of the nationalist or neo-nationalist type is primarily an Indian practice but not without imitators in the ranks of liberal historians in Britain and elsewhere.

2. Both these varieties of elitism share the prejudice that the making of the Indian nation and the development of the consciousness – nationalism – which informed this process, were exclusive or predominantly elite achievements. In the colonialist and neo-colonialist historiographies these achievements are credited to British colonial rulers, administrators, policies, institutions and culture; in the nationalist and neo-nationalist writings – to Indian elite personalities, institutions, activities and ideas.

3. The first of these two historiographies defines Indian nationalism primarily as a function of stimulus and response. Based on a narrowly behaviouristic approach this represents nationalism as the sum of the activities and ideas by which the Indian elite responded to the institutions, opportunities, resources, etc. generated by colonialism. There are several versions of this historiography, but the central modality common to them is to describe Indian nationalism as a sort of 'learning process' through which the native elite became involved in politics by trying to negotiate the maze of institutions and the corresponding cultural complex introduced by the colonial

authorities in order to govern the country. What made the elite go through this process was, according to this historiography, no lofty idealism addressed to the general good of the nation but simply the expectation of rewards in the form of a share in the wealth, power and prestige created by and associated with colonial rule; and it was the drive for such rewards with all its concomitant play of collaboration and competition between the ruling power and the native elite as well as between various elements among the latter themselves, which, we are told, was what constituted Indian nationalism.

4. The general orientation of the other kind of elitist historiography is to represent Indian nationalism as primarily an idealist venture in which the indigenous elite led the people from subjugation to freedom. There are several versions of this historiography which differ from each other in the degree of their emphasis on the role of individual leaders or elite organizations and institutions as the main or motivating force in this venture. However, the modality common to them all is to uphold Indian nationalism as a phenomenal expression of the goodness of the native elite with the antagonistic aspect of their relation to the colonial regime made, against all evidence, to look larger than its collaborationist aspect, their role as promoters of the cause of the people than that as exploiters and oppressors, their altruism and self-abnegation than their scramble for the modicum of power and privilege granted by the rulers in order to make sure of their support for the Raj. The history of Indian nationalism is thus written up as a sort of spiritual biography of the Indian elite.

5. Elitist historiography is of course not without its uses. It helps us to know more about the structure of the colonial state, the operation of its various organs in certain historical circumstances, the nature of the alignment of classes which sustained it; some aspects of the ideology of the elite as the dominant ideology of the period; about the contradictions between the two elites and the complexities of their mutual oppositions and coalitions; about the role of some of the more important British and Indian personalities and elite organizations. Above all it helps us to understand the ideological character of historiography itself.

6. What, however, historical writing of this kind cannot do is to explain Indian nationalism for us. For it fails to acknowledge, far less interpret, the contribution made by the people *on their own*, that is, *independently of the elite* to the making and development of this nationalism. In this particular respect the poverty of this historiography is demonstrated beyond doubt by its failure to understand and assess the mass articulation of this nationalism except, negatively, as a law

and order problem, and positively, if at all, either as a response to the charisma of certain elite leaders or in the currently more fashionable terms of vertical mobilization by the manipulation of factions. The involvement of the Indian people in vast numbers, sometimes in hundreds of thousands or even millions, in nationalist activities and ideas is thus represented as a diversion from a supposedly 'real' political process, that is, the grinding away of the wheels of the state apparatus and of elite institutions geared to it, or it is simply credited, as an act of ideological appropriation, to the influence and initiative of the elite themselves. The bankruptcy of this historiography is clearly exposed when it is called upon to explain such phenomena as the anti-Rowlatt upsurge of 1919 and the Quit India movement of 1942 – to name only two of numerous instances of popular initiative asserting itself in the course of nationalist campaigns in defiance or absence of elite control. How can such one-sided and blinkered historiography help us to understand the profound displacements, well below the surface of elite politics, which made Chauri-Chaura or the militant demonstrations of solidarity with the RIN mutineers possible?

7. This inadequacy of elitist historiography follows directly from the narrow and partial view of politics to which it is committed by virtue of its class outlook. In all writings of this kind the parameters of Indian politics are assumed to be or enunciated as exclusively or primarily those of the institutions introduced by the British for the government of the country and the corresponding sets of laws, policies, attitudes and other elements of the superstructure. Inevitably, therefore, a historiography hamstrung by such a definition can do no more than to equate politics with the aggregation of activities and ideas of those who were directly involved in operating these institutions, that is, the colonial rulers and their *élevés* – the dominant groups in native society – to the extent that their mutual transactions were thought to be all there was to Indian nationalism, the domain of the latter is regarded as coincident with that of politics.

8. What clearly is left out of this unhistorical historiography is the *politics of the people*. For parallel to the domain of elite politics there existed throughout the colonial period another domain of Indian politics in which the principal actors were not the dominant groups of the indigenous society or the colonial authorities but the subaltern classes and groups constituting the mass of the labouring population and the intermediate strata in town and country – that is, the people. This was an *autonomous* domain, for it neither originated from elite politics nor did its existence depend on the latter. It was traditional only in so far as its roots could be traced back to pre-colonial times, but it was by no means archaic in the sense of being outmoded. Far

from being destroyed or rendered virtually ineffective, as was elite politics of the traditional type by the intrusion of colonialism, it continued to operate vigorously in spite of the latter, adjusting itself to the conditions prevailing under the Raj and in many respects developing entirely new strains in both form and content. As modern as indigenous elite politics, it was distinguished by its relatively greater depth in time as well as in structure.

9. One of the more important features of this politics related precisely to those aspects of mobilization which are so little explained by elitist historiography. Mobilization in the domain of elite politics was achieved vertically whereas in that of subaltern politics this was achieved horizontally. The instrumentation of the former was characterized by a relatively greater reliance on the colonial adaptations of British parliamentary institutions and the residua of semi-feudal political institutions of the pre-colonial period; that of the latter relied rather more on the traditional organization of kinship and territoriality or on class associations depending on the level of the consciousness of the people involved. Elite mobilization tended to be relatively more legalistic and constitutionalist in orientation, subaltern mobilization relatively more violent. The former was, on the whole, more cautious and controlled, the latter more spontaneous. Popular mobilization in the colonial period was realized in its most comprehensive form in peasant uprisings. However, in many historic instances involving large masses of the working people and petty bourgeoisie in the urban areas too the figure of mobilization derived directly from the paradigm of peasant insurgency.

10. The ideology operative in this domain, taken as a whole, reflected the diversity of its social composition with the outlook of its leading elements dominating that of the others at any particular time and within any particular event. However, in spite of such diversity one of its invariant features was a notion of resistance to elite domination. This followed from the subalternity common to all the social constituents of this domain and as such distinguished it sharply from that of elite politics. This ideological element was of course not uniform in quality or density in all instances. In the best of cases it enhanced the concreteness, focus and tension of subaltern political action. However, there were occasions when its emphasis on sectional interests disequilibrated popular movements in such a way as to create economistic diversions and sectarian splits, and generally to undermine horizontal alliances.

11. Yet another set of the distinctive features of this politics derived from the conditions of exploitation to which the subaltern classes were subjected in varying degrees as well as from its relation to the

productive labour of the majority of its protagonists, that is, workers and peasants, and to the manual and intellectual labour respectively of the non-industrial urban poor and the lower sections of the petty bourgeoisie. The experience of exploitation and labour endowed this politics with many idioms, norms and values which put it in a category apart from elite politics.

12. These and other distinctive features (the list is by no means exhaustive) of the politics of the people did not of course appear always in the pure state described in the last three paragraphs. The impact of living contradictions modified them in the course of their actualization in history. However, with all such modifications they still helped to demarcate the domain of subaltern politics from that of elite politics. The co-existence of these two domains or streams, which can be sensed by intuition and proved by demonstration as well, was the index of an important historical truth, that is, the *failure of the Indian bourgeoisie to speak for the nation.* There were vast areas in the life and consciousness of the people which were never integrated into their hegemony. The *structural dichotomy* that arose from this is a datum of Indian history of the colonial period, which no one who sets out to interpret it can ignore without falling into error.

13. Such dichotomy did not, however, mean that these two domains were hermetically sealed off from each other and there was no contact between them. On the contrary, there was a great deal of overlap arising precisely from the effort made from time to time by the more advanced elements among the indigenous elite, especially the bourgeoisie, to integrate them. Such effort when linked to struggles which had more or less clearly defined anti-imperialist objectives and were consistently waged, produced some splendid results. Linked, on other occasions, to movements which either had no firm anti-imperialist objectives at all or had lost them in the course of their development and deviated into legalist, constitutionalist or some other kind of compromise with the colonial government, they produced some spectacular retreats and nasty reversions in the form of sectarian strife. In either case the braiding together of the two strands of elite and subaltern politics led invariably to explosive situations indicating that the masses mobilized by the elite to fight for their own objectives managed to break away from their control and put the characteristic imprint of popular politics on campaigns initiated by the upper classes.

14. However, the initiatives which originated from the domain of subaltern politics were not, on their part, powerful enough to develop the nationalist movement into a fully fledged struggle for national liberation. The working class was still not sufficiently mature in the

objective conditions of its social being and in its consciousness as a class-for-itself, nor was it firmly allied yet with the peasantry. As a result it could do nothing to take over and complete the mission which the bourgeoisie had failed to realize. The outcome of it all was that the numerous peasant uprisings of the period, some of them massive in scope and rich in anti-colonialist consciousness, waited in vain for a leadership to raise them above localism and generalize them into a nationwide anti-imperialist campaign. In the event, much of the sectional struggle of workers, peasants and the urban petty bourgeoisie either got entangled in economism or, wherever politicized, remained, for want of a revolutionary leadership, far too fragmented to form effectively into anything like a national liberation movement.

15. It is the study of this *historic failure of the nation to come to its own,* a failure due to the inadequacy of the bourgeoisie as well as of the working class to lead it into a decisive victory over colonialism and a bourgeois-democratic revolution of either the classic nineteenth-century type under the hegemony of the bourgeoisie or a more modern type under the hegemony of workers and peasants, that is, a 'new democracy' – *it is the study of this failure which constitutes the central problematic of the historiography of colonial India.* There is no one given way of investigating this problematic. Let a hundred flowers blossom and we don't mind even the weeds. Indeed we believe that in the practice of historiography even the elitists have a part to play if only by way of teaching by negative examples. But we are also convinced that elitist historiography should be resolutely fought by developing an alternative discourse based on the rejection of the spurious and unhistorical monism characteristic of its view of Indian nationalism and on the recognition of the co-existence and interaction of the elite and subaltern domains of politics.

16. We are sure that we are not alone in our concern about the present state of the political historiography of colonial India and in seeking a way out. The elitism of modern Indian historiography is an oppressive fact resented by many others, students, teachers and writers like ourselves. They may not all subscribe to what has been said above on this subject in exactly the way in which we have said it. However, we have no doubt that many other historiographical points of view and practices are likely to converge close to where we stand. Our purpose in making our own views known is to promote such a convergence. We claim no more than to try and indicate an orientation and hope to demonstrate in practice that this is feasible. In any discussion which may ensue we expect to learn a great deal not only from the agreement of those who think like us but also from the criticism of those who don't.

Notes

1. The author is grateful to all the other contributors to *Subaltern Studies I: Writings on South Asian History and Society* as well as to Gautam Bhadra, Dipesh Chakrabarty and Raghabendra Chattopadhyay for their comments on an earlier version of this statement.
2. For a definition of the terms 'elite', 'people', 'subaltern', etc. as used in these paragraphs the reader may refer to the note printed below.

A note on the terms 'elite', 'people', 'subaltern', etc. as used above

The term 'elite' has been used in this statement to signify *dominant* groups, foreign as well as indigenous. The *dominant foreign* groups included all the non-Indian, that is, mainly British officials of the colonial state and foreign industrialists, merchants, financiers, planters, landlords and missionaries.

The *dominant indigenous* groups included classes and interests operating at two levels. At the *all-India level* they included the biggest feudal magnates, the most important representatives of the industrial and mercantile bourgeoisie and native recruits to the uppermost levels of the bureaucracy.

At the *regional and local levels* they represented such classes and other elements as were *either* members of the dominant all-India groups included in the previous category *or* if belonging to social strata hierarchically inferior to those of the dominant all-India groups still *acted in the interests of the latter and not in conformity to interests corresponding truly to their own social being.*

Taken as a whole and in the abstract this last category of the elite was *heterogeneous* in its composition and thanks to the uneven character of regional economic and social developments, *differed from area to area.* The same class or element which was dominant in one area according to the definition given above, could be among the dominated in another. This could and did create many ambiguities and contradictions in attitudes and alliances, especially among the lowest strata of the rural gentry, impoverished landlords, rich peasants and upper-middle peasants all of whom belonged, *ideally speaking,* to the category of 'people' or 'subaltern classes', as defined below. It is the task of research to investigate, identify and measure the *specific* nature and degree of the *deviation* of these elements from the ideal and situate it historically.

The terms 'people' and 'subaltern classes' have been used as synonymous throughout this note. The social groups and elements included in this category represent *the demographic difference between the total Indian population and all those whom we have described as the 'elite'.* Some of these classes and groups, such as the lesser rural gentry, impoverished landlords, rich peasants and upper-middle peasants who 'naturally' ranked among the 'people' and the 'subaltern', could under certain circumstances act for the 'elite', as explained above, and therefore be classified as such in some local or regional situations – an ambiguity which it is up to the historian to sort out on the basis of a close and judicious reading of his evidence.

2

The Nation and Its Peasants

Partha Chatterjee

The Modern State and the Peasantry

The relationship between the modern state and a peasantry is ambiguous and shot through with tension. In Western Europe, the institutionalization of a modern regime of power coincides with or follows a process of the extinction of the peasantry. Even in France, where it survived as a significantly large mass of the population in the second half of the nineteenth century, the peasantry was associated with such supposedly aberrant political phenomena as Bonapartism and had to be systematically disciplined and transformed into 'Frenchmen'.[1] Hegel, we know, assigned to the class of peasants – the 'substantial class' – an ambiguous position in civil society: it was a part of the class structure produced by the 'system of needs' but had an ethical life that was only immediate. Even when agriculture was conducted 'on methods devised by reflective thinking, i.e. like a factory', Hegel would allow a member of this class only to accept 'unreflectively what is given to him'. The agricultural class had 'little occasion to think of itself' and was 'inclined to subservience'.[2] Further east, the peasantry figured for more than half a century as the hub of a fierce debate between populists and Marxists over its role in a revolutionary Russia. This debate also highlighted the controversy, known in one form or the other everywhere in Europe, between modernizers who thought of peasants as embodying all that was backward and pre-modern and those modern critics of modernity, especially romantics, who saw in a peasantry the rapidly vanishing virtues of simplicity, naturalness and cultural authenticity. In the end, the matter was settled in Russia by the elimination of the peasantry under the collectivization programme of the 1930s.

In the agrarian societies of the colonial East, peasants of course became the repositories of all of those cultural presuppositions that allegedly made those societies incapable of modern self-government and hence justified the paternal authoritarianism of Western colonial rule. In India, the colonial mind thought of Indian peasants as simple, ignorant, exploited by landlords, traders and moneylenders, respectful of authority, grateful to those in power who cared for and protected them, but also volatile in temperament, superstitious and often fanatical, easily aroused by agitators and troublemakers from among the Indian elite who wanted to use them for their narrow political designs. Indian nationalists, not surprisingly, shared similar assumptions. For them, too, the peasants were simple and ignorant, unaware of the fact that their poverty was the result of the exploitative nature of colonial rule and therefore in need of being woken up to a new consciousness, of being guided and led into effective political action by a nationalist organization. This was a necessary task if the opposition to colonial rule was to acquire the form of a mass movement, but it was also a difficult and dangerous task because the ignorance and volatility of the peasantry could easily lead it astray. In thus proceeding towards their opposed political objectives – located, however, within the same historical career of the modern state – both colonial and nationalist politics thought of the peasantry as an object of their strategies, to be acted upon, controlled and appropriated within their respective structures of state power.

What does the history of anti-colonial struggles in India tell us about the relation between the nation and the peasantry? It is now reasonably clear that contrary to the claims of both colonialist and nationalist historiographies, neither the competitive factional interests of Indian elite groups nor the efforts of the Congress leadership to arouse an all-embracing nationalist consciousness among the entire people can explain the dynamics of the involvement of the peasantry in anti-colonial movements. Indeed, several studies published in the 1970s and the early 1980s on the course of the Congress movement among peasants in different parts of India have shown, some explicitly and others implicitly, the existence of a structure of duality in the nationalist mass movement.[3] A coming together of two domains of politics seems to have occurred. On the one hand was the domain of the formally organized political parties and associations, moving within the institutional processes of the bourgeois state forms introduced by colonial rule and seeking to use their representative power over the mass of the people to replace the colonial state by a bourgeois nation-state. On the other hand was the domain of peasant politics where beliefs and actions did not fit into the grid of 'interests' and 'aggregation of interests' that constituted the world of bourgeois representative politics. Seen from the former domain, the latter could appear only as the realm of spontaneity, which was of course nothing more than the acknowledgement that the specific determinants of the domain of peasant political activity remained incomprehensible from the standpoint of bourgeois politics.

Specifically, two major aspects of the mass movement of nationalism were brought out by these studies. First, the meeting of these two domains of politics was marked by an unresolved contradiction. There was undoubtedly a coming together of the two domains, so that the organization, ideology and programmes of the formally constituted political domain underwent considerable transformation with the entry of a mass peasant element, just as the peasantry too became aware of an entirely new world of political issues, languages, leaders and forms of action. And yet the very union of these two domains was of a form which required that they be kept apart. While the nationalist leadership sought to mobilize the peasantry as an anti-colonial force in its project of establishing a nation-state, it was ever distrustful of the consequences of agitational politics among the peasants, suspicious of their supposed ignorance and backward consciousness, careful to keep their participation limited to the forms of bourgeois representative politics in which peasants would be regarded as a part of the nation but distanced from the institutions of the state. On the other hand, while peasants became aware of the hitherto unknown world of nationalist agitation, they made sense of it not in terms of the discursive forms of modern bourgeois politics but rather by translating it into their own codes, so that the language of nationalism underwent a quite radical transformation of meaning in the peasant domain of politics.[4] The meeting of the two domains did not therefore mean that the first domain was able to absorb and appropriate its other within a single homogeneous unity; the unity itself remained fragmented and fraught with tension.

The second aspect of the meeting of the two domains was that it did not bring about a linear development of the consciousness of the peasantry into a new sense of nationhood. While peasants in different parts of India became aware, albeit in varying degrees, of the realities of nationalist politics, their participation in it seemed to be marked by radical breaks and often reversals, for spells of militant anti-colonial action by peasants were often followed by bitter sectarian strife, sometimes in the course of a single movement, and at other times by spells of apparently inexplicable quiescence. Both of these aspects of peasant participation in nationalist politics seemed to point in the same direction: the need for a critique of both colonialist and nationalist historiographies by bringing in the peasantry as a subject of history, endowed with its own distinctive forms of consciousness and making sense of and acting upon the world on its own terms.

Peasant Insurgents of Colonial India

The problem was formulated specifically by Ranajit Guha, using the material on peasant insurgency in the period immediately preceding that of nationalist mass movements.[5] From the series of peasant revolts in colonial India between 1783 and 1900, Guha undertook to isolate the ideological invariants of peasant consciousness and their relational unity – that is to say, its paradigmatic form. He began by assuming that the domination and exploitation under which the peasant lived and worked existed within a relation of power. There was thus an opposed pair: on the one side, the dominators (the state or the landlords or moneylenders), and on the other, the peasants. A relational opposition of power necessarily meant that the dominated had to be granted their own domain of subjectivity, where they were autonomous, undominated. If it were not so, the dominators would, in the exercise of their domination, wholly consume and obliterate the dominated. Dominance then would no longer exist within a social relation of power with its own conditions of reproduction. In this specific case, therefore, the peasantry had to be granted its autonomous domain.

Where was one to locate this domain? If domination is one aspect of this relation of power, its opposed aspect must be resistance. The dialectical opposition of the two gives this relation its unity. This opposition also creates the possibility for a movement within that relation, and thus makes it possible for there to be a history of the relation of dominance and subordination. In searching for the characteristic form of the autonomous domain of peasant consciousness, Guha was led to a study of the aspect of resistance. This did not mean that resistance was more important, or more true, than domination. On the contrary, by placing the forms of peasant consciousness within a dialectical relation of power, peasant consciousness would be assigned its proper theoretical value: its significance was to be established only in relation to its other, namely, the consciousness of the dominator.

If resistance was the aspect of the power relation through which the peasantry expressed its distinct and autonomous identity, as opposed to that of its dominators, where were we to find it in the historical material available to us? Precisely in the material on peasant insurgency, where the insurgent consciousness left its imprint on that of its dominator, and where the dominator was forced expressly to 'recognize' its other. Thus the inquiry into the characteristic forms of peasant consciousness became in Guha a study of the elementary aspects of peasant insurgency. The study of peasant insurgency was, in other words, a methodological procedure by which one obtained an access into peasant consciousness, expressed through its resistance at the point of insurgency and recognized as an antagonistic force in the historical records prepared by the dominant classes. The instituted knowledge of society, as it exists in recorded history, is the knowledge obtained by the dominant classes in their exercise of power. The dominated, by virtue of their very powerlessness, have no means of recording their knowledge within those instituted processes, except as an object of the exercise of power. Thus, Guha used the colonial discourse of counter-insurgency to read, as a mirror image, the discourse of insurgency.

He identified six 'elementary aspects', as he called them, of the insurgent peasant consciousness: negation, ambiguity, modality, solidarity, transmission and territoriality. The insurgent consciousness was, first of all, a 'negative consciousness', in the sense that its identity was expressed solely through an opposition, namely, its difference from and antagonism to its dominators. It was an identity whose limits were fixed by the very conditions of subordination under which the peasantry lived and worked; only the relations were inverted. The signs of domination, such as the imposition of taxes or rent or of the power to punish, now became the targets of resistance. A characteristic feature of peasant rebellions was the urge of the oppressed to assert his resistance to authority 'not in terms of his own culture but his enemy's'. Second, the forms of resistance involved a high degree of ambiguity. Precisely because relations of domination were inverted at the moment of insurgency, the signs of rebellion were liable to be misread by the rulers who would fail to distinguish them from such 'normal' signs of aberrant behaviour as crime. But unlike crime, 'rebellions are necessarily and invariably public and communal events'; 'crime and insurgency derive from two very different codes of violence'. Third, insurgent peasant movements had their characteristic modalities or forms. On the one hand, the political and yet innately negative character of inverting the dominant relations of power took the form of destroying the signs of authority, such as the police station or the landlord's rent-collection office or the moneylender's house. Specifically for the case of colonial India, Guha identified four forms of destruction: wrecking, burning, eating and looting. On the other hand, the negativity of the insurgent consciousness of the peasant was also expressed in the setting up of a rebel authority, in the inverted image of the authority that it replaced, equally public in character and with its own powers to impose sanctions and levies on the community. Fourth, the self-definition of the insurgent peasant, his awareness of belonging to a collectivity that was separate from and opposed to his enemies, lay in the aspect of solidarity. Its specific expression varied from rebellion to rebellion, sometimes even from one phase to another within the same rebellion. Often it was expressed in terms of ethnicity or kinship or some such affinal category. Sometimes one can read in it the awareness of a class. But solidarity was the total expression of the communal character of an insurgency. Fifth, within the solidarity thus defined, the message of insurgency was transmitted with an ease and rapidity that the ruling classes often found bewildering, but this too had its characteristic channels. Rumour, for instance, was one such channel, in which the source of a message was anonymous and unknown and which involved no distinction between the communicator and his audience. Absolutely transitive, rumour, as distinct from news, was 'an autonomous type of popular discourse'. Finally, the solidarity of an insurgent peasantry also occupied a specific geographical space. The limits of this geographical space were determined, on the one hand, negatively by the rebel's perception of the geographical spread of the enemy's authority, that is to say, by a principle of exclusion, and on the other, positively by a notion of the ethnic space occupied by the insurgent community, that is, by the principle of solidarity. The intersection of these two spaces defined the territoriality of the insurgency.

The Notion of Community

In all these aspects that Guha identified, there is a single unifying idea that gives to peasant insurgency its fundamental social character: the notion of community. Every aspect expresses itself in its specific political forms through the principle of community. Whether through the negatively constituted character of the forms and targets of insurgent action, defined by applying the criterion of 'we' and 'they', or whether through the rebel's self-definition of the territorial space of insurgency, a principle of community gives to all these specific aspects their fundamental constitutive character as the purposive political acts of a collective consciousness. This principle, again, enables us to read from the actions of a rebellious peasantry at the moment of insurgency the total constitutive character of a peasant consciousness, to relate those actions to the forms of everyday social existence of the peasantry.

It is important to stress this point, because what the principle of community as the characteristic unifying feature of peasant consciousness does is directly place it at the opposite pole to a bourgeois consciousness. The latter operates from the premise of the individual and a notion of his interests (or, in more fashionable vocabulary, his preferences). Solidarities in bourgeois politics are built up through an aggregative process by which individuals come together into alliances on the basis of common interests (or shared preferences). The process is quite the opposite in the consciousness of a rebellious peasantry. There solidarities do not grow because individuals feel they can come together with others on the basis of their common individual interests: on the contrary, individuals are enjoined to act within a collectivity because, it is believed, bonds of solidarity that tie them together already exist. Collective action does not flow from a contract among individuals; rather, individual identities themselves are derived from membership in a community.

The implication is that peasant consciousness cannot be understood in its own constitutive aspects if we continue to reduce it to the paradigm of bourgeois rationality. We must grant that peasant consciousness has its own paradigmatic form, which is not only different from that of bourgeois consciousness but in fact its very other. This central theoretical proposition is brought out by Guha's book, and it poses a basic challenge to the methodological procedures followed not only by bourgeois economists and sociologists (including those of the Chayanovian and 'moral economy' varieties) searching for the 'rational peasant' (however defined), but also by many Marxist scholars writing on the agrarian question.

This notion of community cannot be immediately assigned a single determinate value based on a determinate social institution such as totemism or caste or religious denomination. The boundaries or forms of solidarity in peasant rebellions have no single determinate character that can be directly deduced either from its immediate socio-economic context or from its cultural world. On the contrary, the cultural apparatus of signs and meanings – the language, in the broadest sense – available to a peasant consciousness, far from being narrow and inflexible, is capable of a vast range of transformations to enable it to understand, and to act within, varying contexts, both of subordination and of resistance. It is precisely this ability that makes insurgency the purposeful political work of a deliberate and active insurgent consciousness. Without it, this consciousness could in fact be 'objectivized' easily, by reducing it to its determinate institutional form – tribe, caste, religious denomination, locality, whatever. Such a reductionism grossly underestimates, and in fact misunderstands, the ideological resilience and innovativeness of peasant consciousness.

The Concrete Forms of Community

Guha, therefore, has proposed a paradigmatic form of the insurgent peasant consciousness. Its contours are drawn from a reading of the material on peasant revolts in colonial India from the point of view of the peasant as an active and conscious subject of history. But because of his objective of isolating an invariant structural form, in line with the structuralism inherent in his method, he has not attempted to give us a *history* of this consciousness as a movement of self-transformation. Rather, having found an access into the structural form of this consciousness in its aspect of autonomy, he has given us a basis to ask the appropriate questions about its history.

The first area where this interrogation can begin is precisely that which binds together the structure of peasant consciousness as described by Guha, namely, the community. We have seen that Guha, quite correctly, does not give to this community any immediately determinate content; or rather, to put it more accurately, while he describes the community in the historical context of a particular peasant rebellion in the relevant terms of clan, tribe, caste, village and so forth, he leaves the theoretical conceptualization of the community in peasant consciousness as a formal construct, abstract and empty. It is necessary now to attempt to give to this crucial concept its proper theoretical content. We already have something to go on. We know, for instance, that the identification of the enemy in peasant revolts, the separation of the 'they' from the 'we', occurs within a framework where distinct communities are seen as being in antagonistic relation with each other. The same framework of communities provides room for the establishment of solidarities and alliances on the side of the rebels (and, for that matter, on the side of the enemy), and even of collaboration and treachery. The alliances are not seen as the result of contracts based on common interests; rather, they are believed to be the necessary duty of groups bound together by mutual bonds of kinship: 'You are our brothers. Do join with all expedition.' This invitation of the first group of rebels in the Rangpur uprising of 1783 to the peasants of neighbouring villages was, in fact, the standard form of insurgent alliance in peasant rebellions all over India. It applied even in the case of a perceived breach of mutual duty; this was no breach of contract. When the villagers of Kallas wrote to those of Akola blaming them for breaking the solidarity of the movement during the Deccan Revolt of 1875, they did not appeal to a mutuality of interest. Rather, they said, 'It is wrong of you people to keep communication with persons who are deemed as excluded from the community of the village . . . As we consider Kallas and Akola as one village, we have made the above suggestions to you.'

We also know that the boundaries of solidarity, the line separating the 'we' from the 'they', can shift according to changing contexts of struggle. Pandey has given us an account of how a strife between Rajput landlords and Muslim weavers in a small town in Uttar Pradesh in the middle of the nineteenth century quickly changed into the solidarity of the entire town in its defence against outside attack and back again to internal strife, all within the space of a few weeks, without any apparent sign that the people of the town saw anything anomalous in these rapid changes in the boundaries of solidarity. Hardiman, Sarkar and Chatterjee have also considered this problem of shifting boundaries of solidarity in terms of the changing context of struggle.[6] What is necessary now is to formulate the concept of community within a set of systematic relationships signifying the mutual identity and difference of social groups.

In the Indian context, the system of castes seems to represent an obvious paradigmatic form for signifying identity and difference. On the one hand, castes are mutually separate as though they were distinct species of natural beings and, on the other, they are mutually bound together as parts, arranged hierarchically, within a social whole. In traditional social anthropology, to the extent that these relations were seen as constituting a system, the dominant view has been that it provides a framework for harmonizing the mutual interdependence of separate groups through the inculcation of a set of shared values about the unity of the system as a whole.[7] What is not recognized is the equally systematic nature of the rejection of the supposedly 'shared' values by groups that are inferior in caste ranking. There seems to be ample evidence to enable us to ground the system of castes within the totality of power relations, because the changing relations between castes and the periodic attempts to redefine the content of ethical conduct in the Indian religions bear the signs of a continuing struggle, and its temporary resolutions, within social relations of domination and subordination. In short, we have here the possibility of linking a history of peasant struggle with a *history* of the caste system, and through it, with a history of religious beliefs and practices.

There are strong reasons to suspect that the system of castes operates as a paradigmatic form not merely in the domain of relations between jātis within the fold of the Brahmanical religion; it is probably the case that it is the general cultural form of conceptualizing and ordering the relations of identity and difference between several kinds of social groupings. Significantly, the word *jāti* in most Indian languages can be used to designate not merely caste, but caste agglomerations, tribes, race, linguistic groups, religious groups, nationalities, nations. Anthropologists have, of course, often noted the existence of caste or caste-like forms not only among religious groups such as Buddhists, Jains or the medieval devotional sects that emerged in opposition to the Brahmanical religion, but also among Indian Muslims and Christians. But this point is of a more general significance: the extent to which a caste-like system provides the cultural form for conceptualizing relations of domination, as well as of resistance, between social groups needs to be examined in its concreteness.

Apart from this question of identifying the boundaries of the community in varying contexts of struggle, there is the other aspect of the internal structure of the community in peasant consciousness. It is clear that the notion of community, especially among the non-tribal agrarian population, is not egalitarian, even in the matter of rights in the basic means of production, namely, land. For most parts of India, in the sector of settled peasant cultivation, something like a fifth or more of the population, belonging to the lowest castes, have never had any recognized rights in land. But the unity of a community was nevertheless established by recognizing the rights of subsistence of all sections of the population, albeit a differential right entailing differential duties and privileges. The point then is that the notion of community as itself a differentiated unity operates not merely between peasants as a community and their dominators, but between peasants themselves. The full range of possibilities of alliances and oppositions, with the boundaries of community shifting with changing contexts of struggle, may then be said to operate in relations between sections of the peasantry. The point goes against a populist idealization of the peasantry as an egalitarian and harmonious community, free from internal dissension and struggle.

An Indian History of Peasant Struggle

Following Guha, the argument of the *Subaltern Studies* group of historians has been that by studying the history of peasant rebellions from the point of view of the peasant as an active and conscious subject of history, one obtains an access into that aspect of his consciousness where he is autonomous, undominated. One thereby has the means to conceptualize the unity of that consciousness as grounded in a relationship of power, namely, of domination and subordination. Peasant consciousness, then, is a contradictory unity of two aspects: in one, the peasant is subordinate, where he accepts the immediate reality of power relations that dominate and exploit him; in the other, he denies those conditions of subordination and asserts his autonomy. It has also been argued that the community is the space where this contradictory unity of peasant consciousness makes its appearance. So far, the community has been characterized only in the abstract and formal sense. But there is sufficient historical material to begin a more concrete conceptualization of the community, itself differentiated, as the *site* of peasant struggle, where respective rights and duties are established and contested.

Already this gives us a path of investigation that is likely to deviate from the conventional ways of studying peasant revolts in Europe. In fact, I will argue that what the recent debates about the role of the peasantry in the nationalist movement lead to is a project to write an Indian history of peasant struggle.[8] In principle, this is a different project from that of a history of peasant struggles in India. The semantic difference signifies a quite radical difference in the approach to historiography. The latter stands for an arrangement of the historical material on peasant struggles in India according to a framework in which the fundamental concepts and analytical relations are taken as given, established in their generality by the forms of a universal history (for example, the theory of transition from feudalism to capitalism, or modernization theory, or the theory of world systems, or the theory of the moral economy of the peasant, and so on). The former seeks to discover in that material the forms of an immanent historical development, fractured, distorted, and forced into the grid of 'world history' only by the violence of colonialism. The framework of this other history does not take as given its appointed place within the order of a universal history, but rather submits the supposedly universal categories to a constant process of interrogation and contestation, modifying, transforming and enriching them. The object is not to resume the course of a pre-colonial history by erasing from historical memory and present reality the experience of colonialism: this would be not only archaic and utopian, it would in fact be reactionary even to pretend that this is possible. Rather, the task is to ground one's historical consciousness in the immanent forms of social development that run through Indian history and from that standpoint to engage our colonial experience in a process of struggle – negating and superseding that experience by appropriating it on one's own terms.

This agenda implies the relegation of the universal categories of social formations into a temporary state of suspension, or rather a state of unresolved tension. But this again is a task fundamental to the historian's practice. The relation between history and the theoretical disciplines of the social sciences is necessarily one where the structural neatness of the latter is constantly disturbed and refashioned by the intransigent material of the former. The plea for an Indian history of peasant politics, then, is also one that calls for the historian to take up his or her proper role as agent provocateur among social scientists.

A calumny was spread by European writers on India in the eighteenth and nineteenth centuries to the effect that because of the lack of a historical consciousness among Indians, there existed next to no material on Indian history, save a few court chronicles, hagiographies and genealogical tables of questionable veracity. This misrepresentation ought not to be attributed solely to the malicious intentions of the colonial mind to tarnish the character of a conquered people. There were more profound difficulties with the very conception of history as a form of knowledge in post-Enlightenment Europe. Judged from the European standpoint, the overwhelming mass of material out of which the institutions and practices of social relations among the Indian people were fashioned, and which survived as palpable evidence of a living past, was simply not recognized as valid historical material. All evidence that did not fit into the linear order of progression of state forms defined by principalities, kingdoms and empires was relegated to the exotic, timeless domain of Indian ethnology, where history played only a marginal role.

We now know that the situation is quite the opposite. The variety of structural forms of social relations in India, the intricacy of their interconnections, the multiple layers and degrees of differentiation, the ideological forms of identity and difference, and the long course of the historical evolution of these forms through social struggle are stamped on the living beliefs and practices of the people. In its sheer vastness and intricacy, this material is incomparably richer than what is contained in the received histories of Europe, a fact that the efflorescence of modern anthropology in the period after the Second World War has brought home to the European consciousness. In fact, the recent attempts to exhume a 'popular history' of Europe from the rubble of a dead past have been provoked precisely by this challenge thrown by the new sciences of anthropology and linguistics, working on the material of non-European societies, to the accepted dogmas of post-Enlightenment European knowledge.

Now that there is a much greater eagerness to face up to this evidence as historical material, its very richness forces us to throw up our hands and declare that it is much too complex. Every practising social scientist of India will confess to this feeling of inadequacy and helplessness. For colonial ethnographers, this was evidence of the orderless *mélange* that was the mysterious Orient, and for colonial administrators, additional proof of the historical necessity to impose linearity and order on an ungovernable society. For Indian nationalists, this was evidence of the greatness of the indigenous tradition which was capable, they said, of absorbing diverse social forms into a single unity without destroying the marks of difference. Needless to say, the colonial view tended to emphasize the inherent disorderliness of Indian society and its lack of a united consciousness, while the nationalists glorified the absorptive capacity without taking notice of the considerable internal struggles that marked the process of absorption.

For those of us who face up to this problem today, the feeling of unmanageable complexity is, if we care to think of it, nothing other than the result of the inadequacy of the theoretical apparatus with which we work. Those analytical instruments were fashioned primarily out of the process of understanding historical developments in Europe. When those instruments now meet with the resistance of an intractably complex material, the fault surely is not of the Indian material but of the imported instruments. If the day comes when the vast storehouse of Indian social history becomes comprehensible to the scientific consciousness, we will have achieved along the way a fundamental restructuring of the edifice of European social philosophy as it exists today.

The second point of strength of the Indian material on peasant struggle arises, curiously enough, from an apparent weakness. There is a common tendency to regard the evidence of open revolts of the peasantry in India as insignificant when compared to the historical experience of medieval Europe or to that of neighbouring China. One must, however, be careful in judging the nature of this insufficiency. It has sometimes been suggested, for instance, that a history of peasant insurgency in India is a non-starter because there has never been a peasant revolt in India which was anything more than local and brief. The fact is, first of all, that the number of such 'local' revolts is quite considerable, and from about the seventeenth century, through the period of British rule and right up to the contemporary period of the postcolonial state, the accounts of several hundred peasant revolts from all over the country exist in the historical records. Second, what appears to be only 'localized' in the context of a vast country like India may often be found to involve a territory and a rebel population larger than those in even the most famous peasant revolts in European history. The crucial difference lies elsewhere. It is undoubtedly true that peasant revolts in India do not seem to have the same political impact on the evolution of state forms or on legal–proprietary relations as they do in Europe or China.[9] An important reason for this is that dominance in Indian society was not exercised exclusively, or even primarily, through the legal forms of sovereign power embodied in the institutions of the state or of feudal estates. Consequently, resistance was not restricted only to the domain of legal–political relations. The study of peasant struggles in India must therefore encompass a field of social relations far wider than what is conventionally regarded as appropriate in European history. Once again, therefore, what the Indian material calls for is an opening up and restructuring of the received disciplinary boundaries for the study of peasant movements.

The Movement of Consciousness

The immediate implications for the project of an Indian history of peasant politics is, first, that the domain of legal–political relations constituted by the state cannot be regarded as the exclusive, perhaps not even the principal, site of peasant struggle. Second, the domain of community will appear as intricately differentiated and layered, with a structural form that affords far greater flexibility, and hence strategic opportunities for both peasants and the dominant classes, in the making of alliances and oppositions than in the 'peasant community' in feudal Europe. Third, in the long intervals between open, armed rebellions by peasants or the spread of the great heterodox religious movements, one is likely to notice, if one looks for it, a continuing and pervasive struggle between peasants and the dominant classes in everyday life. The forms of such struggle will range from absenteeism, desertion, selective disobedience, sabotage and strikes to verbal forms such as slander, feigned ignorance, satire and abuse – the 'Brechtian forms of class struggle', as James Scott has described them.[10] The storehouse of popular culture in India has preserved an enormously rich collection of the material and ideological artefacts of such everyday forms of peasant protest, which have never been incorporated into the study of the processes of subordination and resistance within which Indian peasants have lived and struggled.

This brings us to our final, and crucial, question. If our objective is to write the history of peasant struggle in the form of a history of peasants as active and conscious agents, then their consciousness must also have a history. Their experience of varying forms of subordination, and of resistance, their attempts to cope with changing forms of material and ideological life both in their everyday existence and in those flashes of open rebellion, must leave their imprint on consciousness as a process of learning and development. Some like

Scott have sought to privilege the everyday forms of resistance over those of open rebellion because the former are supposedly more enduring and, in the long run, more effective in their slow and almost imperceptible transformation of the conditions of subordination. It may be premature to dismiss this argument on a priori grounds, but the fact remains that the domain of the quotidian, which is also the domain of the seeming perpetuity of subordination, is circumscribed by a limit beyond which lies the extraordinary, apocalyptic, timeless moment of a world turned upside down. It is the historical record of those brief moments of open rebellion which gives us a glimpse of that undominated region in peasant consciousness and enables us to see the everyday and the extraordinary as parts of a single unity in historical time.

To push the point a little further, we could argue that it is always the spectre of an open rebellion by the peasantry which haunts the consciousness of the dominant classes in agrarian societies and shapes and modifies their forms of exercise of domination. This was true of the colonial state in the period of British rule in India, just as it is true today, notwithstanding the establishment of universal adult franchise. Of course, the nature and forms of domination of peasants have changed quite fundamentally in the last hundred years or so. The older forms of feudal extraction and ties of bondage have been replaced to a large extent by new forms of extraction mediated through the mechanisms of the market and of fiscal policies. These changes themselves have not come about solely through reforms at the top; a whole series of peasant struggles from the days of colonial rule have acted upon the structures of domination in order to change and modify them. Even the new political institutions of representative government, struggling to give political form to the material of social relations of a large agrarian country, are themselves being shaped into figures that would be unrecognizable in the liberal democracies of the West. To give one example, the phenomenon of massive and uniform swings in the vote across large regions, which has been a characteristic of several recent elections in India, is of a magnitude and geographical spread unknown in Western liberal democracies and inexplicable in terms of the normal criteria of voting behaviour. Do we see in this the form of an insurgent peasant consciousness which, having learned in its own way the mechanisms of the new system of power, is now expressing itself through entirely novel methods of political action?

An Indian history of peasant struggle will tell us a great deal more than simply the story of medieval peasant rebellions. For it is a history that constitutes our living and active present. It is a history that will tell us why, when peasants identified the colonial state as their enemy, as they did in 1857 or 1942, they could be so much more radical and thoroughgoing in their opposition than their more enlightened compatriots. It is a history that will educate those of us who claim to be their educators. Indeed, an Indian history of peasant struggle is a fundamental part of the real history of our people; the task is for the Indian historian to perceive in this a consciousness of his or her own self.

Notes

1. A well-known account of this process is Eugen Weber, *Peasants into Frenchmen: The Modernization of Rural France, 1870–1914* (London: Chatto and Windus, 1979).
2. G. W. F. Hegel, *Philosophy of Right*, trans. T. M. Knox (1952; reprint, London: Oxford University Press, 1967), par. 203 and additions 128–9, pp. 131–2 and 270–74.
3. For instance, David Hardiman, *Peasant Nationalists of Gujarat* (Delhi: Oxford University Press, 1981); Gyanendra Pandey, *The Ascendancy of the Congress in Uttar Pradesh, 1926–1934* (Delhi: Oxford University Press, 1978); Majid Hayat Siddiqi, *Agrarian Unrest in North India: The United Provinces, 1918–1922* (New Delhi: Vikas, 1978); Arvind Narayan Das, *Agrarian Unrest and Socio-economic Change, 1900–1980* (Delhi: Manohar, 1983); Atlury Murali, 'Civil Disobedience Movement in Andhra, 1920–1922: The Nature of Peasant Protest and the Methods of Congress Political Mobilization', in Kapil Kumar, ed., *Congress and Classes: Nationalism, Workers and Peasants* (New Delhi: Manohar, 1988), pp. 152–216.
4. A telling example of this can be found in Shahid Amin, 'Gandhi as Mahatma: Gorakhpur District, Eastern UP, 1921–1922', in Ranajit Guha, ed., *Subaltern Studies III* (Delhi: Oxford University Press, 1984), pp. 1–61.
5. Ranajit Guha, *Elementary Aspects of Peasant Insurgency in Colonial India* (Delhi: Oxford University Press, 1983).
6. Gyanendra Pandey, 'Encounters and Calamities: The History of a North Indian *Qasba* in the Nineteenth Century', in Guha, *Subaltern Studies III*, pp. 231–70; David Hardiman, 'The Bhils and Shahukars in Eastern Gujarat', in Ranajit Guha, ed., *Subaltern Studies V* (Delhi: Oxford University Press, 1987), pp. 1–54; Tanika Sarkar, 'Jitu Santal's Movement in Malda, 1924–1932: A Study in Tribal Protest', in Ranajit Guha, ed., *Subaltern Studies IV* (Delhi: Oxford University Press, 1985), pp. 136–64; Partha Chatterjee, *Bengal 1920–1947: The Land Question* (Calcutta: K. P. Bagchi, 1984).
7. Argued most powerfully by Louis Dumont, *Homo Hierarchicus*, trans. Mark Sainsbury (London: Paladin, 1970).
8. For two recent surveys of these debates, see Rosalind O'Hanlon, 'Recovering the Subject: *Subaltern Studies* and Histories of Resistance in Colonial South Asia' (included in this volume); and Mridula Mukherjee, 'Peasant Resistance and Peasant Consciousness in Colonial India: "Subaltern" and Beyond', *Economic and Political Weekly* 23, nos. 41 and 42 (8 and 15 October 1988): 2109–20 and 2174–85.
9. A point made by Irfan Habib, 'The Peasant in Indian History', *Social Scientist* 11, no. 3 (March 1983): 21–64.
10. James Scott, *Weapons of the Weak: Everyday Forms of Peasant Resistance* (New Haven, Conn.: Yale University Press, 1985).

3

Gramsci and Peasant Subalternity in India

David Arnold

In recent years the writings of Antonio Gramsci have been read largely for their insights into the politics of contemporary Western industrial societies and to provide an updated Marxism for the West. By contrast, his discussion of the peasantry and rural society has received far less attention, especially among English-language writers.[1] Perhaps the notorious difficulty of unravelling the meaning of Gramsci's *Prison Notebooks* and drawing a consistent theory from them has proved too great a deterrent. Or perhaps – erroneously, as this article will try to show – it has been felt that he has little to contribute to the empirical investigation and theoretical analysis of peasant society.

For any student of peasant societies who wishes to work within a broadly Marxist tradition of scholarship and enquiry and yet to go beyond the narrowly economistic and mechanistic form that such studies often assume, the writings of Antonio Gramsci must have a strong attraction. At a general theoretical level, his attention to consciousness and to the cultural and ideological dimensions of hegemony[2] and subordination provides a basis for a critical understanding and analysis of the subaltern classes and offers a corrective to the tendency towards a deterministic concentration upon societies' economic 'base'. Moreover, unlike the founders of Marxism, with their confident assumption of the imminent demise of the peasantry in the face of rural and industrial capitalism, and their overemphatic contrast between the 'idiocy of rural life' and peasant barbarism on the one hand and the revolutionary, class-conscious industrial proletariat on the other, Gramsci presents the peasantry as a living force, politically as well as culturally and socially. He sees it as demanding close scrutiny and careful analysis, especially through attention to its historical specificity and the subaltern consciousness revealed in popular beliefs and folklore.

For these reasons and others to be discussed shortly, Gramsci's writings have been taken up by a group of scholars working on the

Indian peasantry, some of whose work has appeared in a series of volumes entitled *Subaltern Studies* and edited by Ranajit Guha (1982, 1983b, 1984). This essay is therefore also an attempt by a member of that group to review the progress made so far in applying Gramscian concepts to India. It is not intended to claim for Gramsci's formulations an unassailable universality and self-sufficiency. Indian historiography has already had too many idols without a Mahatma Gramsci being added to them. Gramsci was himself strongly critical of those who sought to reduce Marxism to a series of rigid axioms and laws of historical inevitability. Rather, the purpose here is to examine Gramsci's ideas relating to the peasantry and then to consider how those ideas, particularly of subalternity, hegemony and passive revolution, might be applied, and have begun to be applied, to the specific case of the Indian peasantry in the nineteenth and twentieth centuries.

Gramsci's Peasantry

Gramsci's interest in the peasantry of his native Italy prompted no detailed study devoted exclusively to it. Indeed, it is unlikely that Gramsci, even without his incarceration, would have undertaken such a study for it is one of the characteristics of his writings that he viewed the peasantry as part of a larger and encompassing socio-political order and not as a discrete entity. Nevertheless, peasants formed a recurrent element in his political and polemical writings of the early and middle 1920s and held an even greater prominence in the more abstract and reflective *Prison Notebooks* written between 1929 and 1935. One source of this interest was clearly Gramsci's own background. Born in Sardinia in 1891 in a lower-middle-class family and resident there until his late teens, Gramsci had first-hand experience of peasant life in one of Italy's most backward regions. At first the young Gramsci was attracted to Sardinian separatism, but on moving to Turin as a student and in becoming increasingly interested in Marxist thought, this early sentiment matured into an enduring political commitment to the resolution of the Southern Question within the framework of an Italian socialist society. He thus came to identify the subordination of the peasants of the southern mainland and islands to the industrialists, bankers and bureaucrats of the North as the central problem not only in Italian national life but also in the formation of the theory and strategy of the Italian Communist Party (Fiori, 1973: 207–11; Davidson, 1977: chapter 2).

Events in Italy and Russia and Gramsci's experience as a political activist enhanced and deepened his appreciation of the political importance of the peasantry. The Russian Revolution of 1917, about which Gramsci became Italy's leading expert, impressed on him the need for peasants to lend their great weight of numbers if the bourgeois state were to be overthrown. The aftermath of the Russian Revolution made him aware, too, of the problems of proletarian hegemony in a society in which, as in Italy, peasants remained numerically predominant (*SPW II*: 430). Gramsci's involvement in the abortive factory councils movement in industrial Turin in 1919–20 was another, more immediate, indication that communism in Italy could not succeed if it relied on the proletariat alone and ignored the peasantry. From his reading of history Gramsci could see how a revolutionary movement originating in the cities was in danger of being isolated and crushed by the surrounding countryside: there was a bitter reminder of this in August 1917 when peasant soldiers from his native Sardinia helped quash proletarian unrest in the city of Turin (*SPN*: 92; *SPW II*: 447–9; Cammett, 1967: 53). To overcome this impasse the countryside had to be won over to the revolutionary cause through an alliance of urban workers with the poorer peasants. Unlike many socialists and communists in Italy at the time, Gramsci insisted that it was essential for the political leadership to understand the conditions and aspirations of the peasantry, especially those of the neglected South (Cammett, 1967: 131–3). The growth of a new assertiveness among the southern peasantry at the close of the First World War suggested the imminent possibility of such an alliance: the rise of fascism in the early 1920s made it appear imperative if communism were to survive as an active political force (*SPW II*: 397). In the 'Lyons theses' of January 1926, in his essay on 'Some Aspects of the Southern Question', unfinished at the time of his arrest in November of that year, and above all in the pages of his *Prison Notebooks*, Gramsci returned again and again to the fundamental issues of the position of the peasantry in Italy's political order. What historically had kept the peasants in subordination to the dominant classes? Why had they failed to overthrow their rulers and to establish a hegemony of their own? By what means could the peasantry become part of a triumphant revolutionary movement?

In posing these questions and in seeking convincing answers to them Gramsci had not abandoned faith in the industrial proletariat as the leading revolutionary class, but he had come to believe that the proletariat could fulfil that role only to the extent that it succeeded in creating a system of class alliances that would mobilize the mass of the working population against capitalism and the bourgeois state. In Italy this meant 'to the extent that it succeeds in gaining the consent of the broad peasant masses' (*SPW II*: 443). In the South the proletariat would achieve this hegemony only if it succeeded in supplanting the hold which the rural magnates and petty bourgeoisie had for generations had over the peasantry. But for Gramsci, associating the peasantry with the proletariat-led revolution was not mere short-term political opportunism with peasants being gulled into aiding a revolution of which they would be early victims. The alliance of worker and peasant was to be as genuine as it was enduring. Peasants would enter voluntarily into this alliance through the realization that both they and the workers shared in capitalists and bureaucrats the same oppressors. In the process of combining to overthrow the bourgeois state and northern capitalism the peasants would become a truly revolutionary class. The formation of this revolutionary bloc further meant for Gramsci the resolution of the deep divide and mutual suspicion between the countryside and the city which had perplexed Italian politics for centuries and which remained powerfully and symbolically entrenched in Italy's North–South divide. For their part the industrial workers were to make the Southern Question their own by identifying with the peasants' grievances and recognizing that the persistent northern belief in the innate backwardness and biological inferiority of the southern peasant was a myth, propagated by the ruling classes to uphold their hegemony and keep the subaltern classes divided (*SPW II*: 443–4; *SPN*: 71, 91). After the revolution the model of the factory council was to be extended to rural collectives to promote co-operation among the peasants themselves and between the city and the countryside. The city's expertise and resources were to be mobilized to free the peasants from the oppression of their technological and material impoverishment.

For Gramsci, then, the peasants were not the doomed breed they so often appear as in the pages of Marx, inherently, even irredeemably, conservative and barbaric in the context of modern society. But neither did Gramsci veer to the opposite extreme: his childhood in Sardinia had been too harsh, his experience of the peasantry too intimate, for him to espouse a romantic or utopian view of peasant life (Davidson, 1977: 45). As his *Letters from Prison*, as well as the *Notebooks*, eloquently testify, the imprisoned Gramsci reflected deeply on his childhood insights into the Sardinian peasantry the better to understand objectively why peasants thought and acted as they did. For him Marxism was above all else 'the philosophy of praxis': it followed that there could be no revolutionary movement in a society unless its distinctive forms of consciousness and subordination were accurately identified, objectively understood and critically appraised by those who aspired to transform it. Peasant culture and society were to be studied, not from a sentimentality for the past or an antiquarian resolve to rescue them from the devouring jaws of industrial capitalism, but because they were a vital factor in the ideas and actions of the contemporary subaltern classes, because they were a crucial element in the control exercised by the rulers over the ruled. Popular beliefs were, accordingly, far from being 'something negligible and inert within the movement of history' (*SPN*: 419). Basing himself upon a somewhat free interpretation of Marx's *Introduction to the Critique of Hegel's Philosophy of Right,* Gramsci held that popular ideas had as much historical weight or energy as purely material forces (*SPN*: 165, 377, 404); in his discussions in the *Prison Notebooks* of specific historical situations the ideologies of the hegemonic and subaltern classes assumed far greater prominence than material determinants. While this has laid Gramsci open to charges from critics like Althusser of idealism, historicism and voluntarism, in the *Prison Notebooks* he repeatedly castigated those aloof 'Marxists' who saw as 'real and worthwhile only such movements of revolt as are one hundred per cent conscious, i.e. movements that are governed by plans worked out in advance to the last detail or in line with abstract theory'. Gramsci's political realism made him well aware that in practice, especially among peasants and other subaltern groups, 'reality produces a wealth of the most bizarre combinations' of beliefs and expectations (*SPN*: 200). It was absurd, in his view, for Marxists to dismiss these movements as useless and irrelevant and to wait until, if ever, a pure revolutionary movement arrived. It was the task of the intellectual to unravel the complexities and to '"translate" into theoretical language the elements of historical life', to search out signs of subaltern initiative and incipient class identity that could be nurtured and educated into true class consciousness and effective political action. To fail to do this, to expect reality to 'conform to the abstract scheme', was for Gramsci 'nothing but an expression of passivity' on the part of Marxist intellectuals (*SPN*: 197–200). Class consciousness, he believed, could only come from within a social group: it could not be arbitrarily imposed from outside. Thus the 'spontaneous' and 'elementary' passions of the subalterns had to be studied, not spurned, developed, not despised. Gramsci validated the study of subaltern beliefs and consciousness, not because he thought them objectively correct but because they were forms and expressions of the life of the masses which no exponent of the 'philosophy of praxis' could afford to ignore.

As Alberto Maria Cirese has shown, one can draw from Gramsci's later writings a series of negative subaltern attributes and in antithesis, or at least in partial qualification, a series of positive or potentially positive attributes (Cirese, 1982). On the negative side are to be found many characteristic weaknesses of the peasantry as a political force familiar from other studies. The dispersal and isolation of peasants make it difficult for them to combine into 'solid organisations' (*SPN*: 75). They are divided among themselves, principally between those who possess land and the sharecroppers and labourers who do not, a division which landlords exploit to their own advantage (*SPN*: 75–6). The Italian masses are said to display a 'traditional apoliticism and passivity' (*SPN*: 203): this facilitates effective hegemonic control, for the ruling classes are able to maintain their position through the consent of the peasantry without recourse to open coercion (*SPN*: 12). It makes it possible for them, too, to recruit soldiers and mercenaries from the subaltern classes and to mobilize the peasants in the service of reactionary and conservative causes (*SPN*: 74, 85, 215). Disunity and the absence of a collective consciousness are also the hallmarks of subaltern ideology. Peasant demands are designated 'elementary' and relate principally to land, its acquisition and defence (*SPN*: 68, 74). Although peasants and other subaltern groups share what Gramsci calls 'common sense' (*senso comune*) (as opposed to 'common sense', meaning 'good sense', in the customary English use of the phrase), this is a rag-bag of assumptions and beliefs with little internal consistency or cohesion. 'Its most fundamental characteristic is that it is a conception which, even in the brain of one individual, is fragmentary, incoherent and inconsequential, in conformity with the social and actual position of the masses whose philosophy it is' (*SPN*: 325–6, 419). Peasants rarely accept new ideas in a pure form, but bundle different ones together into a 'more or less heterogeneous and bizarre combination' (*SPN*: 338). Even when the material structure of subaltern existence is transformed, ideas are slow to change. That 'mass ideological factors always lag behind mass economic phenomena' was for Gramsci an important argument against a crude economic determinism (*SPN*: 168, 324–5). By themselves peasants possess only fragmentary elements of a class consciousness. Peasants participated in their own subordination by subscribing to hegemonic values, by accepting, admiring and even seeking to emulate many of the attributes of the superordinate classes. Such antipathy as peasants showed was often directed against officials as the representatives of the city rather than against the rural landlords and petty bourgeoisie. This antipathy represented merely 'a basic negative, polemical attitude' and constituted no more than 'the first glimmer' of class consciousness (*SPN*: 272–3).

The weaknesses of the peasantry found characteristic expression, too, in such movements as it produced. These were spontaneous, amorphous, violent and destructive (*SPN*: 74, 97, 102, 340; *SPW II*: 397, 454–5). Gramsci described the southern peasants in 1926 as being 'in perpetual ferment, but as a mass . . . incapable of giving a centralised expression to their aspirations and needs' (*SPW II*: 454). Without outside direction subaltern movements were likely to lapse into 'anarchic turbulence' (*SPN*: 94) or to be reabsorbed within the prevailing hegemonic order. Autonomous peasant movements were rare (*SPW II*: 456) except in such limited forms as banditry which he regarded as 'a kind of primitive terrorism, with no lasting or effective results' (Fiori, 1973: 31). Even in rebellion, Gramsci observed, subaltern groups are 'subject to the activity of ruling groups' and would remain so until '"permanent" victory breaks their subordination' and even then 'not immediately' (*SPN*: 55). Indeed, it was central to Gramsci's notion of subaltern (*subalterno*: subordinate, dependent), to which we will return shortly, that such groups lacked autonomy, which was essentially the hallmark of the hegemonic classes.

Even within this array of negative attributes there are contradictions which Gramsci does not attempt to reconcile: between 'passivity' and 'turbulence', for example. One might be tempted to attribute such apparent contradictions to the unfinished nature of Gramsci's prison writings. But it seems more consistent with his overall stance to see them as indicative of the actually contradictory nature of subaltern culture and politics. Thus subalterns might draw from both passive and active aspects of their culture without being entirely and permanently governed by one or the other, though negative, passive attributes were likely, from the very fact of their subordination, to predominate. To put it another way, subaltern society was engaged in a continuing dialectical tussle within itself, between its active and its passive voice, between acceptance and resistance, between isolation and collectivity, between disunity and cohesion. This duality of subalternity (not a word Gramsci actually employs but a convenient term to encompass the material, ideological and political condition of the subaltern classes) will be clearer when we turn to the positive attributes he identifies.

Before that it is worth making two further interjections. Gramsci's interpretation of what constituted positive or negative attributes was necessarily governed by his revolutionary Marxism: it reflected the extent to which those elements, in his view, contributed to or militated against the attainment of a revolutionary class consciousness. Some attributes, read as negative in this context, might appear in a different light as positive. Banditry and peasant 'turbulence' might be ineffective, amorphous and inconsequential in their inability to end peasant subordination and exploitation, but they might not be without important local consequences for relations between an oppressed peasantry and an entrenched landlord class. Gramsci also acknowledged that understanding of the history of the subaltern classes was severely restricted by the paucity of source materials from the viewpoint of the subalterns themselves. It *appeared* that subaltern history was fragmented, episodic and spontaneous but in actuality, if the record were more complete, it might be found that there was greater consistency, cohesion and political consciousness among the subordinate classes. In inviting closer investigation of subaltern history and society, Gramsci left open the possibility of a more positive subaltern dimension than he was personally able to identify (*SPN*: 54–5, 196).

Gramsci located the positive attributes of subaltern groups almost exclusively in the cultural and political realm. He does not appear to have seen any appreciable strengths in the economic activities and social organization of the subalterns, at least not of those in the countryside. Among the positive features he did identify two as particularly noteworthy. Gramsci's hostility to the 'fatalistic' and positivistic determinism of theorists like Bukharin and the elements of a humanistic Marxism in his own thought led him to believe that revolutions were not produced merely as a result of certain material structures or conjunctions: they came about through political action and through the development of class consciousness among the subaltern classes. Gramsci was, as we have seen, critical of those Marxists who sought only pure class-conscious movements. The corollary of this was that the spontaneity and 'elementary passions' of the people, despite their political immaturity and negative qualities, needed to be taken up, educated and brought 'into line with modern theory' (that is, Marxism). They provided the subaltern commitment and energy, the first raw elements from which a genuine class consciousness could emerge (*SPN*: 198).

Second, although he viewed critically the inconsistent and contradictory nature of 'common sense' and popular culture, Gramsci at the same time valued them for the expression they gave to subaltern consciousness. Here, however, one enters difficult straits, for Gramsci's basic attitude was to regard popular beliefs as being largely derivative from ruling-class culture and thus constituting one of the principal props of class hegemony and subordination (*SPN*: 327). But this view was qualified in several ways. Subalterns might receive the substance of their culture from the hegemonic classes but make it their own by impregnating it with non-hegemonic values or by selecting some aspects and rejecting others: thus the Catholicism of the Italian peasantry was vastly different in the world view it embodied from the Catholicism of the hegemonic classes (*SPN*: 420, cf. Cirese, 1982: 226). The mental tenacity of the subalterns, which made them slow to take up revolutionary ideas, also made them resistant to attempts to introduce or impose new hegemonic ideas (*SPN*: 337). Again, and here Gramsci reverted to a more economically deterministic Marxism, since consciousness was (ultimately) a product of material conditions (*SPN*: 324, 326), subaltern ideology, especially as represented by religion, one of its principal forms, was necessarily consistent with, or appropriate to, the subalterns' own material existence. Peasant religion was, accordingly, 'crassly materialistic' or frankly 'pagan' (*SPN*: 420; *SPW II*: 456), reflecting the needs and aspirations of the peasants' own way of life rather than that of the hegemonic classes (*SPN*: 337). Religion was not, therefore, 'self-deception' (or 'false consciousness') (*SPN*: 326–7), but was, for the subalterns, 'a specific way of rationalising the world and real life'; it provided 'the general framework for real political activity' among them (*SPN*: 337), especially in the absence of a socialist party responsive to their needs. It further followed that the possession of a shared subaltern culture could cut across the hegemony of the ruling classes and provide a basis for collective action among the subalterns. For Gramsci, the one-time student of linguistics, language (broadly conceived) was of crucial importance here both in embodying a 'specific conception of the world' (*SPN*: 323) and in constituting the means by which sentiments could be communicated and shared among subaltern groups (*SPN*: 349).

The importance Gramsci attached to the peasantry will, it is hoped, be apparent from the discussion so far. Italy's peasants provided him with historical evidence as to how a subaltern class was held in subjection through its internal weaknesses and through its acceptance of the moral, political and social leadership or hegemony of the ruling classes. Having understood the nature of that subordination, Gramsci believed he could see how it might be broken through an alliance of workers and peasants and through the development of class consciousness among the peasants. Unlike many Marxists, Gramsci did not see the peasantry as a class to be despised and consigned to the mortuary of history. He was convinced that they could become a truly revolutionary class. It was, therefore, the task of Marxists to understand and to develop a critique of subaltern ideology and culture so as to expose its negative features and to educate and strengthen its positive ones.

Seen in this light Gramsci's use of the term 'subaltern' is of singular importance. At a minimal evaluation it can be regarded as little more than a convenient shorthand for a variety of subordinate classes –

industrial workers, peasants, labourers, artisans, shepherds and so forth. Its use in the *Prison Notebooks* may have been prompted by a need to avoid the censorship which a more politically explicit word like 'proletariat' might attract. But Gramsci's choice of alternative terms in the *Notebooks* was seldom mere evasion and concealment: an elaboration or enhancement of meaning was often given, for example by the substitution of 'the philosophy of praxis' for 'Marxism'. Certainly, 'subaltern' is not an altogether happy choice, at least in English where it invites an unwelcome confusion with military terminology (and with junior *officers* at that). Nor does it obviate the need for more specific class designations. But it does have some advantages. It emphasizes the central importance of the relationship of power between social groups: they are not just peasants and landlords but subordinates and superordinates, conscious of the implications and consequences of their respective positions though not necessarily in terms that signify a developed class awareness. In dealing with peasants and other groups in a society, like that of nineteenth-century Italy or India, that had not become wholly capitalistic, the language of subalternity might generally be more appropriate than that of class. Its use is expressive, too, of Gramsci's persistent use of dialectical couplets – hegemony/subordination, force/consent, active/passive – to bring out the conflicts and contradictions (again in opposition to determinist, positivist thought) to be found within actual historical situations.

Gramsci's use of the term 'subaltern' further invites us to appreciate the common properties of subordinate groups as a whole – the shared fact of their subordination, their intrinsic weaknesses, their limited strengths. The special, revolutionary character of the industrial proletariat as envisaged by the Marx and Engels of the *Communist Manifesto* is correspondingly played down. Gramsci does not dispute that the proletariat has certain advantages of organization and consciousness, and, as has been seen, he expected it to establish its hegemony over other subordinate classes. But it, too, has many of the negative attributes of the peasantry – passivity, disunity, spontaneity, etc. (*SPW II*: 453, 462). Experience of the factory movement in Turin showed Gramsci that a spontaneous and autonomous workers' movement was not in itself sufficient to topple the capitalist state: the workers, too, needed political guidance and a party organization. Moreover, modern industrial management, with its Taylorism and its Fordism, had erected new obstacles to the development of a class-conscious, revolutionary working class (*SPN*: 277f.). It is suggestive in this connection to note Gramsci's error, admittedly early in his political career, in attributing Marx's celebrated phrase about 'potatoes in a sack' to urban workers instead of to the peasantry (Pozzolini, 1970: 79–80).

Conversely, the peasants, by Gramsci's account, had certain, albeit underdeveloped, elements of consciousness. What Gramsci offers us in effect is not, therefore, a stark dichotomy between proletarian and peasant, between revolutionary and reactionary, such as appears in Marx's writing on nineteenth-century history and politics, but differences of degrees of consciousness and solidarity between the two, with the ability of both to become revolutionary classes.

Gramsci in India: Autonomy and Subordination

A central issue that arises from attempting to apply Gramscian ideas to the specific historical context of the Indian peasantry is that of autonomy. As we have seen, Gramsci's emphasis was upon the strength of the coercive domination and hegemonic direction which ruling groups exercised over subordinate classes. His purpose was to explain why state power, especially in modern capitalist societies, was so difficult to overthrow and why the subaltern classes appeared to accept their subordination. He saw little evidence of autonomy in peasant movements, both in the specific sense of their failure to generate their own leadership and organization and to formulate their own demands effectively, and in the broader sense of being unable to mount an ideological and political assault capable of overthrowing the domination and hegemony of the ruling classes. 'Subaltern groups', we are reminded, 'are always subject to the authority of ruling groups, even when they rebel and rise up' (*SPN*: 55).

In apparent contrast with this hegemonic theory, Ranajit Guha in the introductory essay to the first volume of *Subaltern Studies* has argued that during the colonial period in India subaltern politics constituted an 'autonomous domain' which 'neither originated from the elite politics nor did its existence depend upon the latter' (Guha, 1982: 4). He sees this subaltern domain as having its roots in the pre-colonial period, but it 'continued to operate vigorously' under the British and even to develop 'new strains in both form and content' (1982: 4). He envisages two essentially discrete political 'domains', that of 'the people' or the 'subaltern classes and groups constituting the mass of the labouring population and the intermediate strata in the town and country' (1982: 4), and that of the elite, used here not in Gramsci's sense of a revolutionary vanguard but as a synonym for hegemonic or ruling classes. In the context of colonial India, the elites consisted of both European administrators, planters, landlords and missionaries, and of indigenous feudal magnates, landholders, merchants and bureaucrats (1982: 8). This bipartite division of a society as complexly hierarchical as that of colonial India is not without its problems. To take but one obvious example, the rich peasants who appear as subalterns in their relations with a landed elite of the *zamindar* type are in themselves an elite in their dominant relations with the poorer rural strata of landless labourers and village artisanal and service groups. Any given society may divide in different ways in different situations, but, consistent with Gramsci's theorization, the central problematic is seen to lie in the fundamental and persistent division of society between the subordinate, labouring, cultivating groups and the classes that exercise economic and political domination over them. The precise location of the elite/subaltern divide needs to be established in each specific regional and historical context in accordance with these general principles (1982: 8).

Guha identifies the subaltern domain of politics as including a wide variety of generally autonomous modes of thought and action, particularly expressed through rebellions, riots and popular movements. It is implied, though not in this particular context explicated, that these are the political expression of a subaltern peasant culture and world view which is in itself largely autonomous from that of the elite. The elite domain of politics consisted during the colonial period of the arena created by the British through their laws, legislatures and other institutions of political society, and of the activities and organizations of formal political parties and movements, pre-eminently the Indian National Congress. Guha does not see these two domains as entirely separate: from time to time they overlap and interact but they never become wholly integrated. They remain two 'domains', two 'streams', because of the failure of the Indian bourgeoisie to overcome this fundamental 'structural dichotomy' and establish an effective hegemony over the entirety of Indian society. 'There were', he writes, 'vast areas in the life and consciousness of the people which were never integrated into their hegemony' (1982: 5–6). When some degree of mixing between the two domains occurred the outcome was often explosive, 'indicating that the masses mobilised by the elite to fight for their own objectives managed to break away from their control and put the characteristic imprint of popular politics on campaigns initiated by the upper classes' (1982: 6). What that 'characteristic imprint' was is revealed more fully in Guha's monograph on peasant insurgency in India (1983a).

It is worth noting at this juncture that scholars working on regions far removed from colonial India have noted similar discontinuities between the politics and culture of the elite and subaltern sections of pre-industrial society. E. P. Thompson has questioned the view that eighteenth-century rural society in England centred almost exclusively on the big house and estate of the local landed magnate. This is merely the view from above, the elitist view, based on the gentry and nobility's estimation of their own importance. It is possible, Thompson argues, to construct quite a different view of rural society from the perspective of the subordinate classes. 'Above all,' he comments, 'there might be a radical disassociation – and at times antagonism – between the culture and even the "politics" of the poor and those of the great' (Thompson, 1978: 136). To this degree, Thompson, like Guha, dissents from Gramsci's hegemony theory in so far as it suggests an almost total political, cultural and ideological control by the elites over the subaltern classes. In stressing the 'immense distance' between 'polite' and 'plebeian' cultures, Thompson remarks: 'Whatever this hegemony may have been, it did not envelop the lives of the poor and it did not prevent them from defending their own modes of work and leisure, and forming their own rituals, their own satisfactions and view of life.' Hegemony did not, in his view, constitute a rigid, automatic and all-determining structure of domination. It merely 'offered the bare architecture of a structure of relations of domination and subordination' within which 'many different scenes could be set and different dramas enacted' (1978: 163). Raymond Williams has similarly warned against interpreting hegemony as a 'totalising abstraction' to be virtually equated with the absolute ideological and political domination of society. 'A lived hegemony', he argues, 'is always a process.' It is not a rigid, all-encompassing, unchallenged structure, but 'has continually to be renewed, re-created, defended, and modified'. There are always non-hegemonic or counter-hegemonic values at work to resist, restrict and qualify the operations of the hegemonic order (Williams, 1977: 112–13). In thus countering a deterministic streak in Gramsci's writing on hegemony, Thompson, Williams, and Guha have reasserted the historical, humanist and dialectical nature of his basic political and philosophical position.

The compatibility of subaltern autonomy with elite domination or hegemony and the dialectical nature of their relationship has been pointed out by Partha Chatterjee. 'Domination', he explains, 'must exist within a relationship. The dominant groups, in their exercise of domination, do not consume and destroy the dominated classes, for then there would be no *relation* of power, and hence no domination.' Without their autonomy the subalterns would have no identity of their own, no domain 'where they can resist at the same time as they are dominated'. They would simply become integrated into the life-history of the dominant classes. 'The point', Chatterjee argues, 'is to conceptualise a whole aspect of human history *as* a history, i.e. as a movement which flows from the opposition between two distinct social forces.'

To deny autonomy to the subalterns would be 'to petrify this aspect of the historical process, to reduce it to an immobility, indeed to *destroy* its history'. This, he concludes, is precisely what the elitist historiography of India has done (Chatterjee, 1983: 59).

The autonomy of the subaltern domain of politics has been a recurrent theme in the essays contributed to *Subaltern Studies*. Gyanendra Pandey, in his account of the peasant movement in Awadh in 1919–22, has shown how it began as an autonomous movement of the peasantry, taking forms determined by the peasants themselves and giving expression to their own sense of grievance against the landlords and, latterly, against the British regime. Far from initiating or leading the movement, the middle-class nationalists led by Gandhi and Jawaharlal Nehru made a belated attempt to contain the movement by opposing its more violent and radical attacks on the landlords in defence of 'national unity' and Gandhian non-violence. In this the nationalists are seen to have been no more than partly successful, and the gulf between their ideology and methods and those of the peasants remained imperfectly bridged (Pandey, 1982).

There are certain similarities of theme and interpretation between the events Pandey discusses and David Hardiman's account of the Devi movement in south Gujarat in 1922–23. This, too, began as an autonomous movement but in this case among *adivasi* (tribal) peasants seeking to throw off the economic domination of Parsi landlords and liquor dealers through the collective reform of their established way of life. As in Awadh, the Congress was at first of no more than marginal importance to the Devi movement. Gradually, however, middle-class congressmen gained some influence over it and encouraged the *adivasis* to adopt some parts of the Gandhian programme while lessening their direct opposition to the economic demands of the Parsis. Although the movement had petered out by 1924, it is seen by Hardiman as showing how even such an oppressed and exploited subaltern group could initiate and sustain a movement of self-assertion against powerfully entrenched economic and political interests (Hardiman, 1984).

In a third specific case study Shahid Amin has shown by a careful analysis of popular rumours current at the time how perceptions of Gandhi by peasants in the Gorakhpur district of the United Provinces in 1921–22 were shaped by their own beliefs, expectations and material culture and thus did not correlate very closely with the political programme Gandhi and his associates were attempting to convey. Although in this instance the political initiative came from outside the peasantry, the peasants were not mobilized by Gandhi's ideas or by the Congress leadership but were responding according to their own notion of what constituted a *mahatma* and the nature of his powers (Amin, 1984).

In each of these case studies the focus of attention is upon the perceptions and activities of the peasants themselves and the rift between their aspirations and methods and those of the indigenous elite. But at the same time they reiterate Guha's point that, although the elite and subaltern domains are in certain vital respects separate and distinct, they are not therefore unconnected with each other. For their part the Congress politicians were striving to mobilize or contain the peasants and to incorporate them into the nationalist movement on their own terms. Their degree of success varied: often the gulf between subalterns and elites was too great to be bridged. On their side the peasants were often willing to seek or to accept outside assistance and leadership in the belief that this would help their own cause but had little interest in the causes of the elites. Sumit Sarkar in an essay on subaltern involvement in the Swadeshi and non-co-operation movements in Bengal has preferred to stress the interactive nature of the two political domains by referring to the 'relative autonomy' of the subalterns. As his essay shows, the occurrence of a subaltern movement, though not initiated or led by elite politicians, might still be prompted by a perceived crisis within the elite domain, awakening hopes of an end to oppression and the advent of an age of freedom and justice. Subaltern militancy in turn, though it might be no more than partially under elite direction, could none the less add to the assertiveness and effectiveness of the anti-colonial movement and contribute to the long-term undermining of colonial power and authority (Sarkar, 1984). Only through close attention to historical specificity can the complex interactions of elites and subalterns be unravelled and the dialectical and developing nature of their exchanges be adequately understood.

The undertaking and presentation of such investigations into subaltern themes is a conscious attempt on the part of these and other contributors to *Subaltern Studies* to overturn the existing historiography of modern Indian and to establish the centrality of subaltern aspirations and actions in the historical process. In this they are faithful to Gramsci's direction to the 'integral historian' to study the subaltern classes and to seek out 'every trace of interdependent initiative on the part of subaltern groups' (*SPN*: 55). But in so doing they are also reacting against much conventional writing about modern India which has defined 'history' and 'politics' almost exclusively in terms of the ideas and activities of the elite. The mass of the population, where mentioned at all in such works, is relegated to the position of mere recipients of elite decision-making, as an otherwise inert populace to be mobilized as and when required in the service of elite objectives. They are reacting, too, against an economistic or positivist approach which, in seeking to quantify and to define the 'reality' of economic and social phenomena, has tended to ignore or to discount the subjectivity of the human participants. Conventional accounts of famine, for example, have generally ignored as of little consequence the perceptions and responses of the subaltern classes to what, after all, was primarily *their* crisis of subsistence and survival (cf. Arnold, 1984). And they have begun to question, too, the representation, derived mainly from structural–functionalist theory, of Indian society as a complex but essentially harmonious whole in which conflict is never so fundamental that it cannot be resolved or assimilated, particularly through the accommodating structure of Hinduism and the caste system. Conflict, in such a view, is even seen to validate and uphold the integral social order by encouraging the development of vertical linkages (patronage networks, factions, political organizations, etc.), rather than opening up irreconcilable horizontal divisions along class lines (cf. Hardiman, 1981: 223; 1984).

It is no accident that most of the contributors to *Subaltern Studies* so far have been historians or have worked from a mainly historical perspective for it is perhaps historians who have most come to feel the inadequacy of Indian studies as they currently exist. Historians of modern India have hitherto been too timid. They have either clung to a familiar tradition of elite historiography or, where they have ventured beyond the elite domain into the history of the Indian masses, they have too readily accepted the static models and positivist definitions of other disciplines. The historians of *Subaltern Studies* have become dissatisfied with the failure of history to come into its own and to tackle the issues of domination and subordination, passivity and resistance, which seem to them central to an understanding of modern India. This is not, of course, to say that historians should sever connections with other disciplines and retreat behind their own intellectual walls. On the contrary, as Ranajit Guha has demonstrated, the historian of the subaltern classes needs in particular to learn from the methods and concerns of structuralist anthropology and semiology in order to 'de-code' the underlying meaning of subaltern actions and beliefs and their representation in elite documentation (see especially Guha, 1983b). But the overriding purpose remains historical – to explain how and why, despite periodic resistance and despite the autonomy of the subaltern domain, the subordinate classes of modern India have remained in subordination and have not succeeded in securing their own freedom.

Such a bold attempt to restate the terms of Indian historical debate is not without its difficulties. In order to counter assumptions of peasant inertia and irrationality, the contributors to *Subaltern Studies* have necessarily been drawn first to those movements, or aspects of movements, that give the clearest evidence of subaltern initiative and self-assertion. The negative and more familiar attributes in Gramsci's observations on the peasantry have been given less emphasis than the positive and more neglected elements of subaltern ideology and organization. But subsequent research and writing is likely to redress this imbalance by giving greater attention to the restraints acting upon the subaltern political domain. The criticism might also be made that in focusing upon peasant movements and rebellions, the contributors have given these episodes undue prominence and paid inadequate attention to the 99 per cent of the time when peasants are not insurgent or assertive. The investigation of other subaltern themes than rebellion will, no doubt, in time illustrate other sorts of elite/subaltern relations and other forms of subaltern initiative and expression. As Gramsci pertinently observed, even fatalism 'is nothing other than the clothing worn by real and active will in a weak position' (*SPN*: 337). That 'fatalism', 'passivity'[3] and 'dependency relations' exist in modern India does not, therefore, negate the crucial importance of understanding all forms of elite/subaltern relations in dialectical terms. But the immediate need was to challenge the assumptions of the existing historiography and this could most effectively be done by showing through peasant movements and rebellions the separateness and the vitality of the subaltern political domain.

The study of rebellion in its various forms is, besides, always likely to command particular interest for the historian of the subaltern classes. It is often only on such occasions that the actions and beliefs of the subalterns enter the records of the elite and thus leave a retrievable trace. More substantially, the very fact that a peasant rebellion occurs at all is evidence of the existence of a separate political domain which elite domination and hegemony has been unable entirely to supersede or suppress. In this way a rebellion (or some comparable crisis like a famine or a major epidemic) can reveal more about the nature of underlying identities and conflicts than studying the 'normality' of everyday life in which such relationships lie dormant or untested. The consequences of rebellion were too momentous for peasants to stumble into it spontaneously, without preliminary and less drastic moves to secure the redress of their grievances. Rebellion was not, therefore, merely some automatic reflex action to external economic or political stimulus: it was 'peasant praxis', the expression through peasant action of the collective consciousness of the peasantry (Guha, 1983b).

At the same time the inability of the peasantry to throw off its subordination *unaided* is clearly indicated in the *Subaltern Studies* essays. The substantial qualification of Gramsci lies, therefore, not in questioning the overall fact of peasant subordination to dominant and hegemonic groups, but in showing the extent to which peasant politics possessed autonomy within that encompassing structure of subordination. During the colonial period the Indian peasantry had a relatively large measure of autonomy in these terms from both the British rulers and indigenous elites. It may be that for identifiable historical and cultural reasons this autonomous element was greater in nineteenth- and early-twentieth-century India than in the post-Renaissance Italy Gramsci was discussing.

From what, then, did the relative autonomy of the subaltern domain of politics arise? If, as Gramsci suggested, subaltern ideology and culture was largely a mosaic made up of fragments of elite culture and hegemonic values how could it at the same time be the case, as Guha claims (1982: 5), that 'a notion of resistance to elite domination' was one of the 'invariant features' of subaltern politics?

In the first place it can be argued that an element of resistance was intrinsic to the peasants' economic and political subordination. Conflict was bound to arise between peasants producing for their own subsistence and exchange and the landlords, officials and other superordinates who laid claim to a share of the crop and made other demands upon the peasants, such as for labour service. Awareness of mutual subordination to this process of extraction might lay the foundations for elementary forms of collective resistance and solidarity among the peasants and related subaltern groups.

But we can go further than this. It can be argued, as Rodney Hilton has done in the context of medieval Europe, that the 'capacity for organisation in pursuit of social and political demands arose naturally from the day-to-day experience of peasants' (Hilton, 1974: 70). Agricultural co-operation over harvesting, grazing and the use of common lands and forests partly countered the isolation of individual peasant households and promoted village collectivity. Such forms of co-operation were not, of course, unknown in India either. Peasant solidarity could develop from other collective activities, too. Guha (1983a: ch. 4) has shown how the language and organization derived from hunting and fishing in rural India could provide a natural basis for peasant co-operation in insurgency. Religious rites closely linked to agricultural cycles and subsistence needs, such as rain-making ceremonies in times of incipient drought (Arnold, 1984), or ceremonies to ward off epidemics of cholera and smallpox, also emphasized and gave expression to the collectivity of the Indian peasant village.

Such activities might define the peasant community narrowly by confining its effective meaning to the village or immediate locality and treating with suspicion or hostility outsiders, including other peasants. But there were other forms of communication and other identities that transcended this extreme localism. Disease propitiation movements, like that which later developed into the Devi movement in south Gujarat (Hardiman, 1984), could cover considerable distances and cross boundaries of caste and even language. Rumours, too, travelled rapidly from village to village, market to market, and could act as powerful agents of peasant self-mobilization, for they gave anonymous voice to widely shared fears and expectations. At times transmission took a physical form, with symbolic objects or offerings passing from one village to another to propitiate a malevolent deity or to call for preparations for insurrection to begin (Guha, 1983a: ch. 6). David Hardiman has shown, too, how the social and cultural solidarities of caste, too often treated as a divisive force in peasant India, facilitated the mobilization of the Patidars in Gujarat in the 1920s and 1930s and enabled them to conduct sustained agitations against the colonial authorities (Hardiman, 1981). Thus, the economic, social and cultural forms of Indian peasant existence in themselves provided, to a far greater degree than Gramsci identified in the Italian peasantry, vital elements of peasant solidarity and collective action.

The extent of peasant cultural autonomy and the ways in which it might inform peasant consciousness are complex issues. But the case of the Indian peasantry suggests that Gramsci's notion of subaltern culture being in essence derived from the elite and thus serving as an ideological agency of peasant subordination is greatly overdrawn. As in early modern Europe (Burke, 1978: ch. 2), there appear to have been two-way cultural exchanges between elite and subaltern groups; but Muslim and then British conquest did create in many parts of rural India a marked cultural and religious disjuncture between some urban, administrative and landholding elites and the mass of the Hindu peasantry. In general, one would wish to give rather more positive emphasis than does Gramsci to the capacity of the rural subaltern classes to sustain a culture consistent with their own needs and experiences rather than mirroring the world view of the elites.

The question of subaltern autonomy also has an important historical dimension in the context of the long-term transition from feudalism to capitalism. India's pre-colonial feudal economic and political structure left a large measure of power in the hands of local rulers and landholders; economically, localities had only limited relations with the outside world. In such an environment of relative isolation, local society, including its peasant segment, held a substantial measure of economic, political and cultural autonomy. As Gramsci remarks of medieval Italy (*SPN*: 54):

> centralisation, whether political–territorial or social (and the one is merely a function of the other), was minimal. The State was, in a certain sense, a mechanical bloc of social groups, often of different race: within the circle of political–military compression, which was only exercised harshly at certain moments, the subaltern groups had a life of their own, institutions of their own, etc.

Much the same could be said of pre-colonial India, and indeed of many parts of colonial India until late in the nineteenth century. But the colonial state, at first continuing or associating itself with Indian feudal forms of administration and extraction, soon developed the forms and functions of a European bourgeois state. The reorientation of the Indian economy to meet the requirements of an international economic system, and changes in the nature and penetration of state power, aided by improvements in transport and communications, began to break down the old feudal systems and to erode the autonomy of local communities. The speed of the transformation varied. In some areas, like the formerly almost inaccessible hill-tracts of the Eastern Ghats, the changes came quickly, within a brief, traumatic period in the late nineteenth century, and drew a sustained and openly hostile response from peasants and their traditional chiefs, faced with the loss or diminution of their ancient autonomies (Arnold, 1982). Elsewhere, the changes were more gradual and the response more mixed or muted. Economic and administrative change and the growth of rural capitalism began to alter relations within the locality. Peasants saw the local elites, from whom they were still inclined to expect leadership, as either becoming the agents and allies of external forces or uncertain protectors against them. The process of economic differentiation began to open up new lines of conflict within the peasantry itself. But, as Gramsci indicated, ideology does not necessarily keep pace with underlying economic change. In Bengal in the 1920s and 1930s, so Partha Chatterjee has argued, many peasants retained a strong sense of their old collective or 'communal' identity, even though external change and internal differentiation had by then undercut much of its former reality. There was, therefore, a cultural and ideological time-lag; and since the notion of community continued to find its most potent expression through religion, action by Muslim peasants commonly took the form of attacks upon Hindu traders and moneylenders and Hindu shrines and hence became 'communal' in the more common Indian usage of that term

(Chatterjee, 1982). Only gradually did perceptions shift from a peasant–communal mode, in which religion was a primary form of self-expression, to one more secular and class-oriented.

Thus during the nineteenth and twentieth centuries the old sets of elite/subaltern relations were being undermined by colonialism and capitalism. Only gradually (and often imperfectly) were new controls being established in their place through the developing power of the colonial state and the rise of the Indian bourgeoisie. During this period of transition, between the decay of the old order and the establishment of the new, the peasantry experienced a time of disorientation and uncertainty, unsure of its old identities and leadership, yet largely hostile to the new forces impinging upon it. In such a transitional situation, the autonomy of the peasantry, the felt need for the peasantry to organize itself to defend its interests, to oppose change or to remind superordinate groups of their obligations to the peasantry, may have assumed exceptional importance.

Of importance, too, to the specific strength of the subaltern domain of politics in late-nineteenth- and early-twentieth-century India was the nature of the nationalist movement. Under Gandhi in particular the nationalism of the middle classes developed a position of ideological independence from the British, a position from which it laid claim to leadership over Indian society as a whole, including the peasantry (Chatterjee, 1984). But, as many of the contributions to *Subaltern Studies* suggest, the bourgeoisie failed to establish a genuine hegemony in the Gramscian sense. Gandhi perhaps came closest to securing the 'consent' of the peasantry for middle-class ideological and political leadership, both through his conscious identification with the lifestyle and (sometimes) the grievances of the peasants and through their receptivity to the figure of a *mahatma* through whom they hoped to achieve their own liberation from oppression and exploitation. But as Pandey's account of the Awadh peasant movement reminds us, the Congress leadership failed to advance beyond its own immediate class interests, as shown by its attachment to Gandhian non-violence and inter-class 'national unity', to associate itself with the peasants' demands. Without effective leadership, the peasantry was unable to develop a more mature political consciousness and was left exposed to the coercive retribution of the colonial state (Pandey, 1982). This verdict is echoed by Guha (1982: 6), who remarks that the initiatives originating from the subaltern domain were not in themselves powerful enough to transform the nationalist movement into 'a full-fledged struggle for national liberation'. The working class had not yet developed fully as a class in terms of either its objective conditions or its consciousness, and was not, therefore, able to lead, or even to be an able ally for, the peasantry. The onus of leadership thus fell heavily on the bourgeoisie, but it failed, he believes, to provide the leadership to raise the peasants' struggles out of their localism and other limitations and to 'generalise them into a nationwide anti-imperialist campaign'.

In this failure of the Indian bourgeoisie to unite with the peasantry and to effect a more radical transformation there are suggestive parallels with Gramsci's analysis of Italian unification in the mid-nineteenth century. In his view unification came about only through the diplomatic and military power of the Piedmontese state. The middle classes, especially what Gramsci calls 'the Action Party' headed by Mazzini and Garibaldi, failed to fulfil its historical ('Jacobin') role of aligning with the peasantry against the old feudal ruling classes and thereby establishing its hegemony over the subaltern classes. Instead, the middle-class intellectuals trailed behind the Piedmontese diplomats and generals, while the peasants either, as in Lombardy and Venetia, fought for the occupying Austrians against the nationalists or, as in Sicily, were crushed when they rose in support of Garibaldi's invasion. Gramsci characterized the outcome as a 'passive revolution', a superficial transformation that, in the absence of mass involvement and effective bourgeois leadership, had succeeded merely in establishing the coercive domination of the Piedmontese state over an imperfectly integrated society. In this failure to create a genuine 'people-nation', Gramsci identified one of the root causes of the later rise of fascism (*SPN*: 52–120).

By comparison with Italy's 'Action Party' India's nationalist leaders seem to have associated themselves more closely with the peasantry, especially its richer stratum. Gramsci's characterization of Gandhism along with Tolstoyism as 'naive theorisations of "the passive revolution" with religious overtones' (*SPN*: 107) is too slighting. But the idea of a 'passive revolution' does help to emphasize the no more than partial engagement of the mass of the Indian peasantry in the independence struggle and the extent to which state power in India since independence has continued to rest upon coercive control rather than upon hegemonic consent. In this, as Guha asserts (1982: 5) one might see 'an important historical truth . . . the failure of the Indian bourgeoisie to speak for the nation'.

Conclusion

Although the fact that Gramsci's observations on the peasantry are scattered throughout his writings and not ordered in any systematic way makes it at times difficult to attribute to him a consistent line of thought, the very disposition *not* to treat the peasantry in isolation is one of the strengths and attractions of his contribution to the theoretical and empirical study of the peasantry. In Gramsci peasants are always represented as a class in relation to others, always a *subaltern* group, subject to others, whether to feudal lords, to the bourgeoisie or, finally, to the leadership of the proletariat. It was the nature and durability of that relationship of subordination that intrigued him. In part he attributed it to material conditions, to the poverty of the peasant, to his location within a feudal or capitalist mode of production. He also recognized the part that the raw coercive power of domination might play in establishing and maintaining peasant subordination. But neither economic determinants nor physical force seemed to him an entirely convincing answer. The concept of hegemony provided him with an alternative (or rather, since Gramsci did not see the actual historical situations in terms of either pure hegemony or pure domination, complementary) explanation of why peasants remained disunited and passive and seemed to consent to their own subordination. Hegemony explained to Gramsci's satisfaction the subjectivity of subordination: it was not just externally imposed (through force, through economic and political structures), but was internalized by the peasants themselves as part of their culture and their consciousness. Carried to a theoretical extreme, the concept of hegemony denied virtually all independence of thought to the subaltern classes: it was a totalitarian conception, as some of Gramsci's detractors have feared it was intended to be.

Shut up in a fascist prison, racked by chronic ill-health, Gramsci was perhaps entitled to err on the side of gloomy exaggeration. His reading of Italian history and the politics of the day led him to believe that hegemony was responsible for the strength of state power and ruling-class supremacy in modern capitalist society and accounted for the seeming reluctance or inability of the masses of the city and the countryside to rise up against them. But if one reads Gramsci closely, and if one is alert to his deeper political and philosophical concerns, it can be seen that he was drawing attention to the importance and tenacity of hegemony the better to understand how to find its weaknesses and to overcome it. Gramsci's belief in Marxism as historical dialecticism was profound and ultimately as optimistic as it was humanistic. Domination and hegemony, however strong, were never absolute. Despite their subordination peasants retained some positive cultural and political attributes of their own which could not be wholly integrated into the domination or hegemony of the ruling classes. In themselves these attributes might be redolent of peasants' political weaknesses – their turbulence, spontaneity, incoherence, passivity and so forth. But, with the right guidance and political education, their positive elements could be nurtured and developed into a mature class consciousness. In alliance with intellectuals and industrial workers, peasants thus had the capacity, in his view, to overthrow the ruling classes and, ultimately, help to free themselves from their ancient subordination. But class consciousness, no more than the hegemony of the old rulers, could not simply be imposed upon the subalterns. It was, therefore, of the utmost importance to Gramsci not only to recognize the nature and strength of domination and hegemony, but also to look for evidence that historically the peasantry had shown, through its 'elementary' demands and by its 'elementary' forms of self-expression and organization, the first glimmerings of an incipient class identity.

The contributors to *Subaltern Studies* have not, as yet, given sufficient attention to the forms that domination and hegemony took in colonial India. Some of these have already been explored, though not in Gramscian terms, in the existing literature. In the context of the prevailing historiography of the region, the first priority was to pursue Gramsci's other concern and to uncover and appraise the neglected history of subaltern consciousness and subaltern initiative and resistance. This was a necessary starting-point in order to establish that elite–subaltern relations were of a dialectical nature and to counter elitist and structural–functionalist assumptions about the one-sidedness of power relations in India and the intrinsic harmony of India's social and political order. Through their empirical findings and the more general theorizations, the contributors to *Subaltern Studies* have tended to go beyond Gramsci in identifying a greater degree of autonomy and internal cohesion in the peasant politics of modern India than he saw in his native Italy. But a society still retaining some of its old feudal autonomies, a society in which a large measure of state power (and in some areas economic power) rested in the hands of an alien ruling group, and in which the emerging bourgeoisie had yet to establish effective control over the mass of the peasantry, was likely to be one in which the autonomy of the peasants was particularly marked. None the less, the contributors have, in general, not lost sight of the need to see the peasantry as a subaltern class, engaged in various relations of subordination with both foreign and indigenous elites and subject to forms of control that were both rankly coercive and more subtly hegemonic. As indicated at the outset, Gramsci's ideas are not necessarily self-sufficient explanations nor universal in their applicability. But they do draw attention to a number of aspects of the nature of subordination and control that are of the greatest relevance to those who seek a greater understanding of peasant subalternity in India.

Notes

1. One notable exception to this has been the work of Eric Hobsbawm, whose discussions of peasant consciousness and peasant politics have clearly been influenced by his enthusiasm for Gramsci (in particular, see Hobsbawm, 1971 and 1973).

2. The Gramscian concept of hegemony has been too extensively discussed to require further detailed comment here. Femia (1975: 31), following *SPN*: 12, defines it as 'the predominance obtained by consent rather than force of one class or group over other classes'. Bates (1975: 352) defines it as 'political leadership based on the consent of the led; the consent which is secured by the diffusion and popularisation of the world view of the ruling class'. Some commentators restrict its usage to modern capitalist and predominantly industrial societies, but it is evident from Gramsci's own discussion of Italian history that he sees *elements* of hegemony existing in earlier times and in rural society even if hegemony reaches its most diverse, developed and effective forms only in modern industrial society.

3. Hobsbawm (1973: 13) likewise interprets 'passivity' to be a common and often successful form of peasant resistance and hence a form of class struggle.

References and Further Reading

Amin, S., 1984, 'Gandhi as Mahatma: Gorakhpur District, Eastern U.P., 1921–22', in R. Guha (ed.), *Subaltern Studies III.*

Arnold, D., 1982, 'Rebellious Hillmen: The Gudem–Rampa Risings, 1839–1924', in R. Guha (ed.), *Subaltern Studies I.*

———, 1984, 'Famine in Peasant Consciousness and Peasant Action: Madras 1876–78', in R. Guha (ed.), *Subaltern Studies III.*

Bates, T. R., 1975, 'Gramsci and the Theory of Hegemony', *Journal of the History of Ideas,* XXXVI.

Burke, P., 1978, *Popular Culture in Early Modern Europe,* London: Temple Smith.

Cammett, J. M., 1967, *Antonio Gramsci and the Origins of Italian Communism,* Stanford: Stanford University Press.

Chatterjee, P., 1982, 'Agrarian Relations and Communalism in Bengal, 1926–1935', in R. Guha (ed.), *Subaltern Studies I.*

———, 1983, 'Peasants, Politics and Historiography: A Response', *Social Scientist* No. 120.

———, 1984, 'Gandhi and the Critique of Civil Society', in R. Guha (ed.), *Subaltern Studies III.*

Cirese, A. M., 1982, 'Gramsci's Observations on Folklore', in A. S. Sassoon (ed.), *Approaches to Gramsci,* London: Writers and Readers.

Davidson, A., 1977, *Antonio Gramsci: Towards an Intellectual Biography,* London: Merlin Press.

Femia, J., 1975, 'Hegemony and Consciousness in the Thought of Antonio Gramsci', *Political Studies*, XXIII.

Fiori, G., 1973, *Antonio Gramsci: Life of a Revolutionary*, New York: Schocken Books.

Guha, R., 1982, 'On Some Aspects of the Historiography of Colonial India', in R. Guha (ed.), *Subaltern Studies I*, Delhi: Oxford University Press.

———, 1983a, *Elementary Aspects of Peasant Insurgency in Colonial India*, Delhi: Oxford University Press.

———, 1983b, 'The Prose of Counter-Insurgency', in R. Guha (ed.), *Subaltern Studies II*, Delhi: Oxford University Press.

———, (ed.), 1984, *Subaltern Studies III*, Delhi: Oxford University Press.

Hardiman, D., 1981, *Peasant Nationalists of Gujarat: Kheda District, 1917–1934*, Delhi: Oxford University Press.

———, 1984, 'Adivasi Assertion in South Gujarat: The Devi Movement of 1922–23', in R. Guha (ed.), *Subaltern Studies III*.

Hilton, R., 1974, 'Peasant Society, Peasant Movements and Feudalism in Medieval Europe', in H. A. Landsberger (ed.), *Rural Protest: Peasant Movements and Social Change*, London: Macmillan.

Hobsbawm, E. J., 1971, 'Class Consciousness in History', in I. Meszaros (ed.), *Aspects of History and Class Consciousness*, London: Routledge and Kegan Paul.

———, 1973, 'Peasants and Politics', *Journal of Peasant Studies*, I.

Pandey, G., 1982, 'Peasant Revolt and Indian Nationalism: The Peasant Movement in Awadh, 1919–1922', in R. Guha (ed.), *Subaltern Studies I*.

Pozzolini, A., 1970, *Antonio Gramsci: An Introduction to His Thought*, London: Pluto Press.

Sarkar, S., forthcoming, 'The Conditions and Nature of Subaltern Militancy: Bengal from Swadeshi to Non-Cooperation, c. 1905–22', in R. Guha (ed.), *Subaltern Studies III*.

SPN, *Antonio Gramsci: Selections from the Prison Notebooks (SPN)*, London: Lawrence and Wishart, 1971.

SPW II, *Antonio Gramsci: Selections from Political Writings (SPW), 1921–1926*, London: Lawrence and Wishart, 1978.

Thompson, E. P., 1978, 'Eighteenth-Century English Society: Class Struggle without Class?', *Social History*, III.

Williams, R., 1977, *Marxism and Literature*, Oxford: Oxford University Press.

4

'The Making of the Working Class': E. P. Thompson and Indian History[1]

Rajnarayan Chandavarkar

The reception and influence of Edward Thompson's historical work has been marked by paradox. It is surprising, for instance, that a historian in whose work the state occupied such an important place should have spawned a vast historiography in which the state was simply left out. Moreover, Thompson's writings were characterized by their Englishness; yet, for one who was quite so attentive to the specificities of a peculiar social and cultural context, it is remarkable that the influence of his work was global, attracting followers in several continents and diverse historiographies. Finally, it is ironical that while Thompson was perhaps best known, and most widely admired, for having demonstrated how the history of a class may be written, his method and style of argument may have contributed substantially to the deconstruction and dissolution of the very concept of class.

In the light of these paradoxes, this essay examines the influence of Thompson's work on the investigation of the working class in Indian history. Its purpose is to consider primarily how historians of India responded to Thompson's inspirational work, how they read it and what they took away from it; and further, how the expectations of social theory were served when confronted with the evidence of Indian working-class history.

The tradition of writing about Indian labour has passed through several shifts in perspective and approach but each has indelibly marked the subject. Until 1918, commentaries about labour in India, produced largely by social investigators, both official and philanthropic, focused upon the physical and moral degradation of the urban poor, and considered the means by which their conditions might be alleviated. The flurry of strikes which followed the First World War stimulated a wave of writing about labour which, in the context of widespread public anxieties about urban poverty and overcrowding, the rise of nationalism and the threat of widespread unrest, disclosed a greater sensitivity to, and apprehension of, the possible political consequences of impoverishment and exploitation.[2] As publicists and philanthropists were drawn into representing workers during industrial disputes, they turned their attention to the growth of strikes and trade unions. They meditated upon the nature and weaknesses of trade unions, the role and effect upon them of 'outsiders' (that is, organizers who were not themselves workers) and the proper place of political programmes and ideology in their activities.[3]

From the late 1920s, the growing influence of communists in the trade union movement pulled this literature in fresh directions. The communists assumed the inherent revolutionary propensity of the working classes and understood their own role to be the realization of this potential. They also took it for granted that the working classes were primarily concerned with real and immediate material issues. By contrast, nationalism appeared to be an effete bourgeois ideology which was unlikely to sustain, even if it was able to muster, mass support. To the extent that the Congress gained a mass following, the communists set themselves the task of entering the anti-imperialist struggle and directing the working classes towards their revolutionary goals.[4] Accordingly, they examined specific working-class struggles to measure the level of revolutionary consciousness and scrutinized bourgeois consciousness for signs of progress. They considered how deeply the Indian bourgeoisie was committed to nationalism and whether its political leadership would develop the anti-imperialist struggle in a radical direction or whether it was more likely to abandon and betray its popular following.[5] These debates among Indian communists, which in part originated in the theoretical preoccupations of the Comintern, exercised a powerful influence upon the subsequent development of Indian nationalist and Marxist historiography.

These lines of enquiry intersected in the 1950s and 1960s with a growing interest in blueprints for 'development' and modernization. Historians now sought to investigate how far the labour force could be, or had been, rendered functional to the needs of industrialization. They focused upon the supply of labour, measured its rates of turnover and assessed its commitment to the factory. Most crucially, historians working from widely divergent assumptions converged upon the mobilization, recruitment and organization of labour in the modern industrial setting.[6] Alternatively, sometimes in addition, they analysed the development of trade unions as the outcome of the conflict between modern institutional forms of organization and the social control of supposedly 'traditional' leaders drawn from the ranks of jobbers, recruiting agents and labour contractors.[7] In this way, the history of the working class was studied in terms of the intentions and objectives of the entrepreneurs or made interchangeable with the history of their leaders, trade unions and political parties. Moreover, the history of the Indian working classes came to be represented as an example of a labour force at 'an early stage of industrialization', which, it was implied, was evolving towards the 'advanced stage' manifested in 'the West'.

In the late 1970s, when Thompson was elected President of the Indian History Congress, and rode into session on the back of an elephant, this was a tribute primarily to *The Making*. Yet, at the time, studies of the Indian working class strongly reflected their long-standing historiographical inheritance. Historians investigated 'the material conditions' of the working classes and explored the relationship between labour and wider political movements. For some, reflecting the elite bias of the historiography or working from evolutionary assumptions about industrialization, the notion of 'the making of an Indian working class' was an invitation to satire. Most historians, and especially Marxists, took it for granted that the working class was essentially a structural formation. The weakness of capitalist development in India and its associated characteristics – the persistence of traditional loyalties of caste, kinship and religion – made the notion of a working class, let alone the prospect of class consciousness, unthinkable.

It would seem that these assumptions about the evolutionary and structural character of class took hold despite *The Making*; but it is also possible to see that they could be affirmed by a particular reading of the ambiguities and contradictions of its arguments about class formation. The conceptual originality of *The Making* was, of course, to have represented class as a historical, rather than a structural, fact, and the outcome of agency and struggle, experience and consciousness. None the less, Thompson refused to surrender the theory – however lightly held – that class and class consciousness was 'largely determined by the productive relations into which men are born – or enter involuntarily'.[8] This determinism strengthened the notion that class and class consciousness were intimately related to the particular character of production relations and implied that 'the working class' only fully existed, and therefore could only properly be studied, in advanced capitalist societies. It is significant, therefore – and a reflection of this orthodoxy – that the major debate in Indian Marxism in the 1970s, conducted primarily by economists, focused upon 'the mode of production' and appeared to miss the issues being raised by social history altogether.[9] More generally, Indian historiography was then characterized by an excessive concern either with the history of elites or with those features of Indian society which seemingly made it unique and exceptional – with British policy or how Indian elites subverted their intentions, with the counter-factual question of whether Britain developed or retarded the Indian economy and with social and cultural responses to 'Westernization' and 'modernization'. The study of the working class fitted uneasily with these dominant tendencies in the wider historiography.

The significance of working-class struggles was not diminished, however, simply because they were shrouded in obscurity by the academy. The Indian working class had scarcely been a negligible force. Between 1918 and 1940, for instance, there had been eight general strikes in Bombay city alone, each lasting long periods, while in 1928–29, the city was brought to a standstill for nearly eighteen months.[10] From 1928, the labour movement passed under the hegemony of a communist leadership, which retained its dominance until the 1960s.[11] These developments in Bombay were exceptional in scale, but not in character. Similarly, long-lasting and bitterly contested strikes had repeatedly brought workers together throughout the subcontinent in the early twentieth century. Moreover, while agrarian revolt was what the British feared most, the great nationalist agitations were largely urban affairs in which poor town-dwellers played a prominent part.

It was only in the late 1970s, with the appearance of Thompson's first eighteenth-century studies, that his influence came to be more directly and tangibly registered in Indian historiography. This had already owed something to the significance of 'moral economy'[12] for interpreting the episodic accounts of mass political action which were offered in the historians' most common, indeed ubiquitous, sources: police and newspaper reports. Since these accounts often described incidents in a rather decontextualized way, they were bound to prove difficult to interpret. 'Moral economy' offered a means of identifying a collective sense of injustice and a legitimizing rationale behind what otherwise appeared to read as rather disjointed and discontinuous tales of an episodic past. Yet, at the same time, the use of 'moral economy' to elaborate these accounts of popular politics did not necessarily challenge some of the basic assumptions upon which historians proceeded. It could be fitted readily into polarities of 'tradition' and 'modernity'. It did not have to disturb the prevailing sense of an undifferentiated 'popular culture'. It provided a convenient formula and a point of reference which enabled some historians – partly because it had the weight of Thompson's accreditation behind it – to describe collective action without looking too closely at its constituent elements.

Perhaps more far-reaching was the significance of Thompson's elaboration of the notion of 'class struggle without class'. The concept of 'class', Thompson now argued, could either describe the development of class and class consciousness 'in the full sense' or it could be deployed as a 'heuristic or analytic category' in the investigation of social conflict and social relations. In this latter sense, class was 'inseparable from the notion of "class struggle"'.[13] Since class consciousness was the product, not the prediction, of historical experience, class struggle preceded its emergence and, indeed, facilitated its development. The ties which bound class to a given stage of capitalism appeared to have been relaxed. In other words, an important implication of Thompson's argument seemed to be that class struggle and the cultural and historical experience which it encompassed could be studied more extensively in societies where capitalism had manifested itself weakly and unevenly.

By the late 1970s there were already signs that historians of India were beginning to turn their attentions to the study of popular movements, their social economy and their political culture.[14] None the less, the most prominent site for the absorption of Thompson's insights was the work produced under the title of *Subaltern Studies.*[15] This work, conducted by scholars based at first in Canberra, Sussex and Oxford, has represented the most influential intervention in Indian history in the past fifteen years. It has disclosed diverse subjects and approaches, some shared themes and, at the outset, a common purpose to investigate the history of the subaltern classes. This common purpose, rather than a set of general arguments or insights about colonial India, has imparted a measure of coherence to Subaltern Studies. In this sense, it should be seen as part of a general, indeed global, interest in social and cultural history which had developed since the 1960s. Its historiographical contribution lies not so much in its collective effort, in a coherent theory or interpretation of Indian history, but in some outstanding monographs produced by individual scholars who have been associated with the project. The most successful of these studies sought to situate local social conflicts and political movements, and the complex social relationships which informed them, in their material and discursive context.[16] Since the achievement of *Subaltern Studies* lies in the particular significance of individual monographs, any attempt to treat the corpus as a whole must leave a trail of exceptions in its wake.[17]

Many of the influences which shaped the development of Indian historiography in general have necessarily left their mark on the

Subaltern scholars. But it is perhaps crucial to note that the Subaltern point of departure was initially to be found in their insistence upon 'the autonomy of peasant insurgency'.[18] Between the 1930s and the 1960s, it was primarily the growth of peasant radicalism, sometimes precisely in those areas which lay beyond the reaches of the party, which breathed life and energy into Indian communism. Yet, by the early 1970s, these revolutionary impulses appeared to have petered out or else they had been confined to their localities. The left, especially the revolutionary left, now had to face up to its failure adequately to engage and mobilize the peasantry. It was perhaps the recognition of, and disillusionment with, the very limitations of the political and intellectual influence of the left that nurtured the perception of 'the autonomy' of the popular domain. However, this insistence on 'the autonomy of peasant insurgency' may now be seen to have opened the way to the reification of collective identities in the work of the Subaltern historians and pushed them often towards an essentialist interpretation of popular culture and consciousness.

While, at first, the Subaltern historians borrowed liberally from Thompson's ideas, rhetoric and example, they seemed to take little account of wider developments in social history and, least of all, the critiques of Thompson's work which had already become fairly widespread.[19] Their particular translation of Thompson's methods and objectives was distorted by the fact that their agenda owed little to the debates and insights of social history. Moreover, the Subaltern interpretation of Thompson and their deployment of his insights was limited primarily by their own problematic. The organizing principle of their research was to be found, following an old convention, in the clash between imperialism and nationalism. At first, they were concerned, primarily in reaction to the 'Namierism' of the Cambridge school,[20] to provide an alternative history of Indian nationalism. To this end, they substituted 'the making of the Indian nation' for 'the making of the working class' and defined nationalism as the 'consciousness' which 'informed this process'. Their aim was to establish the significance of 'the politics of the people' to 'the making of the Indian nation'. This politics was constrained, they explained, by the fact that the working class was 'still not sufficiently mature' whether in its 'social being' or its 'consciousness as a class-for-itself'. Their 'sectional struggles' were thus soon 'entangled in economism' or, alternatively, 'wherever politicized, remained, for want of a revolutionary leadership, far too fragmented to form effectively into anything like a national liberation movement'.[21] Already in 1981, the Subaltern manifesto carried a rather archaic tone. Thompson's echo now reverberated in the leaden language of the Comintern.

Thompson has been poorly represented by his disciples among the Subaltern historians. First, a rather narrow, over-literal and mechanistic interpretation of culture has often led them to deem the investigation of the economy to be 'deterministic'.[22] Second, despite Thompson's own attention to the state, the Subaltern historians, concerned with 'the autonomous domain' of the people, often appeared to emancipate their own historical research from the intrusions of the colonial state. Where its presence was acknowledged, the state appeared simply as a monolithic instrument of oppression and exploitation, whose institutions were closed to political negotiation and conflict.[23] This neglect of the economy and the state precluded the sustained analysis of class formation in Indian society. Third, they often brought from Thompson, in a rather simplistic, undifferentiated and therefore sometimes caricatured form, an emphasis on the cultural traditions and inheritances of particular social groups. Thus, for instance, this 'inheritance' turned in Dipesh Chakrabarty's hands into a static, timeless, indeed Orientalist characterization of a 'traditional' Indian, implicitly 'Hindu' culture – in Bengal, a predominantly Muslim province. Whereas in India, Chakrabarty argues, 'hierarchy and the violence that sustains it remain the dominant organizing principles in everyday life', Britain and the West is, by contrast, characterized by egalitarianism, individualism and democracy.[24] Closely allied, perhaps integral, to this Orientalist conception of a 'hierarchical culture' is, in Chakrabarty's account, its inherently 'pre-capitalist' character. This character is identified not by an examination of the history of Bengal's production relations but by the absence of the properties of capitalism which, according to his reading of Thompson, comprised the historical experience of late-eighteenth- and early-nineteenth-century England. Thus, 'pre-capitalist relationships' are identified by 'the absence of notions of "citizenship", "individualism", "equality before the law" and so on' and by the absence of '"formal equality"' and 'the "formal freedom of contract"'.[25] Bengali society, indeed Indian society, was now represented as England's proverbial 'Other'.

It was also another implication of Thompson's position in the late 1970s that writing the history of the working class must entail disaggregating it into its component parts. Once the residual determinism of *The Making* was relaxed, Thompson's work could be read as an example of a self-confessedly Marxist history concerned to push the analysis of class to its conceptual limits and, indeed, beyond them. In this way, despite his insistence on 'the making of the working class', Thompson's work contributed to the development of a historiography in Britain and elsewhere which has increasingly stressed its fragmentation. It is not difficult to see how Thompson's own style stimulated this deconstruction. Thompson's emphasis on 'experience' and 'the cultural handling' of class and, indeed, his own attention to the specificities of social and cultural context and to the finer discriminations within it, invited the better and closer appreciation of the range and varieties of class experience. His treatment of the collective experience of the working class was often distilled through individual lives, particular events and specific localities, which stressed patterns of differentiation within the working class. The more closely these differences and particularities of social experience were examined, the richer the evidence, the more complex the interpretative possibilities they suggested, so increasingly the more abstract and remote the determination (however weak) of production relations appeared, not only as a framework of explanation, but especially as the source of an immanent solidarity.

Moreover, 'the making of the English working class', it has often been observed, was dominated by the role of radical artisans. Their predominance set the English case apart from virtually every other, where – as in India – the working classes were formed primarily by rural migrants. But, in addition, the significance of the artisanal presence in 'the making of the English working class' served to highlight the contradictions of sectionalism in the process of class formation. If working-class consciousness was shaped by the institutions and ideology of artisans, it was likely to have included other lesser proletarian groups on weaker terms, or sometimes excluded them altogether. The very dominance of artisans in 'the making of the English working class' was bound to direct attention to the difference of skill and occupation or the sectionalism fostered by region and religion, nationalism and gender. As Thompson was recently to complain, 'it is very much the fashion of our own time for intellectuals to discover that working people were (and are) bigoted, racist, sexist, but/and at heart deeply conservative and loyal to Church and King'.[26]

As the determining force of production relations in the formation of class and class consciousness was progressively relaxed by Thompson, so the range and variety of social experience and political conflict through which they could be realized was expanded and diversified. The notion of class struggle without class widened the range of social and political action which was brought into the consideration of class formation. Class and class consciousness, Thompson argued, were the culmination of a process by which 'people . . . identify points of antagonistic interest' and 'commence to struggle around these issues'.[27] Necessarily, these points of antagonistic interest (and their perception as such) and forms of struggle were likely to vary not only with the tensions and conflicts of specific, local contexts, but also among the different groups which populated them; and joining them up could be seen to be a task no less complex for later historians than for the political protagonists of the time.

In India, where the working class was constituted by rural migrants, the line of historiographical reasoning moved in the opposite direction. It was precisely because of the supposedly 'traditional' or pre-capitalist character of Indian society in the late nineteenth and twentieth centuries that historians took it for granted that its working class could not be made.[28] Indeed, the very notion seemed anachronistic, as if Indian society belonged to some previous epoch, through which Britain and the West had already passed. Thus, in the colonial period, Ranajit Guha declared, in launching *Subaltern Studies*, 'The working class was still not sufficiently mature in the objective conditions of its social being and its consciousness as a class-for-itself.'[29] It possessed, we are told, 'an emergent, though elementary, class consciousness'.[30] The urban working classes consisted primarily of rural migrants who, it was often said, brought their peasant ways into the factory. They were rooted firmly in a tradition, it was supposed, which was marked by powerful caste, kinship and religious loyalties. If their experience of modernity and industrialism might help to forge solidarities among them, their cultural inheritance was bound to divide and fragment them. Although the working classes repeatedly demonstrated their ability to forge solidarities and to effect and sustain industrial and political action over very long periods, it was tempting to conclude that this working class represented a particular kind of pre-capitalist social formation whose primordial loyalties were always likely to defeat the possibilities of class solidarity.

The Subaltern followers of Thompson did not resist this temptation. They have often espoused the conventional wisdom, recently restated by Dipesh Chakrabarty, that rural migrants 'imported a peasant culture into the industrial setting'. This conclusion was not the product of an extensive investigation of the nature of labour migration, how workers perceived their rural base or indeed how they organized themselves in the towns into which they migrated. None the less, this 'peasant culture' was, according to Chakrabarty, primarily 'a pre-capitalist, inegalitarian culture marked by strong primordial loyalties of community, language, religion, caste and kinship'.[31] Rural migrants, it was supposed, possessed a tradition of violence, which they brought into the industrial setting; they were said to have an inherent predisposition to crime; and they were readily drawn to religious bigotry which they displayed with vigour in communal (Hindu–Muslim) riots.[32]

Thus, some Subaltern historians mistook the received wisdom and commonplace of colonial officials for interpretative novelty.

Yet few of these suppositions will withstand careful scrutiny.[33] We should be wary, especially in India, of taking a simplistic, bland view of 'rural traditions' or 'peasant culture'. Indian agrarian society was highly differentiated; and rural traditions and peasant cultures were themselves rather varied. Labour migrants were drawn largely from the smallholding peasantry, rather than, necessarily, the landless rural poor; but the coal mines and tea gardens recruited not only from the impoverished peasantry but from various tribal groups as well. Some peasants went to nearby towns in search of work in the short term; most migrated to neighbouring districts to earn wages from field labour; a few travelled substantial distances to the large cities and often, whatever their original intentions, were drawn more permanently into the urban and industrial labour force.[34]

The patterns of labour migration were marked by strong continuities over several generations, which makes nonsense of an evolutionary understanding of class formation. Thus migrants to the large industrial centres were usually adult males who left their families in their village and spent their working lives in the city but maintained close connections with their rural base. Having been born in their villages, they often returned to them in periods of sickness or in old age. This pattern of migration could continue over several generations. It would be misleading to suppose, therefore, that rural migrants were on the point of transition from peasants to proletarians – for we would then have to concede that they remained thus suspended in evolutionary time for over a century.

The aim of most migrants was to earn cash – or gain wider access to credit – to enable them to hold on to or consolidate their stake in the village, by paying off debts, rent arrears or other dues. The predominance of adult males was greater in the case of long-distance migration, urban and industrial employment and indentured labour especially in its early phase. The persistence of this sexual division of labour between town and country scarcely lends plausibility to the simple transference of peasant culture into the cities. Moreover, the strategy of smallholding peasant households to retain their land by sending their male relatives away to earn cash also increased their dependence upon the more intensive exploitation of female and child labour on their village plots. In the urban and industrial context, however, factory legislation to regulate the conditions of women's work after 1881 limited their employment opportunities largely to casual, manual, unskilled and poorly paid occupations. If women's work was confined to the domestic sphere in the peasant household and thus devalued, their alternative employment opportunities carried low status, considerable uncertainty and meagre rewards. The identification of women's work with low status had significant social consequences. Respectability became the exclusive attribute of households which were able to withdraw the labour of women. If women's work was confined to their home, their public presence degraded them. The interplay of the conditions which hedged women's participation in the labour market and their characterization in public discourse necessarily shaped their relationship not only with their employers but also with other workers.[35]

Rural migrants, seeking to conserve their smallholding base in the countryside, entered an overstocked labour market, in which jobs and housing were scarce, wages low and social conditions appalling. Wages were often barely sufficient for the subsistence of the worker and, in most cases, insufficient to support a family. Most workers were hired daily on a casual basis and their hold on employment was always tenuous. Low wages, uncertain conditions of employment and poor housing ensured that most migrants had to leave their families in their villages. But living on the margins of subsistence in the cities also made it essential for them to turn to their rural base for support in times of sickness, unemployment and old age. At the same time, urban employment remained indispensable to secure and maintain their village base. This meant that migrant workers with the strongest rural connections were often the most active in defence of their jobs and their wage levels and among the most 'committed' to the factory and the industrial setting. During strikes, employers found it easiest to recruit blacklegs from the most proletarianized sections of the urban workforce. The communist trade unions in Bombay in the 1930s found their most determined followers among migrant workers who retained close connections with their village base.

This was not, however, the consequence of inherited rural traditions of resistance and violence finding expression in the towns. Migrant workers from Satara, which had a long and continuing tradition of resistance, were among the more quiescent in Bombay; those from Ratnagiri, a district whose political temper by contrast appeared somnolent, were to be found in the vanguard of the workers' movements. Migrants from the turbulent districts of East U.P. and Bihar appeared to be docile in Bombay, but militant in the jute mill towns of Bengal.[36] In neither case, for instance, was the tradition of socialism of the peasant associations in this region in the 1930s registered in the politics of its migrant workers. If anything, the traffic flowed in the opposite direction, but even then as a relatively thin trickle, with some workers organizing their fellow villagers in nationalist agitations or around particular agrarian conflicts.[37] It is possible that migrant workers so firmly committed to the industrial setting, with their families and the retention of their village ties so dependent on their industrial earnings, were reluctant to carry the risks of resistance in the countryside. In any case, rural traditions and inherited cultural practices informed political consciousness in complex ways, and their effects were not manifested directly and immediately in political action.

More significantly, perhaps, this disjunction between rural traditions and urban practice may be attributed to the social and political context into which migrants entered. The urban neighbourhoods and industrial setting had a history and a momentum of their own, capable of transforming the values and expectations of migrant workers. The social organization of the neighbourhood was closely integrated with the workplace. Workers had to use their social connections in the neighbourhood to find employment, secure housing and obtain credit. Jobbers and sirdars, who acted as agents of labour recruitment and discipline, were powerless in the workplace if they did not cultivate a following or cut a figure in the neighbourhood. Strikes which began within the mill gates were often conducted in the streets, where employers sought to hire blacklegs, workers fought to prevent them and the state intervened, often clumsily, to maintain order. Trade unions suppressed at the workplace sought to maintain a presence in the neighbourhood. The political traditions of the neighbourhood were often characterized by reciprocity as patrons – whether landlords, jobbers, grain dealers or creditors – served their clients and could not simply bully, coerce and exploit them (although there was plenty of that, too). Its political traditions were informed not only by antagonisms between landlords and tenants, creditors and borrowers, grain dealers and consumers, but also by a history of active struggle with employers and the state. It was in the public arenas of street and neighbourhood that the interventions of the state were most evident – in quelling a riot, arresting pickets or escorting blacklegs into factories. And it was primarily in relation to the state that the political consciousness of the working classes took shape.

The urban neighbourhoods were not, therefore, the repositories of the primordial loyalties of the working classes. They provided the materials from which wider class solidarities could be forged. Caste and kinship ties were vital to the social organization of workers; but so were the affinities of region and religion, workplace and neighbourhood, trade unions and political parties, all of which cut across each other. To insist that the culture of migrant workers was characterized by 'strong primordial ties of community, language, religion, caste and kinship' is to obscure the extent to which their interaction produced something quite different and it is to remain blind to the extent to which their 'culture' was also informed by work and by politics and, indeed, by the daily struggles of workplace and neighbourhood.

So the sectionalism of the working class was neither simply the corollary of their so-called 'primordial loyalties' nor the expression of a culturally specific 'Indian' tradition. On the other hand, more industrialization did not generate greater homogeneity and class solidarity, as the characterization of their culture as 'pre-capitalist' might suggest. In fact, industrialization often served to exacerbate differences between workers. The impact of trade fluctuations or managerial policies were felt differentially throughout the workforce. Business strategies varied not only between different centres of the same industry but between individual units in the same centre. The diversity of conditions within particular industries accentuated the differences between workers. In the cotton textile industry, for instance, the quality of machinery, the layout of the mill, the policies and attitudes of the managers and the composition of output varied from mill to mill and influenced the wages which could be earned and the working conditions which prevailed in particular mills. Such differences could induce labour mobility and wage competition and they could also stimulate wage demands and collective pressure for improved conditions. Workers within the same mill competed for the supply of the best raw materials, the assignment of the most paying orders and the use of the best machinery. As mill owners attempted to regulate production to the short-term fluctuations in demand, its effects could be to increase the flow of work to some workers and make others redundant. It was rarely the case that changing entrepreneurial strategies affected the entire workforce in the same way. Industrialization did not always reduce, it sometimes intensified, the competition between workers. If it concentrated workers into larger masses, it did not thereby increase their homogeneity but sometimes exacerbated the diversity of their interests. Workers in industry were not involved simply in a single relationship of exploitation with capital but also in relationships of competition with each other. By contrast, the neighbourhood was not the embodiment of their sectionalism nor did the persistence of their rural connections confirm the existence of their primordial loyalties and signify their pre-capitalist culture.

It was once assumed, it sometimes still is assumed, that the interest of Indian society lay in its uniqueness and exceptionalism, in the cultural specificity of tradition, caste and religious community. The sociological and historical evidence of the Indian case is not conventionally expected to provide material for thinking more generally about industrialization and its social consequences. Now it is becoming clear that the sectionalism of the Indian working class was neither a symptom of a pre-capitalist economy nor a derivative of the bonds of village and neighbourhood, caste and religion; rather, it was accentuated and developed by industrialization. On the other hand, an increasing sensitivity among historians of the Western working classes to the competition and conflicting identities of ethnicity and religion, kinship and gender, neighbourhood and nation has focused attention upon the very issues which had, in the conventional view, rendered Indian society exceptional in the first place and sometimes even demanded a culturally specific sociology for its proper analysis.

The legacy of Thompson's work has taken varied forms, often indirect and mediated, in studies of the Indian working classes. One historian has recently adopted his title.[38] In some cases, it has been manifested in attempts to track the development of working-class struggles and working-class consciousness; in others, in attempts to portray the social world which workers inhabited, bringing together material conditions, cultural expression and political action into relation with each other; in yet others, historians have focused upon everyday social relations and everyday resistance, both in relation to work discipline and to their social organization outside the factory, sometimes refracting Thompson's influence through the prism held up by James Scott.[39] Thompson's influence upon the historiography of India has been considerable, but its expression, especially in *Subaltern Studies*, has often been at odds with his own historical method and analytical style. Frequently, the Subaltern historians misinterpreted some of Thompson's concepts or sometimes they simply handled them clumsily. They grasped 'moral economy' far too literally as the obverse of a 'market economy'. Thompson's strictures against determinism led them to avert their gaze from the economy and thus obscured their understanding of class formation. Their determination to restore 'the agency' of the subaltern classes precluded the analysis of the state and the dominant classes, but their commitment to concepts of 'hierarchy', dominance and spectacular and unlimited power left little room for subaltern agency. From Thompson, they derived the significance of custom and inheritance, but applying this mechanistically, they emerged with an understanding of tradition that was often Orientalist, and often in such couplings as 'pre-capitalist culture', crudely determinist. In other words, *Subaltern Studies* frequently produced the kind of historical analysis for which, when he encountered it in English history, Thompson saved some of his most coruscating invective.

How can one explain this monumental misinterpretation? Perhaps it stemmed from a misconceived attempt to find in Thompson's work a set of axioms which could be transposed to India, whereas Thompson himself had refused to subordinate the logic of history to social theory or to wait patiently as a supplicant to catch the whispered wisdom of the Theorist. Perhaps it showed that the revisionist vision of the Subaltern project was too narrow, seeking to throw Thompson and 'popular culture', later Gramsci and Foucault, into the 'absences' and 'gaps' in Indian historiography rather than to engage more fully with arguments within the discipline as a whole. Perhaps it shows simply that outstanding works of history cannot be 'applied' or transposed and that their derivatives are condemned to appear as inferior copies.

By the late 1980s, the Subaltern school had drifted away from Thompson and down the road to postmodernity. Increasingly, their project disclosed little coherence beyond the title that bound their volumes together as a slogan. By 1981, when the first volume of *Subaltern Studies* appeared, Thompson's *Making* had acquired the status of a classic and it remained an inspirational text. But it had already been severely interrogated, sometimes by the research it had inspired, and the subject had inevitably moved on. When *Subaltern Studies* moved towards 'popular culture' in their third volume (1984), its historiographical moment had already begun to pass, not least under the weight of a post-structuralist and Foucauldian critique. They caught Foucault only as the first flush of excitement generated by his work had begun to subside. In relation to these sources, the Subaltern historians had always found themselves a step behind the pack, either applying works whose originality lay in their engagement with historical evidence in specific contexts, usually in the West, or whose conceptual frameworks had already been deployed and sometimes already digested elsewhere. Said's *Orientalism* now offered them a body of 'theory' which dispensed with the need to be subservient to historians writing about other societies and a conceptual framework which could be indigenized.[40] Its lesson was to show how the Orient had been trapped and victimized by the terms in which it was perceived and described, terms which were themselves integral to, and an outcome of, colonial domination. In representing this colonial discourse (even as they sometimes unwittingly replicated it) and its Indian victims, it allowed the Subaltern historians to offer themselves to the growing din of Calcutta's scepticism, as the authentic voice of the subcontinent – even the third world – while at the same time emancipating themselves from the epistemological thraldom of Western historians.[41] By the later 1980s, *Subaltern Studies* turned increasingly to textual, rather than social, analysis and these were texts which, by their nature, had primarily been written or produced not by subalterns but by elites. In 1981, the Subaltern project had set out 'to promote a systematic and informed discussion of subaltern themes'.[42] Its 'historiographical prerogative', according to its champions, had been 'to rewrite the history of colonial India from the distinct and separate point of view of the masses'. As a result, 'the work of the Subaltern scholars' appeared to be nothing less than 'an analogue for all attempts to articulate the hidden or suppressed accounts' of the dispossessed throughout the world. Indeed, Subaltern Studies, it is said, had become 'an extension of the struggle between subaltern and elite and between the Indian masses and the British Raj'.[43] By the end of the 1980s, for all Edward Said's effusions, Subaltern Studies had begun to leave the subaltern out.

This is, perhaps, not in itself entirely surprising. What Sumit Sarkar has called 'the Saidian turn' in Subaltern Studies led to an increasing emphasis upon colonial discourse and, thus, a growing concern with the intellectual foundations of colonialism. Historians deconstructed colonial discourse in order to expose the Eurocentricity of post-colonial scholarship. In fact, however, the unintended consequence was to restore Eurocentricity to South Asian history. Colonial discourse, it was argued, constructed Indian society and represented its subjects in ways which facilitated their subordination and which they absorbed, appropriated and applied to themselves. It was because forms of authority and dominance at work were embedded in 'working-class culture', Chakrabarty has argued, that workers acquired 'an active presence in the whole process of disciplining'. They were, in other words, complicit in their own subordination and active agents in the making of their own powerlessness.[44] Not only did this claim of an encompassing colonial domination deprive the subaltern of any power of agency, but it also suggested that the colonial rulers were the only moving force in Indian history. Thus, the postmodern odyssey beached its crew on familiar shores. Barely three decades ago, there had been a flow of scholarly treatises which held firm to the belief that Indian society sprang from Britannia's helmet. Similarly, the Saidian turn, it has often been suggested, allowed the West to be portrayed in the same essentialized and homogeneous terms in which the Orientalist discourse had cast the East.[45] It was a short step from the homogenization of the West to the assumption that all of India's troubles came from outside. Thus, in Indian history, Sumit Sarkar noted, 'the critique of colonial discourse, despite vast claims to originality, quite often is no more than a restatement in new language of old nationalist positions – and fairly crude restatements at that'.[46]

Moreover, the postmodern critique of universalism has often led, in the hands of the Subaltern scholars, to the unwitting replication of colonial discourse. One aim of the postmodern critique was to release the dispossessed from the universalizing categories of colonial discourse. By stressing fragmentation and plurality, and asserting difference, it sought to enable the suppressed narratives of the dispossessed to be heard and to subvert the dominant discourse which, in particular, had imposed a Eurocentric rationality upon non-Europeans and facilitated their colonization. However, the assertion of difference, with its accompanying search for the true voice of the dispossessed (and not least their authentic representative within the academy), has often led to the reification of subaltern groups and their portrayal in essentialist terms. As Subaltern scholars attempted to assert and claim difference, they have tended to reaffirm assumptions about the culturally specific, unique and exceptional character of Indian society. As a result, they have sometimes been led to restore some of the fondest shibboleths of colonial ideologues – for instance, about the propensity of the working classes to violence,[47] their susceptibility to rumour,[48] the paternalism of the expatriate capitalist and the filial deference of their employees[49] or the centrality of religion to their political consciousness.[50] This replication of colonial discourse, which arose out of the historian's culturalism, occurred most explicitly when scholars, in pursuit of the fragment, neglected to attend sufficiently to its social and political context.

It is not intended to suggest that we should recoil from the shortcomings of the 'Saidian turn' in Subaltern Studies back to the Thompsonian agenda of thirty years ago. Given some postmodern excursions into social and cultural history, we might be excused a nostalgic glance at *The Making*.[51] However, to insist that postmodernism has nothing to offer is to miss the opportunities it has created. Most significantly, it has cut 'grand narratives' down to size. The meta-narratives of class, in any case, had always been rather awkwardly imposed upon the formation of the Indian working classes. There was here no steady evolution of 'peasants into proletarians', no inexorable process of de-skilling and no clear demarcation between factory labour and the casual poor. Industrial and political action on a massive scale often preceded trade union organization and did not necessarily sustain itself in rising class consciousness. Nationalist rhetoric could sharpen the antagonisms of the working classes against the state and consolidate its support for the communists; but widespread collective action, in the context of political and economic competition, sometimes provoked and exacerbated ethnic and sectarian strife. The connections between industrial and non-industrial labour, migrant workers and their rural base, workplace and neighbourhood, gender and skill, caste and the division of labour, trade unions and informal associations suggested that the formation of the working class needed to be examined in its relationship with a wide range of social and political processes.

With its rejection of grand narratives, the postmodern critique had helped to break down the fixity of identities, to decompose social categories and to render their fluidity theoretically explicit. It has – it certainly ought to have – foreclosed the possibility, therefore, that historians might, for instance, too readily adjudicate upon the 'maturity' of the working class whether in terms of its objective conditions or its 'consciousness'. On the contrary, in seeking to allow expression by various groups within the working class, none of them unitary, resistant as groups to further decomposition or incapable of being defined in other terms, the postmodern critique has directed attention to the diversity of relationships which will have to be brought into play in any adequate account of the contingencies, vocabularies and processes by which class was made and unmade. The challenge which it poses is nothing less than how we might write histories of the working classes without assuming the fixity of their multiple and changing identities, or essentializing their popular culture and consciousness. As historians pay closer attention to the shifting, hybrid and plural identities which comprised social relations, so the defining role of politics in class formation, a central and powerful argument of Thompson's *The Making of the English Working Class*, once more becomes increasingly apparent.

Notes

1. This paper was originally written for and presented to the conference on 'E. P. Thompson and the Uses of History' organized by History Workshop in London on 8–9 July 1994. The focus of this paper inevitably derives from the purpose for which it was written. Consequently, it reflects upon Thompson's influence on the writing of Indian working-class history. Although it comments on various trends in Indian historical scholarship, it does not set out to offer a comprehensive review either of the historiography of labour in India or of particular developments within it. I am grateful to Gareth Stedman Jones who first suggested the topic, to those who participated in the conference, and to the editors of *History Workshop Journal*, for their comments, and to Amiya Bagchi, Tony Cox and especially David Feldman, for their suggestions.

2. See the perceptive comments of Sanat Bose, 'Indian Labour and Its Historiography in the pre-Independence Period', *Social Scientist*, 143 (April 1985), pp. 3–10. See R. K. Das, *Factory Labour in India*, Berlin, 1923; J. H. Kelman, *Labour in India: A Study of Conditions of Indian Women in Modern Industry*, London, 1923; G. M. Broughton, *Labour in Indian Industries*, London, 1924; A. R. Burnett-Hurst, *Labour and Housing in Bombay: a Study in the Economic Condition of the Wage-earning Classes of Bombay*, London, 1925; M. Read, *From Field to Factory*, London, 1927; Raj Bahadur Gupta, *Labour and Housing in India*, Calcutta, 1930; R. K. Das, *Plantation Labour in India*, Calcutta, 1931; R. N. Gilchrist, *Labour and the Land*, Calcutta, 1932; Dewan Chaman Lal, *Coolie – The Story of Labour and*

Capital in India, Lahore, 1932; S. G. Panandikar, *Industrial Labour in India*, Bombay, 1933; Radhakamal Mukherji, *The Indian Working Class*, Bombay, 1945.

3. N. M. Joshi, *The Trade Union Movement in India*, Bombay, 1927; B. Shiva Rao, *The Industrial Worker in India*, London, 1939; S. D. Punekar, *Trade Unionism in India: A Study in Industrial Democracy*, Bombay, 1948.

4. Rajnarayan Chandavarkar, 'From Communism to "Social Democracy": the Rise and Resilience of Communist Parties in India, 1920–1995', *Science and Society*, 61:1, Spring 1997, pp. 99–106.

5. Proceedings of the Meerut Conspiracy Case, Statement by S. A. Dange, Made in the Court of R. L. Yorke, I.C.S., Additional Sessions Judge, Meerut, 26 October 1931, National Archives of India; *Communists Challenge Imperialism from the Dock: Meerut Conspiracy Case, 1929–33: The General Statement of 18 Communist Accused: the Statement Made Before R. L. Yorke, Esq., I.C.S., Additional Sessions Judge, Meerut, U. P. India by R. S. Nimbkar, Accused, on behalf of 18 Communist Accused Mentioned Above*, Calcutta, 1967; Rajani Palme Dutt, *India Today*, London, 1947; Indrajit Gupta, *Capital and Labour in the Jute Industry*, Bombay, 1953.

6. Morris D. Morris, *The Emergence of an Industrial Labour Force in India: A Study of the Bombay Cotton Mills 1854–1947*, Berkeley and Los Angeles, 1965; C. A. Myers, *Labour Problems in the Industrialization of India*, Cambridge, Mass., 1958; Ranajit Das Gupta, 'Factory Labour in Eastern India: Source of Supply, 1855–1946: Some Preliminary Findings', *Indian Economic and Social History Review*, 13:3, 1976, pp. 277–328; Colin Simmons, 'Recruiting and Organizing an Industrial Labour Force in Colonial India: the Case of the Coal Mining Industry, c. 1880–1939', *Indian Economic and Social History Review*, 13:4, 1976, pp. 455–85; B. Misra, 'Factory Labour During the Early Years of Industrialization: An Appraisal in the Light of the Indian Factory Labour Commission, 1890', *Indian Economic and Social History Review*, 12:3, 1975, pp. 203–28; Richard Newman, 'Social Factors in the Recruitment of the Bombay Millhands', in K. N. Chaudhuri and C. J. Dewey (eds), *Economy and Society: Essays in Indian Economic and Social History*, Delhi, 1979, pp. 277–95.

7. Dick Kooiman, 'Jobbers and the Emergence of Trade Unions in Bombay City', *International Review of Social History*, 22:3, 1977, pp. 313–28; E. A. Ramaswamy, *The Worker and His Union: A Study of South India*, New Delhi, 1977; E. D. Murphy, *Unions in Conflict: A Comparative Study of Four South Indian Textile Centres, 1918–1939*, New Delhi, 1981; Richard Newman, *Workers and Unions in Bombay, 1918–29: A Study of Organization in the Cotton Mills*, Canberra, 1981.

8. Edward Thompson, *The Making of the English Working Class*, Penguin, 1977 edition, first published London, 1963, p. 10.

9. The debate was conducted in the early 1970s primarily in the *Economic and Political Weekly* and reprinted in Utsa Patnaik (ed.), *Agrarian Relations and Accumulation: The 'Mode of Production' Debate in India*, Bombay, 1990.

10. Sabyasachi Bhattacharya, 'Capital and Labour in Bombay City, 1928–29', *Economic and Political Weekly*, 17–24 October 1981, pp. PE36–PE44; Newman, *Workers and Unions in Bombay*; Rajnarayan Chandavarkar, 'Workers' Politics in the Mill Districts of Bombay Between the Wars', *Modern Asian Studies*, 15:3, 1981, pp. 603–47.

11. Rajnarayan Chandavarkar, *The Origins of Industrial Capitalism in India: Business Strategies and the Working Classes in Bombay, 1900–1940*, Cambridge, 1994.

12. Edward Thompson, 'The Moral Economy of the English Crowd in the Eighteenth Century', *Past & Present*, 50, February 1971, pp. 76–136.

13. Edward Thompson, 'Eighteenth-Century English Society: Class Struggle without Class?', *Social History*, 3, May 1978, pp. 133–65; Edward Thompson, *Customs in Common*, Penguin, 1993, first published London, 1991, pp. 16–96.

14. Eric Stokes, 'The Return of the Peasant to South Asian History', in Eric Stokes, *The Peasant and the Raj: Studies in Agrarian Society and Peasant Rebellion in Colonial India*, Cambridge, 1978, pp. 265–89. These signs were revealed in the work of historians, who later marched under the subaltern banner; notably, Gyanendera Pandey, *The Ascendancy of the Congress in Uttar Pradesh, 1926–1934: A Study in Imperfect Mobilization*, Delhi, 1978; David Hardiman, *Peasant Nationalists of Gujarat: Kheda District, 1917–1934*, Delhi, 1981;

Dipesh Chakrabarty, 'Communal Riots and Labour: Bengal's Jute Mill-Hands in the 1890s', *Past & Present*, 91, May 1981, pp. 140–69; but also in the work of others, who did not – for instance, Majid Hayat Siddiqi, *Agrarian Unrest in Northern India: The United Provinces, 1918–1922*, Delhi, 1978; Chandavarkar, 'Workers' Politics'; Kapil Kumar, *Peasants in Revolt: Tenants, Landlords, Congress and the Raj in Oudh, 1886–1922*, New Delhi, 1984; Chitra Joshi, 'Bonds of Community, Ties of Religion: Kanpur Textile Workers in the Early Twentieth Century', *Indian Economic and Social History Review*, 22:3, 1985, pp. 251–80.

15. The nine volumes of *Subaltern Studies* were published in 1982 (Vol. I), 1983 (Vol. II), 1984 (Vol. III), 1985 (Vol. IV), 1987 (Vol. V), 1989 (Vol. VI), 1992 (Vol. VII), 1994 (Vol. VIII), 1996 (Vol. IX).

16. Notably, David Hardiman, *The Coming of the Devi: Adivasi Assertion in Western India*, Delhi, 1987; Shahid Amin, *Sugarcane and Sugar in Gorakhpur: An Inquiry into Peasant Production for Capitalist Enterprise in Colonial India*, Delhi, 1984; Gyanendera Pandey, 'Peasant Revolt and Indian Nationalism: Peasant Movement in Awadh, 1919–1922', in Guha (ed.), *Subaltern Studies*, Vol. I, pp. 143–97; 'Rallying Round the Cow: Sectarian Strife in the Bhojpuri Region, c. 1888–1917', in Vol. II, pp. 60–129; and '"Encounters and Calamities": The History of a North Indian *Qasba* in the Nineteenth Century', in Vol. III, pp. 231–70; Sumit Sarkar, 'The Conditions and Nature of Subaltern Militancy: Bengal from Swadeshi to Non-Co-operation, c. 1905–1922', in Vol. II, pp. 271–320; and 'The Kalki-Avatar of Bikrampur: A Village Scandal in Early Twentieth Century Bengal', in Vol. V, pp. 1–53; and perhaps the most impressive of all, Shahid Amin, *Event, Metaphor, Memory: Chauri Chaura, 1922–1992*, Berkeley, 1995.

17. *Subaltern Studies*, taken as a whole, as well as its associated monographs, have been extensively reviewed elsewhere. For a post-structuralist critique of the early volumes see Rosalind O'Hanlon, 'Recovering the Subject: *Subaltern Studies* and Histories of Resistance in Colonial South Asia', *Modern Asian Studies*, 22:1, 1988, pp. 189–224; for a thoughtful and measured critique of the influence of Said on Subaltern Studies, see Sumit Sarkar, 'Orientalism Revisited: Saidian Frameworks in the Writing of Modern Indian History' *Oxford Literary Review*, 16:1–2, 1994, pp. 205–24; see also Rosalind O'Hanlon and David Washbrook, 'After Orientalism: Culture, Criticism and Politics in the Third World', *Comparative Studies in Society and History*, 34:1, January 1992, pp. 141–67; on the working classes, see Amiya Kumar Bagchi, 'Working Class Consciousness', *Economic and Political Weekly*, July 28, 1990, pp. PE54–PE60; Vinay Bahl, 'Class Consciousness and Primordial Values in the Shaping of the Indian Working Class', *South Asia Bulletin*, 13:1 and 2, 1993, pp. 152–72; for a recent self-assessment, see Gyan Prakash, 'Subaltern Studies as Post-colonial Criticism', *American Historical Review*, 99:5, December 1994, pp. 1475–90, accompanied by assessments of the impact of *Subaltern Studies* in Latin American and African history by Florencia E. Mallon, 'The Promise and Dilemma of Subaltern Studies: Perspectives from Latin American History', pp. 1491–515, and Frederick Cooper, 'Conflict and Correction: Rethinking Colonial African History', pp. 1516–45.

18. Ranajit Guha, *The Elementary Aspects of Peasant Insurgency*, Delhi, 1983.

19. For instance, Gareth Stedman Jones, 'From Historical Sociology to Theoretical History', *British Journal of Sociology*, 27:3, 1976, pp. 295–306; Tony Judt, 'A Clown in Regal Purple: Social History and the Historians', *History Workshop Journal*, 7, Spring 1979, pp. 66–94; most explicitly, Richard Johnson, 'Thompson, Genovese and Socialist-Humanist History', *History Workshop Journal*, 6, Autumn 1978, pp. 79–100; and the debates which continued through several successive issues of the journal.

20. John Gallagher, Gordon Johnson and Anil Seal (eds), *Locality, Province and Nation: Essays on Indian Politics, 1870–1940*, Cambridge, 1973; Tapan Raychaudhuri, 'Indian Nationalism as Animal Politics', *Historical Journal*, 22:3, 1979, pp. 747–63.

21. Ranajit Guha, 'On Some Aspects of the Historiography of Colonial India', in Ranajit Guha, *Subaltern Studies*, Vol. I, Delhi, 1982, pp. 1–8.

22. This, for instance, is a recurrent refrain in Dipesh Chakrabarty, *Rethinking Working Class History: Bengal, 1890–1940*, Princeton, 1989.

23. For example, David Arnold's largely administrative history of the police, *Police Power and Colonial Rule: Madras, 1859–1947*, Delhi, 1986.

24. Chakrabarty, *Rethinking Working Class History*, p. xii and passim. The research-in-progress by Tony Cox, comparing the jute industries of Dundee and Calcutta, suggests that few of the attributes of 'egalitarianism, individualism and democracy' Chakrabarty found to be missing in Calcutta are to be found in early-twentieth-century Dundee. Tony Cox, 'The Culture of Resistance of Two Urban Working Classes: the Jute Mill Workers of Dundee and Calcutta, 1918–1939', unpublished paper.

25. Chakrabarty, *Rethinking Working Class History*, p. xiii.

26. Thompson, *Customs in Common*, p. 92.

27. Thompson, 'Eighteenth-Century English Society', p. 149; Thompson, *Customs in Common*, ch. 1.

28. It is ironical, therefore, that it was precisely on the basis of asserting the traditional, hierarchical and pre-capitalist character of Indian society that Chakrabarty embarked upon 'rethinking working class history'. Chakrabarty, *Rethinking Working Class History*.

29. Guha, 'On Some Aspects of the Historiography of Colonial India', p. 7.

30. Chakrabarty, *Rethinking Working Class History*, p. 186.

31. Chakrabarty, *Rethinking Working Class History*, p. 69; David Arnold, 'Industrial Violence in Colonial India', *Comparative Studies in Society and History*, 13:2, 1980, pp. 234–55.

32. Arnold, 'Industrial Violence'; Chakrabarty, *Rethinking Working Class History*; Chakrabarty, 'Communal Riots and Labour'; Dipesh Chakrabarty, 'On Deifying and Defying Authority: Managers and Workers in the Jute Mills of Bengal, circa 1890–1940', *Past & Present*, 100, August, 1983, pp. 124–46; Pandey, *The Ascendancy of the Congress*, pp. 131–2, 127–42; Joshi, 'Bonds of Community, Ties of Religion'.

33. The following paragraphs are based upon Chandavarkar, *The Origins of Industrial Capitalism in India*.

34. Jacques Pouchepadass, 'The Market for Agricultural Labour in Colonial North Bihar, 1860–1920', in M. Holmstrom (ed.), *Work for Wages in South Asia*, Delhi, 1990, pp. 11–27; Neeladri Bhattacharya, 'Agricultural Labour and Production: Central and South-East Punjab, 1870–1940', in K. N. Raj, N. Bhattacharya, S. Guha and S. Padhi (eds), *Essays on the Commercialization of Indian Agriculture*, Delhi, 1985, pp. 105–62; Prabhu Mohapatra, 'Coolies and Colliers: A Study of the Agrarian Context of Labour Migration from Chotanagpur, 1880–1920', *Studies in History*, new series, I:2, 1985, pp. 13–42; Crispin Bates and Marina Carter, 'Tribal Migration in India and Beyond', in G. Prakash (ed.), *The World of the Rural Labourer in Colonial India*, Delhi, 1992, pp. 205–47.

35. Chandavarkar, *The Origins of Industrial Capitalism*; Samita Sen, 'Women Workers in the Bengal Jute Industry, 1890–1940', unpublished Ph.D. thesis, University of Cambridge, 1993.

36. For Bengal, in the preceding and subsequent paragraphs, I have drawn upon Sen, 'Women Workers in the Bengal Jute Industry, 1890–1940'; and Subho Basu, 'The Labour Movement in Bengal, 1880–1930', unpublished Ph.D. thesis, University of Cambridge, 1994.

37. For a different view, see Parimal Ghosh, 'A History of the Bengal Jute Millhands: Class, Community and Colonial Experience, 1880–1930', unpublished seminar paper, Centre of South Asian Studies, Cambridge, February 1995.

38. Vinay Bahl, *The Making of the Indian Working Class: the Case of the Tata Iron and Steel Company*, Delhi, 1995.

39. James Scott, *Weapons of the Weak: Everyday Forms of Peasant Resistance*, New Haven, 1985. For an approach which draws upon 'everyday resistance' in Kanpur, see Chitra Joshi, 'The Formation of Work Culture: Industrial Labour in a North Indian City', *Purusartha*, 14, 1992, pp. 155–72. For some recent research on the working classes in India, not already cited, see Dilip Simeon, *The Politics of Labour Under Late Colonialism: Workers, Unions and the State in Chota Nagpur, 1928–39*, Delhi, 1995; Ranajit Das Gupta, *Labour and the Working Class in Eastern India: Studies in Colonial History*, Calcutta, 1994; Parimal Ghosh, 'The Colonial State and Colonial Working Conditions: Aspects of the Experience of Bengal Jute Mill Hands, 1881–1930', *Economic and Political Weekly*, July 30,

1994, pp. 2019–27; Janaki Nair, 'Production Regimes, Cultural Processes: Industrial Labour in Mysore', *Indian Economic and Social History Review*, 30:3, 1993, pp. 261–81; Marina Carter, *Servants, Sirdars and Settlers: Indians in Mauritius, 1834–1874*, Delhi, 1995; Ian Kerr, *Building the Railways of the Raj, 1850–1900*, Delhi, 1995.

40. Sarkar, 'Orientalism Revisited'.

41. For instance, Dipesh Chakrabarty, 'Postcoloniality and the Artifice of History: Who Speaks for the "Indian" Pasts?', *Representations*, 37, Winter 1992, pp. 1–26. Chakrabarty cites with proper demur Inden's lofty judgement that for the first time, with *Subaltern Studies*, 'Indians are showing sustained signs of reappropriating themselves', Ronald Inden, 'Orientalist Constructions of India', *Modern Asian Studies*, 20:3, 1986, p. 445. See also Edward Said, 'Foreword' to Ranajit Guha and Gayatri Chakravorty Spivak (eds), *Selected Subaltern Studies*, New York, 1988; see also Prakash, 'Subaltern Studies as Postcolonial Criticism'.

42. Ranajit Guha, 'Preface' in Guha (ed.), *Subaltern Studies*, Vol. I, p. vii.

43. Said, 'Foreword', pp. vi–vii.

44. Chakrabarty, *Rethinking Working-Class History*, pp. 68–9.

45. James Clifford, *The Predicament of Culture: Twentieth Century Ethnography, Literature and Art*, Cambridge, Mass., 1988, pp. 255–76; Aijaz Ahmed, *In Theory: Classes, Nations, Literatures*, London, 1992; Sarkar, 'Orientalism Revisited'.

46. Sarkar, 'Orientalism Revisited', p. 209.

47. See n. 32 above. I have examined the contemporary discourse of violence, and its consequences for the working classes, more fully in Rajnarayan Chandavarkar, *Imperial Power and Popular Politics, 1850–1950*, Cambridge, 1997, ch. 5.

48. For a critique of the analysis of rumours in epidemics, see Rajnarayan Chandavarkar, 'Plague Panic and Epidemic Politics in India, 1896–1914', in Terence Ranger and Paul Slack (eds), *Epidemics and Ideas: Essays on the Historical Perception of Pestilence*, Cambridge, 1994, pp. 223–6; for an account of such rumours, see David Arnold, 'Touching the Body: Perspectives on the Indian Plague, 1896–1900', in Guha (ed.), *Subaltern Studies*, Vol. V, pp. 55–90. See also Shahid Amin, 'Gandhi as Mahatma: Gorakhpur District, Eastern UP, 1921–2', in Guha (ed.), *Subaltern Studies*, Vol. III, pp. 1–61.

49. Compare Chakrabarty's account of the paternalism affected by Scottish mill managers in Bengal in *Rethinking Working Class History*, ch. 5 and the account of Zoe Yolland, *Boxwallahs: the British in Cawnpore, 1857–1901*, Norwich, 1994, especially her account of her grandfather, Alfred Butterworth, weaving master, Cawnpore Woollen Mills, pp. 249–51.

50. See Shahid Amin, 'Agrarian Bases of Nationalist Agitations in India: An Historiographical Survey', in D. A. Low (ed.), *The Indian National Congress: Centenary Hindsights*, Delhi, 1988, p. 105, in comparison with *Government of India's Despatch on Proposals for Constitutional Reform, dated 20th September 1930, Parliamentary Papers*, 1930–31, Vol. XXIII, p. 695.

51. Marc Steinberg has recently noted that while Thompson's post-structuralist critics 'reify political language in ways quite contrary to the epistemology of the linguistic turn' his 'cultural Marxism at times is truer to the spirit of the revisionist's proffered perspective than their own analyses'. Marc Steinberg, 'Culturally Speaking: Finding a Commons Between Post-Structuralism and the Thompsonian Perspective', *Social History*, 21:2, May 1996, p. 194.

5

Recovering the Subject: *Subaltern Studies* and Histories of Resistance in Colonial South Asia

Rosalind O'Hanlon

In the field of social and cultural anthropology, the issues raised by European representations of non-European 'others' – of the control of discourses, the production of professional canons for the representation of truth about the other, the epistemological and ethical ambiguities in the position of the ethnographic observer – have recently received an enormous amount of critical attention. This intensified critical awareness goes beyond the familiar ethnographic concern with the development of cultural empathy, to a much more fundamental exploration of the epistemological constitution of non-European and colonial societies as objects of knowledge within the disciplines of Western social science. The development of these concerns, and the acceptance and exploration in the last decade of the links between colonialism and the emergence of anthropology as a discipline, are traceable in no small part to the attempted iconoclasms of structuralism and its post-structuralist and deconstructive turns, and to the latter's ferocious and many-sided attack upon the presumed sovereignty and universality of the Western intellectual tradition: in particular, upon the Enlightenment faith in a rational human subject and an effective human agency. These themes have been brought together with greatest political and theoretical effect, of course, in Edward Said's assault upon the production of histories in which 'the one human history uniting humanity either culminated in or was observed from the vantage point of Europe'.[1] These concerns have been rather less well explored for the writing of social history of non-European or colonial societies, except where these social histories are argued, as they are now with increasing frequency, to be most usefully subsumed under the new category of historical anthropology or ethnohistory.[2]

My purpose here is to explore these themes in the context of the social historiography of colonial South Asia, where I think it is now widely accepted that the project of *Subaltern Studies* has provided the most provocative and interesting intervention in recent years. I intend the present article in part to be a general review, but my more central purpose is to rethink the issues raised and fruitfully restated by the series in the context of the themes sketched out above. I aim both to suggest how we may place the series, and what I believe to be its limitations, in a critical and intellectual context, and to indicate some of the further categories and conceptual schemes which must be developed as a part of the project of restoring 'suppressed' histories – of women, non-whites, non-Europeans – as well as the subordinate of colonial South Asia. It needs hardly to be said that a commentary of this kind is in many ways a parasitic exercise, made possible in large part by the insights and critical stance developed by the contributors themselves.

The central concern of the project has been the possibility of writing a history which is not only from Europe's 'periphery' in its rejection of the neo-colonialist, neo-nationalist and economistic Marxist modes of historiography argued to dominate the contemporary field, but which also takes as its focus the dispossessed of that periphery. Their own particular forms of subjectivity, experience and agency, at present subjugated by these universalizing modes, are to be reconstituted and thus restored to history. This project in turn engages the contributors with further issues: with the identification of forms of power in fields and relations far removed from the domain of the political as we familiarly understand it, such as colonialism's production of new forms of knowledge of South Asian societies; with ways of conceptualizing the nature of resistance and its possibilities in a deeply coercive social context; and, in the overt commitments of the project and particularly of its editor, with the political status of the historian or critic. The extraordinary interest of the project viewed in this way is thus that it illustrates both the present possibilities of, and the likely limitations in a challenge to the kind of rationalist and universalizing historicism identified by Edward Said: a challenge which, although it incorporates many of their themes, is made neither from the ground of post-structuralism nor from that of classical Marxism, but from the point of view of the subordinate of colonial society.

Both the rejection of an ethnocentric historicism and, perhaps less uncontroversially, a decentring of our familiar notions of power and the political, seem to me wholly to be welcomed. This does not mean, however, that we enter a world free of determination or necessity, for the emphasis on difference is informed by a much sharper awareness of the various forms which power and domination may take, of the possibility of its appearance even in those social contexts associated in programmatic political radicalism with emancipation. In epistemological terms, moreover, the very focus on ways in which non-European objects of knowledge have been and are constituted in the social scientific disciplines of the West separates this perspective from empiricism. My main concern here, however, is with the nature of the reconstruction attempted in the Subaltern project. At the very moment of this assault upon Western historicism, the classic figure of Western humanism – the self-originating, self-determining individual, who is at once a subject in his possession of a sovereign consciousness whose defining quality is reason, and an agent in his power of freedom – is readmitted through the back door in the figure of the subaltern himself, as he is restored to history in the reconstructions of the Subaltern project. The consequence of this is to limit and distort the conceptualization of the contributors' own chosen themes of domination and resistance. What they raise for us, however, is a critically important question. If we accept, as I assume we should, that no hegemony can be so penetrative and pervasive as to eliminate all ground for contestation or resistance, this leaves us with the question as to how we are to configure their presence, if it is not to be in terms of liberal humanist notions of subjectivity and agency. Much of the material with which the contributors work, particularly that concerning the construction of subjectivity through negation, does help to provide us with some basis for the construction of subjectivities of a kind very different from the universal constitutive subject of the Western tradition. A similar tension appears in the conceptual status accorded to the category of experience. While a Marxist teleology which empties subaltern movements of their specific types of consciousness and experience forms a principal target of the project, the notion of a cumulative subjective change through struggle towards a recognizable class consciousness forms a principal theme in some of the studies. I situate this tension within similar debates among Marxists in the European context and suggest that the problem of experience, separated from that of agency, might be more fruitfully thought without the notion of universal human subjectivities. Finally, I examine the notion of political commitment in the project, and what I see as the tension between the desire to find a resistant presence, and the necessity of preserving difference and otherness in the figure of the subaltern.

In addition to the first four volumes of *Subaltern Studies*, I should also like to make reference to Ranajit Guha's *Elementary Aspects of Peasant Insurgency in Colonial India*, both because Guha is editor of the series and because the two seem to me to illuminate each other in important ways. At the time of writing, some eighteen scholars have contributed to the series, in essays ranging over a period from the early seventeenth century to the 1970s, and including in the subordinate groups surveyed peasants, agricultural labourers, factory workers and tribals. The contributions also range in theoretical sophistication from empirical accumulations of detail concerning these groups and their resistances, to the most ambitious attempts to redraw the basic explanatory procedures of Marxist historical theory. What they all share in common, however, is their critical intent, and indeed it is the critique of the conventional genres of nationalist, colonialist and Marxist historiography which is now the most familiar and impressive feature of the series. The attack upon elite historiography in its three forms is, of course, that these have treated the subordinate peoples of South Asian society as if they had no consciousness of their own, and hence no ability to make their own history. In the case of neo-colonial historiography, as Guha has put it, Indian nationalism is represented 'as the sum of the activities and ideas by which the Indian elite responded to the institutions, opportunities, resources, etc., generated by colonialism'.[3] Of course, this criticism of the Namierite character of much of the history of South Asia written from outside the region is not new, and the 'Cambridge school' is now a familiar figure in a variety of radical demonologies. Yet such criticism has rarely been supported by the systematic and substantive investigation into what went on beyond the narrow circles of elite politics, with which some of the contributors have furnished us.

The attack on neo-nationalist historiography is now also familiar. This genre has read every moment and variety of popular resistance in terms of its own anti-colonial struggle, appropriating all of them to a new 'great tradition' of the Indian freedom movement, in which the Indian National Congress not only spoke for all of the people, but also generated and led all of the 'genuinely' political movements in which they were engaged. In response, the contributors have attempted to establish, in a variety of contexts, the specific rootedness in bourgeois political ambition and ideology of many Congress and Gandhian campaigns, and to show that far from leading movements of subordinate resistance, Congress activists frequently moved in and attempted to appropriate and divert movements which were generated outside and independently of it. This perspective has yielded a number of fine essays. Shahid Amin has documented the ways in which the villagers of Gorakhpur district decoded Congress and Gandhian messages in their own way, rather than on the model of a simple peasant religiosity responding to the sanctified figure of the Mahatma, as party activists assumed. The way in which the figure and message of the Mahatma, particularly the polysemic word *Swaraj*, were contextualized within the villagers' own popular religious culture, helped give birth to a vision of a millennial world which was their own rather than the Congress's, and which was directly political in intent.[4] In his examination of the Kisan Sabha movement in Awadh over the same period, Gyan Pandey reconstructs both the peasants' appropriation of the image of the Mahatma and the ways in which they drew upon their own profoundly moral and religious world view in order to voice their protests against the growing impositions of landlords. This radicalism, culminating in the Eka movement of 1921, was not a product of Congress leadership, but rather of the experience of the peasants themselves: first, of very high rents, debt and severe land shortage in a talukdar-dominated agrarian structure; and second, of the peasant leadership in their encounters with landlords, British officials and the police, whom they came to see as a common enemy. The Congress turned down this radical lead on the ground that it breached national unity. However, Pandey argues, the sort of unity envisioned here was actually of a very specific kind:

> It should be evident that the nature of the Swaraj that eventuated from this struggle would depend very much on the nature of the alliance (the 'unity') that was forged. From this point of view, the Congress' insistence in 1921–2 on a united front of landlords as well as peasants and others, was a statement in favour of the *status quo* and against any radical change in the social set-up when the British finally handed over the reins of power.[5]

The third genre which the contributors have brought under attack is that of conventional Indian Marxist historiography. The perspective of the subaltern group naturally at once calls into question their relationship with Marxist theory. The argument here, which Partha Chatterjee puts most succinctly, is that the teleologies of Marxist historical writing have acted to empty subaltern movements of their specific types of consciousness and practice, and to see in the history of colonial South Asia only the linear development of class consciousness. For the national–colonial opposition of neo-nationalist historiography, Marxists have substituted that between feudal and bourgeois forces, and read all South Asian history in the same totalizing manner.[6] As we shall see, by no means all of the contributors are free from the notion of a progression of consciousness and a teleology which finds some resistances to be backward and primitive, and hence less congenial material for the historian to work on than those which are advanced along the road to an enlightened awareness of class interest. A number of critics have made the point that this conflicts with the proclaimed interest in the historical specificity of subaltern movements.[7] There is indeed a conflict here, and it would be surprising if there were not; it is a genuine difficulty as to how we may discern, in the consciousnesss and practice of those we study, processes of unilinear change, real learning experiences gained in the course of struggle and resistance, and how far we should assign all change to the realm of the reversible and contingent. Much the same issues, of the specificity and irreducibility of experience versus the onward movement of class consciousness and struggle, have been fought out in the context of English working-class history.[8]

Having looked very briefly at some of the main themes in the series' critique of established historiography, I should now like to ask whether the contributors share some more positive common ground or set of assumptions between them – most obviously, of course, in the significance of the term 'subaltern' itself – or whether a dissatisfaction, for all the difficulties attendant on the task of the iconoclast, is all that unites them. First, however, it would be useful to clarify this question of what we might expect in the way of internal consistency or common ground among the contributors, since this has been a point of criticism already. It would be unhelpful of us to expect either that a project of this duration should not shift and develop in its emphases over time, or that a large body of scholars, intent primarily on the task of deconstruction, should hasten to establish a new uniformity. Quite rightly, the contributors have decided that it is positive and useful to work in some respects within a loose rather than a rigid interpretative framework. As Ranajit Guha puts it, the focus on the subaltern provides only 'a new orientation within which many different styles, interests and discursive modes may find it possible to unite in their rejection of academic elitism'.[9] However, I think that it is legitimate to distinguish between a difference of view or interpretation which is clearly stated and understood in public discussion, and inconsistencies which arise as the product of a failure or confusion in debate, which work to obscure both the issues raised in the series, and our ability to respond critically to them.

For – to return to the question of a set of shared assumptions – my argument here, and it may well seem a presumptuous one, is that underlying and making possible the separate essays in the series is indeed a recognizable theory or progression of ideas. The problem, rather, is that it has been inadequately recognized as such, with two consequences. First, some of the contributors have employed these ideas in an unhelpful and confused manner, and this without any clear discussion which is available to a general readership. Second, there has been something of a confusion in the minds of critics, together with a quite inadequate scrutiny of what is important and distinctive in the broader project. This progression of ideas concerns the category of the subaltern itself, and the way in which it is employed to break up the hegemony of the three modes of interpretation mentioned above. It is certainly true, as Sabyasachi Bhattacharaya has remarked, that 'people's history' or 'history from below' has been a category to which historians writing from a very broad range of perspectives – nationalist, liberal, Marxist, Annales school – have laid claim.[10] When, however, the idea of 'history from below' is made to take on the form of a project to 'recover the experience' of those 'hidden from history', in the phrase made classic in feminist historiography, we move to a very specific and powerful set of assumptions indeed. This is a very important point, both because this is the idiom in which a very great deal of contemporary historical writing concerned with the subordinate and the marginal – feminist and black history, as well as regional projects like *Subaltern Studies* – is cast, and because it is an inadequate understanding of these assumptions which gives rise to the widespread idea that writing in this idiom represents only a very general orientation of interest, rather than any specific notion of how the task of recovering lost or suppressed experience is to be carried out.

The Subaltern contributors would, I think, accept the argument that their own project has been cast in these terms: that they have come together in an effort to recover the experience, the distinctive cultures, traditions, identities and active historical practice of subaltern groups in a wide variety of settings – traditions, cultures and practice which have been lost or hidden by the action of elite historiography. What this asserts, against elite historiography's pretensions to comprehensiveness and universality is, of course, that the history of the people is an unknown quantity, an area of darkness which the dominant modes of historical discourse have failed to penetrate, and which mocks their claims to complete or even partial knowledge. This, the first step in what I have referred to above as a progression of ideas, represents an enormously powerful challenge, precisely because of the overwhelming normative value which the identification with 'the majority', 'the people', has assumed in the political and sociological discourses of the twentieth century (of which, of course, the discourse of democracy is only one) and hence in the legitimation of all our cultural and ideological projects. As Jean Baudrillard notes in his provocative commentary on the significance which 'the masses' have taken on in our present political culture: 'They are the leitmotif of every discourse; they are the obsession of every social project.'[11] At the level of our political culture, this consuming ideological imperative makes it intolerable for us to accept publicly that we cannot appropriate the masses to our projects, that there may be only silence where their own authentic voices should be raised in our support: 'This silence is unbearable. It is the unknown of the political equation, the unknown which annuls every political equation. Everybody questions it, but never as silence, always to make it speak.'[12] It is this same value, of course, which allows us to make the term 'elite historiography' itself one of criticism; and which makes that undoubted majority of professional historians who remain pre-occupied with elites of various kinds defend this preoccupation not with a frank disavowal of any interest in 'the people', but with the assertion that it is elites, or those in power, after all, who are most in a position to determine what happens to the people at large, and who therefore remain the best means through which we may understand the changes through which the people must live.

With this reminder of the tremendous ideological significance of an identification with 'the people' – and let us be clear that this remains a matter of the norms of political discourse, rather than of actual historiographical practice – we are in a better position to appreciate the strength of this first step. It is the assertion not just of a space of which dominant historical discourses have failed to take account, but of their fundamental inability to occupy the central ideological ground of our culture. It is this central ground, the masses and the recovery of their own specific and distinctive histories, with all of the legitimating power implied in such a concern, which the Subaltern contributors claim as the hallmark of their project. Their task, and that of all historians who write in the same idiom, thus becomes one of 'filling up': of making an absence into presences, of peopling a vacant space with figures – dissimilar in their humble and work-worn appearance, no doubt, but bearing in these very signs of their origin the marks of a past and a present which is their own. As Partha Chatterjee puts it,

> The task now is to fill up this emptiness, that is, the representation of subaltern consciousness in elitist historiography. It must be given its own specific content with its own history and development . . . Only then can we re-create not merely a whole aspect of human history whose existence elitist historiography has hitherto denied, but also the history of the 'modern' period, the epoch of capitalism.[13]

If this is the task, how is it to be carried out? Not, I would argue, in as many ways as there are contributors. Rather, the very notion of the restoration of an original presence suggests – and particularly so where the presence is an 'insubordinate' or resistant one – the means by which it is to be done, and this constitutes our second step. Essentially, this consists in the recuperation of the subaltern as a conscious human subject-agent. We are to restore him, in the classic manner of liberal humanism, as a subject 'in his own right', by reclaiming for him a history, a mode of consciousness and practice, which are *his own*: which are not bestowed upon him by any elite or external leadership, which have their origins nowhere else but in his own being. We are to recuperate him as an agent, rather than as the helpless victim of impersonal forces, or the blind follower of others, through the recognition of his capacity for purposeful action: for a considerable degree of self-determination in favourable times and, returning to his own inextinguishable subjectivity, possessed at least of his own modes of ideation and practice in unfavourable ones. This, then, I think, is what Gayatri Chakravorty Spivak means when she speaks of the contributors' use of 'a *strategic* use of positivist essentialism in a scrupulously visible political interest'.[14]

Having said that the manner in which the subaltern makes his reappearance through the work of the contributors is in the form of the classic unitary self-constituting subject-agent of liberal humanism, let me at once make three qualifications. The first is that I am not implying by this that any unthinking positivism or empiricism pervades the series. We should see this rather as a strategy although, as I shall argue, it is not completely understood by all those who use it, and its larger significance and, more importantly, its limitations, have yet to receive any proper public discussion. Second, there is some variation in the centrality accorded to this figure. It appears most weakly in the work of Shahid Amin, and particularly in his study of small peasant production of sugarcane in the eastern U.P. at the turn of the century, whose central focus is on agricultural seasonality, its variance with the economic demands made on the peasantry during the year, and the consequences for peasant indebtedness of these structural mistimings.[15] Yet I would argue that it remains the dominant trope in the series, precisely because it is very strongly suggested in the project itself of recovering 'their own' history of the subordinate and the marginal. This brings me to my third qualification. I am not here saying that it is always impossible to write about these groups without transforming them into autonomous subject-agents, unitary consciousnesses possessed of their own originary essence, in the manner which we now understand to be the creation, very largely, of Enlightenment humanism's reconstruction of Man. Put on its own like this, I do not believe that any of the contributors would want to espouse an essentialism of this kind. The difficulty, however, is that in the assertion – which is very difficult *not* to make, without having to abandon the strategy altogether – that subordinate groups have a history which is not given to them by elites, but is a history of *their own*, we arrive at a position which requires some subtlety and skill if it is to be held from slipping into an essentialist humanism. This skill will depend in very large part precisely upon our rejection of humanism's obsessive invocation of origins as its ultimate legitimation and guarantee: of the myth, which gives us the idea of the self-constituting subject, that a consciousness or being which has an origin outside itself is no being at all. From such a rejection, we can proceed to the idea that although histories and identities are necessarily constructed and produced from many fragments, fragments which do not contain the signs of any essential belonging inscribed in them, this does not cause the history of the subaltern to dissolve once more into invisibility. This is, first, because we apply exactly the same decentring strategies to the monolithic subject-agents of elite historiography; and second, because it is the creative practice of the subaltern which now becomes the focus of our attention, his ability to appropriate and mould cultural materials of almost any provenance to his own purposes, and to discard those, however sacred or apparently an integral part of his being, which no longer serve them.

Skill of this kind, the ability to argue for a distinctiveness of practice without slipping into a metaphysics of presence, is clearly very difficult to achieve, and most of all so where our object is a recovery of presence. Some of the contributors possess this skill in greater proportion than others, but in almost all of them, as we shall see, there appears a persistent wavering or slipping between the two positions, which is the most striking evidence of the tension or difficulty in the common strategy which I have argued to be theirs. It is not only the difficulty of maintaining the first position which should make us hesitate before criticizing such an instability. We must also bear in mind the siren attractions of the idea of the self-constituting human subject, in a political culture in which the free and autonomous individual represents the highest value. To lay claim to this highest value for our subaltern peoples represents an overwhelmingly attractive and apparently effective move, creating possibilities for retributive polemic along the lines of primordial being and distinctive identity, which far outstrip any to be had in a nuanced focus upon practice alone. We can be sure, moreover, that none of the genres of dominant historiography, with their own much more towering subject-agents, are about to perform any act of deconstruction upon themselves, thus giving us very little incentive at all to refrain from taking up the same metaphysical weapons in our own cause.

It is also worth noting that very similar dilemmas have beset other projects intent upon restoring the subordinate and the marginal to history. Since the publication of his work on the English working class in 1963, written against what he regarded as a reductive Marxist economism, as well as the silences in official British historiography, Edward Thompson's project has been to rescue the authentic experience of those sections of England's pre-industrial working class absent from official histories, and to employ this recovered experience to show how these groups were able, by recognizing their essential identity and interests as a class, to become active historical agents, to exert some control over the conditions of their own existence. The criticisms of Thompson's work and, by implication, of that of the numerous social historians now writing in the same idiom, range over a set of issues strikingly similar to those raised in the Subaltern project: those of an essentialism arising from the assertion of an irreducibility and autonomy of experience, and a simple-minded voluntarism deriving from the insistence upon a capacity for self-determination.[16] There is another very strong parallel in feminist projects of historical and literary reconstruction. As Toril Moi has pointed out, the framework within which almost all Anglo-American feminist writing in these fields has been cast is that of a search for a history, or a literature, 'of their own': an idiom which contains within it the suggestion of an original female nature or essence, which will provide a firm ground of truth for those engaged in the search, and a means of testing the authenticity of what they find. Moi notes the undoubted polemical advantages of such a suggestion, but is also very clear as to its ultimate limitations as a strategy for restoring the presence of women to literature or to history.[17]

It will be clear, then, that the progression of ideas which I have argued to underlie, and to give unity and coherence to the Subaltern project, is not without great difficulties of its own, to which I shall return. But what is important to note here is the structure of the strategy which is being pursued, the way in which it challenges prevailing orthodoxies, and its strength and potential in a field in which so much value is vested in the autonomous subject, on the one hand, and 'the masses' or 'the people', on the other. Given the strength, the possibilities, and the interest of the issues raised in such a strategy, I find two things puzzling. The first is the refusal of the contributors to own to any set of common suppositions beyond a general orientation of interest. Usually one of the most theoretically astute of their number, Partha Chatterjee, prefaces his important explanatory article by denying any fundamental theoretical position in common between the contributors except for a dissatisfaction with current historiographical orthodoxies.[18] Yet he concludes the article by making just this point, that a most effective way of breaking up the false ideological totalities of nationalist, colonialist and Marxist historiography is precisely by reopening the question of subaltern consciousness.[19] The second puzzle is the weakness and confusion of much critical response to the project, and in particular the failure of Marxist critics to grasp what is distinctive and important about it. The closest that we come to such a recognition is in the collective review published in *Social Scientist* in 1984, where it is pointed out that the contributors have made of the subaltern a subject-agent, in the manner of bourgeois humanism, which accords ill with the structural and materialist emphases of a proper Marxist historiography. Having made this important identification, however, the authors do not pursue the point about the strategic potential, for histories of the subordinate, of subjectivity in a culture which places such supreme value on it, or of the possibilities of restoring presence without essentialism. Rather, the issue of the subject-agent is brushed aside as an old one, and said to have been resolved conclusively by Louis Althusser in his exchange with John Lewis over the discourse of idealist history.[20] Instead, the contributors are enjoined to take a better account of the familiar preoccupations of Marxist historiography: the structure of agrarian society, the importance of activist leadership, the centrality of the anti-imperialist struggle.

Yet misunderstanding of the contributors' work is not simply the product of insensitivity or careless reading. It arises further when the instability in the argument which I noted above is placed in the context of the juxtaposition or dichotomy between elite and subaltern itself, and the associated notion of the 'autonomy' of the latter's experience. It is this juxtaposition or dichotomy, of course, which not only allows us to think about the subordinate as a kind of category, but which introduces the emphasis upon power and dominance in their mutual relations, which is another distinctive feature of the contributors' work. It is important to clarify the purpose of this dichotomy, the ways in which it may most fruitfully be used, in part because it has been so widely taken to represent what is distinctive about the Subaltern project, and in part because the confusion surrounding it reinforces the sense that the contributors do not have any joint theoretical contribution to make, but are brought together only by a diffuse focus on the heterogeneous and analytically unusable category of the subaltern.

Much criticism has been directed, as we shall see, at the apparent implication of a crude social division between those on top and those underneath. Now the point about the dichotomy, I believe, if it is to be used in any effective way, is that it actually contains two separate propositions, the first of which is prior to the second. The first proposition, which we might call the theoretical one, is, as the very generality of the two blocks should indicate, not concerned with categorizing actually existing social groups at all, but with making a point about power. This is that what is fundamental to relationships in South Asian society is not negotiation, consensus or common contribution, but domination: exercised over the weak, where possible, without overt conflict, through modes of hegemonic appropriation and legitimation; and, where necessary, through actual violence and coercion. It is here that the assertion of subaltern autonomy belongs: as Partha Chatterjee indicates, the purpose of this assertion 'is precisely to conceptualise this domination as a relation of power'.[21] The point of making such a general proposition about power is to undermine the liberal assumption of a plurality in social structures and of consensus in a shared culture which, in different ways, underlies both colonial and nationalist historiographies; but to make this point about power in a way which is not immediately assimilable to an economistic Marxism.

The second proposition, which we might call the substantive one, is that we should seek to understand how different forms of domination have operated in the societies of the subcontinent. The categories which we employ in the actual task of analysis will not be those of monolithic blocks at all, since the existence of such totalities has proved so distorting in the genres of elite historiography. Having made the statements about power and domination, rather, the categories which we must employ to understand their workings must be as multifarious and nuanced as the courses and ligaments through which power itself runs.

The confusion surrounding the dichotomy – a confusion which besets critics and some contributors alike – is that the two propositions are not made explicit and kept separate. Rather, some of the contributors employ the first as the instrument of the second, making the dichotomy itself an instrument for direct application to their historical material, so that elite and subaltern groups are made to appear as distinct social entities. This is, of course, to take the argument of subaltern autonomy quite literally, rather than as making a point about power. It is certainly very easy to see how this might be done, in view of what I have identified as the strategic importance of the statement that the subaltern has a history, as identity and practice, that are *his own*. Yet the result is that the argument degenerates into an unhelpful set of assertions to the effect that subaltern groups generated their own traditions and pursued their political projects quite independently of anyone else, and especially of the Indian National Congress. By no means all of the contributors make such a move, and where it is made it does not always result in this reduction to what is sometimes no more than a set of clichés underlying the empirical material. In particular, I want to distinguish Ranajit Guha's work in the book *Elementary Aspects of Peasant Insurgency* here. Yet the literal interpretation of subaltern autonomy, and the use of the dichotomy itself as an instrument for direct social analysis, appear in the contributions with a troubling frequency. Stephen Henningham's article on the Quit India campaign in Bihar and the eastern U.P. places its central emphasis upon

> the revolt's dual quality, whereby it comprised not one but two interacting insurgencies. One insurgency was an elite nationalist uprising of the high caste rich peasants and small landlords who dominated the Congress. The other insurgency was a subaltern rebellion in which the initiative belonged to the poor, low caste people of the region.[22]

Not only was the initiative all their own, 'achieved in the absence of overall co-ordination' with the arrest of most leading nationalist activists,[23] but they also came endowed with their own distinctive modes of consciousness, 'the subaltern world vision'. Their popular nationalism was imbued 'with a charactistically subaltern religious consciousness', while their entry into political action was distinguished by 'the articulation of a moral justification, in terms of their consciousness, for acts of physical force'.[24]

In the fourth volume, both Ramachandra Guha and Swapan Dasgupta take it that the main point of the enterprise should be to delineate a distinctive area of consciousness and initiative, originating with the subaltern, as against those of an elite-dominated Congress. Investigating protest movements against the increasing exactions of the Forest Department and its officials in the village communities of British Kumaun at the turn of the century, one of Ramachandra Guha's main purposes is to demonstrate that these communities mobilized on their own, on the basis of ancient community solidarities and sets of values. Not only was Richard Tucker wrong to assume that these movements were led in any way by nationalist activists from outside[25] but the values which underlay them were absolutely distinct: 'For the Kumaun peasant the cohesion and collective spirit of the village community provided the main spring of political action ... Expressed through the medium of popular protest were conflicting theories of social relationships that virtually amounted to two world views.'[26] Swapan Dasgupta's account of Adivasi politics in Midnapur between 1760 and 1924 sets out to make very similar points. His aim is to demonstrate the existence of the 'autonomous political tradition' of the Adivasis of this area.[27] Despite some links with the local Congress, these communities mobilized themselves essentially from within: 'Elite politics in Midnapur had thus only a very tenuous connection with the autonomous mobilisation of this particular section of the subaltern. Adivasi insurgency belonged on the whole to another domain of politics.' This mobilization arose out of their own original traditions: 'an alternative conception of justice born out of fundamentally different sets of values'.[28] Even Tanika Sarkar, who, as we shall see, displays a very sophisticated sense of the processes of reconstruction and metamorphosis at work in Santal 'tradition', and of the tension and ambiguity with which these were accompanied, still holds on to a notion of Santal identity as in some sense *originary*. The transformations of that tradition represented, albeit in an ambiguous and uncertain way, 'the Santal's flight from himself'[29] and the symbolic battle to appropriate a mosque, with which Jitu Santal's battle ended, leads her to conclude that 'the Santal thus returned to his indigenous code of belief'.[30]

The difficulty arises in examples such as these, as I have argued, from a tension in the progression of ideas which underlies their accounts and which, insufficiently understood, produces the slide towards essentialism which we see here. It is a similar essentialism which Dipankar Gupta has identified in the work of Ranajit Guha: an 'ethnicised history' in Guha's conception of a primordial and autonomous insurgent peasant tradition running right through Indian history, which implies, in almost Hegelian fashion, that the 'independent organising principle of the insurgent's mind' is what actually moves the historical process forward.[31] Gupta pinpoints exactly what are the historiographical difficulties in this undoubted tendency towards idealism. It shuts off the whole field of external structural interaction and determination, so that 'the potentialities of a movement and its final limits are . . . understood in terms of what the culture allows and not in terms of what the structure forecloses'.[32] This 'culturological' style of explanation, present in the work of some of the contributors, is carried to an extreme in Guha's *Elementary Aspects of Peasant Insurgency*, and renders particularly weak his attempts to document any of the 'real' structures outside the subjective world of the insurgent. Guha explains the failure of peasant movements to spread beyond their own limited territories, for example, in terms of their 'habit of thinking and acting on a small and local scale' rather than considering 'what could have been the structural features of colonial societies, or even of pre-modern societies, which could have accounted for the spiritual circumscription of the peasant movements'.[33]

At this level, of course, Gupta is quite right. There is a real historiographical difficulty in this apparent idealism, and in particular in Guha's drive to posit an originary autonomy in the traditions of peasant insurgency. He does at times appear to be approaching a pure Hegelianism, as in his criticism of the way in which, in elite historiography, 'insurgency is regarded as *external* to the peasant's consciousness, and Cause is made to stand in as a phantom surrogate for Reason, the logic of that consciousness'.[34] Yet Gupta does not, it seems to me, grasp that this drive towards the originary is the outcome of a tension in the difficult strategy which underlies the Subaltern project, but sees it only as an old-fashioned idealism which is the product of an uninformed employment of anthropological concepts and methods. The problem with Gupta's reluctance to consider the broader issues which the strategy raises in any other way is not only that he hastens what is intended to be a project of deconstruction and critique too rapidly back to a world of determination with whose deficiencies it is all too familiar. It is also that we are left with the unfortunate, and I think unintended, impression, that the historiographical issue at stake is that of man's freedom as against the determining power of his external world. But this very juxtaposition, of the free man as against the man determined, is itself an idealist conception, in which the mode of existence of the unitary subject-agent is never called into question. Man under this conception can either be free or he can be bound; but in either case, he himself looks very much the same. A Subaltern strategy, reconstructed along the lines I have suggested, might be used to recover the presence of the subordinate without slipping into an essentialism, by revealing that presence to be one constructed and refracted through practice, but no less 'real' for our having said that it does not contain its own origins within itself. Such a strategy would not only be able to subvert the self-constituting subject of idealism, but much more subtly and effectively to address the undoubted historiographical problem of determination. Other critics, however – and this seems to me quite understandable, in view of the confusion over the purpose of the dichotomy and the assertion of subaltern autonomy which I have described – have written rather less perceptively than Gupta. In a review of the second volume, Anand Yang takes its authors to task for not having precisely and rigorously defined the concept of the subaltern as a substantive social category: for their apparent application of the term to anyone and everyone oppressed by the Raj, whereas in actuality very significant differences existed within such an enormous mass of humanity, making the dichotomy quite inadequate as an instrument of social analysis.[35] Of the third volume, Majid Siddiqi asks how the possibility of subordinate groups being exploiters in one context, and exploited in another, can be consonant with any idea of genuine autonomy.[36]

I want now to turn to these same issues in Ranajit Guha's work, where the drive to identify the peasant insurgent as a conscious subject-agent appears to be made, not in any wavering semi-awareness of its significance and consequences, but with great deliberation and purposefulness. For – and this is a passage insufficiently noted by his critics – Guha makes it clear at the start of *Elementary Aspects of Peasant Insurgency* that 'it is rebel consciousness which will be allowed to dominate the present exercise. We want to emphasise its sovereignty, its consistency and its logic in order to compensate for its absence from the literature.'[37] It is clear that Guha construes the category of the subaltern to be a substantive social one. The subaltern classes literally represent '*the demographic difference between the total Indian population and all those whom we have described as the elite*'.[38] The repressiveness of elite historiography, itself generated by the counter-insurgency concerns of the colonial state, consists precisely in its refusal to the peasant of 'recognition as a subject of history, even for a project that was all his own'.[39] The insurgent consciousness or mind of this collective subject-agent, its essential unity and autonomy, and its pervasion of all particular historical forms, are explained with the help of references to Hegel's *Logic*. The common form of insurgency

> is not a generality which is 'something external to, or something in addition to' other features or abstract qualities of insurgency discovered by reflection. On the contrary, 'it is what permeates and includes in it everything particular' – a pervasive theoretical consciousness which gives insurgency its categorical unity.[40]

Yet this deliberate drive towards unity and origins, the prerequisites of humanism's subject-agent, is not without its own tensions and contradictions, not only in the assumptions on which it is made, but in the rich documentation of the insurgent peasant's subjective world which constitutes the main body of the book. The assumptions which underlie it become clearer if we look at Guha's attacks on what he regards as elitist theories of causation. We have already noted his hostility to the way in which 'insurgency is regarded as *external* to the peasant's consciousness'. What he confuses here, it seems to me, is the reduction of insurgent consciousness to its causes, to which he is certainly quite right in objecting, with the matter of externality. His fear seems to be that any suggestion of such an externality, that the peasant does not bear the founding *causes* of his insurgency within his own consciousness, will be enough to empty or extinguish that consciousness, to deny its existence in the manner of elite historiography. Seen from this perspective, his forceful insistence upon humanism's unitary subject-agent in its most extreme form, and his use of Hegelian ideas to make of insurgency a 'mind' which draws all particular historical forms into its own founding unity, become comprehensible. In not seeing beyond humanism's myths of origin to the possibility of a presence without essence, he assumes that the latter alone will be enough to secure the return of the insurgent peasant to history.

A further paradox, and one that is not confined to Guha's work, is that the process by which the insurgent actually arrives at a sense of himself is through negation: as Guha says, 'not by the properties of his own social being, but by a diminution, if not negation, of those of his superiors'.[41] This, more than anything, should suggest that this self was constantly in the process of production, and that, too, mediated through symbols and signs which were external to it, those of elite authority. Within the limits of this contradiction, however, Guha and others have entered and begun to chart what must be a vital area for anyone concerned with relationships of power and the possibilities and limitations of resistance. The idea of 'identity' is itself a highly problematic one, always implying the duplication of an original whose locus and manner of existence remain elusive. Analysis of the process whereby the subject arrives at a sense of 'identity', and the place of an 'otherness' in that capacity to identify is, of course, the concern of a very large field of psychoanalytical theorizing, as well as having been a central preoccupation of existentialist thought. The insights generated in these two fields have been applied most successfully to non-Western contexts, to explore the tortuous relationship between the colonizer and his other, the native, between the projection of the former's repressed desire and the latter's dehumanization in the discourses and forms of knowledge which colonialism produces, by Frantz Fanon and then, more recently, by Edward Said.[42] It hardly needs to be emphasized what an important and complex field is this production of the self in the colonial context, particularly of the self of the colonized. For we have not only the approved selves which the colonizer attempts to produce for the native and to constitute as the sole area of legitimate public reality, but the continual struggle of the colonized to resolve the paradoxes which this displacement and dehumanization of indigenous processes of identification sets up in his daily existence. Moreover, as Homi Bhabha points out, the desire of the native to supplant the colonizer is not thereby a desire simply to extinguish himself as a slave but, in a splitting of the self always associated with the dominated in the colonial context as elsewhere, to stand in two places, and 'keeping his place in the slave's avenging anger', to witness himself triumphant.[43]

The explorations of the theme of negation in the series have much to contribute to this field, and also, I think, something further to glean from it. With the focus on the subaltern's negativity, we include another dimension in the conflicted process of identification under colonialism: that of the subordinate within the ranks of the colonized. The theme of negation runs right through *Elementary Aspects*, and Guha draws on a most impressive range of exemplary material to illustrate the purposefulness and discrimination with which peasants violated the symbols of the dominant, both indigenous and colonial: speech, both verbal and written; bodily gestures and social space, clothing, means of transport, the ostentation of wealth in domesticity.[44] His grasp of the importance of the violation of signs, precisely as a process of identification, is a wonderful antidote to an instrumentalist notion both of the way in which power works upon its object, and of fixed categories of action themselves which are 'symbolic', as opposed to real or material. Tanika Sarkar's study of the reconstruction of Santal identity during Jitu Santal's movement draws our attention very importantly to the fact that it was not only through the negation of the signs of elite authority that the Santal moved towards a sense of his own identity. Jitu also expressed a strong hostility and contempt for Muslims and Hindu low castes and untouchables. Thus,

> the 'other' that defines the subaltern's self-consciousness need not then only be the elite groups exerting dominance; it may equally be the classes and groups that lie even lower in the hierarchy, and the striving to maintain a distance from them may be the most important content of his self-image and self-respect.[45]

Yet we should note a further point, which needs to be made a little clearer in the contributors' treatment of negation. This is that the insurgent did not invariably wish to destroy the signs of authority, but very often preserved and appropriated them for himself. This was not merely the kind of discrimination between friend and foe which Guha describes, emerging out of the peasant's obscure sense of the real connections of power between the disparate groups who wielded authority over him.[46] Rather, it was the symbols of the latter which were at issue, forming the object alternately of the peasant's anger, and of his desire: negation took the form of 'the peasants' attempt to destroy or appropriate for themselves the signs of the authority of those who dominate them'.[47] David Arnold records this complex mingling between desire and destructiveness in the *fituris* of the late nineteenth century among the hillmen of Andhra Pradesh, and describes the inversion which it brought about:

> To seize and burn a police station, to brandish weapons or to don the uniforms of the vanquished constables, was a spectacular inversion of the oppression hillmen had so recently suffered: they were on top now, and it was the policemen who begged for their lives to be spared.[48]

'Inversion' is, of course, the figure which many of the contributors use to describe negativity in action. Yet Arnold's account here gives us something further, a sense of the importance of desire in negativity, of precisely that wish to stand in two places at once, which underlies it and makes it comprehensible. For, as he points out, inversion viewed thus constitutes not only resistance, but also the limits of its own particular form, the peasant's 'incapacity for real revolution, that is structural, change'.[49]

For all of Guha's emphasis, quite deliberately made, on the internal world of the subaltern, we should note that he is not content to leave this as an overt idealism. Rather – and here one can only admire his furious pursuit of consistency and comprehensiveness – he brings idealism and materialism together in a wrenching move which eliminates any of the mediations between consciousness and structure which are the stuff of most conventional historical narratives. The polarization of consciousness between elite and subaltern, and the long history of hostility between them, are nothing other than the reflection of a long-standing divide in the material structures of Indian society itself: between the peasant on the one hand and the collusive forces of landlord, moneylender and colonial state on the other, who established 'a composite apparatus of dominance' over him.[50] And it is this dominance in the end, it seems, which is the source not only of the ways in which insurgents organize themselves, but of insurgent consciousness itself:

> What the pillars of society fail to grasp is that the organising principle lies in nothing other than their own dominance. For it is the subjection of the rural masses to a common source of exploitation and oppression that makes them rebel even before they learn how to combine in peasant organisations.[51]

Thus, insurgent subjectivity and the determination of material structures of dominance stand mutually opposed, but in a curious disconnection: the latter appearing, in a highly deterministic fashion, responsible not only for the existence, but for the very form of the first, while the former, in its prescribed sovereignty, forbids us to make any such allusion to a cause beyond itself. It is very likely, indeed, that this is precisely the effect Guha intends: contradictory, no doubt, but no more so than much of the historiographical field in which he has to work.

Before leaving this issue of autonomy, I should like to make two further points. The first is that the Althusserian phrase, 'relative autonomy', taken up by Sumit Sarkar and Partha Chatterjee, among others, as a way of attempting to avoid the implications of an absolute disjunction between the worlds of the elite and the subaltern, seems to me further to confuse the issue.[52] Certainly, we want to find ways of connecting the classes and communities of South Asian society, and the idea of relative autonomy certainly suggests a connectedness, although with an air of analytical power which is quite specious, since its employment to suggest relationships within the social field is quite alien to the purpose for which Althusser developed it, in his suggestion of the modified determining power operating between the three 'instances' – economic, political, ideological-cultural – which compose the social formation, in place of Marxism's conventional base–superstructure model. Implying that it is a modification in the autonomy of the subaltern which is required only serves to reinforce the misconception that it is intended as a substantive social category, rather than a statement about power, and gives us no way out of the essentialism to which such a misconception tends to lead.

The second point is that while I have laid great emphasis on this constitution of the autonomous subject-agent, we should also notice that there is a theme in some of the essays to which several critics have pointed, and which appears to cut across it. This is, as Dipankar Gupta points out in his critique of Guha's work, the imposition of what looks very like the kind of unsophisticated Marxist teleology, assigning value and significance in the extent to which consciousnesses are more or less 'developed' which was supposed to be one of the objects of the Subaltern project's attack.[53] Such a tendency, an attempt to trace a unitary 'learning' process, undoubtedly exists in Guha's work. However, we can hardly accuse him of ignoring in consequence the specificity of the forms of nineteenth-century peasant insurgency, even if he does assign them places on a notional evolutionary curve. As I remarked earlier, moreover, the problem of mapping what on the surface look like quite fundamental transformations of mentality, of noting their origins and their consequences for the peasant in his relationship to the state or to organized religion, without slipping into a rigid teleology or a denial of historical specificity, is a genuine problem for all historians of the recent non-European world and Guha seems to me to have made strenuous efforts to tread between these two.

Less wary contributors do not make this negotiation quite so successfully. In his reconstruction of agrarian protest in twentieth-century Bihar, Arvind Das sees nothing very mysterious or difficult to understand in the nature of peasant consciousness or practice. What peasants want is perfectly clear, and that is land; the problem is whether or not they should seek alliances in the organized political world to try to get it. This seems to me a good example of a large genre of well-intentioned scholarly concern with economic welfare in contemporary India whose unfortunate, and ironically impoverishing assumption is that for the poor of modern India, questions of strategy and instrumentality have succeeded those of culture or value. In Das's case, this is in spite of concerns not reducible in this way, which he himself gives us, such as the Bhojpuri widow whom he quotes as saying that for her the struggle against landlords and police was a matter of dignity or honour.[54] For Das, such concerns, and the peasant's diffusion of energy over a heterogeneous collection of issues, such as exploitation by indigo planters, the unjust settlement of a landed estate, social degradation and low wages, are misguided and regrettable. They lead the peasants 'to ignore the basic question of land distribution, and to take up other, subsidiary issues in its place'.[55] Very interestingly, the subaltern's sense of 'dignity' is something that crops up again in N. K. Chandra's essay on agricultural workers in Burdwan, where the concern is also primarily with 'welfare' questions of wages, working conditions, nutrition and education. Chandra records the growing insistence of labourers that they should be able to eat their meals in their own homes, even if these had actually been prepared in their employers' kitchens. Explained only as the product of 'poverty and a desire to assert their independence' this insight is lost beneath the drive to gather information about the externals of the labourer's existence, on the assumption that he is now the proper subject of the welfare worker and the local activist.[56] Whatever his pressing need for their services, such an assumption is as impoverishing and oppressive, in its own way, as the material deprivations of which he is the victim.

Having argued there to be a recognizable strategy underlying the work of the contributors, and identified some of its difficulties, I turn now to its consequences for the treatment of two themes absolutely central to the project: those of domination or hegemony in South Asia, and the nature and possibilities of resistance to it. From the invocation of Gramsci in the category of the subaltern itself, and from the general emphases of the project, we would expect this theme to be one of its greatest strengths. Before we go on to look at this in detail, it is worth reminding ourselves of the formidable Western critique, both of traditional Western philosophy's essentializing search for origins, and of its product in humanism's self-constituting subject, against which this attempt at recuperation of a non-Western subject-agent is made. This critique, which had its most important origins in Marx and Nietzsche, is now, of course, a dominant theme in many fields of theory: perhaps best represented in political theory of a conventional kind by Louis Althusser, and in history and theory of a less easily classifiable sort, in the work of Michel Foucault. There can be little doubt, moreover, that this attack on humanism's subject – encountered in history as the agent who produces it, and of whose experience all history is the continuous expression, in literature, in the notion of the author and his autonomous creativity, and in philosophy, in the assumption of a unitary sovereign consciousness – has been extremely fruitful and liberating. Critics have attempted to dismantle this figure – which is, needless to say, a masculine one – in very varied ways, but all of which recognize in its insistence upon us all as fundamentally free, equal and autonomous selves, a profoundly repressive strategy of power. For the Marxist tradition, Althusser has been most effective in pointing out its consequences, in masking the real constraint and inequality which is at the foundation of capitalist society, and in making 'responsible' for their own history classes whose real powerlessness must forever condemn them to failure within its terms. Marx's theoretical anti-humanism meant

> a refusal to root the explanation of social formations and their history in a concept of man with theoretical pretensions, that is, a concept of man as an *originating subject* . . . For when you begin with man, you cannot avoid the idealist temptation of believing in the omnipotence of liberty or of creative labour – that is, you simply submit, in all 'freedom', to the omnipotence of the ruling bourgeois ideology, whose function is to mask and to impose, in the illusory shape of man's power of freedom, another power, much more real and much more powerful, that of capitalism.[57]

Yet it is Foucault, of course, who has constructed our most powerful critique here, not only of Man as a universal category, but of the way in which modern societies discipline and subjugate their populations through the production, in the discourses of the human sciences, of norms of thought and behaviour which lay down the sort of subjects that we are, and prescribe to us the law of our being. More than anyone, Foucault has documented the repressiveness of this imposition of 'normality', with its fastening of subject-natures to us which are ever open to its gaze, and its insistence, both individualizing and totalizing, upon their fundamental sameness:

> This form of power applies itself to immediate everyday life, which categorizes the individual, marks him by his own individuality, imposes a law of truth on him which he must recognize and which others have to recognize in him. It is a form of power which makes individuals subjects. There are two meanings of the word *subject*: subject to someone else by control and dependence, and tied to his own identity by a conscience or self-knowledge. Both meanings suggest a form of power which subjugates and makes subject to.[58]

With Nietzsche, Foucault exposes the obsession with origins which underlies the search for a self-constituting universal human nature, for 'the existence of immobile forms that precede the external world of accident and succession'.[59] With the dissolution of the universal human subject goes also, of course, the seamless narrative movement of history, from the past to our present, which we continually attempt to construct and to recognize ourselves in.

As Rashmi Bhatnagar has very perceptively traced, moreover, these themes in Western critical theory have already borne rich fruit in the attempt to understand the nature of colonial power and the way in which it operated upon its subjects, most of all in the work of Edward Said. This is first in the documentation of the way in which colonized peoples were endowed with identities, made into subjects, in the great scholarly apparatuses, both discursive and institutional, of Orientalism. The second is in the very obsession with origins which these discourses of colonialism, themselves formed around the dominant humanist themes of traditional Western philosophy, unleashed upon their subjects: 'In effect the search for Aryan/Islamic/Semite origins becomes for the colonised people a longing for an impossible purity and a yearning for the fullness of meaning' which is not only fundamentally misguided, but leads, in the Indian context, to revivalism and thence towards communalism.[60]

What are the implications of this fruitfulness, the severity and evidently liberating effects of this critique of the constitutive subject-agent, for what I have identified as the strategy underlying the Subaltern project, and in particular for its potential for our understanding of the themes of domination and resistance? Let us be clear as to the importance of this question: the most fruitful one which the contributors raise for us, and one which is at the heart of all efforts to comprehend not merely the possibilities for resistance within coercive or hegemonic structures, but also the very constitution of those structures themselves, whose power to coerce we can only comprehend as it acts upon its objects. I have argued above that the assumptions underlying the work of the contributors do not consist straightforwardly in the recuperation of the subaltern as subject, but that their very structure, and especially the emphasis, very difficult to avoid making, on the subaltern's action *on his own*, have led many of the contributors towards such an identification, while Guha proceeds very deliberately in this direction. We must examine here, therefore, not only the consequences of such an identification for understanding power and resistance, but whether the strategy itself is the best way to restore the subaltern to history. There is undoubtedly an enormous dilemma here, precisely because of our difficulty in envisaging any other form which such a presence might take except the virile figure of the subject-agent, and in the resulting temptation to appropriate the categories of dominant discourse, in the form of a distinctive subaltern self and tradition.

We should also note that to do this might in its own way become a profoundly authoritarian exercise, and this, ironically, precisely in the framing of a concern to recover subaltern experience itself. For it is this focus on experience in all its authenticity which resolves the problem of how the subaltern is to be 'represented', in the political as well as the descriptive sense of the term; which enables the contributors to distinguish their project from the master discourses which have failed to make the silence of the subordinate speak, but only enclosed it within a hegemony which may be broken up through the very indication of that fact. Through the restoration of subjectivity and the focus on experience, the conceit is that a textual space has been opened up in which subaltern groups may speak for themselves and present their hidden past in their own distinctive voices, whose authenticity in turn acts as the guarantee of the texts themselves. We recognize that this is a conceit, of course, but it is a very powerful one, and we must ask ourselves whether we are in danger in using it to turn the silence of the subaltern into speech, but to make their words address our own concerns, and to render their figures in our own self-image. For my contention here is not only that the recuperation of the subject-agent imposes real limitations on our ability to comprehend the workings of power upon its object, but that its unguarded pursuit produces a diminution in the only constant feature of the subaltern's 'nature' which we can identify with any certainty, which is its alienness from our own. It can become a drive just as Baudrillard says, 'to keep the masses *within reason*',[61] a joining in that common abhorrence, which marks our own age, that they should remain mute before all our meanings and ideals: 'Everywhere the masses are encouraged to speak, they are urged to live socially, electorally, organisationally, sexually, in participation, in free speech, etc. The spectre must be exorcised, it must pronounce its name.'[62] We will return to this theme in our conclusion, and turn now to examine the contributors' treatment of the themes of power and resistance.

The first difficulty refers to the way in which the contributors represent the collective traditions and cultures of subordinate groups. Dipankar Gupta has already criticized very perceptively the tendency to attribute a timeless primordiality to these: not only in Guha's work, but also in, for example, Dipesh Chakrabarty's notion of the 'primordial loyalties' of religion, community, kinship and language which was the 'essence' of the pre-capitalist culture of the Calcutta jute-mill worker,[63] in Sumit Sarkar's assumption of a timelessness in the cultural significance of the figure of the *sannyasi* or of Stephen Henningham's invocation of the 'traditional consciousness' of the peasant insurgent in Bihar and the eastern U.P.[64] This is not merely poor historical or anthropological practice; it undermines just that sense of power which it is the contributors' concern to restore. We can best see how this is so in Partha Chatterjee's notion, developed in essays in the first and second volumes of the series, of a 'peasant-communal ideology'. This ideology, 'acting as a live force in the consciousness of the peasantry' held the community itself to possess an authority over the land which was prior to that of any single individual, so that legitimate political power was itself 'organised as the authority of the entire collectivity'. These shared values acted above all to mediate the peasant community's relations with the potentially threatening political forces of the world beyond it, through

> norms of reciprocity, formulated in an entire system of religious beliefs – origin myths, sacred histories, legends – which laid down the principles of political ethics and were coded into a series of acts and symbols denoting authority and obedience, benevolence and obligation, or oppression and revolt.[65]

This model of collective political authority holds good for all peasant communities: 'When a community acts collectively, the fundamental political characteristics are the same everywhere.'[66]

The important and deleterious consequence of this portrayal is that it restores, within a redrawn and smaller notion of the collectivity, exactly that impression of unity and consensus, of the absence of relationships of power, which is intended to be the object of attack. The ideology of the collective authority of the peasant community is seen primarily as providing strategies for resistance to external coercion. There is very little sense that the same ideology might be employed within the collectivity, for the suppression of those not counting as the 'individuals' of which Chatterjee speaks: women, untouchables, labourers and so on. Certainly, he says, these bonds of affinity offer 'possibilities of manipulation'. But

> the point which distinguishes the communal mode from other modes or organisations of power is this: here is not a perception of common interests which compels organisation to achieve unity; there is rather the conviction that bonds of affinity *already exist* which then become the natural presupposition for collective action.[67]

Presumably Chatterjee does not wish to imply a perfect equilibrium of material and political forces within any peasant community: in which case, we are entitled to ask, whose conviction is this and how widely is it actually shared as a 'natural' assumption, rather than as a product of anything similar to the calculation of interests and formation of alliances which he regards as the essential feature of the differently constructed realm of 'organised politics'. The point is that if the contributors are to maintain the radical impetus of their emphasis on power, it is vital that it should not be brought to a halt through a static idea of the subaltern collectivity: whether in the shape of this apparently 'natural' community, or in the unitary 'moral economy' of which many contributors speak, or in any other laying down of a pre-ordained subject-position which can stand outside the fluctuations of human existence to impose an order of value or of narrative. I do not mean to imply by this that we should thereby surrender the search for the regularities of practice or the schemes of value through which subordinate groups attempt to bring order and coherence into their existence, but rather that we should not forget that such order can only ever represent the contingent and temporary creation of this practice, a creation capable of being turned to effect in repressive ways within their number, as well as of conducing to their mutual understanding and solidarity. What is interesting, indeed, is that just the same issue, of the attempt to reintroduce homogeneity and consensus within a redrawn idea of an essential collectivity, has arisen in feminist debate. Toril Moi describes how minority feminist groups have forced white heterosexual feminists 'to re-examine their own sometimes totalitarian conception of "woman" as a homogeneous category'. To maintain the radical thrust of feminist criticism, she argues, these groups 'ought to prevent white middle class First World feminists from defining their own preoccupations as *universal* female (or feminist) problems'.[68]

From this strategic weakness in the treatment of power, I come now to the discussion of resistance, and to a difficulty which arises out of the way in which contributors envision and classify fields of activity –

the political, the economic, the cultural–symbolic. There has been a criticism of the project, from without as well as within, that the contributors have dwelt largely on moments of overt resistance and revolt.[69] This tendency is, of course, the product of the insistence on agency itself: the demand for a spectacular demonstration of the subaltern's independent will and self-determining power. This means, as has been accepted, that there has been little sustained focus upon the continuities in subaltern culture. The nobable exception here would be Gyan Pandey's study of the town of Mubarakpur in the eastern U.P., seen through the eyes of two very different chroniclers: an obscure weaver, Abdul Majid, and the member of a local zamindari family, Ali Hasan. Pandey employs the comparison not only to suggest the differences between what these accounts, and the narratives of official records, identified as 'events', but to illuminate what was shared between these representatives from very different areas of Muslim society. What emerges most interestingly from both accounts is that although their authors possessed a strong sense of community,

> this consciousness of community was an ambiguous one, straddling as it did the religious fraternity, class, qasba and mohalla. Here, as in Ali Hasan's account, the boundaries shift all the time. It is difficult to translate this consciousness into terms that are readily comprehensible in today's social science – Muslim/Hindu, working class/rentier, urban/rural – or even to argue that a particular context would inevitably activate a particular solidarity. What is clear is that Ali Hasan is quite untroubled by the problems that confound the modern researcher as he moves from one notion of the collective to another through the eighty-nine pages of his manuscript.[70]

Pandey's reference to the habitual dichotomizing of conventional social science, and its tendency to obscure the real ambiguity and contingency of the fixed identities for which we continually search, brings our attention to another pressing question in the contributors' treatment of cultural continuities, that of the classifications between fields referred to above. Beneath the tremendous variety in the empirical material upon which the contributors draw, there very frequently appears a quite similar basic model of explanation: a long tradition of exploitation, or a shorter-term economic dislocation, which provokes resistance and rebellion: challenges to landlords or the agents of the state, the appropriation or destruction of the signs and instruments of their authority. This action, which is independently generated and pursued, draws on the insurgents' own original culture for its values, its symbols and its means of organizing. This is to state the argument as a caricature, of course, but not, I believe, to render it unrecognizable. The central limitation of such a model – a model which is very much the product of the unguarded pursuit of subjectivity and agency – is that it fails adequately to displace familiar classifications of activity – the economic, the political and the cultural – from their familiar and respected roles: roles which, in their insistence on a clear distinction between the material and the ideal, the instrumental and the symbolic, have themselves been a formidable ally in elite historiography's denial of a political significance to a whole range of subaltern activity. In making this criticism, I do not in the least want to suggest that the contributors themselves lack such an awareness of the political: such an awareness is, indeed, one of the hallmarks of the project. The essays display, moreover, a very sharp sense of the employment of symbols, either as negation or as appropriation, as an integral part of political practice. We have already noted Ranajit Guha's treatment of these themes. David Hardiman's study of the drive towards purification and cleanliness which marked the Devi Movement in south Gujarat is also exemplary in this respect. Rejecting the depoliticizing categories of sanskritization or revitalization, Hardiman is clear that the desire for these symbols of dominance was a desire for power itself:

> The values which the adivasis endorsed were those of the classes which possessed political power. In acting as they did, the adivasis revealed their understanding of the relationship between values and power, for values possess that element of power which permits dominant classes to subjugate subordinate classes, with a minimum use of physical force.[71]

The point, however, is that where resistance is concerned, the model which I have described above acts as a constraint upon our ability to incorporate into our material just this awareness of the real interpenetration of fields of activity conventionally separated as the instrumental and the symbolic. Tanika Sarkar has called attention to our need 'to be able to explain the attitudes of acceptance and submission which remain as strong if not much stronger than subaltern resistance'.[72] This is undoubtedly true, yet it is not the case that after we have exhausted the overt and violent revolts of the subaltern, all that remains to us is to document his submission. The very problem of the model is its tendency to suppress strategies and efforts at resistance which do not take the masculine form of a full-blooded rebellion by a subject-agent such as it tends to have enshrined within it. To make this point, let us turn to N. K. Chandra's attempts to understand why there has been so little protest among agricultural workers in Burdwan, despite the wretchedness of their conditions. Yet the protest which he seeks is of a very conventional 'political' kind: of organized labour, of a vigorous effort at political mobilization, of a direct blow against the collusion of landlord and state. Yet evidence of resistance, of a kind which this implicit and instrumentalist classification of fields tends to overlook, is present in his own text: as we have already noticed, in the labourer's insistence on eating in his own home, but also in a wonderful description of the labourer and his wife's strategies for resisting conformity to the norm of conscientious worker – a norm, let us note, urged upon them by the local kisan leader and social worker:

> A local worker, according to him, is rather inefficient and tries to take time off on one pretext or another. In the middle of the morning he wants to have a rest of between thirty-five and forty minutes in order to smoke a couple of *bidis* at leisure or go off to drink water. Even when both are supplied to him in the field, his wife may come by on the plea that he must attend to some urgent work at home. Constant supervision is needed to make him work properly. On top of this, barely an hour after he goes out to work, his wife appears almost everyday at the *malik*'s residence demanding the daily wages in kind for her man. She keeps waiting and nagging until she gets it, but the *malik*'s wife resents it. As soon as she gets the rice, the worker's wife runs down to the field to inform her husband who now slackens his pace. On occasion the latter goes home around ten in the morning to find out if his wife has got the rice.[73]

We seem to be turning here, no doubt, to forms of resistance which are modest in the extreme: inscribed in small everyday acts, made in fields apparently quite disconnected from the political as it is conventionally understood, and as it is unfortunately and, I am sure, unintentionally made to appear in the model referred to above. Yet it is in its own way a series of negations, a refusal of approved forms of behaviour, even if these are made within a coercive framework which is not itself directly challenged. Moreover, we should not allow a desire to see direct or violent challenges to the basic matrix of domination either to lead us to assume that such challenges will always be the most effective means of the latter's subversion, or, indeed, that we should assign significance to the categories of resistance according to a pre-set standard of the spectacular and the successful. For, as Jean Comaroff has noted of tribal life in another highly coercive political order, 'If we confine our historical scrutiny to revolutionary success, we discount that vast proportion of human social action which is played out on a humbler scale. We also evade, by teleological reasoning, the real questions that remain as to what *are* the transformative motors of history.'[74]

If, therefore, we were to ask whether the focus on the subject-agent and his experience has enabled the series to contribute in any systematic or collective way towards understanding the operation of power on its objects in colonial South Asia, the answer would have to be largely in the negative, in spite of the undoubted richness of the specific insights which many essays contain. Certainly, there is no concerted attempt to construct a theory of domination as *hegemony*, as the invocation of Gramsci might have led us to expect, and in this sense the critics Suneet Chopra and Javeed Alam seem to me quite accurate in their observation that the series has not turned out to be a Gramscian project at all.[75] If there is a reason outside the intentions of the contributors for this foreclosure, it seems very likely that it lies precisely in the common slippage which I identified above, towards using the dichotomy itself to supply a ready but crude framework for direct social application. The concepts of power which have actually been developed in the series are fragmentary and somewhat disconnected. I should like to mention two here. The first is Partha Chatterjee's notion of 'modes of power', developed in his two essays on the Bengal peasantry. This concept, most fully elaborated in the idea of the 'peasant-communal' mode of power, is offered as a means of theorizing 'the political instance' in a social formation, or rather, in the transition from one mode of production to another, and he is very explicit about his debt to Althusser here.[76] The concept of 'modes of power' has been the subject of extensive disagreement and, as Chatterjee says, still remains an abstract concept in his work. I shall not discuss this further, therefore, but make just two comments. The first is that we have returned with a vengeance to the world of impersonal structure and external determination. Recalling Althusser's own anti-humanism, it would have been useful if we could have had some overt public discussion of Chatterjee's differences with the humanist strategy of the project at large. The second, as I have indicated above, is that it is very often just this assumption that we can readily identify autonomous – or, in Althusser's phrase, 'relatively autonomous' fields or 'instances': the economic, the political, the ideological–cultural – which has arisen as an impediment to our understanding of the way in which power takes effect: as a play of forces which continually moves across and bursts through our efforts to establish coherent fields of activity. Indeed, such efforts bear an uncomfortable similarity precisely to that conventional division between politics and culture, the instrumental and the symbolic, which operates in society at large, and in elite historiography, to mask the real mobility of power.

The second concept of power employed in the series is that of knowledge, given a field of structure and possibility in the form of discourse: a concept most associated, of course, with Foucault. We would expect that the contributors should be much aware of the potential power of discourses over those about whom they speak, for it is the dismantling of discourse, in the form both of historiography and of the texts produced by colonialism, which constitutes their main aim. Yet there is a problem here, which I believe is insufficiently noted in much contemporary theorizing about the power of discourse, which does not find a resolution in the essays which discuss it here. This problem is of describing the process through which knowledge, structured, given legitimacy and a proper field for its operation in discourse, operates upon its objects: those 'subjects' who come within its jurisdiction. Within this analytic mode we frequently make reference to a very similar range of phenomena and processes as are more conventionally classified under the title of ideology. While Foucault's conception has the great advantage of its emphasis upon the material and institutional forms in which discourse is invested, it lacks the first concept's apparatus, well-worn though it is, for theorizing or explaining the manner in which it has its effects upon its objects. Of course, almost all contemporary discussion of discourse stresses – and herein lies its appearance of great explanatory power – that it imposes a total milieu, institutional as well as intellectual and informational, to whose hegemonic sway its subjects must inevitably succumb. Colonial power thus derives its strength from two sources: from the material ability to coerce which it brings with it in its armies, and from the Orientalist discourses of its second, shadow army of textual scholars, linguists, historians, anthropologists and so on. Now there can be no doubting the ability of colonial power, documented in Edward Said's classic work, to give material effect to its efforts to structure and provide fields for knowledge, through the establishment of a powerful institutional infrastructure. The problem with the argument as it is more generally employed, rather, is its tendency to assume that discourses have an existence which is prior to, and hence unsullied by, the interventions of those over whom they are to have jurisdiction. Rather, colonialism's discourses came into being as attempts at fields of knowledge precisely as a struggle between at least three parties: the Orientalist scholar, the native informant successful in convincing him of his authority to represent, and those others among the colonized unable to do so, but grievously aware of the potential disadvantages in which this would place them in any future political structure established under the colonial power. This struggle was the site not only of contested understandings, but also of deliberate misrepresentations and manipulation, in which the seemingly omnipotent classifications of the Orientalist were vulnerable to purposeful misconstruction and appropriation to uses which he never intended, precisely because they had incorporated into them the readings and the political concerns of his native informants. It is this sense of mutuality – not as common contribution, but as struggle and contestation – which is missing from much contemporary discussion of discourse, with its assumption that new fields of knowledge had only to be enunciated, for them to elicit mute obedience from those whom they purported to know. It is, indeed, this lack of any exploration of the theme of simultaneity and struggle which is responsible for the criticism most frequently levelled at Foucault's own conception: that it allows no room and no possibility for resistance to the fine meshes of knowledge's disciplinary and normalizing power.[77] This is an absence, indeed, which is all the more surprising in view of his own stress on the mutuality, the ever-present possibility of reversal, in the play of power itself between agents.

This is not an issue which is very much illuminated in Bernard Cohn's study, carried out within an overtly Foucauldian framework, of the 'invasion of an epistemological space' which took place in the Orientalist production of knowledge about Indian law, language and textual traditions.[78] This essay contains a most impressive documentation of the latter's compilatory and exegetical endeavours, and a wonderfully funny account of European attempts to arm themselves with fragments of the vernacular sharp-edged enough to cut decisively through the soft but treacherous world of Indian servanthood and populace. Yet it seems to me written a little too respectfully in the shadow of its own Foucauldian frame, in its assumption that we can capture a discursive formation before it is markedly affected by those over whom it exerts its power. The Indians, he concludes his study, who 'increasingly became drawn into the process of transformation of their own traditions and modes of thought' were 'far from passive'; but 'the delineation of the cumulative effect of the results of the first half-century of the objectification and re-ordering through the application of European scholarly methods of Indian thought and culture is beyond the scope of this essay'.[79]

On the other hand, exactly this struggle and mutuality in the formation of knowledge is the subject of Dipesh Chakrabarty's examination of the relationship between the generation of colonial texts – in this case, the Calcutta jute mills' records about its workers – and their eventual contents. Chakrabarty refers to Foucault's point, that authority – in this case, the government of India and the capitalist mill owners – 'operated by forming "a body of knowledge" about its subjects'.[80] Yet as he investigates the symptomatic absences and inaccuracies in the knowledge produced in registers of labourers and their hours of work, in reports on housing, health and educational conditions, what is actually most striking is precisely the impotence, in different ways, both of the government of India and of the capitalists themselves, to generate documentation whose classifications and framed intent the objects of its knowledge would respect. Thus, the owners of the jute mills remained largely oblivious to the government's drive to amass information on a scale comparable to the detailed documentation available for the English factory worker, because the primitive nature of the production process itself demanded a constant supply of labour, rather than a stable and trained workforce, whose health and housing might have aroused a more deliberate concern.[81] The capitalists, on the other hand, faced the continual frustration that the information generated within the factories, mostly through factory registers, was always 'corrupted' and inaccurate: because, as Chakrabarty describes, the sardars responsible for maintaining them drew upon pre-capitalist notions of authority and community in their relations with the workforce, which accorded ill with bourgeois standards of legality, factory codes and service rules.[82] The effect of such a contextualization is to situate the colonial pursuit of knowledge within a process which circumscribes and sets conditions upon it: involving not merely the administrator's effort at control through knowledge, but also material production and the limitations and resistances to such control set up in the practice of its hoped-for objects.

Let us return now to the larger themes and questions under discussion, and to note that while in some respects the strategy for recovery employed in the Subaltern series has been strikingly fruitful, in others, especially the key area of power and resistance, the effect has tended to be one of a slow theoretical paralysis. Is this, then, another irony of history, doubly confirming the appropriative powers of the dominant discourse: that like the subaltern himself, those who set out to restore his presence end only by borrowing the tools of that discourse, tools which serve only to reduplicate the first subjection which they effect, in the realms of critical theory? If this is indeed the case, we should certainly hesitate before accepting Gayatri Chakravorty Spivak's suggestion that the strategy of the Subaltern series 'in claiming a *positive* subject-position for the subaltern might be re-inscribed as a strategy for our times'.[83] Nevertheless, this is the vital question which the contributors have raised for us: that of what form the presence of the subaltern might take, if it is not to be that of the autonomous subject-agent.

In speaking of the presence of the subaltern, we are, of course, referring primarily to a presence which is in some sense resistant: which eludes and refuses assimilation into the hegemonic, and so provides our grounds for rejecting elite historiography's insistence that the hegemonic itself is all that really exists within the social order.

Our question, therefore, must in part be what kind of presence, what kind of practice, we would be justified in calling a resistant one: what is the best figure for us to cast it in, which will both reflect its fundamental alienness, and yet present it in a form which shows some part of that presence at least to stand outside and momentarily to escape the constructions of dominant discourse. Let us note that we are engaged in two parallel projects here, between which there is a significant degree of tension: a tension which raises in the most pressing way the political status of our historical practice. As indeed the contributors have always been clear, theirs is a political project, as are in their different ways the genres of elite historiography. Yet to draw the conclusion, as Ranajit Guha does, that our efforts can be coterminous with the struggles of the dispossessed, feeding directly into them by making sense of them, seems to me fundamentally misconceived.[84] We may wish in all faith for their freedom from marginality and deprivation, and do our best to cast our insights in a form which they will be able to use. But if we ask ourselves why it is that we attack historiography's dominant discourses, why we seek to find a resistant presence which has not been completely emptied or extinguished by the hegemonic, our answer must surely be that it is in order to envisage a realm of freedom in which we ourselves might speak. This is not to say that our project becomes thereby a private and merely selfish one: it is precisely on the predication of such a realm that we can think of our practice as a provider of insight and clarification. Our political concern is thus differently constructed from that of the subaltern. It contains a contradiction; but in such circumstances our best practice is to let it stand, as indeed Guha himself does in many other cases. To seek ways out of it, back to the realms of the absolute, whether in the form of post-structuralist critic, or of the historian *engagé*, serves only to reinforce the myth that there can be such a transcendent subject-position. It is this contradiction, containing a conceit of the profession which is very difficult to escape, which means that our desire to find a resistant presence will always be in tension, rather than as we might think convergent with, the need to preserve alienness and difference in the figure of the subaltern himself. It will only be a scrupulous respect for this tension, moreover, which will keep our practice from slipping into what Baudrillard described as the obsessive demand of our political culture: from making the subaltern's voice heard, but construing it in the image of our own.

Let us turn back, then, to that category of the autonomous subject-agent, into which the discourse of liberal humanism invites us to step, under the appearance of that realm of liberty and of the universal, from which the dispossessed of our societies have been excluded, and whose restoration there will signal the end of dispossession. The idea of the self-constituting, self-determining individual, his reason enshrined in his sovereign consciousness, came into its full expression, as Michel Foucault has argued, during the European Enlightenment of the eighteenth century. The same period saw the culmination of another crucial process in the evolution of the modern state: the notional separation from it of 'civil society'. This is the sphere of private interests in general: the family, the church, the institutions of learning, trades unions, the media and cultural life, civic institutions; where the individual may exercise his rights and liberties, free from the immediate authority of the state: an authority which itself receives its legitimacy from its respect for and protection of those rights and liberties. It is Gramsci's distinctive contribution to political theory to have tried to map how this intermediary area between structure and superstructure, rather than the institutions overtly identified with the state alone, provides the terrain where classes contest for power and where hegemony is exercised. This is most powerfully, in our own society, precisely because of the legitimating power of the sphere of civil society itself, the symbol in all its inviolability of the achievements of the Western political tradition, and what marks its politics off from those still enslaved to the state in its traditional form, or caught up in authoritarian dogma.

Where, in this field of civil society, with its myth of independence and political neutrality, does the figure of the sovereign subject-agent enter? Absolutely centrally, because he is its modal figure. It is for him that it is called into existence to provide the ground on which he realizes the central features of his being: his liberty and his rights; in his unique individuality, his happiness; and, most importantly, the fact that he possesses a double existence, one led in the private sphere of his home and his family, his personal interests and his leisure, and the other in the public realm of civil society. For the latter is not, in its overt distinction from the state, thereby relegated to the sphere of the private. On the contrary, precisely because of its power over the state, as the source of the latter's value and its legitimacy, civil society, the well-being and nourishment of its multiplicity of cultural, economic and civic institutions, becomes the focus of public concern *par excellence*: and this, too, in a manner which endows the individual who has, in all legitimacy, his practice and his interest within these institutions, with a public voice, of a different but equally powerful kind from that which he exercises within the overtly political institutions of the state. It seems to me impossible to place too much emphasis on this double characteristic of civil society, its capacity for political legitimation, and the space for public concern and deliberation which it creates, just at the moment when it seems to be distancing itself from the formal political structures of the state. We should not assume, either, that these classifications are now just a matter of the history of political theory. One has only to note the huge critical acclaim and discussion which have surrounded John Rawls's *A Theory of Justice*, since its publication in 1971 – a work which structures itself around a theory of social contract, of rights, liberties and rationality inherent in individuals – to appreciate their continuing centrality to our political culture.[85]

It is through this double characteristic that the marginalization of the subaltern acquires its particular character, and one that is distinct from what I have tried to suggest is, in the problems of recuperation it faces, a parallel dispossession – that of women. The latter is accomplished, as very many critics have noted, through the assimilation of large areas of female existence and concern into the private sphere of the family, and their exclusion from the field of public political culture in civil society. The subaltern is rendered marginal in quite a different way – in part through his inability, in his poverty, his lack of leisure and his inarticulacy, to participate to any significant degree in the public institutions of civil society, with all the particular kinds of power which they confer; but most of all, and least visibly, through his consequently weaker ability to articulate civil society's self-sustaining myth.

If these dispossessions are constructed in different ways, however, surely their resolution will be the same: that of stepping into the realm of civil society as sovereign subject-agent, and into the full enjoyment of its double persona. This is, of course, one of the central conceits of the modern Western state in its dealings in this field: that it has been able to realize and to preserve such a realm of neutral freedom, but that obstacles have arisen in the way of all of its population reaching it. We should also note that this conceit has been reproduced exactly in the impression that feminist issues, or indeed regional concerns such as the Subaltern project, represent essentially *neglected* areas, presently the concern of a worthy minority of historians and critics, but which require only to be restored to the whole for matters to be put right. We might also say that it has been reproduced in the delineation of ex-colonial societies themselves as an area of special interest, which will be ended in their restoration to the proper form and fruits of the modern Western state. Yet, as Sabyasachi Bhattacharaya has pointed out, no such proposals can be made without calling into question the structure and limitations of the whole.[86] For the figure of the subject-agent is not a universal, but a highly specific one, whose autonomy and self-determination will always render it unobtainable to all but the privileged. Not only is it unobtainable, but it also mocks the dispossessed, impressing upon them that it is only their shortcomings – their fecklessness as subalterns, their closeness to nature as women, their helpless addiction to authoritarian traditionalism as ex-colonial societies – which prevent them from being welcomed into its own numbers. It is this perspective above all which should make it clear to us that the concern with the subaltern, or indeed with women, is not a special interest. Rather, they provide both the theoretical means, and the historical material, through which we may examine and call into question the very stuff of which civil society is made, to appreciate the strategies of power at work in its most cherished figures and self-images. Thus, the documentation of resistance, and that of a hegemony which does not believe in its own omnipotence, ultimately converge and are part of the same task. Resistance – those moments in which the prizes and incentives of the dominant are refused, held inadequate or simply uncomprehended before the pressure of material want – leads us into the structures and appropriative tactics of the hegemonic itself, to demonstrate both the manner in which it works upon its object, and the limits of its power.

What, however, if hegemony is right to insist on its own omnipotence: if our project, rooted ultimately in our own striving to create an area of freedom in which we might conduct our own practice, is quite misplaced before its ability to appropriate and assimilate all real resistance? We must certainly take account of the argument that a hegemonic culture so conditions and mediates resistance, not only giving it its goals, but even marking its approval on its ends, that its appearance can only be an illusion, which underwrites that culture's own liberal self-image. In denying that this is the case, however, it seems best not to follow Partha Chatterjee when he says that

> the dominant group, in their exercise of domination, do not consume and destroy the dominated classes, for then there would be no relation of power, and hence no domination. For domination to exist, the subaltern classes must necessarily inhabit a domain that is their own, which gives them their identity, where they can exist as a distinct social form.[87]

This is misleading precisely because it rests upon the essentialism which we have noted: the notion that there is something inherently inextinguishable in the very form of the subaltern's own subjectivity. Rejecting the idea of inherent being, we must certainly face the possibility that the subaltern may be subject to such an intensity of ideological and material pressure that his consciousness and practice are indeed completely pervaded and possessed by it. It is possible to find fault with this argument, but on other grounds. This is in its assumption, very similar to what I identified in contemporary discussions of discourse, that the monolith of hegemony *precedes* resistance: that it will always provide the matrix or set the arena in which resistance will have to operate, and from which will spring its moulding power. This, what we might call the Swiss cheese theory of hegemony in its assumption that resistance can only crawl through the holes, is in its own way a myth of origins, for hegemony does not spring fully formed into being to be followed by a resistance which must always operate within its pre-given confines. Rather, we should call to mind Gramsci's own insistence that the hegemonic is the articulation of a number of historic blocks, in the ability of a fundamental class to become, in its awareness that its own corporate interests transcend the purely economic, the spokesman of other, subordinate, groups, and to articulate the latter's overt interests to its own. For Gramsci, the specific moment of the political is enacted precisely on this site: through the struggle, in which, as he calls them, 'philosophies' or 'conceptions of the world' play a vital role, to exert leadership over a variety of groups, and to conform to its sway the institutions of civil society as well as the overtly political ones of the state. Thus each form of the hegemonic comes into existence around diversities of interest and potential sites for resistance which fracture and constrain it even as it exerts its conforming power.

If it is possible to postulate a site for resistance, therefore, this still leaves the larger problem of how we are to configure its presence. Many answers are possible to this question, which is no less than that of attempting to conceive of presence and agency outside the approved categories of our conventional social sciences. We have been given a valuable lead in the work of some of the contributors, in their emphases upon the ambiguous and constructed nature even, indeed, especially, of the most apparently fixed subject-position. My own further emphasis would be that the very dichotomy between domination and resistance, as we currently conceive it, bears all the marks of dominant discourse, in its insistence that resistance itself should necessarily take the virile form of a deliberate and violent onslaught. Rejecting this, we should look for resistances of a different kind: dispersed in fields we do not conventionally associate with the political; residing sometimes in the evasion of norms or the failure to respect ruling standards of conscience and responsibility; sometimes in the furious effort to resolve in ideal or metaphysical terms the contradictions of the subaltern's existence, without addressing their source; sometimes in what looks only like cultural difference. From this perspective, even withdrawal from or simple indifference to the legitimating structures of the political, with their demand for recognition of the values and meanings which they incessantly manufacture, can be construed as a form of resistance. As Baudrillard notes, 'ordinary life, men in their banality, could well not be the insignificant side of history – better: that withdrawing into the private could well be a direct defiance of the political, a form of actively resisting political manipulation'.[88] These, then, would be forms of resistance more 'feminine' than masculine, those of Chandra's labourer and his wife: which are only half perceived as 'resistance', but which are not, on the other hand, accepted as matters of personal guilt and failure.

In insisting that what may look like idiosyncrasy, passivity and even indifference should be included thus, it is not intended to antagonize those who properly insist on the subaltern's capacity for an acute consciousness of the political. It is only to note that this marks the point where our own political project runs into the subaltern's fundamental otherness, which may render his consciousness of the political in forms alien or even antipathetic to us. Moreover, we should stress that this kind of emphasis does not condemn the subaltern to a half-light of faint understanding and fainter effort, outside the moments of his revolutionary heroism. It is one of the deepest misconstructions of the autonomous subject-agent that its own masculine practice possesses a monopoly, as the term signifies, upon the heroic: that effort and sacrifice are to be found nowhere but in what it holds to be the real sites of political struggle. As Raymond Williams has remarked,

> it is a fact about the modes of domination, that they select from and consequently exclude the full range of human practice. What they exclude may often be seen as the personal or the private, or as the natural or even as the metaphysical. Indeed, it is usually in one or other of these terms that the excluded area is to be expressed, since what the dominant has effectively seized is indeed the ruling definition of the social.[89]

We can comprehend and contest this seizure by noting just this most fundamental and least visible level of its operation: its classification, through this certification of resistances, of the range even of heterodox human practice according to the seemingly universal values of endeavour, courage and sacrifice. Although they are at one level separate tasks, that of contesting this definition, its ruling figure and mystifying conceits, and that of carrying the concern with the subaltern out of the realm of special interests, they surely converge for the present to provide a recognizable and crucially important field of exploration, from whose implications very few of us can afford to remain detached.

Acknowledgements

I am indebted to David Arnold, Crispin Bates, Chris Bayly, Nick Dirks, David Hardiman, Gyan Prakash and David Washbrook for having taken the time to provide detailed commentaries on the arguments made here and also to the participants at seminars where parts of it were presented as papers: at the South Asian Studies seminar at St Antony's College, Oxford, at a workshop on popular culture in South Asia held at the Centre of South Asian Studies, Cambridge, in March 1986, and at a symposium on colonialism and the nation-state at the California Institute of Technology in May 1987.

Notes

1. Edward Said, 'Orientalism Reconsidered', in Francis Barker *et al.*, *Literature, Politics and Theory: Papers from the Essex Conference* (Methuen, London 1986), p. 223. The most useful recent statement of the difficulties of representing non-European 'others', which draws on the themes of post-structuralism, is James Clifford and George Marcus (eds), *Writing Culture: The Politics and Poetics of Ethnography* (University of California Press, Berkeley, 1986). Good critical introductions to these themes are Richard Harland, *Superstructuralism: The Philosophy of Structuralism and Post-Structuralism* (Methuen, London, 1987) and John Fekete (ed.), *The Structural Allegory: Reconstructive Encounters with the New French Thought* (Manchester University Press, Manchester, 1984).

2. For a recent exploration of these arguments, see Hans Medick, '"Missionaries in the Row Boat"? Ethnological Ways of Knowing as a Challenge to Social History', in *Comparative Studies in Society and History*, 29, 1, 1987. A provocative argument in favour of the value of ethnographic work for social history within the South Asian context is Nicholas B. Dirks, *The Hollow Crown: Ethnohistory of an Indian Kingdom* (Cambridge University Press, 1987).

3. Rananit Guha, 'On Some Aspects of the Historiography of Colonial India', *SS* I, 1982, p. 2.

4. Shahid Amin, 'Gandhi as Mahatma: Gorakhpur District, Eastern U.P., 1921–2', *SS* III, 1984.

5. Gyan Pandey, 'Peasant Revolt and Indian Nationalism: The Peasant Movement in Awadh, 1919–22', *SS* I, 1982, p. 187.

6. Partha Chatterjee, 'Peasants, Politics and Historiography: A Response', *Social Scientist*, no. 120, May 1983. This brief note, written in response to a critical review article, written from a Marxist perspective by Javeed Alam, in *Social Scientist*, no. 117, February 1983, is useful for clarifying a number of issues.

7. See, for example, the review article by Dipankar Gupta: 'On Altering the Ego in Peasant History: Paradoxes of the Ethnic Option', *Peasant Studies*, vol. 13, no. 1 (Fall 1985), p. 15. I thank Majid Siddiqi for bringing this article to my attention.

8. Most notably, of course, in the debates surrounding the work of E. P. Thompson, since his publication of *The Making of the English Working Class* in 1963, and in his exchanges with British Marxist historians who had drawn on the work of Louis Althusser. See especially E. P. Thompson, *The Poverty of Theory, and Other Essays*, Merlin (London, 1978); and the riposte by Perry Anderson: *Arguments within English Marxism*, New Left Books (London, 1979).

9. Ranajit Guha, Preface, *SS* II, 1983.
10. Sabyasachi Bhattacharaya, 'History from Below', *Social Scientist*, no. 119, April 1983, p. 6.
11. Jean Baudrillard, *In the Shadow of the Silent Majorities . . . or the End of the Social and Other Essays*, translated by Paul Foss, Paul Patton and John Johnston, Foreign Agents Series (New York, 1983), pp. 48–9.
12. Ibid., p. 29.
13. Partha Chatterjee, 'Peasants, Politics and Historiography', p. 62.
14. Gayatri Chakravorty Spivak, 'Discussion: Subaltern Studies: Deconstructing Historiography', *SS* IV, 1985, p. 342.
15. Shahid Amin, 'Small Peasant Commodity Production and Rural Indebtedness: The Culture of Sugarcane in Eastern U.P., *c.* 1880–1920', *SS* I, 1982.
16. For references to parts of this debate, see n. 8.
17. Toril Moi, *Sexual/Textual Politics: Feminist Literary Theory* (Methuen, London, 1985). See especially Part I, 'Anglo-American Feminist Criticism'.
18. Partha Chatterjee, 'Peasants, Politics and Historiography', p. 58.
19. Ibid., p. 61.
20. See the collective review of *Subaltern Studies* II, in *Social Scientist*, no. 137, October 1984, p. 12.
21. Partha Chatterjee, 'Peasants, Politics and Historiography', p. 59.
22. Stephen Henningham, 'Quit India in Bihar and the Eastern U.P.: The Dual Revolt', *SS* II, 1983, p. 137. The emphasis is the author's.
23. Ibid., p. 149.
24. Ibid., p. 153. See the criticism of this essay in *Social Scientist*, no. 137, October 1984, pp. 23–9.
25. Ramachandra Guha, 'Forestry and Social Protest in British Kumaun, *c.* 1893–1921', *SS* IV, 1985, pp. 92–4.
26. Ibid., pp. 99–100.
27. Swapan Dasgupta, 'Adivasi Politics in Midnapur, *c.* 1760–1924', *SS* IV, 1985, p. 102.
28. Ibid., pp. 134–5.
29. Tanika Sarkar, 'Jitu Santal's Movement in Malda, 1924–32: A Study in Tribal Protest', *SS* IV, 1985, p. 154.
30. Ibid., p. 10.
31. Dipankar Gupta, 'On Altering the Ego in Peasant History', p. 9.
32. Ibid., p. 10.
33. Ibid., p. 13.
34. Ranajit Guha, 'The Prose of Counter-Insurgency', *SS* II, 1983, p. 3.
35. See the review in *Journal of Asian Studies*, vol. XLV, no. I, Nov. 1985, p. 178.
36. See the review in *Indian Economic and Social History Review*, vol. 22, no. 1, 1985, p. 94.
37. Ranajit Guha, *Elementary Aspects of Peasant Insurgency in Colonial India* (Oxford University Press, Delhi, 1983), p. 13.
38. Ranajit Guha, 'On Some Aspects of the Historiography of Colonial India', p. 8. The emphasis is the author's.
39. Ranajit Guha, *Elementary Aspects of Peasant Insurgency*, p. 3.
40. Ibid., p. 334.
41. Ibid., p. 18.
42. Especially in Fanon's *Black Skin, White Masks*, translated by C. L. Markman (Grove Press, New York, 1967), and, of course, in Said's *Orientalism* (Pantheon Press, New York, 1978).
43. See his foreword to the new edition of Fanon's *Black Skin, White Masks*: Pluto Press, London, 1986, pp. xv–xvi.
44. Ranajit Guha, *Elementary Aspects of Peasant Insurgency*, esp. pp. 18–76.
45. Tanika Sarkar, 'Jitu Santal's Movement in Malda', pp. 152–3.
46. Ranajit Guha, *Elementary Aspects of Peasant Insurgency*, pp. 20–28.
47. Ibid., p. 28.

48. David Arnold, 'Rebellious Hillmen: The Guden–Rampa Risings, 1839–1924', *SS* I, 1982, p. 131.

49. Ibid., pp. 131–2, fn 106.

50. Ranajit Guha, *Elementary Aspects of Peasant Insurgency*, p. 8.

51. Ibid., p. 225.

52. Sumit Sarkar, 'The Conditions and Nature of Subaltern Militancy: Bengal from Swadeshi to Non-co-operation, *c.* 1905–22', *SS* III, 1984, p. 273; Partha Chatterjee, 'Agrarian Relations and Communalism in Bengal, 1926–1935', *SS*, I, 1982, p. 36.

53. Dipankar Gupta, 'On Altering the Ego in Peasant History', pp. 15–16.

54. Arvind Das, 'Agrarian Change from Above and Below: Bihar 1947–78', *SS* II, pp. 225–6.

55. Ibid., p. 226.

56. N. K. Chandra, 'Agricultural Workers in Burdwan', *SS* II, 1983, p. 237.

57. Louis Althusser, 'Is it Simple to be a Marxist in Philosophy?' in *Essays in Self Criticism* (New Left Books, London, 1976), p. 205. The emphasis is the author's.

58. Michel Foucault, 'The Subject and Power', in Hubert L. Dreyfus and Paul Rabinow, *Michel Foucault: Beyond Structuralism and Hermeneutics* (Harvester Press, 1982), p. 212.

59. Michel Foucault, 'Nietzsche, Genealogy and History', in Paul Rabinow (ed.), *The Foucault Reader* (Penguin, 1984), p. 78.

60. Rashmi Bhatnagar, 'Uses and Limits of Foucault: A Study of the Theme of Origins in Edward Said's "Orientalism"', *Social Scientist*, no. 158, July 1986, p. 5.

61. Jean Baudrillard, *In the Shadow of the Silent Majorities*, p. 9.

62. Ibid., pp. 23–4.

63. Dipesh Chakrabarty, 'Conditions of Knowledge for Working-Class Conditions: Employers, Government and the Jute Workers of Calcutta, 1890–1940', *SS* II, 1983, p. 308.

64. Dipankar Gupta, 'On Altering the Ego in Peasant History', pp. 9–12.

65. Partha Chatterjee, 'Agrarian Relations and Communalism in Bengal, 1926–35', *SS* I, pp. 12–13 and p. 18.

66. Ibid., p. 35.

67. Partha Chatterjee, 'More on Modes of Power and the Peasantry', *SS* II, 1983, p. 343. See the exchange between Chatterjee and Sanjay Prasad on these points, in *Social Scientist*, no. 141, February 1985, and no. 151, December 1985.

68. Toril Moi, *Sexual/Textual Politics: Feminist Literary Theory*, p. 86.

69. See, for example, Sumit Sarkar, 'The Conditions and Nature of Subaltern Militancy', pp. 273–4.

70. Gyan Pandey, '"Encounters and Calamities": The History of a North Indian *Qasba* in the Nineteenth Century', *SS* III, 1984, p. 269.

71. David Hardiman: 'Adivasi Assertion in South Gujarat: the Devi Movement of 1922–3', *SS* III, 1984, p. 217.

72. Tanika Sarkar, 'Jitu Santal's Movement in Malda', p. 153.

73. N. K. Chandra, 'Agricultural Workers in Burdwan', *SS* II, 1983, p. 250.

74. Jean Comaroff, *Body of Power, Spirit of Resistance: The Culture and History of a South African People* (University of Chicago Press, 1985), p. 261.

75. See their reviews in *Social Scientist*, no. 111, August 1982, and no. 117, February 1983.

76. Partha Chatterjee, 'Modes of Power: Some Clarifications', *Social Scientist*, no. 141, February 1985, pp. 56–7. See also his tribute to Althusser, in the Preface to his *Bengal 1920–1947: The Land Question*, CSSSH Monograph (Calcutta, 1985), pp. xviii–xxxv.

77. See, for example, Mark Poster, *Foucault, Marxism and History: Mode of Production versus Mode of Information* (Polity Press, Cambridge, 1984), pp. 111–15; Mark Philp, 'Michel Foucault', in Q. Skinner (ed.), *The Return of Grand Theory in the Human Sciences* (Cambridge University Press, 1985), p. 79.

78. Bernard S. Cohn, 'The Command of Language and the Language of Command', *SS* IV, 1985, p. 283.

79. Ibid., p. 329.
80. Dipesh Chakrabarty, 'Conditions for Knowledge of Working-Class Conditions', p. 262.
81. Ibid., pp. 289–91.
82. Ibid., pp. 294–310.
83. Gayatri Chakravorty Spivak, 'Discussion: Subaltern Studies: Deconstructing Historiography', *SS* IV, 1985, p. 345.
84. Ranajit Guha, *Elementary Aspects of Peasant Insurgency*, pp. 336–7.
85. John Rawls, *A Theory of Justice* (Cambridge, Mass., 1971).
86. Sabyasachi Bhattacharaya, 'History from Below', p. 7.
87. Partha Chatterjee, 'Peasants, Politics and Historiography', p. 59.
88. Jean Baudrillard, *In the Shadow of the Silent Majorities*, p. 39.
89. Raymond Williams, *Marxism and Literature* (Oxford University Press, 1977), p. 125.

6

Rallying Around the Subaltern

C. A. Bayly

Rereading *Subaltern Studies,* volumes I to IV now [1988], almost a decade after the Subaltern project was conceived, one is struck by the high quality of many of the individual essays. For instance, Gyanendra Pandey's delicate handling of the mental history of the small town and of religious conflict in Azamgarh, taken alongside his essay on the 1920s peasant movement and other writings in journals, comprises a significant contribution to the history of colonial U.P. Shahid Amin's essay on debt and agricultural seasonality in Gorakhpur pointed towards his important book on the sugar economy of the region. David Hardiman's exploration of the moral economy of the *adivasis* (tribals) in Gujarat and the pieces by Ramchandra Guha, David Arnold and Swapan Das Gupta marked the beginning of the reclamation for Indian history of tribal and marginal people which has become an important agenda for the latter 1980s.

The question of what constitutes the Subaltern project as a historiographical revision remains, however, as difficult to answer as it did on the appearance of the first volume. If, as one of the jacket blurbs says, all those working on Indian social history are now classified according to whether they are 'subalterns or not', how would one decide? It is true that the most unregenerate of 'elitist' historians or economic reductionists among Marxists might now leave a larger 'analytical space' for the autonomous action of the non-elite in deference to the Subalterns' polemic. But here the Subalterns acted mainly as a catalyst, speeding the development of what was the interest of a substantial minority in the field and elevating it into a major concern. The work of those who pioneered the investigation of peasant rebellion as far back as the 1950s – Walter Hauser, Peter Reeves, Eric Stokes and A. R. Desai – had already done much to form our view of rural colonial India and they had paid more attention to the periodic revolt of the poor and marginal than has sometimes been assumed. Equally important have been the works by the many contemporaries of the Subaltern authors who had studied peasants and workers but sometimes seem to have been denied attention by the onrush of the Subaltern wave: Majid Siddiqi, Jim Masselos, Raj Chandavarkar, Anand Yang, Rajat Ray, David Ludden and several contributors to *The Journal of Peasant Studies* in the 1970s, among many others.

Wherein lies the change in historical orientation: in source material, theory or empirical evidence? The Subaltern authors have not yet deployed a mass of new statistical material and indigenous records nor have they made much use of the techniques of oral history to supplement the colonial documentation. It is American historians, influenced by the anthropology of Geertz, Turner, Sahlins and Cohn, who have been most active in recovering and using indigenous sources (including popular ballads), even though not everyone likes the whiff of 'cultural essentialism' in their work. By contrast the Subalterns' forte has generally lain in rereading, and mounting an internal critique, of the police reports, administrative memoranda, newspapers and accounts by colonial officials and the literate, which earlier historians had used for different purposes. The C.I.D. report on 'The Kisan Sabha [peasant association] in U.P.', for instance, is rapidly replacing Macaulay's Minute as the most quoted document in Indian history. Some of these authors are indeed working towards a reconstitution of the mental history of the forgotten people of colonial history, but they have hitherto been impeded by the need to feel to concentrate on 'resistance'.

Nor, apparently, has there been any sustained development in 'theory' running throughout these volumes (Ranajit Guha's monograph, *Elementary Aspects of Peasant Insurgence in Colonial India*, Delhi, 1983, is not at issue here). If anything, there has been a retreat from theory and overarching argument, on the grounds that these foster economism or deny the poor a voice. Braudelian conjunctures, demography, neo-classical price–wage analyses, Marxian concerns with modes and relations of production: these have all been marginalized and appear only fitfully in the pages of *Subaltern Studies*. The theoretical underpinnings of these books are highly eclectic. I would not myself advance this as criticism; only as a refutation of a popular notion that there has in some ways been a significant and demonstrable advance in 'progressive' historical theory. Instead, the Subalterns' essays have provided important missing pieces to add to a picture which must still be constructed from many different materials, and in which quantitative economic and 'elite' history along with the history of the state remain critical.

In fact, the Subaltern authors generally use theory as the elite historians used it, as a piquant garnish for footnotes, though in the process Foucault, Gramsci and Derrida have been stirred in with Weber, Marx or Pareto. The historical analysis here does not really appear to accord wholeheartedly with the stance of the French post-structuralists or 'anti-humanists'. The emphasis on 'moral economy' and on 'sovereign consciousness' would fit uneasily with the arguments of the French (cf. O'Hanlon, *Modern Asian Studies*, vol. 22, 1988, pp. 189–224; Spivak, *Subaltern Studies*, IV). Again, if Gramsci is to be the model, one would presumably have to see a more consistent analysis of the origins and limitations of ruling-class hegemony. In this connection the degree to which the authors wish to retain or reject various different notions of 'social control' remains unclear because of the very heavy concentration on periods of revolt and violence among the non-elites. Some of the ways in which the poor and marginal appropriated and used elite ideologies for their own purposes appear in the essays by Amin, Pandey and Hardiman, but it appears as a gloss on empirical evidence, not as an argument which can be generalized and tested.

What appears mainly to distinguish the Subalterns from their predecessors and co-workers in the field of popular and rural history is a rhetorical device, the term 'subaltern' itself, and a populist idiom. The first question seems to be, then: why has this change of historiographical style and idiom seemed to be congenial to so many in the field and outside it in recent years? When the intellectual history of modern Indian historiography comes to be written, the emergence of the Subaltern group and the wide interest that it aroused will provide a fascinating vignette. Ronald Inden (*Modern Asian Studies*, vol. 20, 1987, p. 445), believes rather romantically that there is a move afoot for Indians to 'reappropriate their own past', and it is true that some of the energy behind this writing was generated by the frustration of young Indian historians that many years after independence, the field was still in the 1970s dominated by what they saw as version of neo-colonialism ('faction theory'/'casteism'/the 'Cambridge school') and by American Orientalism ('community' and the search for the 'South Asian mind'). But the roots were both narrower and broader than this implies. Nearer to home Indian intellectuals found comfort, amid all the signs of embourgeoisement, in the Maoist violence of the Naxalites. Later in the 1970s many who were not on the pro-Chinese left sniffed danger in the hegemonic ideology of the Indian National Congress, elevating national unity into an icon which could keep it permanently in power (the Subaltern group, it must be remembered, came together not long after Mrs Gandhi's Emergency). There was concern that, in official discourse, tribal resistance movements, poor peasant protest and working-class rising could be bundled into the category of archaic disturbance, communalism or 'Naxalism'. The ease with which many elements of the old left, particularly in Bengal, compromised with the authoritarian claims of some in the Congress, and the way in which their orthodox Marxist–Leninist theorists were able to accommodate this to economistic developmental theories of class struggle set alarm bells ringing.

Yet the move away from 'social structure' to 'consciousness', autonomy and 'difference' clearly had a much wider background and one which went beyond the left. It reflected a broad intellectual shift in Western (though not yet in Soviet) social thought. French philosophers and literary critics were influential. But the insistence on the complexity of the 'savage mind' reflects Lévi-Strauss; the blend of semiotics and revived folklorism is reminiscent of the 'post-structural' anthropology of 'many voices, many vantage points' which now dominates the American Anthropological Association conferences. Although 1970s chic demanded that Indian intellectuals quote French not Anglo-Saxon gurus, there is also a great deal of Edward Thompson here, especially the impression one gets that peasant or subaltern action is morally approved and wholesome by comparison with the subterfuges and self-interest of the 'elites' (although one notes that Thompson's concern with the nature of the state and forms of property receives much less attention). It may be no coincidence that at least two of the Subaltern authors were less than ten miles from the Oxford University Church on the night that Thompson debated his famous jeremiad on the poverty of theory in the city. For it is often not so much the notion of the subaltern as an autonomous subject-actor which comes through here but the 'moral community' whether in the guise of systems of folk religious values (Amin, vol. III) or a more abstract notion of the peasant commune (P. Chatterjee, vol. I).

Yet these are all influences on the centre and left of politics. The interesting point is that the new right in both Britain and the United States have a very similar ideological ploy at about the same time as the Subalterns and some of their audience. According to the new right among English historians, for instance, their predecessors 'stood helplessly mired in positivism, teleology and economic or other forms of materialist determinism' (J. Innes, *Past and Present,* 115, p. 172). The difference is that 'consciousness', cut free from its teleological, positivist and economistic groundings, appears for the right in the guise of religion, paternalist values and nationalism, rather than as subaltern struggle.

And that thought is quite a sobering one, given that the notion of deep consciousness, religious symbolism in revolt, the self-help and righteous violence of the oppressed which appear in several of these essays could be quite easily appropriated by the new breed of communal publicist in India, if they were a little less crass than they actually are. If that did happen, one wonders, how would the Subaltern historians be able to attack and differentiate themselves from such ideas by critical historical analysis? If indeed peasant or worker 'consciousness', whether construed as a dynamic system of popular culture, a semiotic network of meanings or a past and future kingdom, can be severed from its particular historical context and invested with essential continuities, why should not be 'caste', 'nation' or 'religious community'?

In this context it would be interesting to see how the Subaltern authors handled the ethnic and communal conflicts of recent, post-colonial India. What has 'gone wrong' if, as is often the case, peasant or worker struggles have transformed themselves into chauvinist movements? Is it that there has been some split, or some malformation within the subaltern category, or more concretely within the peasant or worker community? This would seem to be Partha Chatterjee's position – though it would surely require a more sustained analysis of class and group formation *within* the peasantry to fill this out. Or is it that the intervention of elite politics and dominant institutions has caused this shift? If so, one would surely need, in many of these essays (or in my imaginary projections of them into post-colonial India), to reconstruct the world of elite politics and concerns in order to specify the limits of the autonomy of various elements of the peasantry or working class. Above all, the nature of the state and its relations to prevailing political and economic forces would need to be invoked to explain the context and timing of many subaltern actions, or indeed the very nature of the subaltern as a social actor. Gyan Pandey, I believe, says as much when he implies that the further development of 'communalism' in U.P. after the 1900s was a function of institutional and elite politics. How then does institutional politics 'form' mentality at some level in a way which does not deny the subaltern his autonomy? If in the contests over ideology, the political autonomy of the subaltern is constantly subverted, in what does it reside except occasional and diverse moments of resistance?

This brings us to the question of the historical dynamics hidden within *Subaltern Studies*. Any historical thesis must surely address itself to the question of historical change, and in this particular case to the question of why peasant, tribal or workers' movements occurred at particular times and not at others; what were the major determinants of change; to what extent was peasant solidarity enhanced over time; more importantly, why did it decline at others? Institutional historians argued, not unconvincingly, for the importance of government action, rent laws and so on; economic historians located change in conjunctures or in class struggle over specific resources. How do the Subaltern historians view change? It is not so easy to answer this question. Ranajit Guha's own approach (set out more fully in his monograph) seems sometimes to postulate the existence of an unchanging peasantry and unified peasant consciousness defined by struggle with colonialism. Shahid Amin, retreating from his social structuralist argument about economic dominance in Volume I, seems to adopt a notion of an essential peasant 'moral economy' or ' popular culture'. This is constituted out of religious symbolism and given coherence by rumour. In 1920 it seizes and appropriates Gandhi's message unto itself. It is difficult to tell here what were the specific moral and material conditions which affected the peasants of Gorakhpur. For all its empirical richness the feel of the argument is sometimes not dissimilar from the 'oriental peasant mentality' postulated by contemporary district officers.

Pandey and Hardiman, among others, have much more on change. But their concern to emphasize peasant autonomy seems to have deflected them from moving towards a 'total history' in which elite politics, institutions and economic and social distinctions among the peasantry play a critical role in limiting and forming subaltern action. This, then, is perhaps the greatest weakness of the Subaltern orientation: that it tends to frustrate the writing of rounded history as effectively as did 'elitism'. Yet within Pandey's interesting work in particular lie the seeds of a possible resolution of the historiographical conflicts between the Subaltern historians and their critics, and it is for this reason that much of the rest of the review is concerned with his chapters. That analysis must be an empirical one, because it is in their use of empirical evidence to illustrate historical movements, not in general debate, that the Subaltern historians excel.

Pandey's 'Rallying Around the Cow', taken with some of his other articles and the work of other historians, begins to specify the limits of subaltern autonomy, while at the same time insisting on its importance – under some historical circumstances; this is a useful development, but one which needs to be taken further. A rereading of the chapters seem to indicate that there are several basic parameters of change which lie outside the subaltern world but continually inform it. First, there was a gradual escalation of the economic conflicts of late colonial rule as a result of economic stagnation, changes in the international economy and the colonial state's endorsement of large landowners in Awadh and high caste yeomanry in the permanently settled areas adjoining it. The economic conjuncture was also marked by the de-industrialization of the small towns and the decline of the weaving and service communities, which were often Muslim. This process may have speeded up with the development of railway communication after 1880.

There was another, ideological parameter of change: the desire of marginal communities such as poor weavers or middle agricultural castes (Kurmis, Kacchis and Koeris) to improve their respectability or ritual status. This was achieved in Pandey's analysis by 'rallying around the cow' and also by other modes of self-improvement such as caste associations and temperance movements. The equivalent among Muslims was a tendency to seek status and honour by adopting the piety and modesty supposedly associated with the *ashraf* (pious Muslim gentlemen). For Muslims, this concern for status sometimes resulted in the reinvention of the tradition of ritual slaughter of cattle. Caste, religious and peasant identities are contingencies forged out of the conflicts and contradictions implicit in this situation. But all the same, the markers of 'respectability' appear to have been set by ideologies and institutions which influenced peasant mentalities. Although Pandey (and other authors dealing with similar issues) emphasizes the automony of the non-elites and the contingent status of 'consciousness', it does appear that the *dynamics* in their accounts are provided by processes not very different from 'sanskritization', 'Islamization' or even 'modernization', as they would have been understood by earlier historians and sociologists. Surely indeed Pandey's correct insistence that rural and poor people cannot simply be assigned a priori to self-conscious communities reinforces the importance of the role of the state and of elite politics in the eventual triumph of communalism? We should not always be concerned about 'success' in history, but at the same time historians' primary aim must surely be to specify the locus of change.

To be more complete, Pandey's analysis would also need to take fuller account of material conditions and differentiation within the peasantry, in this case of the *relative* prosperity of many groups of Kurmis, Kacchis and Ahirs in the later nineteenth century throughout U.P. and Bihar. Again the context of brief periods of peasant insurgency can best be related to the policies of the state and the way in which external influences bore on the conditions by which peasants ensured the survival of their households. Some Kurmis, for instance, had taken service under the Raj; others had benefited from the slow and inequitable growth associated with the railways, urban demand, or opium and even sugar production. Kurmis, even in south Awadh, were among the biggest agricultural moneylenders according to the Banking Enquiry Committee of 1930. Movements for self-respect among Kurmis had been common in east U.P. and Bihar, for this was more than a struggle for simple material improvement. Their fragmented protest against the system in the 1920s and 1930s was the protest of a peasantry whose success was constantly being snatched from their grasp by the agents of the colonial government, the state of the world economy or by struggling higher-caste landholders who had a head start over them in the competition for resources.

This last group, the large body of petty landholders and tenants of higher-caste status (Rajputs, Jats, Bhumihars and other rural Brahmins, even Muslims in the Gangetic Plain) would also play a critical part in a fuller history of Indian rural movements in the twentieth century. But they get short shrift in the works of the Subaltern historians because they occupy an uneasy marginal role between the elite and the subaltern, crossing and recrossing the conceptual boundary according to the precise historical circumstances under discussion. Also, while their politics was assertive it was rarely violent. They provided a meeting ground for the accommodation of elite and peasant politics and the contests between them, and it was from this group that much rural political activity emanated.

This stratum of peasantry was important in the areas which Pandey, Amin and Henningham study. Close to Pandey's Rai Bareilly District, peasant associations had been established well before 1914 and had been active in parts of rural Allahabad and Fatehpur since the outbreak of war. The activity of the more radical wing of Allahabad and Lucknow politicians and their confrères in south Awadh cannot be ignored here. The Sewa Samiti, the Allahabad 'Hindu populists' had been holding meetings urging a permanent settlement, security of tenancy, expansion of education and government aid. Many peasants had been active in their meetings and agitations; these were often people from subdivided high-caste joint villages near the Doab small towns and in the Benares region.

There is no reason to assume that such people were simply 'manipulated' by elite politicians. On the contrary, there is cause to see here a sophisticated political consciousness. It was one which was prepared to use pressure, petition and even electoral politics in the District Board and, after 1920, in the Legislative Councils, to advance its aims. These forms of rural organization were well represented in the 1919 and 1920 Indian National Congress. In the 1930s the Congress '*tahsil* dictators' who organized the no-rent and no-revenue campaigns were often drawn from their number and received their support. This emphasizes the point that elite and peasant politics were not separate domains; they continuously intervened in and informed each other.

Such a level of rural politics and protest had emerged before 1920 in several Indian provinces. It was foreshadowed in some social reform movements in the 1870s and 1880s, and had many common features with cow-protection and caste reform movements in the 1890s. Very often it was associated with 'conversions' to the Arya Samaj or to Krishna bhakti (devotional) movements. It reflected neither the total autonomy of 'the peasant' nor elite manipulation, but a constant transaction between the countryside and the small town, speeded by the development of the market, the commercialization of the larger villages and the spread of ideas which constantly brought the peasant and townsmen together. If one looks at the location of the most important rural radical movements both before and after the First World War it is from this pressured but mobile social stratum that the most significant responses emerged: from the Mahishyas, a relatively literate stratum in Midnapur and surrounding districts; from the upper Patidars of Kaira and Ahmedabad who linked themselves into the cotton markets and joined the Arya Samaj; from the Bhumihar and other relatively high-caste groups who supported Swami Sahajananad within the Bihar Kisan Sabha through until the 1930s. This level of peasantry were economically distinct from, and sometimes hostile to, the organization of the middle peasant castes beneath them. From a rural perspective it was these petty landlords and secured tenants, concerned with property and stability, which 'captured' the Congress in the 1930s. Since independence the lineal descendants of these groups have been able to re-create their power, sometimes in alliance with the rural and urban poor or Muslims, sometimes working against them. Very often they are found in political or economic competition with the middle-caste groups, Kurmis, Koeris or Ahirs, who form the main actors in several of these essays.

The arguments for the relative autonomy of peasant protest in the case of the Kurmi peasant associations and the Ekka movement in parts of Awadh after the First World War are well taken. At times these associations broadened out to include a much wider range of peasants. But this subaltern solidarity was evanescent. The most striking fact was how quickly the sectionalism which ultimately represented different interests and different statuses among the peasantry reasserted itself at every point in rural protest during late colonial India.

This is at least as important an answer to that most fundamental of the Subalterns' problems – 'why the revolution didn't happen' – as is the problem of Congress hegemony and colonial repression. Gyan Pandey, for instance, implies that peasants were betrayed by the elite Congress politicians; that what was in fact a movement against the whole structure of landed property was diluted by Gandhi and the Congress leadership's insistence on a joint front with the landlords; and that this 'was a statement in favour of the *status quo* and against any radical change in the social set-up when the British finally handed over the reins of power' (vol. I, p. 187). This argument finds echoes in Sumit Sarkar's piece on Gandhi in Volume III.

More important, however, was the fact that the rural movement fell apart under the weight of its own internal conflicts and that propertied elements within the peasantry as much as the small landed class took a hand in suppressing the movement. The colonial state and the Congress merely helped promote a 'white terror' in the countryside in which tenants and small landlords as much as larger *taluqdars* were already leading agents. For that faction had its own autonomous origins. Sectional conflicts within 'the peasantry' had the same degree of autonomy as the kisan movement itself. For a start, in culture and economic interest, the higher-caste tenants and petty landlords who were often drawn from declining coparcenary communities never merged with the Kurmi peasant associations and the Ramchandra movement. They were as much concerned with Permanent Settlement as with security of tenancy. It was noted that several officials of the Oudh Kisan Sabha argued for security of tenure for themselves but wished to deny it to those beneath them. In Bihar Swami Sahajanand began to lose support among the higher-caste tenants in the mid-1930s when he began to articulate the interests of the lower-caste peasantry beneath them.

Next – during the early 1920s – the incidence of *swarajya* riots in which very low-caste landless or near-landless labourers (Pasis and Chamars) played an important role, frightened the middle castes and the upper castes. The occasional call for land redistribution worried the landed peasantry as much as the new pretensions of the unclean scandalized the clean castes. Since many Pasis were also village watchmen (testifying to the deep penetration of the colonial state into their lives), strikes by village servants enhanced the general fear of anarchy. It cannot unambiguously be said that 'The interests of the landless labourers and the smaller, unprotected tenants of Awadh converged to a large extent' (vol. I, p. 179).

By 1923 the immediate post-war economic crisis had passed. The combination of better prices, some measures to limit ejectment (the major issue in Awadh) and the fact that the labour market moved back in favour of the landlords was tending to force the middle peasantry to come to terms with the landlords. Again, communal tensions were beginning to split rural society. The main feature which guaranteed rural 'order' in the Doab was not so much Congress betrayal or even the violence of the colonial police, it was the violence of small landlords (many of whom were also tenants in other villages) supported by their poorer dependants from local bazaars against the demonstrations of the middle peasant castes. This was what happened in places like Mahgaon in the Allahabad Doab. Here, however, the fight was between Muslims and Kurmis. Congress fear of mounting rural violence was in large part motivated by the fact that by summer 1922 rural radicalism (like town radicalism) was beginning once again to take a communal form.

One final point concerns the relative propensity of peasants to violent protest, a theme which runs throughout these volumes. Even at the height of these spectacular disturbances only a minority of villagers were involved in prolonged violent disturbance. In a paragraph from the much-quoted C.I.D. report on the Kisan Sabha which does not find its way into the analysis in *Subaltern Studies*, the writer remarks that it is 'only a very foolish landlord who cannot build up a party to support him in his own villages'. Again, at the height of the Depression and no-rent movements in 1931 a remarkably high proportion of peasants still paid up. It is not at all clear that resistance, let alone violence, is a defining characteristic of the poor or exploited. This may be an unfortunate fact, but it is not one that historians can ignore.

What emerges from this is that a critical analysis of rural movements (and for that matter, working-class movements) will be flawed if it fails to take into account the sectionalism of workers and peasants. The investment of the Congress in defence of the social status quo was paralleled by the concern of high and middle peasant groups for property, status and dominance, however poverty-stricken they were in reality. Even if many were prepared to demonstrate and confront the colonial state and landlords in order to get intergenerational security of tenure and lower rents (or land revenue), they did not necessarily seek security or greater bargaining power for those beneath them in resources and status. Down almost to the very bottom of society every subaltern was an elite to someone lower than him. Close attention has therefore to be paid to the form of appropriation and ritual subordination within villages, to relative access to land, and to broader economic conjunctures. Stressing the autonomy of 'the peasant', as the Subaltern authors have done, has served a valuable purpose in enriching what was in danger of becoming a somewhat mechanical and abstract historiography. Simply to stress that autonomy, as they are sometimes inclined to do, however, is not very helpful in any attempt to specify the nature of historical change. In practice the Subaltern historians quite often allude to these issues, but the rhetorical devices of 'subaltern' and 'peasant resistance' often impede them in this more subtle analysis. If, however, the great volume of good work in *Subaltern Studies* can now be taken and reintegrated with other types of history, then something very interesting might well emerge.

7

Moral Economists, Subalterns, New Social Movements and the (Re-) Emergence of a (Post-) Modernized (Middle) Peasant

Tom Brass

Introduction

This essay follows a doubly unpopular path. First, it constitutes an attempt to reassert the value of a chronologically old and increasingly unfashionable Marxist analysis of the peasantry. And second, it utilizes a comparative framework that stresses certain similarities between some recent agrarian mobilizations in Latin America and India, when the trend nowadays is in the opposite direction: that is, towards an absolute relativism which stresses the complexity and uniqueness (almost, even, the autonomy) of the individual subject in terms of ideological formation, social composition, and (thus) political interest and disposition.

Just as sociological theory generally can be described as a continuing dispute with Marx, so the study of agrarian change is similarly a confrontation with Lenin. Hence the political importance of the long-standing debate between Marxism and neo-populism on the agrarian question involves not just the issue of peasant differentiation *per se* but rather its implications for the role played by rural mobilization in the transition to socialism. The hostility of neo-populism to the latter, and the resulting conflict between it and Marxism, is embodied historically in the theoretical opposition between Chayanov and Lenin concerning both the socio-economic differentiation and the politico-ideological disposition of the peasantry. In contrast to Marxism, therefore, neo-populism views the peasantry as an undifferentiated *sui generis* economic category ('peasant economy', 'peasant mode of production') which both reproduces itself regardless of, and simultaneously resists, all social systems.

It is claimed here that the more important epistemological components – together with their political implications – of precisely such a neo-populist lineage can now be traced directly from Chayanov through the 'middle peasant thesis' and the 'moral economy' argument of Wolf, Alavi and Scott, to the current studies of agrarian mobilization that use a postmodern Subaltern Studies and New Social Movements framework. These frameworks, it is further argued, also provide Chayanovian theory about the peasant economy with its missing politico-ideological dimension: in so far as the Subaltern Studies and New Social Movements approach is structured by the increasingly fashionable methodology of discourse analysis and resistance theory, therefore, its conceptualization of ideology and action is decoupled from class and revolution. It becomes pluri-vocal, and is diffuse in its origins, causation, effect and, ultimately, in its political direction. Finally, the theoretical efficacy of these frameworks is evaluated with regard to recent agrarian mobilizations in Colombia, Peru and India.

Neo-populism, Middle Peasants and Moral Economists

According to Lenin (1960, 1966) – and also Trotsky (1962, 1969) – the peasantry discharges a twofold role in the process of revolutionary transformation. The first stage occurs in the course of the transition to capitalism, and entails a process whereby an economically declining feudal landowning class is challenged and overwhelmed by a peasant movement reflecting the interests of a rising and economically dominant rich peasantry (= rural capitalists). The second stage occurs under capitalism itself, when a rural mobilization led by poor peasants and agricultural workers in turn challenges and overthrows the capitalist peasantry who successfully led the movement against the landlord class. On the agenda at this stage, therefore, is the possibility of a transition to socialism, in that poor peasants and particularly agricultural workers will demand the further socialization of the means of production, and specifically the collectivization of all rural property. The middle peasantry is not involved – let alone leads the peasant movement – in either of these two stages, for the simple reason that in Lenin's model this particular stratum disintegrates (or is 'depeasantized') in the course of capitalist development.[1]

By contrast, in the neo-populist vision of Chayanov (1966), it is precisely the middle peasant which reproduces itself in the form of the family labour farm, regardless of the presence/absence of feudalism, capitalism or indeed socialism. Implicitly challenging Lenin's view regarding the occurrence of socio-economic differentiation within the peasantry, Chayanov argued instead that the reproduction of the family labour farm is unaffected by wages, interest, rent and profit. Consequently, work organization and intensity on such units is determined not by internal/external surplus appropriation leading to capital accumulation, but rather by the producer–consumer balance within the peasant family itself.[2] Based on the development cycle of the domestic group that cultivates the economically self-sufficient smallholding, rural change is endogenous and takes the form of demographic differentiation linked to the consumption requirements of family members.

However, while Chayanov outlines the *economic* logic of the peasant family farm, he tells us nothing about the nature of the *political* action which corresponds to and follows from this economic role. And it is this very gap that the theory advanced not only by Scott, Alavi and Wolf but also by the Subaltern Studies and New Social Movements framework concerning the nature and object of individual or collective action undertaken by the peasantry fills so neatly. In other words, it is Chayanov's peasant family farm which, as the 'eternal' middle peasant, either engages in revolutionary action against capitalism, or simply resists it on a day-to-day basis, the object in both instances being to restore the status quo ante.

Unlike the Lenin view, the 'middle peasant thesis' propounded by Wolf (1971) and Alavi (1979) allocates a revolutionary role to its subject, and thus opens up a *politico-ideological* space for the economic theory of Chayanov. Superficially, the seminal texts by Wolf and Alavi covering twentieth-century peasant movements in Mexico, Russia, China, India, Vietnam, Algeria and Cuba appear to be compatible with a Marxist framework. Thus agrarian mobilizations are regarded as a response to the impact of capitalist development, and the peasantry itself is differentiated on the basis of rich, middle and poor components. Wolf's analysis of peasant movements has been endorsed by no less a person than Desai (1979: 760ff.), who not only maintains that he uses 'some of the major elements of a Marxist approach [and] adopts an approach which comes closest to a Marxist [framework]' but goes so far as to commend the resulting break with ahistorical anthropology in which peasants 'are treated as passive, unchanging . . . traditional and . . . major obstacles to the modernization of the Third World'.[3] However, both Alavi (1979: 673ff.) and Wolf (1971: 291f.) share the (un-Leninist) belief that the middle peasant is not located between the rich and poor peasantry but much rather corresponds to a different sector of the rural economy, composed of independent smallholders who own their land which they cultivate with family labour. Both also share the (un-Leninist) view that poor peasants are the least militant elements of the peasantry as a whole because of patron–client ties which bind them to their masters, and similarly that the most militant elements are the middle peasantry.[4]

The mutually reinforcing theoretical overlap between the 'middle peasant thesis' and the 'moral economy' argument provides Chayanov with two additional forms of superstructural material. First, it constitutes a break with the Leninist concept of revolutionary action and the role of different peasant strata in this process (the political significance of which will become clear below). Instead of revolutionary or insurrectionary activity involving peasants as a mass, rural mobilization in the 'moral economy' argument has been recast by Scott (1976, 1985, 1989) as 'everyday forms of peasant resistance'. The latter refers to small-scale and apparently innocuous activity undertaken by peasants on an individual basis, corresponding to 'generalized non-compliance by thousands of peasants' (1989: 11), and consists of actions such as foot dragging (or go-slows), dissimulation, desertion, false compliance, feigned ignorance, slander, arson and sabotage (1985: xvi). The importance of such actions, Scott argues, lies in the fact that they require little or no co-ordination or planning (in a word, spontaneous), they make use of implicit understandings and networks, they often represent a form of individual self-help, and they typically avoid any direct confrontation with authority. He concludes that in many ways 'everyday forms of peasant resistance' are a more effective form of action, in that through them peasants are more likely to achieve the goals they fail to obtain in the course of the more dramatic large-scale rural mass mobilizations.

And second, just as the Chayanovian subject is reconstituted theoretically in the 'middle peasant' thesis, so the 'moral economy' argument emphasizes its ahistorical character (or 'naturalness') in protecting the subsistence ethic against an external capitalism.[5] A theoretical position which this time Wolf shares with Scott, the 'moral economy' argument maintains that peasants are moved to protest when capitalist penetration of the countryside leads to the loss of subsistence as a result of the breakdown in patron–client relations linking them to elites.[6] The 'moral economy' element consists of the fact that pre-capitalist relationships and institutions protect the peasantry against hardship and starvation, and it is this pre-existing form of insurance or subsistence guarantee which is destroyed by capitalism. Therefore, Scott and Wolf claim, the object of peasant resistance against capitalism is to protect this traditional source of provision. Unlike Lenin, for whom capitalist development not only benefits rich and poor peasants in different ways but also prefigures socialism, for 'moral economists' it merely provokes a return to the pre-capitalist socio-economic structure, and thus cannot prefigure anything.[7]

Postmodernism, Subalterns and New Social Movements

At first sight, both the Subaltern Studies and New Social Movements theory seem to have little in common in terms of time and space. Thus the Subaltern Studies series is basically a critique of the historiography of colonial India, and focuses on issues connected largely with rural transformation; by contrast, the emphasis of the original New Social Movements texts is on urban social mobilization in contemporary Latin America, which is regarded as a response to new forms of social subordination (commodification, bureaucratization and massification).[8] More recently, however, the scrutiny of New Social Movements theory has not only shifted from urban to rural mobilizations – for example, Eckstein (1989), Redclift (1988), Fox (1990) – but has also begun to combine with the 'middle peasant thesis', the 'moral economy' argument and 'everyday forms of resistance' theory, where it finally (and logically) joins forces with Subaltern Studies.[9]

Postmodernism and Its Effects

It is impossible to situate the theoretical concerns and political direction of Subaltern Studies and New Social Movements without reference to the way in which their discourse is structured by the postmodernist project. The latter has transformed the disillusion of 1968 into a Nietzschean pessimism which licenses and in politico-ideological terms epitomizes the reactionary conservatism of the 1980s (see, *inter alia*, Sarup, 1988; Callinicos, 1989). In rejecting totalizing/Eurocentric metanarratives, postmodernism also denies thereby the possibility of a universal process of socio-economic development embodied in the notion of history-as-progress (regardless of whether or not this is actually realized).[10] Such a view necessarily signals the abolition of the Enlightenment project, or emancipation as the object and attainable end of historical transformation, and along with it socialism and communism.[11]

The epistemological link between on the one hand the 'middle peasant thesis' and the 'moral economy' argument of Wolf, Alavi and Scott, and on the other the postmodern underpinnings of Subaltern Studies and New Social Movements theory, is evident from the positive/negative thematic classification that structures their discourse. In general terms, therefore, Eurocentrism, universalism, together with the emancipatory object of history-as-progress all constitute methods/processes/concepts the efficacy of which is denied. The collective is replaced by the autonomous/fragmented individual subject, and the latter is defined not by production but by consumption. The realm of 'the economic' gives way to 'the cultural', while Lenin and Marx are similarly pushed aside by Gramsci and Foucault. Action is guided not by class structure/formation/struggle but by subaltern/elite identities and/or those based on ethnicity/gender/religion/region; a change in the very nature of action itself entails that revolution be replaced by resistance, and in terms of the desirable/(possible) outcome of such action socialism is displaced by bourgeois democracy.

This nihilistic and anti-systemic/anti-progressive position derives in part from the methodological underpinnings of postmodern theory itself. In methodological terms, postmodernism is the mirror image of historical materialism: its unit of analysis is the individual, and its sphere of intervention/determination 'the ideological'.[12] As with language itself, each and every discursively constituted subject in postmodern theory is in ideological terms fragmented and hence autonomous: instead of people speaking univocally (as a class), the individual speaks plurivocally (as a gender/ethnically/regionally specific subject).[13] In contrast to the Marxist analysis of, for example, Volosinov (1973), for whom language is a materially determined arena of class struggle, whereby rival significations are reproduced or transcended and meanings constructed inter-subjectively, for postmodernism the subject is unproblematically constituted by and through language, outside of which there is no existence and therefore no meaning.[14]

In common with two of its theoretical precursors, Gramsci and Foucault, the analytical focus of postmodernism is on 'the ideological': unlike historical materialism, however, an important socio-*economic* concept such as 'power' is theorized by Foucault as an ideological phenomenon, as an end in itself (an innate human characteristic), and thus not as a means to an end (ownership/control of the means of production).[15] Accordingly, the determining role of 'the economic' is either denied or downgraded: ethnic- or gender-specific sociological categories are decontextualized economically, only to be reconstituted in postmodern discourse as cultural subjects.[16] In the case of Subaltern Studies, this methodological procedure results in the depeasantization of tribals (or the tribalization of peasants), which in turn licenses the dei-/rei-fication of the 'other' (see below).

In rejecting history-as-progress, postmodernism is nevertheless required to identify a less alienating version of the present, and (its ahistoricism notwithstanding) unsurprisingly retrieves from the past an idealized version of a world we have lost. Accordingly, the postmodernist philosopher Lyotard expresses nostalgia for a pre-modern (traditional) society, which rests on non-scientific knowledge such as myth, magic, folk wisdom, while the 'New Philosopher' Nemo makes a similarly unfavourable contrast between the dehumanized anonymity of commodity relationships under capitalism and the (more desirable) personal bond between master and servant under feudalism (see Sarup, 1988: 132; Dews, 1980: 10). This advocacy by postmodernism of a return-to-nature both merges neatly with and simultaneously reinforces not only the 'moral economy' argument and the 'middle peasant thesis' but also the neo-populist vision of Chayanov that lies behind them. In denying either the possibility or even the desirability of emancipation, therefore, postmodern theory supports the view of an 'eternal' peasant economy as a 'natural' category outside and against history, and thus confers politico-ideological acceptability on the struggle of its constituent subjects to remain the same.[17] Postmodernism also reproduces and reinforces the theoretical emphasis placed by Chayanovian theory on the role of consumption (as distinct from production) in defining the subject.

Subalterns, New Social Movements, Class and Consciousness

In typically postmodern fashion ('a plague on all your houses'), the critiques undertaken by Subaltern Studies, New Social Movements and Scott all object to a similar combination of overarching theoretical frameworks. Thus the trinity composed of 'conservative paternalism ... populist manipulation [and] the technicist understanding of history by Latin American Marxists' (Evers, 1985: 45; see also Slater, 1985: 4, 5) against which New Social Movements theory argues is analagous to the tripartite model of colonial/nationalist/Marxist interpretations challenged by Subaltern Studies (Ranajit Guha, 1983: 4).[18] In much the same vein, Scott (1989: 4) rejects both 'conservative officialdom and revolutionary vanguard'.

In Subaltern Studies and New Social Movements texts, as well as in the work of Alavi, Wolf and Scott, the concept 'class' is either used incorrectly, questioned, downgraded or rejected. Although he uses the terms 'rich', 'middle' and 'poor' peasants, therefore, Alavi (1979: 672–3) nevertheless questions the utility of such concepts. In a similar vein, Wolf (1971: 289) claims that peasant interests override class alignments, as demonstrated by the fact that rich and poor peasants unite as kinsfolk (kinship = affective relation) rather than divide as economic subjects. For Scott (1985: xvi–xvii; 1989: 5, 7), the concept of 'class' is synonymous with the category 'peasant' (see also Ranajit

Guha, 1983: 92–3), and seemingly radical notions such as 'ordinary means of class struggle' together with 'everyday forms of class resistance' thus refer mainly to conflict between the peasantry as a whole and the state (see below).[19] Significantly, because of this 'conflation' ('class' = 'peasant'), Scott is then able to claim that, as a 'class', peasants are able to discharge an *independent* historical role.

The irrelevance of class differentiation in relation to the peasantry emerges most clearly in a recent collection celebrating Scott's concept of 'everyday forms of resistance', where the editor unambiguously asserts that:

> For the sake of convenience the rural poor are described as peasants. Numerous discussions about what constitutes a peasant remain inconclusive. At times it is important to acknowledge the heterogeneity of the rural poor. Not so here. Thus the definition adopted is broad, with only two easily satisfied characteristics: (1) the peasant works in agriculture, and (2) he or she has a subordinate position in a hierarchical economic and political order. (Colburn, 1989: ix)[20]

Much the same is true of the approaches which adhere to the New Social Movements and Subaltern Studies framework. Because it is tainted with universalism and Eurocentrism, and hence deemed to be inapplicable to the third world, both deprivilege class as an analytical category; see, for example, Ranajit Guha (1983: 166ff.), Evers (1985: 62), Laclau (1985: 29, 30), Slater (1985: 5, 15).

Instead of class differences, the opposition is rather between the 'elite' and its 'state' on the one hand, and on the other the 'masses'/ 'popular masses'. Thus Ranajit Guha's (1982a: vii–viii) category of the 'subaltern' encompasses all forms of 'subordinate' who do not belong to the 'elite'; that is, all those 'of inferior rank . . . whether this is expressed in terms of class, caste, age, gender and office or in any other way' (see also Sen, 1987: 203). It is these same 'subalterns' who correspond approximately to Scott's (1989: 5) 'weaker party' or 'relatively powerless groups' that engage in 'everyday forms of resistance' against the state. The politically and sociologically problematic nature of the 'subaltern' is evident from its all-embracing social composition: among its ranks, therefore, are to be found 'the lesser rural gentry, impoverished landlords, rich peasants and upper middle peasants'. The fact that it includes those whose *class* position and interest correspond to those of an agrarian petty-bourgeoisie, and as such are opposed to those of a rural proletariat, rightly identifies the 'subaltern' as an all-encompassing *neo-populist* category.[21]

The political and analytical deprivileging/demise of class that characterizes the theoretical approaches under consideration stems from a particular epistemological chain of causation. Because classical Marxism – with the exception of Lukács (1971) – failed to develop an adequate theory of class-determined ideological forms and practice, this terrain has been annexed by non-Marxist postmodernists who now use it to throw doubt on the current and historical existence of class itself. Thus Subaltern Studies and New Social Movements theory argue that, as agrarian mobilization and resistance to colonialism/capitalism has more to do with the experience and ideology of gender, ethnicity, region, ecology or religion, these kinds of 'difference' cannot be understood by (and are therefore not reducible to) the class position of the subject. This incompatibility between ethnic/gender/religious/regional identity and experience on the one hand, and class-specific ideological forms on the other, leads in turn and inevitably to the non-emergence of class consciousness, which is then taken as evidence for the non-existence of class itself. Within such an unambiguously idealist framework there is no need to probe the surface appearance of non-class idioms/language/identity/experience, and hence no contradiction is perceived to occur between the latter and the socio-economic position of the subject(s) concerned. Accordingly, the question of precisely what ideological forms constitute consciousness of class, together with the reasons for their absence, is never (and indeed cannot be) posed.[22]

In the case of Latin America, therefore, the argument is that as peasants are unable to make the transition from a 'class-in-itself' to a 'class-for-itself', any attempt to analyse rural mobilizations in terms of 'class' is consequently inappropriate (see, for example, Wolf, 1971: 289; Redclift, 1988: 250). At no point do such texts consider what ideological forms such a transformation (class-in-itself ⇒ class-for-itself) would entail, let alone the possibility that for the leading strata such movements are actually a success.[23] As a number of other texts have pointed out (for example, Sánchez, 1982; Mallon, 1983), the operationalization of apparently politically 'innocent' pre-/non-capitalist ideological forms serve to disguise and simultaneously to advance the *class*-specific objectives of rich peasants, since only in this way can relationships which in economic terms are unequal be represented ideologically as equal. Similarly, in the case of India politico-ideological inversions in which 'Brahmans . . . would behave like Sudras and Sudras like Brahmans' (Ranajit Guha, 1983: 30ff.) that seem to reverse (and hence subvert) the existing hierarchy, may in certain situations also serve to obscure the presence of economically opposed subjects within the category of the subaltern/subordinate itself.[24] A consequence of accepting the surface appearance of these relationships is to endow them with a false concreteness, a reification which not only results in the (mis-) recognition of middle peasants as the sole agents and benefactors of agrarian mobilization but also sustains thereby a rejection of history-as-progress.

This acceptance of the surface appearance of relations of production, which derives from the epistemological impossibility of admitting the presence of false consciousness, also structures the Subaltern Studies critique of the non-fulfilment of the liberal bourgeois project on the part of the British Raj. That the latter did not displace pre-capitalist social forms in its colony, as embodied in the contrast between the introduction of Liberalism/Democracy/Liberty/Rule-of-Law, etc., leading to the elimination of unfreedom in the metropolitan context yet the absence of the very same combined with the persistence of unfreedom in the Indian subcontinent (Guha, 1989: 235–7, 273–4, 277), is regarded as evidence for the failure of the totalizing capitalist project and implicitly confirms the impossibility of history-as-progress.[25] Because the issue is theorized largely at the level of the superstructure, however, even a perceptive Subaltern Studies contributor like Ranajit Guha fails to distinguish between the spread of capitalism as an *economic* project, and Liberalism/Democracy/Liberty/Rule-of-Law, etc., as contingent *politico-ideological* aspects of this process, any or all of which may be absent without necessarily hindering the reproduction of the capital relation itself.

Accordingly, capitalism does not everywhere need – and indeed sometimes cannot operate with – the superstructural forms that constitute the liberal bourgeois project: much rather, in specific contexts and at particular moments, the accumulation process actually depends on their absence. Unfree (or 'feudal') relations of production constitute a good example of this paradox, since both historically and currently the development of a specifically *proletarian* class consciousness linked to the existence of the free wage relation not only threatens the profitability of capitalism in the short term but also confronts this socio-economic system with the possibility of its own demise in the long terms.[26] In such circumstances, therefore, the continuation of pre-capitalist socio-economic forms in non-metropolitan contexts is in fact a *realization* and not a negation of the universalist project of capitalism.

Revolution and Resistance

As has already been noted, Marxism denies middle peasants an independent historical role in any revolutionary process. As small capitalist producers, rich peasants are in the vanguard of the struggle against the landlord class in the course of a capitalist transition, only to be displaced in turn by the proletariat and poor peasantry in the course of a transition to socialism. Because of its continuous 'depeasantization', the middle peasantry does not – and indeed *cannot* – discharge a similar historical role, and for this reason is not considered by Marxism to constitute an independent revolutionary force. Having recuperated this very same subject for the historical process, Wolf and Alavi nevertheless experience difficulty in reconciling the innate dissonance between, on the one hand, its revolutionary political action and, on the other, its conservative socio-economic disposition.[27] The work of Scott offers a plausible solution to this contradiction, in so far as it shifts the locus of peasant action from revolution to 'everyday forms of resistance', thereby banishing or downgrading revolution from the historical agenda and simultaneously restoring to the middle peasant an independent historical role embodied in this kind of all-pervasive and continuous political activity.

Scott is in many ways a pivotal figure in the whole discourse under consideration here; his methodology based on 'everyday forms of resistance', together with its theoretical effects, forms a crucial (and continuing) link between earlier texts by Wolf and Alavi and the later texts belonging to the Subaltern Studies and New Social Movements framework. Thus the micro-level responses embodied in Scott's ubiquitous concept, deployed by Wolf (1971: 282) to describe peasant reaction to capitalist penetration, reappear as the 'new forms of struggle and resistance' (Laclau, 1985: 27) undertaken by New Social Movements which in turn lead to 'new socio-cultural patterns of everyday sociability . . . the embryos of a popular counter-foundation' (Evers, 1985: 63). As an organizational form, the concept of 'everyday forms of resistance' also structures the actions undertaken by subalterns: in contrast to the elite, whose activity is legalistic/constitutional, cautious and controlled, and consists of vertical mobilization (Ranajit Guha, 1982b: 4–5), subalterns engage in spontaneous violent (= 'natural') action that entails the operationalization of traditional horizontal linkages based on kinship and territoriality.

Most importantly, the element of hegemony, implied in the work of Wolf and Alavi, is challenged and displaced by Scott. The latter thereby transforms peasants from passive accepters of existing ideology into its active challengers. Hence middle peasants are not just occasionally engaged in overt conflict, such as going to war, rioting, rebelling or engaging in revolutionary activity to stay middle peasants, but are now depicted by Scott as being actively and continuously engaged in covert struggle to remain middle peasants. In short, the periodic and defensive action attributed by Wolf and Alavi to middle peasants in order to preserve their status as such is in the work of Scott transformed into incessant and offensive action.

As significant is the fact that in the course of this epistemological break, the central focus of peasant resistance has shifted from withstanding capitalism (as in the work of Wolf and Alavi) to opposing socialism (in the work of Scott, Subaltern Studies and New Social Movements), thus not only reinforcing the Chayanovian concept of the peasantry as a socio-economic form which reproduces itself independently, regardless of the mode of production but also licensing opposition by rich peasants to attempts at the further socialization of means of production. As Kitching (1982: 21ff.) points out with regard to the political difference between neo-populism and populism, the latter was principally a critique of nineteenth-century capitalism arising from opposition to its human costs; moreover, populism did not deny the possibility of economic development *per se*, arguing only that this could be achieved without large-scale industrialization and urbanization. Neo-populism, by contrast, is a twentieth-century phenomenon opposed not so much to capitalism as to socialism, and to the collectivization of smallholding peasants in particular.

The shift from revolution to resistance as the main type of peasant action licenses a break not just with the revolutionary form itself but also with its political content. A consequence of downgrading the act of revolution in this manner is a corresponding denial of history-as-progress linked to and dependent on the revolutionary process itself; in short, a procedure which banishes emancipation generally, and in particular abolishes not merely the inevitability but even the possibility of socialism as the outcome.

Bourgeois Democracy, Socialism and the State

As the focus of New Social Movements is the individual subject, the target of whose activity is the state apparatus, it is unsurprising that its postmodern discourse is unequivocally anti-state. Thus New Social Movements, for whom the 'question of a reappropriation of society from the state has become thinkable' (Evers, 1985: 61), are characterized as generally 'anti-authoritarian, anti-institutional' (Slater, 1985: 3). Wolf (1971: 294–5), Scott (1989: 23) and Redclift (1988: 251) all identify the state as the object of action undertaken by peasants. Since without knowing the class composition of a movement against the state it is impossible to say what kind of socio-economic contradictions permeate its political programmes and objectives, the decoupling of state and class immediately raises a number of politically important issues.

At a general level, this decoupling generates a certain amount of conceptual confusion; for example, the claim (Redclift, 1988: 250) that in Latin America during the 1970s and 1980s the state has replaced the landlord as the source of repression in the agrarian sector allocates to the state (an administrative apparatus where – as is the case here – the class interests are unspecified) the role previously filled by the landlord *class*. It also obscures the *class* origin and object of action against the state. Hence a simplistic peasant/state opposition reproduces and reinforces the all-powerful-state/all-subordinate-peasantry dichotomy, which in turn conceals the extent to which it is *rich* peasants who successfully resist the attempts by a capitalist state to impose controls on the direction of their own accumulation project.[28] Similarly, 'everyday forms of resistance' can be undertaken by any and all socio-economic agents against the state, a point conceded by Scott (1989: 23). He attempts to rescue his characterization of this kind of action as resistance-from-below by claiming that it usually involves a 'weaker' party struggling against an 'institutional' opponent that controls the state apparatus, and that all those engaged in such action operate with the concept of injustice-which-needs-rectifying (Scott, 1989: 24). The problem with this is that landlords and capitalists are not only capable of undertaking 'everyday forms of resistance' but – like poor peasants and workers – also do this on the basis of 'injustice' (for example, state expropriation of privately-owned factories or latifundia). A further problem is that, although New Social Movements are directed against the state, both their mode (resistance-not-revolution) and form (the aestheticization of revolt, or cultural opposition) of mobilization effectively preclude a realistic challenge to the power and existence of the state itself. This point is recognized by Evers (1985: 43), who observes that New Social Movements are basically about 'everyday social [and socio-cultural] relations' and *not* about the capture of political power.

That the state apparatus remains intact in this manner – for the bourgeoisie to (re-) occupy – is unsurprising, since the political objective of New Social Movements and Subaltern Studies framework is an understanding of the difficulties associated with the realization not of socialism or communism but bourgeois democracy.[29] Hence the project of Subaltern Studies has been defined by Guha as 'a "new democracy" – *it is the study of this failure which constitutes the central problematic of the historiography of colonial India*' (original emphasis), while that of the New Social Movements similarly addresses issues relating to the (re-) construction of a hegemonic democracy encompassing the 'popular sectors'.[30] However, the rejection by Scott (1985: 314f.) of 'hegemony' indicates the difficulty of reconciling 'everyday forms of resistance' with any social structure, since the element of politico-ideological acceptation implicit in the concept is by its very nature incompatible with this kind of (almost nihilistic) peasant activity.[31]

The long-term political direction of a theoretical framework with a socially non-specific state at its core, and thus as the focus of peasant action, finally emerges when it becomes clear that it licenses resistance not only to the capitalist state but also to a socialist state and behind this socialism itself.[32] Hence the observation by Slater (1985: 7) that: 'we must not assume that there exists a linear relationship between new social movements and a progressive political orientation, because obviously it cannot be assumed *a priori* that every new struggle or demand will somehow automatically express a socialist content'. This point is reiterated elsewhere by Slater (1985: 14) and also by Evers (1985: 63), who comments that 'some observers have pointed to the puzzling fact that some of the new impulses coming out of these base level groupings have similarities with the ultra-liberal ideology of [Milton] Friedman'. Significantly, in rejecting revolution as a means of securing change, Scott (1989: 3–4) argues that socialist revolutions are more exploitative than capitalism and, like Laclau and Mouffe (1985), make no distinction between Leninism and Stalinism (Scott 1989: 18). For Scott, therefore, the focus of peasant opposition has now become the socialist state, and his most recent examples of 'everyday forms of resistance' embodying state/peasant conflict are all drawn from non-capitalist contexts: the Soviet Union in the 1920s and 1930s, Hungary during the 1940s and 1950s, and China 1949–78 (1989: 15ff.).

Although this particular development in the work of Scott constitutes a fundamental break with Wolf, for whom the focus of peasant opposition is the capitalist state, it nevertheless licenses an equally important continuation with the earlier views of Chayanov. Thus the type of peasant he defends in general terms against the socialist state is precisely that which Chayanov was accused of protecting in the Soviet Union, and for much the same reasons. At first sight, therefore, the self-sufficient family farmer, whose 'autonomy' is threatened by the socialist state, whose life-sustaining link between production and consumption is broken by collectivization, and who because of this engages in 'everyday forms of resistance' (Scott, 1989: 15), exhibits all the socio-economic characteristics associated with – and indeed appears to be nothing other than – the middle peasant. However, just as Chayanov (1966: lxx, 43ff.) conflated middle peasants and kulaks, thereby providing the latter with a politico-ideological defence that permitted them to resist further socialization of the means of production under the guise of petty commodity producers rather than rich peasants, so Scott (1989: 17) tacitly acknowledges that in socialist Hungary 'everyday forms of resistance' was a defensive strategy adopted by kulaks to block state procurements.[33] Despite being aware of the petty bourgeois disposition and element among the peasantry in such contexts, therefore, Scott refuses to make a political distinction between the action by incipient/actual agrarian capitalists against the socio-economic system attempting to prevent them from becoming once more, or continuing as, small capitalists, and that undertaken by workers and poor peasants against capitalism. Whereas both activities share the same form, the political content of the former is reactionary, and must be differentiated from resistance against capitalism which seeks to go beyond it and establish socialism.

Agrarian Mobilization in Latin America and India

The epistemological continuity between on the one hand the postmodernized New Social Movements and Subaltern Studies approach, and on the other the work of Scott, Wolf and Alavi, and the neopopulism of Chayanov, together with the consequent theoretical difficulties inherited by the former from all the latter, is best illustrated with regard to the way in which these frameworks analyse and account for three recent examples of agrarian mobilization in Latin America and India: ANUC in Colombia during the 1970s, Sendero Luminoso in Peru during the 1980s, and Naxalism in West Bengal during the early 1970s.[34]

ANUC in Colombia

Zamosc charts the rise and fall of the peasant movement in Colombia over a period of two decades, a process which began with the formation of the National Peasant Association (*Asociación Nacional de Usuarios Campesinos*, or ANUC) in 1967, reached a peak with the land invasions of 1971, and ended in the late 1970s when the struggle for land ceased. Because it did not result in a substantial 'repeasantization', Zamosc regards this movement as a failure. Although in the course of this struggle and the subsequent agrarian reform some 66,000 families had obtained land by the end of the 1970s, a greater number had in fact become landless during the two previous decades (1986: 149, 203; 1989: 124).

Despite containing much important information on the political economy of Colombia, the opposing politico-ideological positions in debates concerning rural transformation, and the peasant movement itself, Zamosc's analysis is marred by an idealized view of the peasantry, which in turn leads to a misrecognition of the reasons for the agrarian struggles he describes. Apart from a few token footnote references (1986: 215–16), no attempt is made to address the existing literature on and debate about capitalist development, rural socio-economic differentiation, and the peasant economy.[35] Instead of differentiating the peasantry in terms of class, Zamosc follows Shanin – whose enthusiastic endorsement precedes the main text (1986: xi–xiv) – and (like Scott) adopts a neo-populist framework in which not only is the peasantry itself recast in terms of 'class' (1986: 2, 27, 37, 39, 46, 50ff.; 1989: 115, 123, 127) but the self-sufficient peasant family farm is regarded as a non-capitalist alternative form of development (1986: 7, 215–16 footnotes 1–2). That such a theoretical framework is impossible to sustain rapidly becomes apparent, since Zamosc's view of peasants as a class soon begins to co-exist uneasily with references to the presence of rich, middle and poor peasants (1986: 41, 124–5, 140, 231 footnote 81, 224 footnote 83). Subsequently he admits that the existence of a socio-economically differentiated peasantry undermines the peasant movement (1986: 170–71) and concludes by noting that the demise of ANUC was due largely to this factor (1986: 204–5).

Although his argument is based on the Chayanovian concept of the independent peasant family farm, Zamosc actually tells us little about its internal socio-economic structure, organization and dynamic. For example, he omits to provide data on crucial points such as changing household composition, the kinds and amounts of labour employed (personal, family, hired), cropping patterns and per hectare yields, and whether or not such units generated production surpluses. Instead, the defining criterion is land, a methodological procedure which, when coupled with the unproblematic adoption of census landholding categories, involves Zamosc following 'the accepted convention that . . . considers units smaller than twenty hectares to be peasant units' (1986: 23; see also 1989: 109). That the economic interests of those at the top of this category might not be the same as those at the bottom is a question Zamosc never poses. According to the 1960 agricultural census, cultivators owning under 20 hectares accounted for 61 per cent of total output and, more significantly, for half the output of coffee, the principal cash crop exported by Colombia (1986: 25). This undifferentiated landholding category would therefore have included not only poor peasants, whose main income derived from the sale of their labour-power, but also small agrarian capitalists producing coffee for the international market.[36]

The theoretical contradictions inherent in Zamosc's neo-populist teleology are perhaps nowhere more evident than in his assessment of the agrarian reform that followed the peasant movement. Trapped by his essentialist concept of a peasant 'class' composed of family farms whose main objective and defining characteristic is landownership for subsistence cultivation, it is necessary to depict the peasant movement in Colombia during the 1970s as an attempt to realize this goal by establishing a 'peasant economy' (1986: 130, 146, 149ff., 163, 165, 202; 1989: 103, 109). Thus the failure of the co-operative institutional structure (*empresas comunitarias*) set up by the Colombian agrarian reform agency INCORA after the land struggles is attributed principally to the external agency of 'adverse state policy' (1986: 160ff.), despite acknowledgement that 'an individual economy of small entrepreneurs and affluent peasants' (1986: 162) operated inside the co-operatives. However, Zamosc regards the existence of the latter subjects not as evidence of capitalist development in Colombian agriculture but much rather as an indication of 'distorting repeasantisation' and 'a failure of the peasant economy' (1986: 146, 165). Symptomatically, he blames such deviations from the path of peasant essentialism on the decline of a (non-existent) peasant 'class solidarity' (1986: 163).

Like many of the New Social Movements theorists who write about the peasantry, Zamosc also makes explicit the political practice consequent on his analysis. Notwithstanding the inescapable weight of evidence against his essentialist view of the peasantry, therefore, Zamosc continues to argue against the 'indiscriminate use of such notions as "emergent peasant bourgeoisie"', and insists on reaffirming his neo-populist vision that 'the first task of a sensible opposition [in Colombian politics] is to restore the spirit of autonomy among the peasants' (1986: 212, 213; see also 1989: 127). In his most recent text, Zamosc (1990: 47, 48, 52) still talks of making a 'free peasant economy viable', noting that, among other things, 'in the 1980s the Colombian peasants have been fighting for . . . the defence of the small peasant economy'.

Sendero Luminoso in Peru

Much the same kinds of difficulty confront the attempt by McClintock to theorize the support received by the Sendero Luminoso guerrillas in rural Peru throughout the 1980s in terms of a combined 'moral economy', 'middle peasant', and New Social Movements framework. Invoking both Scott and Wolf to sustain her argument (1984: 58f., 74, 82; 1989a: 67–70, 95), McClintock claims that economic decline, population growth and ecological crisis in locationally remote Ayacucho (1984: 63, 76–7) have all resulted in a threat to the subsistence of 'smallholders . . . relatively unintegrated into the capitalist market' (1984: 49, 74) from among whom Sendero consequently draws its support. Although not categorized as such, these smallholding proprietors are clearly regarded as middle peasants, a point which McClintock confirms in another text (1989b: 358). Since peasant proprietors remain socio-economically undifferentiated, are all regarded as uniformly impoverished and downtrodden, and undertake action merely to defend the status quo, little or no attempt is made to account for the changing socio-economic composition of Senderista support in rural areas and to link this in turn to the *class*-specific acceptability of Sendero's ideology.[37]

The problematic nature of McClintock's analytical framework emerges clearly when she attempts to explain the changed socio-economic composition of Senderista backing in the Peruvian countryside. With the exception of one particular location, the Upper Huallaga valley in the department of Huánuco, rural support for Sendero in the Andean region declined over the 1983–86 period. McClintock is clearly baffled by this development, and observes (1989a: 87–8):

> Many analysts were surprised at the appearance of Sendero in this zone. In contrast to the Southern highlands, this valley is prosperous. The people living on these lower Andean slopes are less likely to be descendants of the Incas than the people in the Southern highlands. Sendero apparently chose to recruit in the Huallaga Valley to take advantage of the popular opposition to the coca-eradication programs sponsored by the US and Peruvian governments. Sendero did mobilize and support coca-growers, and became the dominant authority at several sites.

Since most of the texts dealing with the cocaine economy tend to focus only on the large amounts of money generated in the course of and as the rewards linked to the high-risk marketing/distribution from Colombia of the already processed drug, little reference is made to the profitability of the first stage in its production, the cultivation in Peru (and elsewhere) of the coca crop itself. From the viewpoint of cocaine production in the Andean region, the highest-yielding coca leaves are to be found in the Upper Huallaga Valley, where during the mid-1980s a peasant producer might expect to gross on average an astonishing US$ 12,600 per hectare of coca cultivated (Morales, 1989: 55–6).[38] In contrast to McClintock's 'moral economy' and New Social Movements argument, therefore, it is clear that in the Upper Huallaga valley rural support for Sendero no longer corresponds to a struggle by uniformly impoverished middle peasants belonging to the same ethnic group in defence of a threatened subsistence base but much rather involves rich peasant colonists who grow and benefit substantially from the coca crop.

This shift in the socio-economic composition of Senderista backing raises the additional issue of precisely why the same politico-ideological position is apparently acceptable to such different agrarian class subjects. In short, the question concerns the seeming incompatibility betwen the Maoism of Sendero and the class interests of coca-growing rich peasants in the Upper Huallaga valley. Two opposed views exist regarding the political and ideological position of Sendero. One maintains that what is important about Sendero's rural appeal is not so much its Maoism as Andean messianism, the latter invoking a mythical Incaic past where the traditional pre-Conquest cultural values of the Quechua population will once again dominate (for example, Taylor, 1983: 20–21). The other, which includes New Social Movements theorists such as McClintock and Gianotten *et al.*, rejects the claim that Sendero is attempting to re-create an archaic cultural tradition. In support of this view, McClintock (1989a: 83) points out that: 'Words such as "feudalism", "bourgeoisie", "imperialism" are common, whereas references to the Incan past, indigenous customs, and popular anecdotes are non-existent.' Similarly, Gianotten *et al.* (1985: 192ff.) argue that: first, because the Andean peasantry is now integrated into the market, Sendero is faced with the impossibility of reconstituting the self-sufficent rural community; and second, Sendero has anyway attempted to break the existing political and economic structures of the Andean peasant community by replacing communal authorities with its own militants.

In so far as they are mutally exclusive, however, neither of these positions is wholly correct; much rather, the ideology of Sendero ought to be perceived as a *synthesis* of Maoism and Andean messianism. Thus, the objection made by Gianotten *et al.* regarding the impossibility of reconstituting the eroded material base of the peasant economy together with the Andean rural community overlooks the extent to which it is possible for Sendero to obtain support as a result of an *ideology* based on the desire to recuperate this materially impossible objective. Furthermore, it is significant that Sendero does not challenge the concept and structure of 'community' *per se*, but merely replaces its personnel.

Neither view considers the degree to which and the reasons why Sendero Luminoso's Maoism is compatible with the more important politico-ideological components of Andean traditional beliefs, either by reproducing the latter directly or merely by not challenging them. Thus the anti-urbanism, anti-imperialism, ethnic chauvinism and peasant essentialism (*campesinismo*) of Sendero not only possess strong affinities with the politico-ideological form and content of indigenous Andean beliefs such as the town/country opposition, nationalism and ethnic chauvinism, but also reproduce the central tenet of neo-populism, 'urban bias'.[39] In short, they contribute to and reinforce the mythical existence of a middle peasantry while at the same time permitting a rich peasant stratum to operate.[40]

One important consequence of classifying the Peruvian social formation as 'semi-feudal', therefore, is that the principal contradiction is located not between capital and labour but between, on the one hand, an external imperialism coupled with its internal ally, the 'feudal' landlord class, and, on the other, an anti-imperialist alliance composed of peasants, workers and a 'progressive' bourgeoisie, in which the peasantry constitute the dominant element. Not only are Maoism and nationalism interchangeable in this discourse, but its specifically Maoist component also allocates the main role in the defence of the nation against 'outsiders' to an undifferentiated peasantry. Thus in politico-ideological terms 'the nation' ('the people', 'the popular masses') is equated largely with the peasantry as a whole, while 'outsiders' – or non-peasants – of whatever kind (urban dwellers, technocrats, bureaucrats, foreigners) are unproblematically associated with 'imperialism' (peasants: outsiders:: nation: imperialism).

From the viewpoint of prosperous coca-growing peasants in the Upper Huallaga valley, the politico-ideological acceptability of Senderista Maoism/messianism lies precisely in the fact that, when combined with the historical image of coca as a 'traditional' crop associated with subsistence/survival and the Incaic past, an outside enemy permits rich peasants to externalize capitalist exploitation and thus to deflect/suppress any reference to the occurrence of socio-enonomic differentiation and surplus appropriation within the peasantry itself. Accordingly, when linked with anti-urbanism, ethnic chauvinism and peasant essentialism in this manner, the anti-imperialism of Sendero Luminoso reinforces not politically progressive internationalist/socialist concerns but a more narrow and reactionary set of nationalist/conservative beliefs that is compatible with and indeed reflects the *class* position of rich peasants.

Like other texts on Sendero, McClintock (1984: 49, 77ff.; 1989a: 76ff.) emphasizes the discontinuity between the rural guerrilla movements of the 1960s and those of the 1980s, pointing to the failure of the former when compared with the continuing success of the latter. By contrast, it is argued here that, in at least one important respect, significant continuities do exist between these two periods; as in the 1980s, therefore, there are instances of Peruvian agrarian movements during the 1960s that were a success for rich peasant subjects, and similarly not despite but much rather because of a seemingly radical ideology.[41] It is tempting to speculate in passing that, just as the Latin American guerrilla movements of the 1960s were linked to the profitability of the coffee crop (see Gott, 1970: 151), so those of the 1980s in Peru and Colombia may be linked similarly to the profitability of the coca grown for cocaine production.

Naxalism in West Bengal

Turning to the case of India, since peasant movements in the subcontinent have been examined in a large number of texts, it is intended here to consider just one aspect of the Subaltern Studies framework: the theoretical implications of the 'tribalization' of agrarian struggles.[42] In the case of rural mobilizations during the colonial era, for example, Ranajit Guha (1983: 166ff.) downgrades the concept 'class' on the grounds that it was overdetermined by religious or ethnic solidarities; however, one important theoretical effect of this position is the conceptual reproduction of the 'tribal', paradoxically a central emplacement of colonial discourse (the demystification of which is Guha's objective).[43] As O'Hanlon (1988: 196) rightly hints, behind the deconstructed subject of the Subaltern Studies project necessarily lurks another (or 'an other') subject, potentially or actually reconstituted; the latter, it is argued here, is none other than the 'other' which the totalizing discourse of historical materialism had apparently dismantled earlier.

Hence the *ideological* difference embodied in (and recognized by Marxism as) 'ethnicity' not only reappears in Subaltern Studies discourse but can now be recuperated as a *material* difference, occupying the terrain previously held conceptually by 'class'. Accordingly, in rejecting/displacing historical materialism, with its univeral/totalizing *economic* analytical categories, and then contrasting the 'degenerate'/ 'corrupt'/(sinful) Eurocentrism of the latter with the immanent 'goodness'/'naturalness' of the *ideological* categories that constitute 'indigenous' discourse, the Subaltern Studies framework creates a theoretical space for the rescue of the 'tribal' from the dustbin of (colonial) history, and thus breathes new life into the Rousseauesque myth of the 'noble savage' who, together with its contemporary variant, the middle peasant, is everywhere to be found engaged in 'everyday forms of resistance' to remain the same.[44]

Neither isolated culturally from the rest of the population nor economically undifferentiated, tribals in north-east India have participated historically in agrarian struggles not just as producers in their own traditional areas but also as agricultural workers (for higher wages, better working conditions, etc.) in the Assamese tea plantations and in the coal mines of Bihar.[45] The extent to which class differentiation operates within the tribal population emerges clearly from a study by Bose (1985) in 1980 of five districts of West Bengal (Birbhum, Bankura, Burdwan, Midnapore and Purulia).[46] Not only were the beneficiaries of government reservation schemes in this context rich peasant tribals, who composed only 1 per cent of all households yet owned 16 per of the land, 44 per cent of which was irrigated, but they also engaged in moneylending, owned more livestock, and used more chemical fertilizer than any other peasant strata.[47] Middle peasants, who constituted 7 per cent of households, owned 23 per cent of the land, 22 per cent of which was irrigated, while poor peasants who amounted to 68 per cent of all households, owned 60 per cent of the land only 20 per cent of which was irrigated (Bose, 1985: 75, 80, 84, tables 3.10, 3.14, 3.16).

A quarter of middle peasants and three-quarters of poor peasants in these West Bengal villages purchased no labour-power, whereas all rich peasants employed outside labour (Bose, 1985: 86–7); by contrast, no rich peasant, a few middle peasants, most poor peasant and all agricultural labour households sold labour-power (Bose, 1985: 51, 88–9). Tribal peasants who hired tribal wage labourers treated them no better, and in some cases worse, than non-tribal peasants hiring tribals as agricultural labour (Bose, 1985: 94–5). Rich peasant tribals also employed young labourers (*bagels*) to herd their cattle, either without paying them wages or merely on the promise of meeting their marriage expenses when they came of age.[48] In politico-ideological terms, variations in tribal kinship patterns were determined by class, as was intra-kin conflict; there was little evidence of intra-tribal unity, rich tribals being regarded by their poorer counterparts as possessing not just different but antagonistic interests (Bose, 1985: 112–13, 118–19, 121–2).

Significantly, these same West Bengal districts of Midnapore, Birbhum and Bankura were also areas of Naxalite guerrilla activity over the 1967–71 period (Duyker, 1987). Formed in 1969 after a split with the pro-Moscow CPI(M), the Maoist CPI (M-L) initiated the Naxalite guerrilla movement in this region, and drew its main support from the tribal population. Just as in the case of Sendero Luminoso in Peru, Naxalite Maoism in West Bengal exhibited millenarian characteristics that were ultimately not only compatible with but supportive of the existing tribal structure (Duyker, 1987: 110, 124), regardless of the extent to which it might be differentiated socio-economically.[49] Claiming that India was a semi-colonial/semi-feudal social formation, therefore, rural Naxalites externalized capitalist exploitation on the one hand, and on the other emphasized tribal cultural particularism together with the element of continuity between the politico-ideological objectives of the present struggle and those of the past (Duyker, 1987: 101–2, 117).[50] Claims by Duyker (1987: 118) to the contrary notwithstanding, such an appoach leads inevitably to the displacement of class struggle (which licenses intra-ethnic conflict) by ethnic struggle (which licenses intra-class conflict) as the primary focus of Naxalism.[51]

In contrast to the claim by Subaltern Studies texts regarding the irreducible nature of ethnic categories, the Naxalite movement in West Bengal provides evidence that at the bottom end of the social structure proletarian class solidarity does indeed transcend tribal/caste distinctions. Following the introduction of the Green Revolution package in this region during the mid-1960s, there was an increase in the incidence of *de facto* proletarianization as landholders not only no longer leased out land to new tenants and rotated existing ones in order to prevent them claiming ownership rights, but also increased product rents and decreased wage levels (Duyker, 1987: 50ff.). On the basis of a common experience as sharecroppers and agricultural labourers, therefore, Santals united with other tribals (Munda, Mals, Rajbansi, Oraons) and lower-caste Hindus (Bagdi, Bauri, Doms).[52]

While such evidence confirms the existence of and the reasons for the transcendence of ethnic divisions by class solidarity at the lower end of the social structure, the same study only hints at the occurrence of a similar differentiating process at its top end. Duyker (1987: 60ff.) notes the emergence of rich peasantry following the Green Revolution, but omits to indicate whether or not this stratum extended to include Santals. However, nearly half the killings carried out by Naxalites in Birbhum were of peasants with less than 25 acres, while those who owned more than this amount accounted for only 22 per cent of annihilations, a point underlined by one CPI (M-L) leader who observed that 'the fundamental contradiction was not between (big) landlords and their sharecroppers, tenants and labourers, but between *jotedar*-kulaks and sharecroppers, labourers and tenants', (Duyker, 1987: 62–3). The significance of this lies in the fact that, as the study by Bose demonstrates, a numerically small but economically important stratum of precisely this kind of peasant was to be found *within* the tribal population itself.

The existence of actual/potential Naxalite targets among the Santals themselves raises in turn the crucial issue of the reasons for an absence of intra-tribal class struggle. Why, if a *de facto* Santal proletariat was able to unite with other tribals and/or non-tribals along class lines, was it not also capable of directing subsequent action against those of a different class inside the same ethnic group? As with Sendero Luminoso, the answer to this question must necessarily address the complicity between the politico-ideological position of the CPI (M-L) itself and that of the 'traditional' tribal authorities, the corresponding failure to challenge – let alone break – the strong ties of authority inside the village community, and the resulting deflection of class struggle by ethnic conflict.

Duyker (1987: 89, 103–4) suggests that in both Midnapore and Birbhum districts the CPI (M-L) micro-level organization 'owed more to indigenous cultural factors than to its April 1969 resolution on political organization'. Accordingly,

> Naxalite cells and action squads had hierarchies, lines of communication and logistic support which were rooted in the local kinship system . . . as whole families of Santals joined the movement, kinship organization began to parallel guerrilla organization . . . the natural authority of the elders, i.e. fathers, uncles and husbands, appears to have become a political and military authority over sons, nephews and wives who also joined the movement.

In other words, guerrilla activity mobilized through the kinship system was actually structured by – and thus could not but reflect the interests of – the *existing* socio-economic order, as embodied in the authority of tribal elders.[53] The difficulty with this is that even in a tribal context (as Bose, Pathy and others show), such authority can also correspond to that exercised by rich peasants over agricultural labourers and sharecroppers (all of whom happen to be tribal kinsfolk), and would therefore not only not be 'natural' but in class terms could not be neutral. In the (unlikely) event of their own socio-economic position being challenged/threatened, therefore, rich peasant tribals would be able to counter any attempt on the part of the CPI (M-L) to mobilize Santals as class subjects (landless labourers, poor peasants, sharecroppers) by proclaiming a politico-ideological unity based on ethnicity.

Conclusion

It has been argued here that the way in which peasant action and peasant movements are theorized, initially in the work of Alavi and Wolf, and then in the work of Scott, and most recently in the approach which characterizes texts on the New Social Movements and Subaltern Studies, provides neo-populist theory about peasant economy with its missing politico-ideological dimension. To a large degree, this process is structured by the de-/re-constructions effected as a result of post-modern epistemology.

Mediated through the Subaltern Studies and New Social Movements framework, the postmodern project is in a number of important ways particularly supportive of the 'middle peasant thesis' and 'moral economy' argument advanced by Wolf, Alavi and Scott, and behind them the neo-populism of Chayanov himself. On the one hand, therefore, postmodernism attacks the telelogical roots belonging to the traditional political opponents of neo-populist visions of a self-sufficient peasantry: the overarching metanarratives of Marx and Lenin on the universality of class and class struggle, collectivization and socialism as outcomes of the latter, the necessity/desirability/possibility of emancipation which structures the notion of history-as-progress, and the state as the object of revolution. On the other hand, it attempts to recuperate conceptually a politico-ideological project which sustains that very same neo-populist vision: the ideological pluralism of the subject, the autonomy of the individual, the political importance and acceptability of (self-defined) relativism as embodied in 'the cultural' ('the tribal', 'the peasant'), the wholesale legitimacy of any/all 'everyday forms of resistance', and bourgeois democracy.

In keeping with their postmodern antecedents, therefore, analyses based on a New Social Movements or Subaltern Studies framework claim that the object of peasant activity – whether 'everyday forms of resistance' or large-scale mobilizations – is unconnected with socialism because the latter is unrealizable/undesirable. While it is true that peasant activity may not necessarily lead to socialism, this is *not* for the reasons indicated by the Subaltern Studies and New Social Movements framework. These imply that all smallholders are middle peasants interested only in remaining as such, and as a result adhere to non-class-based ideologies which stress regionalism, ethnicity or gender.

By contrast, the case of ANUC in Colombia, Sendero Luminoso in Peru, and Naxalism in West Bengal suggests that rich and not middle peasants are in the forefront of rural mobilization, and also that apparently radical socialist idioms may in particular contexts be compatible with more conservative meanings which themselves support (or do not challenge) the politico-ideological objectives of rich peasants. It is one thing to maintain that class struggle has not developed as predicted; it is quite another to argue that class is of little or no relevance to the understanding of the formation/reproduction of politico-ideological consciousness and the (equally class-specific) kinds of conflict this permits subsequently. Thus the transcendence of ethnic solidarity by class solidarity among poor peasants and agricultural workers, and the subsequent displacement either of class consciousness by ethnic identity or free wage labour by 'semi-feudal' relations of production, is itself an integral part of the class struggle, and constitutes evidence only of the resort by rich peasants to 'traditional' institutional forms supportive of their economic power when/where necessary, and not of the undesirability of socialism or the impossibility of historical progress *per se*.

Acknowledgement

This essay is based on a paper presented in Session 2 (Social movements in Developing Countries) at the XIIth World Congress of Sociology in Madrid during July 1990. The writer thanks the Managers of the Smuts Memorial Fund at Cambridge University for a grant towards the cost of attending the Congress.

Notes

1. While a few middle peasants join the rich peasant stratum and become agrarian capitalists, the majority join the poor peasantry and become *de facto* agricultural workers. The middle peasants that remain must be neutralized in the course of the struggle between the proletariat and the bourgeoisie (Lenin, 1966: 156ff.)

2. It should be noted that the theoretical provenance of Chayanovian arguments concerning the peasant family labour farm is neo-classical economics. Hence the categorization by the latter of the wage received by the industrial worker as a 'reward' for the disutility of labour finds a direct parallel in Chayanov's drudgery-averse peasant, whereby a timeless–static (and thus) 'natural' producer–consumer equilibrium results from a subjective evaluation by the peasant family of the balance between the drudgery of labour and the satisfaction of wants. The political significance of this is as follows: whereas classical economics stressed the role of socio-economic conflict between classes over an exogenous concept of value generated in the sphere of production, neo-classical economics which emerged during the 1870s was by contrast an explicitly anti-Marxist response to the development of the labour movement, and thus emphasized social harmony premised on the existence of an equilibrium in which a psychologistic (and therefore relative) notion of value is conceptualized internally by each individual subject and located at the level of exchange. In his critique of the latter position, Bukharin (1927: 32) observed that the 'methodological difference between Karl Marx and [the Austrian marginalists] may be summarized . . . as follows: objectivism–subjectivism, an historical standpoint – an unhistorical standpoint, the point of view of production – the point of view of consumption'. Not only was adherence to the Austrian marginalist school one of the charges levelled against Chayanov by his Marxist critics (see Chayanov, 1966: lxix, 84–5, 220), but the terms used by Bukharin to describe the way which neo-classical economics diverges from Marxism could be used verbatim to differentiate the latter from postmodernism (see below).

3. As will become clear below, Wolf adheres closely to the anthropological framework that is supposed to have been transcended, and in fact reproduces those very concepts which Desai claims are absent. For the significance of this, see n. 17 below.

4. Wolf and Alavi both acknowledge a mutual influence, and each claims that his own hypothesis concerning the peasantry is supported by the work of the other (cf. Wolf, 1971: 291; Alavi, 1979: 716, footnote 2).

5. The generally opaque link between the 'moral economy' argument and the micro-economic theory that structures the Chayanovian concept of a subsistence-oriented, risk-avoiding, choice-making, utility-maximizing peasantry can be seen most clearly in the work of Scott (1976: 13–15).

6. For a useful critique of the 'moral economy' theory, see Popkin (1979). Although strictly speaking Alavi cannot be categorized as an adherent of the 'moral economy' position, some of its more important concepts are nevertheless present in his work: for example, the view that peasant response is triggered by the violation of traditional norms (1973: 35), together with the crucial role of patron–clientage in peasant–master relations (1979: 714).

7. From the Marxist viewpoint, one of the main objections to the 'moral economy' argument is that it denies the *active* striving of the different components of the rural population as *class* subjects; that is, either by rich peasants to become small agrarian capitalists or by poor peasants and agricultural labourers to improve their position as workers (by organizing in pursuit of higher wages, better working conditions, a shorter working day, etc.). Without this capitalist struggle, together with the equally specific kinds of socio-economic contradictions to which it gives rise, there can be no transition to socialism.

8. While the Subaltern Studies series is about the peasantry in the colonial era, some contributions cross the boundary into the post-colonial period (for example, Chandra, 1983; Das, 1983; Chakrabarty, 1984), while others claim that its methodological/theoretical approach transcends the colonial/post-colonial divide (for example, Chatterjee, 1983: 77). Implicitly or explicitly, therefore, the Subaltern Studies framework can also serve as a model for analysing contemporary peasant movements.

9. The publication in both *Subaltern Studies IV* and the volume edited by Colburn of the same text by Ramachandra Guha (1989) underlines this trend towards theoretical (and political) cross-fertilization and compatibility. Interestingly, the rejection by Scott of 'hegemony' (see below) on the grounds that, while peasants may accept the inevitability of their overall subordination, this does not imply that they regard it as just, finds a strong echo in a recent text by Ranajit Guha. The latter similarly displaces 'hegemony' with a variant of the 'moral economy' argument, whereby 'dharmic protest' or 'rightful dissent' by peasants derives from a pre-colonial Indian tradition that legitimizes 'the morality of struggle against . . . [the ruler's] failure in his protective function [towards the ruled]' (Guha, 1989: 266ff.). The antithesis between 'hegemony' and 'resistance' is another reason why Guha (1989: 299), like Scott, questions its existence.

10. For the rejection of universalism and/or Eurocentrism by Subaltern Studies, see Ranajit Guha (1983: 6; 1989: 272ff.). The latter, however, then goes on to base his concept of 'negative class consciousness' on Hilton's study of *European* peasant movements (Ranajit Guha, 1983: 20).

11. New social movements texts that question emancipation include Evers (1985: 61) and Redclift (1988: 254).

12. For the link between Subaltern Studies and 'the ideological', see Ranajit Guha (1983: 13).

13. Thus Laclau (1985: 28) observes that 'the social agent's positions become autonomous – it is this new autonomy which is at the root of the specificity of the new social movements'. Similar views regarding the autonomy of the subject are expressed by Slater (1985: 5) and Evers (1985: 59). The fragmentation of the subject's consciousness is identified by Evers (1985: 45, 61) as the main characteristic of postmodern discourse, while the effects of the 'individualizing techniques of power' on peasant resistance are noted by Redclift (1988: 251–2). For the importance of ethnic/gender/regional identity/inequality in the discourse of the Subaltern Studies and New Social Movements framework, see Ranajit Guha (1982: vii), Slater (1985: 3), Gianotten *et al.* (1985: 185) and Redclift (1988: 252). Significantly, Wolf attributes a similarly important

role to the element of regionalism in the 'middle peasant thesis'. Accordingly, the location of a middle peasantry in geographically peripheral areas is regarded as one of the main reasons why such 'tactically mobile' peasants are able to engage successfully in revolutionary action (Wolf, 1971: 291).

14. This difference is encapsulated in the comment by Volosinov (1973: 13) that: 'Individual consciousness is not the architect of the ideological superstructure, but only a tenant lodging in the social edifice of ideological signs'.

15. Among those who endorse/invoke/apply Foucault's theory with regard to peasants are Chatterjee (1983: 348–9), Redclift (1988: 252–3) and Scott (1989: 8), while those who do the same with regard to Gramsci include Ranajit Guha (1983: 10, 19ff.) and Chatterjee (1989).

16. This emphasis on culture permeates all the texts under consideration here: for Wolf (1971: 279), the transformation of non-capitalist contexts as a result of capitalist penetration entails a corresponding change from a cultural system to an economic system, while the 'everyday forms of resistance' undertaken by New Social Movements are similarly presented as manifestations of popular culture, 'an alternative moral universe in embryo – a dissident subculture', or the defence of cultural identity (Evers, 1985: 43, 49, 50; Gianotten *et al.*, 1985: 183; Scott, 1976: 240; 1989: 24).

17. In part, the penetration of peasant studies by postmodern discourse has been effected via anthropology in general and the ahistorical structuralism of French 'Marxist' anthropology in particular. From the latter emerged both Clastres (1977), who in true postmodern fashion counterposed an idealized image of the (non-Western) acephalous primitive society to the (Western) state, and the high priest of postmodernism Baudrillard, for whom (1975) a dematerialized political economy of production has symbolic meaning only. In many ways it is unsurprising that postmodernism has been embraced so enthusiastically by anthropology, since the latter regards the project of the former as a vindication of its own specific theoretical/methodological practice, elements of which include both superstructural autonomy and the reification of the peasant and/or tribal as an ever-present 'other'. Of particular significance in this respect is the trajectory followed by Sahlins, whose initial attempt to recuperate Chayanovian theory in the form of the 'domestic mode of production' (Sahlins, 1972: 102ff.) has now culminated symptomatically in postmodern cultural determinism (Sahlins, 1985); for other examples of texts which apply Chayanovian theory to the peasantry, see Durrenberger (1984) and Maclachlan (1987). In terms of methodological and theoretical emphasis, the differences between anthropology and historical materialism on the one hand and the similarities between postmodernism and anthropology on the other may be illustrated by the following set of oppositions:

Anthropology (*Postmodernism*)		*Marxism*
micro-level	:	macro-level
relativism	:	universalism
myth	:	history
culture	:	economy
community	:	state
individual	:	class
resistance	:	revolution
stasis	:	change

Postmodernism might be described as the revenge wreaked by anthropology on development theory for the theft by the latter of the object belonging to the former.

18. In keeping with the New Social Movements theoretical approach, Redclift (1988: 249) dismisses the applicability to Latin American peasant movements of the 1960s of both the modernization paradigm as exemplified by Landsberger and Hewitt (1970) and the Marxist framework of Quijano (1967). This point is echoed by Ranajit Guha

(1989: 270), who observes that '[the popularity of] a dynamic modernity ... has declined with the end of the development illusions generated by post-war capitalism to "modernize" an archaic Third World'.

19. The reference by Scott (1989: 23) to class as 'social stratification' rather than relations of production confirms his non-Marxist use of this term. In his introduction to a recent collection of texts on Peru, Miller (1987: 14) rejects class as a determinant of peasant struggles during the colonial period in preference to the 'moral economy' approach.

20. That Scott himself does not subscribe to a concept of an internally differentiated peasantry is evident from his resort to inverted commas when using the word '"kulak"' (1989: 17, 32 footnote 28). Zamosc (1989: 122) also puts inverted commas round the term '"rich peasantry"'.

21. Significantly, the 'subaltern' category shares this characteristic with the Maoism of Sendero Luminoso and the Naxalites (see below); that is, the heterogeneous nature of the class elements subsumed under its rubric. For the analogous usage of a dichotomy composed of 'elite' and 'rural poor'/'popular masses' in the case of Latin America, see Fox (1990) and Zamosc (1990).

22. Part of the difficulty here is that such a procedure is epistemologically impermissible, since consciousness of class is an Eurocentric concept that involves an 'outsider' imputing a politically appropriate, logically consistent and historically necessary set of universalistic beliefs to particular socio-economic agents.

23. Anti-landlordism constitutes a particularly potent example of one politico-ideological component mobilized by rich peasants, for instances of which in Peru and India, see Brass (1989) and Krishnaji (1986).

24. Although Ranajit Guha agrees that in so far as they 'empty rebellion of its context and reduce it to a routine of gestures in order to reinforce authority by feigning defiance ... ritual inversion stands for continuity turned into sacred tradition' (1983: 31, 36), such reversals may in fact be supportive of the status quo by *deflecting* rebellion, he nevertheless fails to consider the extent to which *successful* uprisings do not similarly incorporate symbolic inversions that also reinforce the existing social order, thereby subverting the act of rebellion/opposition itself.

25. Ranajit Guha (1989: 272–3) poses the central question thus: 'Why did the universalist drive of the world's most advanced capitalist culture, a phenomenon that corresponded to the universalizing tendency of the most dynamic capital of the time, fail, in the Indian instance, to match the strength and fulness of its political dominion over a subject people by assimilating, if not abolishing, the pre-capitalist culture of the latter?'

26. In the course of acute class struggle between agrarian capital and its workers, therefore, the former introduces/reintroduces unfree relations in an attempt to maintain control over the cost/availability of the latter by pre-empting/undermining/reducing their bargaining power (see, for example, Brass, 1986, 1990; Cohen, 1987; Miles, 1987). That poor peasants do in fact struggle to become or remain a proletariat in the face of landlord and/or rich peasant attempts to prevent this, refutes the 'moral economy'/'middle peasant' position of Alavi and Wolf (see above) which maintains that subjects from this particular rural stratum are too downtrodden and oppressed to do this. For the role of unfree agrarian relations in colonial India, see *inter alios*, Patnaik (1985), Prakash (1990) and Sarkar (1985).

27. This dilemma is signalled in the observation by Wolf (1971: 292) that 'it is the very attempt of the middle and free peasant to remain traditional which makes him revolutionary'. This same view – that it is middle peasants reacting to external change rather than rich or poor peasants challenging the existing social order – is implied in the wish of Redclift to reconstruct the 1960s peasant mobilizations in the image of New Social Movements theory. Hence the comment (1988: 251) that '[i]t is easier today to see the [Latin American] peasant movements of the 1960s as a symptom of transformation than the *agency* of transformation ...' (original emphasis).

28. This is illustrated by the case of Peru, where the state has been unable to stop rich peasants either from privatizing co-operative land and assets (see Gonzales and

Torre, 1985) or from growing coca for and profiting from cocaine production (see below).

29. That the control of the state is not the object of anti-colonial conflict is the theme of Ranajit Guha's most recent contribution to the Subaltern Studies series, where he argues (1989: 213–14) that 'the indigenous bourgeoisie . . . abjured and indeed resolutely opposed all forms of armed struggle against the raj, and settled for pressure politics as their main tactical means in bargaining for power'.

30. See, for example, Ranajit Guha (1982b: 7), Slater (1985: 5, 9, 16, 18), Evers (1985: 46, 58, 63), Redclift (1988: 251). By contrast, both Miller (1987: 11) and McClintock (1989a: 73) talk of 'landlord hegemony' [*sic*]. That democracy ('citizenship') and not socialism is to be regarded as the main object of mobilization by the 'rural poor' in Latin America emerges clearly from a recent collection edited by Fox (1990). In his contribution to the latter, Zamosc (1990: 45) observes symptomatically that 'democracy can still provide a substantial part of the remedy for Colombia's ills'.

31. Ranajit Guha (1989) also rejects the concept 'hegemony', but mainly on the grounds that British colonial rule in India failed to displace pre-capitalism with the liberal bourgeois project (Liberty/Democracy/Rule-of-Law, etc.) of capitalism itself.

32. Hence the observation by Evers (1985: 63) that: 'States themselves have fallen into discredit'.

33. Decollectivization and the introduction of the family responsibility system in post-Maoist China is described symptomatically by Scott (1989: 16) as an effect of peasant resistance, the object of which was 'subsistence and survival'. Another text (Chossudovsky, 1986: 75), however, attributes this same process to a very different cause. Since the People's Commune 'failed to eliminate the rich peasantry as a class, decollectivization emerged from *within* the structure of collective agriculture, leading initially to the collapse of the collective work process and to the restoration of private production under the household responsibility system' (original emphasis).

34. The analysis of Sendero by McClintock appears in the collection edited by Eckstein, as does a contribution by Zamosc on ANUC in Colombia.

35. Where he does address the issue of the agrarian question, Zamosc (1989: 103, 108–9) poses it in terms of a two-paths development process characterized by 'peasant agriculture' on the one hand and by 'entrepreneurial landlords' on the other, thereby banishing peasants from the ranks of capitalist producers.

36. The extent of economic differentiation among Colombian peasants owning/operating less than twenty hectares of land emerges most clearly from a recent study of the 1970s agricultural modernization in and its effects on a rural community in the south west of the country. One result of the green revolution programme applied in the latter context was that the average value of per farm marketed output of those with more than 12 hectares of land was twice that of peasants owning 3–12 hectares, eight times that of peasants owning 1½–3½ hectares, and 21 times larger than peasants with less than 1½ hectares of land (calculated from data presented in Reinhardt [1988: 166, Table 6.1]).

37. The element of class is similarly ignored in the presentation of Senderista–state relations by Bourque and Warren (1989), which is based on Taussig's postmodern 'culture of terror' thesis, and accordingly emphasizes the regional and ethnic dimensions of this conflict (1989: 13f.). For a critique of the postmodern discourse of Taussig (1987), who is aptly described as a 'Castenada for the 1980s', see Kapferer (1988: 81f.).

38. According to another and more conservative estimate, by growing coca for cocaine production a peasant is able to earn seven and a half times the amount per hectare that can be made from the cultivation of even profitable cash crops such as coffee or cocoa ('Peru: State of Fear', *Internationalist*, no. 197, July 1989, p. 17).

39. For an excellent account of the way in which categories such as 'nationalism', 'regionalism', and 'ethnicity' both permeate and simultaneously displace 'class' in Senderista ideology, see Montoya (1986). For the connection between Lipton's concept of 'urban bias' and neo-populism, see Kitching (1982: 84ff.).

40. Even this middle peasant disguise has been discarded by Maoism elsehere. During the 1980s, therefore, the Chinese Communist Party no longer sees a

contradiction between the re-emergence of rich peasant capitalists and building socialism (Chossudovsky, 1986: 59).

41. For a case study of one such peasant movement in Peru, see Brass (1989).

42. For a useful critique of the tribalization (and hence abolition) of peasant movements, see Sengupta (1982, 1989). For an example of the tribalization of peasants in Latin America, see Burger (1987). Texts on agrarian movements in India include Desai (1979, 1986), Dhanagare (1983), Gupta (1986), Karna (1989), Nadkarni (1987), Pavier (1981), Pouchepadass (1980), S. Sen (1982) and Wood (1987). The New Social Movements framework has been applied by Lindberg (1990) to farmers' struggles taking place in India during the 1980s, on the grounds that these unite all peasants as consumers as well as producers of commodities against the state which controls input/output prices and thus their economic reproduction, whereas pre-independence peasant movements were solely about landownership. Accordingly, he maintains that the principal contradiction is no longer to be found within the different peasant strata but between all the latter on the one hand and the urban-industrial sector and the state on the other, and therefore rejects the claim by Nadkarni (1987) and Banaji (1990) that agitation by landholders' organizations, such as the *Shetkari Sangatana* of Maharashtra led by Sharad Joshi and the *Bharatiya Kisan Union* of Uttar Pradesh led by M. S. Tikait, corresponds to the mobilization of a kulak lobby. Of the many difficulties faced by this argument, three can be referred to here. First, in keeping with the neo-populist epistemological lineage stretching from Chayanov to Baudrillard, peasants and peasant movements are defined not in terms of production relations but in terms of consumption. Second, since the use of commodified agricultural inputs itself depends on adequate landholding size and secure tenure, property relations not only continue to be an issue but divide rather than unite rich, middle and poor peasants who own/control vastly different amounts of land. And third, in spite of the fact that agricultural workers also depend on the state for inputs (prices of goods consumed) and output (wages for the sale of labour-power), they have not joined with the farmers' movement on this issue, much rather the opposite: it is the peasant proprietors themselves, not the state, who are regarded by rural labour as the source of exploitation and thus the main enemy (see, for example, Brass, 1990).

43. For a similar view to that of Ranajit Guha, see Sen (1987: 204). Although Guha (1983: 15, 26) hints at the existence of intra-tribal socio-economic differentiation, he fails to explore this in terms of ethnic identity as false politico-ideological consciousness in the process of agrarian class struggle. The colonial origins of the concept 'tribe', together with the way in which it was used by the British to divide and rule, are discussed by, *inter alios*, J. Pathy (1984: 2) and Singh (1985: 104ff.).

44. For a useful analysis of the way in which Orientalism involves the attempt to recuperate precisely this 'primitive Other', see Baudet (1965).

45. On tribal migration in north-east India see, for example, Badgaiyan (1986), Bhowmik (1981), Choudhury and Bhowmik (1986), and Vidyarthi (1970). Until the development in the 1940s of pan-tribal movements, Santal and Bhumij culture had for a long time been incorporating Hindu beliefs and behaviour, while Munda ceremonial and religion had similarly been influenced by both Hinduism and Christianity (Bose, 1985: 22f.).

46. Similar observations concerning the socio-economic differentiation of tribal peasants in other parts of India are made by, *inter alios*, Datta (1989), Mishra (1987), J. Pathy (1976) and S. Pathy (1987).

47. J. Pathy makes much the same observation about the fact that welfare measures aimed at tribals invariably benefit the better-off elements, and thus paradoxically intensify and hasten the very differentiation process they are designed to prevent (1984: 25, 185ff.).

48. Tribals who are rich peasants engage in productive moneylending to secure labour-power cheaply, and 71 per cent of tribal agricultural labour households are in debt to such landholders. The economic object of this activity is described by Bose (1985: 95, 102–2) in the following terms: 'all the rich peasants advance money to tribal labourers so that during the peak season, when the demand for labour is high, they get

them at comparatively cheaper rates . . . [t]he loans are mainly consumption loans, which labourers take during the lean period . . . [these have] to be repaid [in the form of] labour during the peak agricultural season.'

49. Despite maintaining that Santals expected a classless society to emerge from the Naxalite movement, Duyker (1987: 123) furnishes no evidence to support this assertion.

50. One CPI (M-L) leader noted that: 'When we went to the Santals we used to emphasize their [1855 Insurrectionary] heroes . . . we told them that Sidhu and Kanhu were our predecessors and that "New Democracy was no different from what they had fought for"' (Duyker, 1987: 118).

51. The Maoist Communist Centre, which Duyker (1987: 152) notes as consolidating its position in West Bengal from the 1970s onwards, was by 1987 engaged not in class but caste struggle in neighbouring Bihar, a communalization that culminated in the killings of Rajputs by Naxalite-led Yadavs in Aurangabad district. Although the Rajput caste has traditionally consisted of substantial proprietors, a few of the latter are now also to be found among the ranks of the traditionally lower-caste Yadavs. As one commentator observed, 'Over the years, the new, better-off class among the backward castes transformed itself into the kulak lobby. Today, the same people who were once in the forefront of the Kisan Sabha movement are the oppressors.' Another source makes much the same point, commenting that 'Yadavs occupy a peculiar position on the socio-economic scale in this part of Bihar. They are both exploiters and exploited. Many of them own land and are said to maltreat Harijan agricultural workers.' Cf. Kanchan Gupta, 'Communism Through Caste in Bihar', *The Statesman*, 16 June 1987; Chandan Mitra, 'Caste-Class War in Bihar to Go On', *The Times of India*, 3 June 1987.

52. See Duyker (1987: 133ff.).

53. Significantly, in the case of the farmers' agitation in Uttar Pradesh, the organizational success of the BKU has been attributed by Dhanagare (1988: 30) to caste and clan solidarity among the Jats, clan heads having acquired leadership of BKU units.

References and Further Reading

Alavi, H., 1973, 'Peasant Classes and Primordial Loyalties', *Journal of Peasant Studies*, vol. 1 no. 1.

———, 1979, 'Peasants and Revolution', in A. R. Desai (ed.).

Badgaiyan, S. D., 1986, '19th Century in Chota Nagpur and Santal Parganas: Political Economy of Migration', in M. S. A. Rao (ed.).

Banaji, J., 1990, 'Illusions About the Peasantry: Karl Kautsky and the Agrarian Question', *Journal of Peasant Studies*, vol. 17 no. 2.

Baudet, H., 1965, *Paradise on Earth: Some Thoughts on European Images of Non-European Man*, New Haven, CT: Yale University Press.

Baudrillard, J., 1975, *The Mirror of Production*, St Louis, MO: Telos Press.

Bhowmik, S., 1981, *Class Formation in the Plantation System*, New Delhi: People's Publishing House.

Bose, P. K., 1985, *Classes and Class Relations among Tribals of Bengal*, Delhi: Ajanta Publications.

Bourque, S. C., and K. B. Warren, 1989, 'Democracy without Peace: The Cultural Politics of Terror in Peru', *Latin American Research Review*, vol. 24 no. 1.

Brass, T., 1986, 'Unfree Labour and Capitalist Restructuring in the Agrarian Sector: Peru and India', *Journal of Peasant Studies*, vol. 14 no. 1.

———, 1989, 'Trotskyism, Hugo Blanco and the Ideology of a Peruvian Peasant Movement', *Journal of Peasant Studies*, vol. 16 no. 2.

———, 1990, 'Class Struggle and the Deproletarianization of Agricultural Labour in Haryana (India)', *Journal of Peasant Studies*, vol. 18 no. 1.

Bukharin, N., 1927, *The Economic Theory of the Leisure Class*, New York: International Publishers.

Burger, J., 1987, *Report from the Frontier: The State of the World's Indigenous Peoples*, London: Zed Press.
Callinicos, A., 1989, *Against Postmodernism: A Marxist Critique*, Cambridge: Polity Press.
Chakrabarty, D., 1984, 'Trade Unions in an Hierarchical Culture: The Jute Workers of Calcutta, 1920–50', in Ranajit Guha (ed.), *Subaltern Studies III*, Delhi: Oxford University Press.
Chandra, N. K., 1983, 'Agricultural Workers in Burdwan', in Ranajit Guha (ed.), *Subaltern Studies II*, Delhi: Oxford University Press.
Chatterjee, P., 1983, 'More on Modes of Power and the Peasantry', in Ranajit Guha (ed.), *Subaltern Studies II*, Delhi: Oxford University Press.
———, 1989, 'Caste and Subaltern Consciousness', in Ranajit Guha (ed.), *Subaltern Studies VI*, Delhi: Oxford University Press.
Chayanov, A. V., 1966, *The Theory of Peasant Economy*, Homewood, IL: The American Economic Association.
Chossudovsky, M., 1986, *Towards Capitalist Restoration? Chinese Socialism after Mao*, London: Macmillan.
Choudhury, N. C., and S. K. Bhowmik, 1986, 'Migration of Chota Nagpur Tribals to West Bengal', in M. S. A. Rao (ed.).
Clastres, P., 1977, *Society Against the State*, Oxford: Blackwell.
Cohen, R., 1987, *The New Helots*, Aldershot: Gower Publishing Co.
Colburn, F. D., 1989, 'Introduction', in F. D. Colburn (ed.).
———, (ed.), 1989, *Everyday Forms of Peasant Resistance*, New York: M. E. Sharpe.
Das, A. N., 1983, 'Agrarian Change from Above and Below: Bihar 1947–78', in Ranajit Guha (ed.), *Subaltern Studies II*, Delhi: Oxford University Press.
Datta, P. S., 1989, 'Emerging Differentiation in a Traditional Tribal Economy (The Case of the Khasi-Jaintias of Meghalaya)', in M. N. Karna (ed.).
Desai, A. R., 1979, 'Unconventional Anthropology of "Traditional" Peasantry', in A. R. Desai (ed.).
———, (ed.), 1979, *Peasant Struggles in India*, Delhi: Oxford University Press.
———, (ed.), 1986, *Agrarian Struggles in India After Independence*, Delhi: Oxford University Press.
Dews, P., 1980, 'The "New Philosophers" and the End of Leftism', *Radical Philosophy*, 24.
Dhanagare, D. N., 1983, *Peasant Movements in India 1920–1950*, Delhi: Oxford University Press.
———, 1988, 'An Apolitical Populism', *Seminar*, No. 352.
Durrenberger, E. P. (ed.), 1984, *Chayanov, Peasants, and Economic Anthropology*, London: Academic Press.
Duyker, E., 1987, *Tribal Guerrillas: The Santals of West Bengal and the Naxalite Movement*, New Delhi: Oxford University Press.
Eckstein, S., 1989, 'Power and Popular Protest in Latin America', in S. Eckstein (ed.).
———, (ed.), 1989, *Power and Popular Protest: Latin American Social Movements*, Berkeley, CA: University of California Press.
Evers, T., 1985, 'Identity: the Hidden Side of New Social Movements in Latin America', in D. Slater (ed.).
Fox, J. (ed.), 1990, *The Challenge of Rural Democratization: Perspectives from Latin America and the Philippines*, A Special Issue of the *Journal of Development Studies*, vol. 26 no. 4.
Giannotten, V., *et al.*, 1985, 'The Impact of *Sendero Luminoso* on Regional and National Politics in Peru', in D. Slater (ed.).
Gonzales, A., and G. Torre (eds), 1985, *Las Parcelaciones de las Cooperativas Agrarias del Peru*, Chiclayo: Centro de Estudios Sociales 'Solidaridad'.
Gott, R., 1970, *Guerrilla Movements in Latin America*, London: Nelson.
Guha, Ranajit, (ed.), 1982, *Subaltern Studies I*, Delhi: Oxford University Press.
———, 1982a, 'Preface', in Ranajit Guha (ed.).
———, 1982b, 'On Some Aspects of the Historiography of Colonial India', in Ranajit Guha (ed.).

———, 1983, *Elementary Aspects of Peasant Insurgency in Colonial India*, Delhi: Oxford University Press.

———, 1989, 'Dominance without Hegemony and Its Historiography', in Ranajit Guha (ed.).

———, (ed.), 1989, *Subaltern Studies VI*, New Delhi: Oxford University Press.

Guha, Ramachandra, 1989, 'Saboteurs in the Forest: Colonialism and Peasant Resistance in the Indian Himalaya', in F. D. Colburn (ed.).

Gupta, A. K. (ed.), 1986, *Agrarian Structure and Peasant Revolt in India*, New Delhi: Criterion Publications.

Kapferer, B., 1988, 'The Anthropologist as Hero: Three Exponents of Post-Modernist Anthropology', *Critique of Anthropology*, vol. 8 no. 2.

Karna, M. N. (ed.), 1989, *Peasant and Peasant Protests in India*, New Delhi: Intellectual Publishing House.

Kitching, G., 1982, *Development and Underdevelopment in Historical Perspective: Populism, Nationalism, and Industrialization*, London: Methuen.

Krishnaji, N., 1986, 'Agrarian Relations and the Left Movement in Kerala', in A. R. Desai (ed.).

Laclau, E., 1985, 'New Social Movements and the Plurality of the Social', in D. Slater (ed.).

———, and C. Mouffe, 1985, *Hegemony and Socialist Strategy*, London: Verso.

Landsberger, H., and C. Hewitt, 1970, 'Ten Sources of Weakness and Cleavage in Latin American Peasant Movements', in R. Stavenhagen (ed.), *Agrarian Problems and Peasant Movements in Latin America*, New York: Anchor Doubleday.

Lenin, V. I., 1960, 'The Development of Capitalism in Russia', *Collected Works*, vol. 3, Moscow: Foreign Languages Publishing House.

———, 1966, 'Preliminary Draft Theses on the Agrarian Question', *Collected Works*, vol. 31, Moscow: Progress Publishers.

Lindberg, S., 1990, 'Civil Society Against the State? Farmers' Agitation and New Social Movements in India', paper presented at the XII World Congress of Sociology, Madrid.

Lukács, G., 1971, *History and Class Consciousness*, London: Merlin Press.

Mallon, F., 1983, *The Defense of Community in Peru's Central Highlands*, New Jersey, NJ: Princeton University Press.

McClintock, C., 1984, 'Why Peasants Rebel: The Case of Peru's Sendero Luminoso', *World Politics*, vol. XXVII no. 1.

———, 1989a, 'Peru's Sendero Luminoso Rebellion: Origins and Trajectory', in S. Eckstein (ed.).

———, 1989b, 'Peru: Precarious Regimes, Authoritarian and Democratic', in L. Diamond *et al.* (eds), *Democracy in Developing Countries: Latin America*, Boulder CO: Lynne Rienner Publishers.

Maclachlan, M. D. (ed.), 1987, *Household Economies and Their Transformations*, New York: University Press of America.

Miles, R., 1987, *Capitalism and Unfree Labour: Anomaly or Necessity?*, London: Tavistock Publications.

Miller, R., 1987, 'Some Reflections on Foreign Research and Peruvian History', in R. Miller (ed.).

———, (ed.), 1987, *Region and Class in Modern Peruvian History*, Liverpool: Institute of Latin American Studies.

Mishra, S. N., 1987, 'Private Property Formation among the Highland Tribal Communities of North-East India', *Social Science Probings*, vol. 4, no. 4.

Montoya, R., 1986, 'Identidad étnica y luchas agrarias en los Andes Peruanos', In L. T. Briggs *et al.* (eds), *Identidades andinas y lógicas del campesinado*, Lima: Mosca Azul Editores.

Morales, E., 1989, *Cocaine: White Gold Rush in Peru*, Tucson, AR: The University of Arizona Press.

Nadkarni, M. V., 1987, *Farmers' Movements in India*, New Delhi: Allied Publishers Private Ltd.

O'Hanlon, R., 1988, 'Recovering the Subject: *Subaltern Studies* and Histories of Resistance in Colonial South Asia', *Modern Asian Studies*, vol. 22, no. 1.
Pathy, J., 1976, 'Political Economy of Kandhaland', *Man in India*, vol. 56, no. 1.
———, 1984, *Tribal Peasantry: Dynamics of Development*, New Delhi: Inter-India Publications.
Pathy, S., 1987, 'Class Formation in an Indian Tribe: The Saora', *Social Science Probings*, vol. 4 no. 4.
Patnaik, U., 1985, 'Introduction', in Patnaik and Dingwaney (eds).
———, and M. Dingwaney (eds), 1985, *Chains of Servitude: Bondage and Slavery in India*, Madras: Sangam Books.
Pavier, B., 1981, *The Telengana Movement 1944–51*, New Delhi: Vikas Publishing House.
Popkin, S. L., 1979, *The Rational Peasant*, Berkeley, CA: University of California Press.
Pouchepadass, J., 1980, 'Peasant Classes in Twentieth Century Agrarian Movements in India', in E. J. Hobsbawm *et al.* (eds), *Peasants in History: Essays in Honour of Daniel Thorner*, Calcutta: Oxford University Press.
Prakash, G., 1990, *Bonded Histories: Genealogies of Labor Servitude in Colonial India*, Cambridge: Cambridge University Press.
Quijano, A., 1967, 'Contemporary Peasant Movements', in S. M. Lipset and A. Solari (eds), *Elites in Latin America*, New York: Oxford University Press.
Rao, M. S. A. (ed.), 1986, *Studies in Migration*, New Delhi: Manohar.
Redclift, M., 1988, 'Agrarian Social Movements in Contemporary Mexico', *Bulletin of Latin American Research*, vol. 7 no. 2.
Reinhardt, N., 1988, *Our Daily Bread: The Peasant Question and Family Farming in the Colombian Andes*, Berkeley, CA: University of California Press.
Sahlins, M., 1972, *Stone Age Economics*, Chicago, IL: Aldine-Atherton Inc.
———, 1985, *Islands of History*, Chicago, IL: University of Chicago Press.
Sánchez, R., 1982, 'The Andean Economic System and Capitalism', in A. D. Lehmann (ed.), *Ecology and Exchange in the Andes*, Cambridge: Cambridge University Press.
Sarkar, T., 1985, 'Bondage in Colonial India', in Patnaik and Dingwaney (eds).
Sarup, M., 1988, *Post-Structuralism and Postmodernism*, Hemel Hempstead: Harvester.
Scott, J. C., 1976, *The Moral Economy of the Peasant: Subsistence and Rebellion in Southeast Asia*, New Haven, CT: Yale University Press.
———, 1985, *Weapons of the Weak: Everyday Forms of Peasant Resistance*, New Haven, CT: Yale University Press.
———, 1989, 'Everyday Forms of Resistance', in F. D. Colburn (ed.).
Sen, A., 1987, 'Subaltern Studies: Capital, Class, and Community', in R. Guha (ed.), *Subaltern Studies V*, Delhi: Oxford University Press.
Sen, S., 1982, *Peasant Movements in India: Mid-Nineteenth and Twentieth Centuries*, Calcutta: K. P. Bagchi.
Sengupta, N., 1982, 'Background of the Jarkhand Question', in N. Sengupta (ed.).
———, 1989, 'From Peasant to Tribe: Peasant Movements in Chotanagpur', in M. N. Karna (ed.).
———, (ed.), 1982, *Fourth World Dynamics: Jharkhand*, Delhi: Authors Guild Publications.
Singh, K. S., 1985, *Tribal Society in India*, Delhi: Manohar Books.
Slater, D. (ed.), 1985, *New Social Movements and the State in Latin America*, Amsterdam: CEDLA.
Taussig, M., 1987, *Shamanism, Colonialism, and the Wild Man: A Study in Terror and Healing*, Chicago, IL: University of Chicago Press.
Taylor, L., 1983, *Maoism in the Andes*, Liverpool: Centre for Latin American Studies, Working Paper 2.
Trotsky, L., 1962, *The Permanent Revolution and Results and Prospects*, London: New Park Publications.
———, 1969, 'The Three Conceptions of the Russian Revolution', *Writings, 1938–39*, New York: Merit Publishers.
Vidyarthi, L. P., 1970, *Socio-cultural Implications of Industrialisation in India: A Case Study of Tribal Bihar*, New Delhi: Research Programmes Committee, Planning Commission.
Volosinov, V. N., 1973, *Marxism and the Philosophy of Language*, London: Seminar Press.

Wolf, E. R., 1971, *Peasant Wars of the Twentieth Century*, London: Faber.
Wood, C., 1987, *The Moplah Rebellion and Its Genesis*, New Delhi: People's Publishing House.
Zamosc, L., 1986, *The Agrarian Question and the Peasant Movement in Colombia*, Cambridge: Cambridge University Press.
———, 1989, 'Peasant Struggles of the 1970s in Colombia', in S. Eckstein (ed.).
———, 1990, 'The Political Crisis and the Prospects for Rural Democracy in Colombia', in J. Fox (ed.).

8

Writing Post-Orientalist Histories of the Third World: Perspectives from Indian Historiography

Gyan Prakash

To ask how the 'third world writes its own history' appears, at first glance, to be exceedingly naive. At best, it reaffirms the East–West and Orient–Occident oppositions that have shaped historical writings and seems to be a simple-minded gesture of solidarity. Furthermore, in apparently privileging the writings of historians with third-world origins, this formulation renders such scholars into 'native informants' whose discourse is opened up for further disquisitions on how 'they' think of 'their' history. In short, the notion of the third world writing its own history seems to reek of essentialism. Seen in another way, this formulation can be construed as positing that the third world has a fixed space of its own from which it can speak in a sovereign voice. For many, this notion of a separate terrain is rendered problematic by the increasing rapidity and the voracious appetite with which the post-modern culture imperializes and devours spaces.

In view of the above objections, it appears hazardous even to pose, let alone answer, the question as to how the third world writes its own post-Orientalist history; and, given the fire drawn by well-intentioned attempts to locate this third-world voice,[1] such an enterprise seems positively foolhardy. I persist precisely because the call for mapping post-Orientalist historiographies also acknowledges that the knowledge about the third world is historical. The attention to the historicity of knowledge demanded by the invitation to chart post-Orientalist historiography, therefore, runs counter to those procedures that ground the third world in essences and see history as determined by those essential elements. It requires the rejection of those modes of thinking which configure the third world in such irreducible essences as religiosity, underdevelopment, poverty, nationhood, non-Westernness; and it asks that we repudiate attempts to see third-world histories in terms of these quintessential principles. Thus, the previously mentioned objections, instead of invoking essentialism, unsettle the calm presence that the essentialist categories – East and West, first world and third world – inhabit in our thought. This disruption makes it possible to treat the third world as a variety of shifting positions which have been discursively articulated in history. Viewed in this manner, the Orientalist, nationalist, Marxist and other historiographies become visible as discursive attempts to constitute their objects of knowledge, that is, the third world. As a result, rather than appearing as a fixed and essential object, the third world emerges as a series of historical positions, including those that enunciate essentialisms.

This essay is an attempt to map the different positions occupied by India in the post-Orientalist historiographies. To do so, however, requires that we begin by defining and situating Orientalism. For this purpose, nothing is more suitable than Edward Said's general definition of Orientalism as a body of knowledge produced by texts and institutional practices.[2] According to him, Orientalism was responsible for generating authoritative and essentializing statements about the Orient and was characterized by a mutually supporting relationship between power and knowledge. As I reflect on Said's analysis, there are three key elements that in my view gave Orientalism its coherence: first, its authoritative status; second, its fabrication of the Orient in terms of founding essences invulnerable to historical change and prior to their representation in knowledge; and third, its incestuous relationship with the Western exercise of power over what we call the third world. This essay analyses Orientalism in India with respect to these three elements in order to sketch in what ways and in which contexts Orientalism has survived and changed, and describes histories that can be called post-Orientalist.

Orientalism's India

Orientalism was a European enterprise from the very beginning. The scholars were European; the audience was European; and the Indians figured as inert objects of knowledge. The Orientalist spoke for the Indian and represented the object in texts. Because the Indian was separated from the Orientalist knower, the Indian as object – as well as its representation – was construed to be outside and opposite of self; thus, both the self and the other, the rational and materialist British and the emotional and spiritual Indian, appeared as autonomous, ontological and essential entities. Of course, the two essential entities, the spiritual India and the materialistic West, made sense only in the context of each other and the traces of each in the other, which suggested that heterogeneity and difference lay beneath the binary opposition, although the process of rendering India into an object external both to its representation and to the knower concealed this difference. It also made the colonial relationship – the enabling condition of British Orientalism – appear as if it was irrelevant to the production of knowledge. As a result, although colonial dominance produced the East–West construct, it looked as if this binary opposition not only predated the colonial relationship but also accounted for it. In other words, Orientalist textual and institutional practices created the spiritual and sensuous Indian as an opposite of the materialistic and rational British, and offered them as justifications for the British conquest.

To be sure, the above representations underwent considerable change over time, but Orientalism's basic procedures of knowledge remained remarkably stable. They were developed soon after the East India Company conquered Bengal in 1757. Since the company required that its officers have a knowledge about the conquered people, administrators learned Persian and Sanskrit and soon began to publish texts. Alexander Dow, an army officer, translated one of the standard Persian histories into English, *The History of Hindustan* in 1768–71; and N. B. Halhead compiled and translated the Sanskrit *Dharmashastras* as *A Code of Gentoo Laws, or Ordinations of the Pundits* in 1776.[3] With the involvement of more officials – notably, William Jones, H. T. Colebrooke, John Shore and Francis Gladwin – this process of learning Sanskrit and Persian, as well as that of publishing texts and commentaries, gathered speed and led to the founding of the Asiatic Society of Bengal in 1784. From then on, a number of research journals emerged, such as the *Asiatik Researches* (1788), the *Quarterly Journal* (1821) and the *Journal of the Asiatic Society* (1832). Orientalist knowledge spread to European universities; and scholars with no direct contact with India, Max Müller in London and the Romantics on the continent, saw Europe's origins or childhood in India.[4] In this developing discourse, the discovery of affinities between Sanskrit and European languages provided the premise for formulating the belief in an 'Aryan race' from which the Europeans and Brahmans were seen to originate.[5] This search and discovery of European origins in the India of Sanskrit, the Brahmans and texts essentialized and distanced India in two ways. First, because it embodied Europe's childhood, India was temporally separated from Europe's present and made incapable of achieving 'progress'. As an eternal child detached altogether from time, India was construed as an external object available to the Orientalist's gaze. Second, composed of language and texts, India appeared to be unchanging and passive. These distancing procedures overlooked the European dominance of the world that provided the conditions for the production of this knowledge and that had constituted this discursive dominance. The India of the Orientalist's knowledge emerged as Europe's other, an essential and distanced entity knowable by the detached and distanced observer of the European Orientalist.

While essentialism, distancing and the centrality of the opposition of Europe and India deployed in the formative phase of Orientalism outlived the early Orientalists, the specific configurations of knowledge did not. As the genuine respect and love for the Orient of William Jones gave way to the cold utilitarian scrutiny of James Mill, and then to missionary contempt, the picture changed.[6] Sanskrit, texts and Brahmans were no longer attractive in the harsh light thrown by the liberal reformers and critics. Instead, they became accountable for India's lack of civilization, moral obligations, good government and historical change. Such revisions and refigurations of representations were occasioned by debates over such major policy questions as land revenue settlements, educational and administrative policies and the renewal of the charter for the East India Company.[7] These were occasions when the ideas current in Europe were most conspicuously applied to India. In the course of time, the application of Eurocentric ideas added to the stock of images available for representing India, but the on-the-spot official reports, parliamentary inquiries and papers, and detailed surveys during the first half of the nineteenth century exponentially crowded the representational field. These became regularized and professionalized in the late nineteenth century, as linguistic, ethnological, archaeological and census surveys and the district gazetteers emerged. With these, the older India of Sanskrit, texts and Brahmans was pushed off centre by details on peasants, revenue, rent, caste, customs, tribes, popular religious practices, linguistic diversity, agro-economic regimes, male and female populations and other such topics. In this enlarged but congested picture, the India of William Jones was less relevant.

The enormous growth, change and the increasing complexity of Orientalist knowledge was of crucial importance; for, committed as British rule was to a government based on accurate knowledge of facts, changes in knowledge had direct implications for the technologies of rule. For example, when the ethnographic surveys and census operations commenced in the late nineteenth and early twentieth centuries, they broke society into groups, households and individuals, making them available for piecing together through statistics. Because the society aggregated from the new units was constituted by an apparently objective and culturally neutral classificatory system of individuals, households and occupations, it became available to more extensive administrative penetration. This brought the older debates on the nature of Indian village communities, culminating in Baden-Powell's 1892 publication of *The Land Systems of British India*, to an end. The government no longer considered the indirect systems of rule – consisting of contractual agreements with village leaders as necessary – and it reached down to the individuals configured by their caste and tribal status.[8]

The discursive space for such changes in knowledge was provided by the Orientalist construction of India as an external object knowable through representations.[9] Because the government viewed knowledge contained in official documents as a representation of reality or, in one official's words in 1860, as a 'photograph of the actual state of the community',[10] it was always possible to argue that the photograph did not represent the external reality adequately, thus requiring more adequate representations. This representational model of knowledge, coupled with the exigencies of colonial government, enabled the scholarly field of Orientalism, or Indology, repeatedly to refigure itself. The consequent refiguration, however, did not unsettle the authority of the Orientalist, the essentialization of India, and its representation as an object in binary opposition to Europe. The lines were drawn clearly, with separate authentic and autonomous essences – India and Europe (or England) – clearly reflected in that knowledge. The old Orientalist, buried in texts and devoted to learning Sanskrit and Persian, was replaced by the official, the scholar and the modernizer. The new Orientalist administered the fruits of modern knowledge and government while being careful not to upset the Indian's presumed outmoded and traditionalist beliefs. Such actions and projections reaffirmed India's representation as a religiously driven social organism and found that the Indian's disinterest in modern politics and historical change was reflected in Sanskritic Hinduism and popular 'animism'. This representation allowed the British to see themselves as engaged in managing and changing such arenas as politics and the economy in which the Indian social organism and thought was incapable of operating.[11]

Nationalist Historiography

The first significant challenge to this Orientalized India came from nationalism and nationalist historiography, albeit accompanied by a certain contradiction. While agreeing to the notion of an India essentialized in relation to Europe, the nationalists transformed the object of knowledge – India – from passive to active, from inert to sovereign, capable of relating to History and Reason.[12] Nationalist historiographers accepted the patterns set for them by British scholarship. They accepted the periodization of Indian history into the Hindu, Muslim and British periods, later addressed as the ancient, medieval and modern eras; relegated caste to sections on 'Society', that is, to the history of society with politics left out; and reiterated the long and unchanging existence of Sanskritic Indic civilization.

In the 1920s and the 1930s, when nationalism became a mass phenomenon, a professional Indian historiography emerged to contest British interpretations. It is significant that these historians chose ancient India as the ground for this contest. If some of the early Orientalists had seen Europe's origin in the India of the texts, the nationalists saw the origin of the modern nation in that same ancient India; and for such historians, the old Orientalist scholarship's sympathetic remarks on the India of the texts, such as Max Müller's studies, became objective and authoritative statements that affirmed India's great past.[13] Nationalist historians, such as H. C. Raychaudhuri, K. P. Jayaswal, Beni Prasad, R. C. Majumdar and R. K. Mookerjee, studied ancient emperors and saw the rise of a nation-state in the creation of these ancient empires. Furthermore, as Romila Thapar points out, it was important for this historiography to claim that everything good in India – spirituality, Aryan origins, political ideas, art – had completely indigenous origins. In fact, Southeast Asian cultures were seen as outgrowths of the glorious Indian civilization, and the period of the Gupta empire (320–540 A.D.) came to symbolize the 'Golden Age', when Hinduism prospered, national unity soared, and economic wealth, social harmony and cultural achievements reached a state of plenitude. Later, the Muslims came (in the eleventh to twelfth centuries), and it was all downhill after that.

This abbreviated account of nationalist historiography does not do full justice to its achievements and complexity. These historians forced debates on sources and brought out much that was unknown, and thus regional histories came into focus. The assumption that all that was valuable in world civilizations originated in Greece was challenged. The Orientalist authority to speak for India was also contested, and Hindu chauvinist interpretations did not go unquestioned. Jawaharlal Nehru's *The Discovery of India*, for example, was marked by an awareness of cultural and historical diversity, and argued that it was 'undesirable to use Hindu or Hinduism for Indian culture'.[14] Although for him, too, spirituality also defined India's past essence and that the Gupta age represented the blossoming of nationalism, the Hindu revivalist historiography was too parochial for his secular and cosmopolitan outlook. The India that he discovered and presented was a secular entity, not a Hindu nation, that had cradled a variety of religions and sects through centuries, and had acquired a degree of unity while surviving conquests and conflicts. His *Discovery of India* was a documentation of this unity through history; and, for him, the nationalist movement was designed to free this unity so that India could join the world-historical march towards modernity.

Clearly, the differences between Nehru and the nationalist interpretations of Hindu chauvinistic historians were important. There can be no doubt that the concept of India as essentially Sanskritic and Hindu – glorious in ancient times, then subjected to Muslim tyranny and degeneration in the Middle Ages, which made it an easy target for British conquest – had and continues to have deadly implications in a multi-ethnic country like India. While recognizing the importance of these differences, I also want to highlight that which was common to nationalism as a whole: the assumption that India was an undivided subject, that is, that it possessed a unitary self and a singular will that arose from its essence and was capable of autonomy and sovereignty. From this point of view, the task of History was to unleash this subjectivity from colonial control; and historiography was obliged to represent this unleashing. The nationalists acted on this assumption by questioning the authority of Orientalists. They accused the older Indological knowledge of biases and judged it as being inadequate for representing reality. In its place, nationalist historiography offered more adequate portraits. A good example of this was the interpretation of the 1857 revolt in north India. For British historians, mutiny was the correct term because the revolt was nothing but an uprising of disaffected soldiers; calling it anything other than a mutiny meant conceding that it had some legitimacy. In 1909, a Hindu nationalist, Vinayak Damodar Savarkar, wrote a book entitled *The Indian War of Independence, 1857* and argued that it was a national revolt.[15] Nationalist historiography's commitment to the idea of India as an essential and undivided entity, and to knowledge as more or less adequate representation of the real, underlay such revisions. In spite of such complicities in Orientalist procedures, nationalism broke the exclusivity of Indology as a European discipline. In the discourse of the nationalists, the objects of description did not owe their meanings only to their opposition to European essences; rather, it was the ontological being of India as a nation – no doubt barely visible and, for the most part in its history, enslaved – that was the most evident element in providing meaning to historical events and actors. So, when politicians spoke of a nation in the making, they were referring to the task of making the masses conscious of a nation already in existence as an objective reality.

The nationalist historiography's narrativization of Indian nationalism, brought to a successful conclusion in the achievement of independence in 1947, represents one trajectory in the writing of post-Orientalist history, despite its complicity in many of the categories of thought and procedures of Orientalism; however, burdened with the task of articulating an anti-colonial national view, it could not but be different from Orientalism. Thus, the nationalists produced impressive scholarship on the 'drain' of wealth from India to Britain, on the de-industrialization of the country by British manufacturing interests, the neglect of Indian industrialization, and other such questions.[16] For this economic and nationalist historiography, as for cultural and political historians, the subject was always India, and the interests of the nation were always at stake. Powerful pronouncements of these kinds established India as an active subject. Therefore, we need to recognize it as one of the ways in which the 'third world writes its own history'. The nationalist writing of history – both before and after independence – did not, however, break free from two elements of the Orientalist canon. First, the nationalists, like the Orientalists, also assumed that India was an undivided entity but attributed it a sovereign and unitary will that was expressed in history. India now emerged as an active and undivided subject that had found its expression in the nation-state and transcended class and ethnic divisions, rather than being the inert object of Orientalist representations. Second, India was given an ontological presence prior to and independent of its representations which followed the procedures of Orientalism. Nationalism's confinement within the Orientalist problematic should not be surprising. As Partha Chatterjee argues, the nationalists opposed colonialism in the name of Reason through their claim that India's ancient history had followed, if not pioneered, a universal spirit leading to the nation-state, republicanism, economic development and nationalism that reaffirmed the cunning of Reason; and their assertion that a 'backward' country like India could modernize itself, if liberated from colonial slavery. The latter reaffirmed, however, the projects of modernity, making India ideologically incapable of transcending the Orientalist problematic.[17] Nationalism hijacked even Gandhi's anti-modern ideology in its drive to create a nation-state devoted to modernization, and turned him into a figure revered for his ability to appeal to the 'irrational' peasants and for the mystical bond that he was seen to have with the masses. That historiography became a part of this project should cause no wonder. History, as a discipline, was, after all, an instrument of the post-Enlightenment regime of Reason; and the Indian nationalist historians, being Western-educated elites, were its eager proponents.

The Refigurations of Essentialized India

Nationalist historiography so discredited some of the specific representations of Orientalism that the image of a sensuous, inscrutable and wholly spiritual India no longer enjoys academic prestige. More important, it made histories centred on India as the norm. The post-war decolonization, anti-colonial sentiments and upsurges against neo-colonialism also created a congenial political and intellectual climate for an orientation based on India. This orientation was institutionalized in the United States by the establishment in the 1950s of study programmes on the South Asia area. Scholarship founded on this basis did much to bring new evidence on history and culture to light by historians who moved rapidly from the study of imperial policies to 'realities on the ground', and social and cultural anthropologists who broke new ground in the analysis of caste and village society. Implicit in these moves, however, was the search for an authentic India. With colonial rule finished and cultural relativity ascendant, the research centred on India assumed that an authentic history and culture unaffected by the knower's involvement in the object of knowledge could be recovered. This research naively assumed that its valorization of India freed the scholar from colonial discourses, released to write, as it were, on a clean slate. Acting on this assumption, the knower could once again be construed as separate from knowledge, thereby overlooking that this position itself had a long history; but because this scholarship did not take cognizance of this history, it obviously could not reflect upon the consequences of its belief that the scholar was external to the object of inquiry. As a result, the operation of a whole battery of interests (academic disciplines, ideologies, institutional investments) was concealed, and old ideas reappeared in new guises. This was true, for instance, of the concept of a caste-driven and other-worldly India, which was reformulated as 'traditional India' by modernization theory in the 1960s. In the postcolonial context, the reappearance of such essentializations had two implications. First, in so far as a focus on India and cultural relativity enabled the represented object to appear as a vibrant and independent entity, the nationalist project was endorsed. Second, the attribution of this identity-in-itself made an Orientalist refiguration also possible. Anthropological studies of the 1950s and the 1960s illustrate these two tendencies and are worth considering because they came to command a prominent place in South Asia area-study programmes quite early, preceding the recent liaison between history and anthropology by at least a decade.

Unlike the traditional Orientalists, anthropologists studied people rather than texts and observed culture in action rather than studying its textual remnants. Moreover, as a discipline that specialized in scrutinizing the other, it was particularly suited to pursue studies centred on India. Studies of caste by anthropologists and, to a lesser extent, historians influenced by them became the most prominent aspect of this scholarship.[18] Louis Dumont argued that caste, after all, was a vital part in envisioning the essence of India, and this was also the assumption in the vigorous debates and theorizing about its place.[19] After the publication of Dumont's *Homo Hierarchicus* in English, very few could resist the argument that caste was the centrepiece of Indian society. Even Marxists, who had always had some trouble dealing with caste in their analysis of Indian society and history, were forced to take note and could no longer dismiss it as superstructural or as 'false consciousness'. For others, Dumont's all-encompassing theory provided a very elegant framework for explaining the forces of continuity, if not 'unchangeability', in Indian history. All this is not to imply that studies on caste did not yield important insights. On the contrary, they did explode the older myths about the unchangeability of the caste system, show its links to economy and polity, and trace patterns of social mobility.[20] Imbued as these works were with a great deal of empathy for India, their depictions of vibrant realities fell in line with the nationalist celebration of India's autonomous and unitary subjectivity.

The attribution of cultural and social essences was, however, also open to Orientalist recuperation. The obsessive focus on caste, for instance, served to affix it as the one essence of India. In doing so, it shared the Orientalist project of constituting India as the other – an other whose difference from self recuperated the latter as self-same, autonomous and sovereign. This was a far cry from the avant-garde ethnographic surrealism of Paris in the 1920s, when the other had corroded the reality of self.[21] The Paris of Louis Dumont in the 1960s, on the other hand, represented *homo hierarchicus* (India) in affirming the reality of *homo aequalis* (West). What was taken to be Dumont's distinct and crucial insight – namely that caste was a religious hierarchy that encompassed the economic and the political – turns out to be not all that different from the colonial view that India's essence lay in social organisms separated from the sphere of power.[22] In this respect, Dumont's work, the most celebrated and authoritative post-war anthropological scholarship on India, illustrates the vulnerability of essentialism to Orientalist refiguration.

These post-decolonization refigurations and recuperations in the scholarly field, particularly in anthropology, ought to be seen as materializations of a context marked by what may be called developmentalism. As new nations emerged from the shadow of colonial rule, the older project of colonial modernity was renovated and then deployed as economic development. As such a new nation-state, India looked upon science and technology as universal forces and deployed them in transforming its society. The boom in post-war anthropological fieldwork and studies began and then pushed forward this reformulation of modernizing projects by providing a social-scientific knowledge of 'traditional' social structures and beliefs targeted for modernization. The subdiscipline of economic development within the field of economics also emerged during these decades to formulate and further the modernization project by furnishing knowledge on the ways that existing economic institutions worked and by outlining strategies that could transform them. The area studies programmes united these social-scientific fields with Indological pursuits in creating knowledge which was no longer bounded by the old East–West definitions. Drawing regional rather than the old Orient–Occident boundaries, these area studies provided a distinct, yet subtler understanding of cultural relativity, although they could not provide postcolonial scholarship with the means to escape nationalist and Orientalist essentialisms. Indeed, it was precisely the lens of cultural relativity that, as Johannes Fabian points out, made the world appear as culture gardens separated by boundary-maintaining values – as posited essences.[23] Furthermore, the erection of these boundaries visualized the separateness of the subject from the object and defended anthropology's claim to represent an external other. In this regard, professional training and expertise allowed the researcher to claim that participant-observation protected the observer's externality that had been compromised in fieldwork. Conditioned by these methods of denying involvement in the construction of its object of knowledge, neither anthropology nor area studies could escape the nationalist and Orientalist recuperations of their essentalisms. These entities became represented as 'traditional' beliefs and structures, which were posed in opposition to modernization and were useful both in formulating culturally sensitive development projects and in evolving the 'appropriate' technology. To be sure, the methodological conventions devised and the questions posed by anthropology, development studies and area studies cannot be reduced to some crude political determination: we can trace the particular configurations of these fields to the dicussions and debates within them; rather, my point is that these scholarly conventions and questions helped in configuring the post-war context of developmentalism – in so far as they highlighted the essences (for example, Dumont's essentialization of ritual hierarchy) that could be evaluated for their adaptability to modernization.

Post-Nationalist Foundational Histories

It is a tribute to the resilience of the modernizing project inaugurated by Orientalism that the legitimacy of its proponents was challenged before its hegemony was threatened. Thus, nationalism accused colonialism of deliberately failing to live up to its own promise; and Marxists, in turn, viewed both colonialism and nationalism as structurally incapable of fulfilling the tasks of modernization in the colonies. In Marxist analysis, the notion of India as an undivided subject, separated and observable in relation to an equally undivided Europe, was suspect because it denied the class relations underlying these entities. These class relations led to an unequal and uneven development that neither colonial rulers nor their nationalist successors could overcome; so, the Marxists regarded the nationalist representation of India as an undivided and autonomous subject as ideological. A somewhat similar critique has been developed by social historians oriented towards world history. In their accounts, India is released from the restricting lens of national history and is placed in the larger focus of world history. Although the emergence of a professional Marxist historiography of India preceded the rise of world-history analysis in the late 1970s and early 1980s by roughly two decades, the two can be treated together because both interpret India in terms of a world-historical transition, despite the many differences between them. With their shared emphasis on political economy, they hold questions of production systems and political control to be of paramount importance in specifying the 'third worldness' of India.

In the Marxist case, the issues relating to political economy were, above all, expressed by social classes. The consequent advocacy of class histories – often contesting Marx's writings on India – cracked the image of an undivided India. While other scholars approached

India from the institutional context of an academic discipline, Marxists adopted the perspective of engaged critics, which enabled them to adopt a combative stance *vis-à-vis* the disciplines of Indology and South Asia area studies. Convinced that non-class histories suppress the history of the oppressed and stress consensus over conflict, Marxists wrote contestatory histories of domination, rebellions and movements,[24] in which they accused others of biases and claimed that their own biases were true to the 'real' world of class and mode of production. In place of the notion of a homogeneous Indic civilization, the Marxists highlighted heterogeneity, change and resistance.[25] The postcolonial Marxist historiography, in particular, replaced the undivided India of the nationalists with one divided by classes and class conflict; but because its enquiries were framed by a narrative about the transition of the mode of production, this scholarship viewed the activities of classes within the context of India's passage to capitalism (or, more accurately, to an aborted capitalist modernization). Take, for example, the Marxist readings of the so-called 'Bengal renaissance' during the first half of the nineteenth century, when brilliant Bengali reformers had defied conventions and produced new visions of Hinduism. Long heralded as the beginning of a new India (with one of the earlist reformers, Rammohan Roy, called 'the father of modern India'), Marxist reinterpretations stressed the failure of this project.[26] Arguing against the widespread belief that this 'renaissance' was entirely a Western influence, the existence of an indigenously born rationalism was discovered and shown to turn conservative through contact with the West. As for the modernity inspired by the West and promoted by the 'Bengal renaissance', these scholars contended that, in the absence of an organic class to serve as its basis, the reformers could not but fail in their project. In short, the 'renaissance' represents the case of aborted or colonial modernity. Without belittling the value of these reinterpretations, I think it is fair to say that the construction of India in terms of this and other failures represents a foundational view. While it highlights the paradoxes of 'renaissance' in a colonial context, the interpretation of these events as aborted or failed modernity defers the conclusion of the modernization narrative but does not eliminate the teleological vision. We are thus led to see the 'third worldness' of India in its incomplete narrative and unfulfilled promise, which invites completion and fulfilment.

A somewhat related interpretation has emerged also in recent social history writings that place modern Indian history in a world-historical framework. Like Marxist historiography, these social histories have dislodged the undivided and essential India of the Orientalists and nationalists. From the works in this genre, the Indian nation appears as a recent and tenuous creation whose artificiality, shown by the earlier 'Cambridge school' historians in the intrigues and stratagems of the nationalists,[27] is quite evident in eighteenth-century history. Descriptions of that century by those social historians decompose India into coasts which look outwards and face the Indian Ocean, and hinterlands composed of regional systems of social and political interests, trade and agriculture. Coasts and hinterlands connect and disconnect, fragment and rejoin; but the multiplicity of interests and perspectives disallows the articulation of a unitary India. C. A. Bayly's study is perhaps the most complete and original work of this genre.[28] His work revises, with a wealth of detail and insights, the older notion of eighteenth-century India as a period of chaos and decline into which the British just stepped in to pick up the pieces. Instead of explaining the conquest as the victory of a technologically superior and stronger Britain over a backward and weaker India, he offers a persuasive accout of how tendencies within the north Indian society interacted with the East India Company's activities in creating an empire. Stressing parity rather than disparity in technological level and economic organization, he analyses the British conquest as a conjunctural combination of social, economic and political conditions and interests. In this story, the rise of the Indian nation appears not as an eruption of a previously existing entity but rather as a historical creation attributable to the transformation of the late-eighteenth-century empire into a classic colonial relationship by the mid-nineteenth century.

There is no denying the richness of Bayly's narrative and the importance of its revisionist insights. Other studies have added support to this story, and a more explicitly Marxist elaboration of this interpretation has been offered,[29] and although it differs from the Marxist accounts on many substantive issues, it provides a more fully developed and substantiated version of the transition story than that formulated in the older Marxist accounts. Whereas the Marxists write from the position of engaged critics and thus stress domination and struggle, historical sociology underplays conflict and traces the development of structures. We have the echoes here of the now familiar contrast between agency and structure. More significant than this contrast, however, is their common immersion in foundational historiography. For both of them, writing history implies recapturing the operation of classes and structures, with the usual caveats about the historian's biases and ideology. I do not mean by this that this historiography makes simple-minded claims to objectivity, and I do not intend to get bogged down in a sterile debate over subjective versus objective accounts; rather, when I call this form of historical writing foundational, I refer to its assumption that history is ultimately founded in and representable through some identity – individual, class or structure – which resists further decomposition into heterogeneity. From this point of view, we can do no better than document these founding subjects of history, unless we prefer the impossibility of coherent writing amid the chaos of heterogeneity. Any change in historical writing becomes primarily a matter of interpretative shifts – new concepts replace old and unworkable ones. This vision excludes a critical return to the scene of writing history and carries an objectivist bias with it, however provisional. Take, for example, the narrativization of Indian history in terms of the development of capitalism. How is it possible to write such a narrative, but also contest, at the same time, the homogenization of the contemporary world by capitalism? How can the historians of India resist the totalizing claims of the contemporary nation-state if their writings represent India in terms of the nation-state's career? The second question is now easier to handle for most people because nationhood can more easily be shown as 'imagined' and fictive.[30] The decomposition of the autonomous nation into heterogeneous class, gender, regional, linguistic and cultural divisions is easy to show.

The refusal of foundational categories that construct the theme of global modernity, however, has proved difficult, but the tenuous presence and the very historicity of class structures that anchor the transitional narrative cannot be fully acknowledged without the rejection of the stability occupied by the theme of transition in the discourse of historians. Without such an acknowledgement, the Marxist and social historians can only envision that India's 'third worldness' consists of its incomplete or underdeveloped development. India, which is seen in this history as trapped in the trajectories of global modernity, is doomed to occupy a tragic position in these narratives. Such a vision cannot but reproduce the very hegemonic structures that it finds ideologically unjust in most cases, and occludes the histories that lie outside of the themes which are privileged in history.

Towards Post-Foundational Histories

The preceding account of how the 'third world writes its own history' makes it clear that historiography has participated in constituting shifting positions. The nationalists, who were opposed to the Orientalist representation of India as a separate and passive other, gave it autonomy and a national essence. Cultural anthropology and area studies programmes in the post-war period, particularly in Europe and the United States, orientalized this essence in terms of the cultural concept and left an undivided India intact. Marxists and social historians broke up this entity in terms of founding class and structural subjects, but narrativized India in contemporary hegemonic terms. If nothing else, these multiple positions suggest how the third-world subject escapes being fixed. Lest this recognition of non-fixity be appropriated as another form of fixing, I hasten to add that the gesture that frames the endorsement of heterogeneity refuses the language of fixing. By way of elaborating and concluding my account of the post-Orientalist Indian historiography, I will refer to Edward Said's *Orientalism* as an argument for an anti-foundational history and discuss examples of attempts in this direction.

Several scholars have noted that Edward Said's work rejects an essentialist reversal of Orientalist constructions.[31] He does not envision the task of post-Orientalist scholarship as consisting of substituting the 'real' Orient for the 'myth' of the Orientalists; rather, his work articulates a post-Orientalist interpretative position that would trace third-world identities as relational rather than essential. This rules out a mere inversion of the Hegelian dialectic so that, instead of the Orientalist's assertion of the Occident's primacy, the self–other opposition could be used to assert the autonomous presence of the Orient. In its place, a post-Orientalist historiography visualizes modern India, for example, in relationships and processess that have constructed contingent and unstable identities. This situates India in relationships and practices that organized its territory and brought it under an international division of labour, assembled and ordered cultural differences into a national bloc, and highlighted it as the religious and spiritual East opposed to the secular and materialist West. I am not suggesting that Indian historiography is yet to study these relational processess. On the contrary, as my account has noted, the Marxist and social historians, for example, have shown in considerable detail that the global history of capitalism has articulated the identity of modern India; but such historical writings do not explore and expose the alterity which underlies this identity – other than calling it pre-capitalist, proto-industrial (or feudal and semi-feudal, as opposed to capitalist), unfree labour (as opposed to free labour), and traditional (not modern).[32] This strategy cannot historicize the emergence of a modern, colonial-capitalist Indian nation because it does not displace the categories framed in and by that history. The historicization of this process requires (as Said, for example, accomplishes in his study of the Orientalist essences) unsettling these identities, disrupting their self-same presence.

The most prominent example of such an attempt in Indian historiography is to be found in the volumes of the *Subaltern Studies*: a series of fiercely combative historical accounts written by a group of Indian and British Marxist historians scattered between India, Britain and Australia – almost all of them having had first-world academic training or experience.[33] Arguing that much of the existing historiography reproduced the colonial, nationalist and Marxist teleologies, the *Subaltern Studies* group aims at recovering the history of subaltern groups. In doing so, it disrupts, for example, the nationalist narrative that considers all colonial revolts as events in the becoming of the Indian nation and contests the older Marxist accounts which see these episodes as preludes to the emergence of full-fledged class consciousness. In carrying out this project, several essays in the series employ the familiar 'history-from-below' approach. Furthermore, the teleological effects of the Hegelian dialectic that they employ, as well as the notion of recovering and restoring the subaltern that they use, do not mesh very well with their structuralist decoding of the sign systems.[34] These limitations, however, should not be allowed to obscure what is truly novel and theoretically refreshing in their work – the deployment of the concept of subalternity. This concept is particularly defined and used the most fruitfully in the work of Ranajit Guha, the editor of the series,[35] who views subalternity as an essential object in place of class – an effect of power relations and expressed through a variety of means – linguistic, economic, social and cultural. This perspective, therefore, breaks the undivided entity of India into a multiplicity of changing positions which are then treated as the effects of power relations. The displacement of foundational subjects and essences allowed by this also enables Guha to treat histories written from those perspectives as documents of counter-insurgency – those seeking to impose colonial, nationalist, transitional (modernizational) agendas. Writing subaltern history, from this point of view, becomes an activity that is contestatory because of its insurgent readings.

From the constitution of subalternity as effects, as identities dependent on difference, it should be clear that the *Subaltern Studies* project shares some of the structuralist and post-structuralist critiques of the autonomous and sovereign subject. In fact, the influence of French and Soviet structuralist semiotics is quite explicit in some of the writings. Indeed, a recent collection consisting of selections from several volumes aims at making an explicit connection with Michel Foucault's writings.[36] Notwithstanding these connections, the Subaltern project is somewhat different because, while it rescues the subaltern from the will of the colonial or nationalist elite, it also claims autonomy for the subaltern consciousness. However this tension is ultimately resolved in their studies, the significance of their project lies in the writing of histories freed from the will of the colonial and national elites. It is this project of resisting colonial and nationalist discursive hegemonies, through histories of the subaltern whose identity resides in difference, which makes the work of these scholars a significant intervention in third-world historiography.

If the recent rise of post-structuralist theories, particularly in the United States, is partially responsible for the recognition of *Subaltern Studies* scholarship, its influence is also evident in the new post-Orientalist historiography. With a somewhat different focus than *Subaltern Studies* and with explicit reference to post-structuralism, this scholarship is marked by its attempts to make cultural forms and even historical events contingent, above all, on power relations. In considering nationalist identity for example, it points to the differences suppressed and the power exercised even as colonial domination was challenged. In studying criminality, it points to power relations at work in classifying and acting upon 'criminal tribes' even as threats to life and property were countered; and in examining the nineteenth-century reformist attempts to suppress and outlaw the institution of widow sacrifice (*suttee*), it reveals how gendered ideas were formulated and used by the colonial rulers and Indian reformers even as they questioned the burning of widows.[37] Rather than seeing these events as important because they were so well regarded in the past, it interrogates the past's self-evaluation. It attempts to disclose that which is concealed when issues are posed as India versus Britain; crime versus law and order; and traditional, reactionary and oppressive treatment of women versus their modern and progressive emancipation. The purpose of such disclosures is to write those histories that history and historiography have excluded.

The emerging historiography, as the above account makes evident, can be located at the point where post-structuralist, Marxist and feminist theories converge and intersect. In understanding this scholarship, however, it is not enough to trace its links with these theories. Equally relevant is some of the earlier historiography. Take, as examples, Romila Thapar's searching scrutiny of Orientalist and nationalist constructs in her work on ancient India and Bernard Cohn's historicization of cultural forms essentialized during colonial rule.[38] Such earlier work of clearing and criticizing essentialist procedures anticipated the contemporary trend of making cultural forms contingent and of highlighting the complicity of colonial and nationalist knowledge in constituting the objects of enquiry. The work by Nicholas Dirks illustrates this point.[39] Like earlier scholars, he also traces the genealogy of a widely accepted idea – namely, that the caste system was primarily a religious phenomenon that encompassed the political; but his argument is framed by contemporary theories in showing that British rule depoliticized the caste system, which then gave rise to the idea that it was primarily a religious entity. Thus, he historicizes the conventional notion of caste by showing its shifting position in a south Indian kingdom. This unstable and changing position of caste and kingdom is accentuated in turn by the repeated interruptions of the narrative and its movement in and out of different historical periods and disciplines. The overall result forces the reader to reflect upon the procedures and rhetoric of the academic disciplines in which the book is located.

This historiography's critical focus on epistemological procedures and institutional interests makes it somewhat different from the *Subaltern Studies*, which targets the colonial or nationalist will. While the former analyses power relations in the context of academic disciplines and institutions, the latter sees itself disrupting and derailing the will of the powerful. Although both ultimately aim critical reflections upon discursive formations, the emphasis is clearly different. In view of the role that Western academic institutions play in studying and marginalizing the other, it is not surprising that the post-Orientalist historiography targets academic disciplines. It is precisely for this reason also that Indology and area studies in Europe and North America have been less than enthusiastic, if not hostile, to Said's interpretation as disciplines devoted to representing the other. Because the demystification of India as an undivided and separate object calls for the decomposition of the undivided and autonomous West, disciplines instituted to represent the binary opposition are understandably reluctant. Interestingly, it is in those fields not associated with Indology – such as literature – and in institutions without strong programmes in South Asian area studies that Said's book has stimulated much new work; but even traditional centres of Indology are beginning to take account of challenges posed by critiques of Orientalism.[40]

The story of Indian historiography that I have been telling has certain evident themes. First, the 'third worldness' of India has been conceived in a variety of different ways by historiography. These shifting conceptions testify to the changing history of India and locate historiography in that history, contributing to as well as being a part of it. This rules out the comfort of assuming that India, or the third world, will finally speak in a voice that will render all previous ones inauthentic. Second, the identification with the subordinated's subject position, rather than national origin, has been the crucial element in formulating critical third-world perspectives. Of course, as subordinated subjects, Indian historians have obviously developed and embraced the victim's subject-position more readily; but because the experience and expression of subordination are discursively formulated, we are led back to the processes and forces that organize the subordinate's subject position. Third, the formation of third-world positions suggests engagement rather than insularity. It is difficult to overlook the fact that all of the third-world voices identified in this essay speak within and to discourses familiar to the 'West' instead of originating from some autonomous essence, which does not warrant the conclusion that third-world historiography has always been enslaved, but that the careful maintenance and policing of East–West boundaries has never succeeded in stopping the flows across and against boundaries and that the self–other opposition has never quite been able to order all differences into binary opposites. The third world, far from being confined to its assigned space, has penetrated the inner sanctum of the first world in the process of being 'third-worlded' – arousing, inciting and affiliating with the subordinated others in the first world. It has reached across boundaries and barriers to connect with the minority voices in the first world: socialists, radicals, feminists, minorities. Although such crossings and interruptions of boundaries have become more insistent now, the turmoil in the field and attempts to write post-Orientalist histories are not new. Historians of India have previously questioned and unsettled dominant paradigms. Fine examples of non-Orientalist histories already exist; to think otherwise would mean attributing a totalizing power to Orientalism. The existence of earlier precedents, however, does not mean that the present historiography is completing the tasks left unfinished and that we are now witnessing the end of Orientalism; such a perspective entails the notion of a continuous history and assumes an essential similarity between different historiographies. Neither entirely new nor completely the same, the present ferment gets its specificity from the ways in which a new post-Orientalist scholarship is being currently conceived lies in the difference from previous contexts; and the particular insights generated by the emerging historical writing can be attributed to the larger field of social experience articulated in discourses.

The present critical appraisal of concepts, disciplines and institutions associated with the study of South Asia forms a part of contemporary challenges to beliefs in solidly grounded existence and identities, if not their loss. Jacques Derrida's disclosure of the 'metaphysics of presence' and Michel Foucault's genealogical accounts of the disciplinary constitution of criminal and sexual subjects have certain general affinities with Edward Said's analysis of Orientalism's suppression of difference in favour of stable and hierarchical East–West identities. These resemblances, which do not diminish significant differences among them, arise from their common espousal of post-structuralist methods. It is argued that these methods form theories about the practices of the earlier literary and aesthetic modernism (such as the latter's break from the belief that language was a transparent medium) and that the kinship with modernism accounts for its obsessive concern with language and writing, which displaces political questions to the aesthetic arena.[41] While the trace of modernism's transgressive impulses may well be discerned in post-structuralism's decentring methods, the current prominence of these theories is better understood as a moment in the postmodern valorization of blurred genres and off-centred identities. Fashioned by denials of grand totalizing theories, postmodernism defies and refuses definition. Only a laundry list of conditions can be offered – TV images, fashion magazines, Salman Rushdie, Talking Heads, challenges to universalist and essentialist theories, architectural irreverence and playfulness, transnational capitalism. The list is endless, without a beginning or end; and any gesture towards classification and distillation would be contrary to postmodernism, which exists only as a combination of conjunctural conditions.[42] This conjuncture includes the post-structuralist disavowal of the essentialist categories and modes of thought in the 'Western tradition' – a position that overlaps with the third-world scholarship's combative stance with respect to the legacies of the application of this tradition of non-European cultures.

This repudiation of the post-Enlightenment ideology of Reason and Progress is also what distinguishes the present historiography from the anti-Orientalism of nationalism. Earlier, when nationalism challenged Orientalism, it staked the subjected nation's claim to the order of Reason and Progress by showing, for instance, that India had a history comparable to that of the West; that it too had produced a proto-republican political order; and that it had achieved economic, cultural and scientific progess. The older Marxist historians, as well as the more recent social historians, broke up the nationalist's undivided India into an entry permeated with class conflict, but their global mode-of-production narratives did not fully confront the universalism of the post-Enlightenment order of Reason. What we are witnessing now in the post-Orientalist historiography is a challenge to the hegemony of those modernization schemes and ideologies that post-Enlightenment Europe projected as the *raison d'être* of history, an assault on what Ashis Nandy calls the 'second colonization'. This is because, as Nandy argues:[43]

> Modern colonialism won its great victories not so much through its military and technological prowess as through its ability to create secular hierarchies incompatible with traditional order. These hierarchies opened up new vistas for many, particularly for those exploited and cornered within the traditional order. To them the new order looked like – and here lay its psychological pull – the first step towards a more just and equal world. That was why some of the finest critical minds in Europe – and in the East – were to feel that colonialism, by introducing modern structures into the barbaric world, would open up the non-West to the modern critical-analytical spirit. Like the 'hideous heathen god who refused to drink nectar except from the skulls of murdered men,' Karl Marx felt, history would produce out of oppression, violence and cultural dislocation not merely new technological and social forces but also a new social consciousness in Asia and Africa.

Today, ideologies of science, progress and hypermasculinity that the Age of Reason brought to the third world riding on the back of colonialism, have lost their seductive appeal; but in reflecting on this history in which Descartes defined rationality and Marx defined social criticism, we must, Nandy argues, listen to the voices contained therein and write 'mythographies' that we did not before. This is not only a plea for a recognition of the plurality of critical traditions but a claim for the liberating nature of the victim's discourse, particularly for that of the colonized. Although both the colonizer and the colonized have been the victims of colonialism, the colonized have a special story to tell because they not only had to confront the 'West' on its own terms of robust hypermasculinity but also to construct and connect with the other subordinated selves of the 'West'. This call for a writing of mythographies, therefore, provides an appreciation not only for the colonized's construction of their subjected self but also the colonized's appeal to and affiliation with the subordinated selves of the colonizer. Such mythographic accounts revealing the previously hidden histories of the subordinated selves of first and third worlds will also expose the mythic quality of colonial and postcolonial fables of modernity. This invocation of the mythic in disclosing the fable-like character of 'real' history calls to mind Salman Rushdie's fabulous history of postcolonial India and Pakistan in *Midnight's Children.*[44] In the novel, Saleem Sinai, a child fathered by history, melts the apparent solidity of history single-handedly and – through his long nose, face, casual talk and telepathy – causes border wars, violent demonstrations and ethnic riots. The very extravagance of myths, dreams and fantasies elicits belief in its truthfulness and defamiliarizes the real. While Rushdie spins his tale around pepperpots and spittoons, Nandy's mythography of history has unheroic heroes – the saintly Gandhi and the comical Brown Sahibs – and through these unlikely figures the tragic tale of colonialism is told, its alliance with psychopathic technologies exposed, its fantastic quality revealed.

Such a strategy of privileging the 'mythic' over the 'real' has turned the historiographical field topsy-turvy. The entities upon which South Asian studies were based – India and the West – can no longer be unquestionably accepted as entirely separate and fixed. After all, if Gandhi's saintliness and non-violence – those quintessential 'Indian' qualities – had counterparts in the 'West' (albeit marginalized); if the Brown Sahibs' imitation of the British was an 'Indian' strategy of survival and even resistance; and if, in spite of its clear-headed realpolitik, modern anti-colonial Indian nationalism fell prey to a 'second colonization'; then what is left of the neatly separated 'India' and the 'West'? Such destabilization of identities and crossing of carefully policed boundaries promise a new third-world historiography that will resist both nativist romanticization and Orientalist distancing. This post-foundational move, implicit in the emerging writings, affiliates the new third-world historiography with post-structuralism, and together they both echo the postmodernist decentring of unitary subjects and hegemonic histories.

This common articulation of the postmodern condition, however, cannot be taken to mean that the fragmentation and proliferation of identities, histories, cultures and the failure of representations and the existence of ironic detachments do not have regional configurations and contextual resonances (American? French? Parisian? German? Continental philosophy? Marxism?). This being so, the post-Orientalist scholarship, while sharing certain common features with post-structuralism and postmodernism, cannot but be different from them. This is particularly important because the third world was defined as marginal from the very beginning. The new post-Orientalist scholarship's attempt to release the third world from its marginal position forms a part of the movement that advocates the 'politics of difference' – racial, class, gender, ethnic, national and so forth.[45] Two points are worth noting about this phenomenon. First, it posits that we can proliferate histories, cultures and identities arrested by previous essentializations. Second, to the extent that those made visible by proliferation are also provisional, it refuses the erection of new foundations in history, culture and knowledge. Seen in this light, this politics of difference evinces impulses similar to those manifested in what is generally referred to as cultural criticism today, although cultural critics have different concerns in that they take the 'Western tradition' as their starting point. Their principal aim is to unlock the 'closures' in 'high' literary and philosophical texts and release meanings trapped by beliefs in essences.[46] Often, their interests are not directly focused on political questions and demonstrate an aestheticist bias, although this is not true of feminist theories and the advocates of the politics of difference.

The post-Orientalist historiography, on the other hand, is much more directly concerned with the question of domination because its very subject – the third world – is defined by its dominated status.[47] The attempt to unlock history from the 'closures' is thus not so much a question for these scholars of taking pleasure in the revealed Bakhtinian carvinalesque but an issue of engaging the relations of domination. Thus, the representation of India as an other defined by certain essences – tradition, spirituality, femininity, other worldliness, caste, nationality – becomes a site of contest. In these contests, the maintenance and the subversion of the relations of domination discursively reproduced by the lack of a clear break from the legacies of Orientalism, nationalism and the ideologies of modernization are at issue. The power attributed to the knowledge about the past makes historical writing into a political practice and turns the recent post-Orientalist historical accounts into contestatory acts. Such a clearly political vision is what distinguishes this historiography in a context in which the third world is widely recognized as a signifier of cultural difference but is rapidly appropriated and commodified as cultural surplus (the Banana Republic stores being the most offensive contemporary example in this respect)[48] or serves as an other in a hermeneutic exercise devoted to the exploration of blurred genres and decentred realities validated by postmodernism.[49] Enabled by, but also in resistance to, these contemporary postmodernist tendencies, the self-consciously political visualization of writing history as a site of contest acquires a distinct significance; but if the postmodern conjuncture accounts for the attention currently paid to how the 'third world writes its own history', it also threatens to envelop it in the larger project of dislodging the 'Western tradition'. If that happens in the present flurry of conferences and seminars on the third world, we will lose sight of the crucial fact that the 'Western tradition' was a very peculiar configuration in the colonial world; and the old axiom – that the third world is a good thing to think with about the 'West' – will once again be proven correct. Such a turn of events will bring the post-Orientalist historiography's promise to contest hegemonic structures and reveal new histories to an ironic end.

Acknowledgements

This essay was originally presented as a paper in a panel entitled 'After Orientalism: the Third World Writes Its Own History' at the American Historical Association's annual meeting in Cincinnati, December 1988. I am thankful to Carol Gluck, whose imagination and organizational efforts made this panel possible and whose invitation prompted me to think about these broader questions. Remarks by others on the panel – Ervand Abrahanian and Edward Said in particular – and the questions and comments from the audience, clarified the issues involved. Comments from Nicholas Dirks, Joan Scott and Carol Quillen were extremely useful in rewriting the original paper, and the criticisms and suggestions of the revised paper offered at the workshop on 'Colonialism and Culture' by *Comparative Studies in Society and History* at Ann Arbor, Michigan, May 1989, particularly by Roger Rouse and Vicente Rafael, were of great help in writing the present version.

Notes

1. A recent example is the exchange between Fredric Jameson and Aijaz Ahmad, in which Jameson's well-intentioned but 'first-world' gesture drew deserved criticism. See Jameson's 'Third-World Literature in the Era of Multinational Capital', *Social Text*, 15 (Fall 1986), 65–88; and Ahmad's 'Jameson's Rhetoric of Otherness and the "National Allegory"', *Social Text*, 17 (Fall 1987), 3–25; and Jameson's reply on pp. 26–7.
2. Edward W. Said, *Orientalism* (New York: Vintage, 1979).
3. On these Orientalist writers, see Bernard S. Cohn, 'Notes on the History of the Study of Indian Society and Culture', *Structure and Change in Indian Society*, Milton Singer and Bernard S. Cohn, eds (Chicago: Aldine, 1968), 7. On Halhead, see Rosane Rocher, *Orientalism, Poetry, and the Millennium: The Checkered Life of Nathaniel Brassey Halhead* (Delhi: Motilal Banarasidass, 1983). For a discussion of Persian historiography and for more on the early British treatments of how eighteenth-century British writings dealt with pre-history, see *Historians of Medieval India*, Mohibbul Hasan, ed. (Meerut: Meenakshi, 1968).
4. Wilhelm Halfbass, *India and Europe: An Essay in Understanding* (Albany: State University of New York Press, 1988), 69–83. Also, Ronald Inden, 'Orientalist Constructions of India', *Modern Asian Studies*, 20:3 (1986), 401–46.
5. Martin Bernal, *Black Athena: Afroasiatic Roots of Classical Civilization* (New Brunswick, N.J.: Rutgers University Press, 1987), 227–9, 330–36.
6. James Mill, *The History of British India* (1817; rpt Chicago: University of Chicago Press, 1975). On missionaries, see Ainslee Thomas Embree, *Charles Grant and British Rule in India* (New York: Columbia University Press, 1962).
7. On how European ideas were applied to India, see Ranajit Guha, *A Rule of Property for Bengal: An Essay on the Idea of Permanent Settlement* (Paris: Mouton, 1963); Eric Stokes, *The English Utilitarians and India* (Oxford: Clarendon Press, 1959).
8. Richard Saumarez Smith's 'Rule-by-Records and Rule-by-Reports: Complementary Aspects of the British Imperial Rule of Law', *Contributions to Indian Sociology* (new series), 19:1 (1985), 153–76, is an excellent study of this process in Punjab.
9. See Ronald Inden, 'Orientalist Constructions' on the use of representation in

Orientalism. Timothy Mitchell's *Colonising Egypt* (Cambridge: Cambridge University Press, 1988) contains a fascinating interpretation of representation in British and European knowledge about Egypt.

10. Cited in Smith, 'Rule-by-Records', 153.

11. Nicholas B. Dirks's *The Hollow Crown: Ethnohistory of an Indian Kingdom* (Cambridge: Cambridge University Press, 1987) is a powerful argument against this thesis. See also, Ronald Inden, 'Orientalist Constructions'.

12. Compare Partha Chatterjee, *Nationalist Thought and the Colonial World – A Derivative Discourse?* (London: Zed Books, 1986), 38.

13. Much of this account is based on Romila Thapar's excellent 'Interpretations of Ancient Indian History', *History and Theory*, 7:3 (1968), 318–35, which contains a critical discussion of these nationalist historians. For more on this phase of historiography and on individual historians, see *Historians and Historiography in Modern India*, S. P. Sen, ed. (Calcutta: Institute of Historical Studies, 1973).

14. Jawaharlal Nehru's *The Discovery of India* (New York: John Day Company, 1946), 65.

15. Interestingly, Marx and Engels's writings in the *New York Daily Tribune* on the 1857 revolts were put together and published in the Soviet Union as *The First Indian War of Independence 1857–59* (Moscow: Foreign Languages Publishing House, 1959).

16. R. C. Dutt's *The Economic History of India*, 2 vols (1901, rpt London: Routledge and Kegan Paul, 1950) is the classic of this genre. For a detailed treatment of this line of nationalist historiography, see Bipan Chandra, *The Rise and Growth of Economic Nationalism in India* (Delhi: People's Publishing House, 1966). For a debate on the 'de-industrialization' question, see M. D. Morris *et al., Indian Economy in the Nineteenth Century: A Symposium* (Delhi: Indian Economic and Social History Association, 1969).

17. Chatterjee, *Nationalist Thought*, 30, 168–9.

18. The list is huge, but for some representative examples, see Frederick J. Bailey, *Caste and the Economic Frontier* (Manchester: Manchester University Press, 1957), and M. N. Srinivas, *Social Change in Modern India* (Berkeley: University of California Press, 1966). David G. Mandelbaum, *Society in India*, 2 vols (Berkeley: University of California Press, 1970) summarizes and cites much of the scholarship on caste. Fine historical studies of caste include the following: Ronald B. Inden, *Marriage and Rank in Bengali Culture: A History of Caste and Clan in the Middle Period Bengal* (Berkeley: University of California Press, 1975); Frank F. Conlon, *A Caste in a Changing World: The Chitrapur Saraswat Brahmans, 1700–1935* (Delhi: Thomson Press, 1977); and Karen I. Leonard, *Social History of an Indian Caste: The Kayasths of Hyderabad* (Berkeley: University of California Press, 1978).

19. Louis Dumont, *Homo Hierarchicus* (Chicago: University of Chicago Press, 1970); McKim Marriott, 'Hindu Transactions: Diversity without Dualism', in *Transaction and Meaning: Directions in the Anthropology of Exchange and Symbolic Behavior*, Bruce Kapferer, ed. (Philadelphia: Institute for the Study of Human Issues, 1976); and Michael Moffat, *An Untouchable Community in South India* (Princeton: Princeton University Press, 1979). Although Dumont's work no longer enjoys the influence that it did in the 1970s, his formulation that ritual hierarchy defines India continues to draw adherents. For example, Donald E. Brown's *Hierarchy, History and Human Nature* (Tucson: University of Arizona Press, 1988) employs the Dumontian essentialization of caste and hierarchy to explain the absence of 'real' historiography in India.

20. See, for example, *Social Mobility in the Caste System of India*, James Silverberg, ed. (Paris: Mouton, 1968).

21. James Clifford, 'On Ethnograhic Surrealism', *The Predicament of Culture* (Cambridge, Mass.: Harvard University Press, 1988), 117–51.

22. Compare Nicholas Dirks, *The Hollow Crown*, 3–5. For other critiques, see Arjun Appadurai, 'Is Homo Hierarchicus?', *American Ethnologist*, 13:4 (1986), 745–61; and 'Putting Hierarchy in Its Place', *Cultural Anthropology*, 3:1 (1988), 36–49.

23. Johannes Fabian, *Time and the Other: How Anthropology Makes Its Object* (New York: Columbia University Press, 1983), 47.

24. The notable examples include: P. C. Joshi, ed., *1857 Rebellion* (Delhi: People's Publishing House, 1957), which tried to reclaim the 1857 revolt as a moment in popular revolutionary movement; A. R. Desai, ed., *Peasant Struggles in India* (Delhi: Oxford University Press, 1979) interprets revolts and movements spread over two centuries as part of the wider struggle of the dominated; and Irfan Habib's masterly *The Agrarian System of Mughal India* (London: Asia Publishing House, 1963), which argues that the peasant revolts led by the local notables plunged the Mughal empire into a paralysing crisis in the eighteenth century.

25. D. D. Kosambi's works on ancient India mark the beginning – and remain stellar examples – of a professional Marxist historiography of this genre. See his *Culture and Civilization of Ancient India in Historical Outline* (London: Routledge and Kegan Paul, 1965).

26. See Sumit Sarkar, 'Rammohum Roy and the Break with the Past', in *Rammohun Roy and the Process of Modernization in India*, V. C. Joshi, ed. (Delhi: Vikas, 1975), 46–68; Barun De, 'The Colonial Context of the Bengal Renaissance', in *Indian Society and the Beginnings of Modernization c. 1830–1850*, C. H. Philips and Mary Doreen Wainwright, eds (London: School of Oriental and African Studies, 1976), 119–25; and Asok Sen, *Iswar Chandra Vidyasagar and His Elusive Milestones* (Calcutta: Rddhi–India, 1977).

27. See John Gallagher, Gordon Johnson and Anil Seal, eds, *Locality, Province and Nation* (Cambridge: Cambridge University Press, 1973); and David Washbrook, *The Emergence of Provincial Politics* (Cambridge: Cambridge University Press, 1976).

28. C. A. Bayly, *Rulers, Townsmen, and Bazaars: North Indian Society in the British Expansion, 1770–1870* (Cambridge: Cambridge University Press, 1983).

29. For example, David Ludden, *Peasant History in South India* (Princeton: Princeton University Press, 1985); and Muzaffar Alam, *The Crisis of Empire in Mughal North India: Awadh and the Punjab 1707–1748* (Delhi: Oxford University Press, 1986). For a Marxist version of this narrative, see David Washbrook, 'Progress and Problems: South Asian Economic and Social History', *Modern Asian Studies*, 22:1 (1988), 57–96.

30. Compare Benedict Anderson's *Imagined Communities: Reflections on the Origin and Spread of Nationalism* (London: Verso, 1983). The brilliance of its insights is somewhat marred by a lapse into sociological determinism and by its overemphasis on 'print capitalism'.

31. Compare James Clifford, 'On Orientalism', in *The Predicament of Culture*, 255–76.

32. My *Bonded Histories: Genealogies of Labor Servitude in Colonial India* (Cambridge: Cambridge University Press, 1990) shows how the free–unfree opposition appropriated and reorganized different forms of labour.

33. *Subaltern Studies*, vols I–V, Ranajit Guha, ed. (Delhi: Oxford University Press, 1982–85). The reference to national origins and to the 'first world' site of academic training and experience is not meant to be invidious; rather, my intention is to show that national origin is not a necessary requirement for the formulation of a post-Orientalist position.

34. Rosalind O'Hanlon's 'Recovering the Subject: *Subaltern Studies* and Histories of Resistance in Colonial South Asia' (see above) argues persuasively that an essentialist and teleological thinking also exists in their work. For an 'against the grain' reading that attempts to capture what is novel and contestatory in the *Subaltern Studies*, see Gayatri Chakravorty Spivak, 'Subaltern Studies: Deconstructing Historiography', in *Subaltern Studies*, vol. IV, 330–64.

35. See, in particular, his *Elementary Aspects of Peasant Insurgency in Colonial India* (Delhi: Oxford University Press, 1983).

36. *Selected Subaltern Studies*, Ranajit Guha and Gayatri Chakravorty Spivak, eds, with the Foreword by Edward W. Said (New York: Oxford University Press, 1988). The last section in this volume, for instance, is called 'Developing Foucault'.

37. See Partha Chatterjee, *Nationalist Thought and the Colonial World*; Veena Das, 'Gender Studies, Cross-Cultural Comparison and the Colonial Organization of Knowledge', *Berkshire Review*, no. 21 (1986), 58–76; Lata Mani, 'Contentious Traditions: The Debate on Sati in Colonial India', *Cultural Critique*, 7 (Fall 1987), 119–56; and Sanjay Nigam, 'The Social History of a Colonial Stereotype: The Criminal Tribes and Castes of

Utter Pradesh, 1871–1930' (Ph.D. disser., Department of History, School of Oriental and African Studies, London, 1987).

38. See Bernard Cohn, *An Anthropologist Among Historians and Other Essays* (Delhi: Oxford University Press, 1987); and Romila Thapar, *Ancient Indian Social History: Some Interpretations* (Delhi: Orient Longman, 1978).

39. Nicholas Dirks, *The Hollow Crown.*

40. The South Asia Regional Studies Department, University of Pennsylvania, held a year-long seminar in 1988–89 entitled 'Orientalism and Beyond: Perspectives from South Asia'.

41. Andreas Huyssen, *After the Great Divide: Modernism, Mass Culture, Postmodernism* (Bloomington: Indiana University Press, 1986), 206–16.

42. Andrew Ross, 'Introduction', in *Universal Abandon? The Politics of Postmodernism,* Andrew Ross, ed. (Minneapolis: University of Minnesota Press, 1988), x.

43. *The Intimate Enemy: Loss and Recovery of Self under Colonialism* (Delhi: Oxford University Press, 1983), ix.

44. Salman Rushdie, *Midnight's Children* (New York: Avon Books, 1980).

45. For a statement of this position from a feminist perspective, see Joan Wallach Scott, *Gender and the Politics of History* (New York: Columbia University Press, 1988). This politics of difference is called 'minority discourse' by Abdul JanMohamed and David Lloyd in their 'Introduction: Minority Discourse – What is to Be Done?', *Cultural Critique,* 7 (Fall 1987), 5–17.

46. These concerns are stated, for example, in Dominick LaCapra's *Rethinking Intellectual History: Texts, Contexts, Language* (Ithaca: Cornell University Press, 1983), and *History and Criticism* (Ithaca: Cornell University Press, 1985).

47. Compare Gayatri Chakravorty Spivak, 'Can the Subaltern Speak?' in *Marxism and the Interpretation of Culture,* Cary Nelson and Larry Grossberg, eds (Urbana and Chicago: University of Illinois Press, 1988), 271–313, in which she argues that even politically oriented Western post-structuralists, like Foucault, are marked by a certain blindness to the reality of imperialist domination.

48. See Paul Smith's 'Visiting the Banana Republic', in *Universal Abandon?,* 128–48.

49. Stephen A. Tyler's 'Post-Modern Ethnography: From Document of the Occult to Occult Document', in *Writing Culture: The Poetics and Politics of Ethnography,* James Clifford and George Marcus, eds (Berkeley: University of California Press, 1986), 122–40, exemplifies this tendency. Note, for instance, that he conceives postmodern ethnography's task as invoking 'the fantasy reality of a reality fantasy' and 'the occult in the language of naive realism and of the everyday in occult language'. This invocation, according to him, 'provokes a rupture with the commonsense world and evokes an aesthetic integration whose therapeutic effect is worked out in the restoration of the commonsense world' (p. 134). In this view, the off-centring of the ethnographer, as in the cover photograph of *Writing Culture,* becomes the purpose of postmodern ethnography.

9

After Orientalism: Culture, Criticism and Politics in the Third World

Rosalind O'Hanlon and David Washbrook

Over the 1980s, studies of 'third world' histories and cultures came to draw to a very considerable extent upon the theoretical perspectives provided by post-structuralism and postmodernism. With the publication in 1978 of Edward Said's work, *Orientalism*, these perspectives – now fused and extended into a distinctive amalgam of cultural critique, Foucauldian approaches to power, engaged 'politics of difference', and postmodernist emphases on the decentred and the heterogeneous – began to be appropriated in a major way for the study of non-European histories and cultures. Certainly in our own field of Indian colonial history, Said's characteristic blending of these themes has now become virtually a paradigm for a new generation of historians and anthropologists. These directions have been most recently and sharply endorsed in Gyan Prakash's discussion, 'Writing Post-Orientalist Histories of the Third World: Perspectives from Indian Historiography'.[1]

We share Prakash's concern with the emancipation of previously submerged colonial histories and identities. However, we are deeply concerned at the way in which his 'post-foundational' history would set about these tasks. Prakash sees this history, and the postmodernist and post-structuralist perspectives that underlie it, as our best future hope for a genuinely critical understanding of the Indian past. We question this, given the manner in which these perspectives have come to be interpreted and absorbed into the mainstream of historical and anthropological scholarship, particularly in the United States. We argue that post-foundational history offers us ways of 'knowing' the Indian past that are quite inadequate to its supposed political concerns. In emancipating ourselves from what Prakash calls 'foundationalism', we need also to ask rather more carefully what oexactly we are emancipating ourselves into. We argue that these approaches prescribe remedies which actually create new and in many cases much more serious difficulties of their own, in part because they have, of course, as much to do with arguments about the politics of representation in Western intellectual and academic circles as they do with imposing that manner of representation on the third world's history. We discuss what we see to be the difficulties of these approaches in the context of Indian and other non-Western historical writing and suggest that they have arisen in part from the widely shared but mistaken assumption that Edward Said's work provides a clear paradigm for a history that transcends older problems of representation.

Post-Foundational History: Dilemmas and Problems

Taking Edward Said's definition of Orientalism as his starting point, Prakash moves through a range of approaches for the study of Indian society, showing how each has inherited and reproduced some of Orientalism's key assumptions and techniques of representation. Indian nationalist historiography, for example, has been unable to transcend Orientalism's preoccupation with essences and its teleologies of modernity. Its historians understood knowledge as a 'more or less adequate representation of the real', and India itself as having an existence independent of its representations.[2] India itself appeared for them as an undivided subject struggling to transcend colonial backwardness and to realize itself as a modern national state. Likewise, the area studies programmes that dominated South Asian history and anthropology from the 1950s seached for an authentic Indian history and culture, fixing on caste as Indian society's essence and scrutinizing its structures in terms of their potential as vehicles for political and economic modernization.

Prakash then turns to 'post-nationalist foundational histories'. By this he means Marxist and what he calls 'social historians oriented toward world history', such as C. A. Bayly, who have been concerned with Indian political economy, particularly in its relationship to world-historical transitions. Although Prakash carefully points out their gains, he finds them ultimately unsatisfactory because their histories are 'foundational'. They use categories which are at some level fixed and essential, as if history were 'ultimately founded in and representable through some identity – individual, class, structure – which resists further decomposition into heterogeneity'. Such categories cannot but have an 'objectivist bias' built into them.[3] Their emphasis on the theme of capitalist transition leads, moreover, to a teleological account that sees India principally as an instance of aborted capitalist modernity and cannot

> explore and expose the alterity which underlies this identity – other than calling it precapitalist, protoindustrial (or feudal and semi-feudal as opposed to capitalist), unfree labor (as opposed to free labor), and traditional (not modern). This strategy cannot historicize the emergence of a modern, colonial-capitalist Indian nation because it does not displace the categories framed in and by that history.[4]

These approaches can only in the end legitimate the structures of capitalist modernity they describe; for, Prakash asks, how is it possible to understand Indian history in terms of the development of capitalism, 'but also contest, at the same time, the homogenization of the contemporary world by capitalism?'[5]

In the last part of his discussion, Prakash considers what he calls 'post-Orientalist' histories, which try to move towards post-foundational approaches. These utilize the insights of Edward Said and Michel Foucault and draw further on themes from postmodernism, feminism, minority discourses and other advocates of the 'politics of difference'. These approaches share Prakash's concern to show how knowledge about the third world is historically produced. They seek 'to make cultural forms and even historical events contingent, above all, on power relations'.[6] Avoiding the temptation to return to essential identities, they work instead to displace foundational subjects and essences, to break up notions of a unitary India into a multiplicity of contingent and unstable identities which are the effects of changing power relationships. They refuse the privileged themes of global capitalist modernization and focus instead off-centre on what those themes exclude: histories of the subordinate whose identity, like all identity, resides in difference. Postmodernist perspectives are important in shaping these approaches, with their 'blurred genres and off-centred identities' and their hostility to systematizing theories:

> Fashioned by denials of grand totalizing theories, postmodernism defies and refuses definition. Only a laundry list of conditions can be offered – TV images, fashion magazines, Salman Rushdie, Talking Heads, challenges to universalist and essentialist theories, architectural irreverence and playfulness, transnational capitalism.[7]

Nor do the new histories limit their vision to India or other third world societies. They forge links with subordinate others in Western contexts, with radicals, feminists, ethnic and other minorities, in a common challenge to teleologies of modernization and their constituent themes of Reason and Progress. Above all, they do not draw back from political engagement. They identify with the subject-position of the subordinate, concern themselves with relationships of domination, and self-consciously make their own historical accounts into contestatory acts. In these respects they differ from the often depoliticized perspectives of postmodernism, while at the same time sharing its emphasis on the provisionality of all identities, its resistance to all systematizing or totalizing theory and its refusal to set up 'new foundations in history, culture and knowledge'.[8] Prakash points to examples of these new approaches. Although he notes their limitations, he commends Ranajit Guha and the *Subaltern Studies* project for deploying post-structuralist arguments and the concept of 'subalternity'. This has enabled them to get away from the older frameworks of colonialism and nationalism within which Indian history was studied and to break up their associated foundational categories, revealing India instead as 'a multiplicity of changing positions which are then treated as effects of power relations'.[9] The work of Bernard Cohn and Nicholas Dirks reveals in different ways how colonial rule created and froze social institutions which the British took to be immutable features of India as a primarily religious society. In common with post-modernists, Ashis Nandy's work on the culture and psychology of colonialism has repudiated the 'post-Enlightenment ideology of Reason and Progress', in which 'Descartes defined rationality and Marx defined social criticism'.[10] To escape these tyrannies, we must turn to 'mythographies', the hidden stories of colonialism's victims, which will 'expose the mythic character of colonial and postcolonial fables of modernity'. Salman Rushdie likewise shares postmodernism's hostility to 'grand totalizing theories', disclosing in *Midnight's Children* the 'fable-like character of real history'.[11]

But we see many problems here. The critique of foundational categories derives in large part from the work of Jacques Derrida, although Derrida's work contains very little to indicate how we should go about the basic, inescapably active, and interventionist task of historical interpretation. Derrida's particular approach to the problem of the conventional and non-objective nature of our categories and schemes of interpretation may actually represent something of an intellectual cul-de-sac, at least for those who would offer forms of historical understanding. As John Searle has argued,

> Derrida correctly sees that there aren't any such foundations, but he then makes the mistake that marks him as a classical metaphysician. The real mistake of the classical metaphysician was not the belief that there were metaphysical foundations, but rather the belief that somehow or other such foundations were necessary, the belief that unless there are foundations something is lost or threatened or undermined.[12]

In the absence of such foundations, Derrida can do little more than reveal, over and over again, the subjective and arbitrary nature of our categories and the uncertainty of the knowledge derived from them. He misses, in effect, the crucial point that we cannot actually do without some categories and some means of evaluating orders of certainty, in order to comprehend, to explain, to elucidate and to do. That these categories are conventions, Searle further argues, is no bar to our continuing to use them provided we recognize them for what they are, inventions of our own necessity. However, this recognition involves a change in the way that we conceive and test them – not against metaphysically conceived standards of objectivity but against their adequacy in serving the purposes for which we want and need to use them. Such considerations of course include ourselves and the reasons why we require particular kinds of knowledge. Preoccupied as he is with the non-problem of objectivity at the expense of questions of purposive adequacy, Derrida has rather little to offer us on these key questions of method. If Prakash's aim were simply to render our existing knowledge of Indian and other third world societies uncertain and unstable, there would indeed be a point in his invoking Derrida's attack on foundational forms of knowledge. Because he actually intends a highly purposive agenda of historical reconstruction and political engagement, however, this invocation seems to us starkly inappropriate.

Prakash's critique of Indian historiography and his prognoses for its future reflect these contradictions. Most who fall into his category of Marxist and social historians of India have long recognized the irreducibly subjective element in their interpretations, seeing that the historian is inescapably a part of what they study as a constant process of movement and transformation.[13] Most would be thoroughly mystified by the charge that they operate with reified and ahistorical categories of class, individual and structure. Such categories are usually contextualized in terms of their making and unmaking, their emergence and decline. Bayly, for example, presents eighteenth-century India in terms of the making and unmaking of a particular and contingent set of relations, which threw up a distinctive and ultimately transient structure of class, on the basis of which colonial rule was initially established. He plainly sees class, along with other forms of structure and identity, as historically contingent, unstable, and given to change – certainly not as immutable in some way. It is also not obvious that these historians understand capitalist transition merely in terms of Western development and Asian underdevelopment. Within the Marxist discourse, debates around the themes of comparative feudalism, the articulation of modes of production and the work of Robert Brenner have all explored the specific dynamics of non-British and wider non-Western relations of production and social formation.[14] Equally, a major thrust of research on the Indian past has for a considerable time now been precisely to break down East–West dichotomies by exploring the indigenous forms of capitalism and their associated military and mercantile institutions that were developing in India from the late seventeenth century. This research describes how these indigenous dynamics powerfully and importantly shaped the East India Company's initial engagement with the economies and societies of the subcontinent and its own subsequent development as a colonial state.[15] Bayly himself sets this against a sharply redrawn picture of early-nineteenth-century British society designed to reveal the precise ways in which its forms of modernity were not only partial and limited but created out of and sustained by wider imperial relationships.[16]

Prakash also contends that any historian who writes about India's history in terms of capitalism's development must in the end be complicit in the very hegemony so described. Rather, we must aim for a 'refusal of foundational categories that construct the theme of global modernity'.[17] The implications of this seem somewhat unclear. If the complicity arises from a tendency to present the world of capitalism as homogeneous, it must be pointed out that most Marxist social history critiques capitalist modernity precisely in order to challenge the self-images and pretensions to the universality of Western social theories of modernization. Lumping the two together because both appear to address the same problem of the forms and forces of capitalist modernity is deeply misconceived. Prakash and the other postmodernist theorists on whose work he draws apparently have the view that merely engaging the question determines our understanding of it so that we ought actually to assume that it does not really exist in any systematic form. What his position leaves quite obscure is what status exactly this category of 'capitalist modernity' occupies for him. If our strategy should be to 'refuse' it in favour of marginal histories, of multiple and heterogeneous identities, this suggests that capitalist modernity is nothing more than a potentially disposable fiction, held in place simply by our acceptance of its cognitive categories and values. Indeed, Prakash is particularly disparaging of Marxist and social historians' concern with capitalism as a 'system' of political economy and coercive instrumentalities. Yet in other moments Prakash tells us that history's proper task is to challenge precisely this 'homogenization of the world by contemporary capitalism'.[18] If this is so, and there is indeed a graspable logic to the way in which modern capitalism has spread itself globally, how are we to go about the central task of comprehending this logic in the terms that Prakash suggests?

These problems seem further compounded if we turn to the work of historians whom Prakash recommends as exemplars of post-foundationalist approaches. What is puzzling is that many of these historians themselves put forward timeless or undifferentiated conceptions of the Indian past, often in a particularly glaring way. Bernard Cohn has undoubtedly done much to disassemble monolithic notions of a traditional India advanced in colonial social theory. Yet in his account of how these notions were fabricated, he describes a class between European and Indian forms of knowledge which are both undifferentiated, the former located in time somewhere between the seventeenth and the nineteenth centuries and the latter not at all.[19] Ashis Nandy identifies the psychological damage and 'loss' associated with the colonial experience. Yet his strategy for the recovery of an 'Indian self' seems merely to invert a range of what were originally Orientalist conceptions about India and to generalize the cultural experience of Bengali literati to that of the whole nation.[20] Ranajit Guha may well criticize 'bourgeois' Indian nationalism for its failure to identify with the very different needs of subaltern classes, but he does take the central question of modern Indian history to be the 'historic failure of the nation to come to its own', a question that plainly derives from the nationalist paradigm that Prakash condemns so strongly.[21] Many theories about Indian personality and social structure which Guha uses to test the consequences of colonial domination bear a strong resemblance to those of Louis Dumont, whose ideas Prakash elsewhere deems to be 'refigured essentialisms'. Indeed, Guha has of late taken to referring to the (undifferentiated) Indian nation as 'us'.[22] Prakash dismisses 'totalizing' understandings of the Indian past in favour of the alternative and the marginal and commends Nicholas Dirks's attack on Dumont's ahistorical theories of caste for making this possible. Yet Dirks himself presents us with a counter-theory of caste that is scarcely less generalizing that Dumont's own. He erects it, moveover, very largely on the basis of the world view and self-images of locally dominant groups.[23] Prakash himself does what he tells us not to. He warns us against writing history around the major themes of global transition but then writes about Indian historiographical development in precisely these terms, seeing the determinants of its progression passing from imperialism to nationalism to a liberal hegemony centred on the United States.

This all makes it very difficult to grasp the character of post-foundationalist understandings of the past or to see what they are meant to achieve. These confusions seem to us to arise out of a wish to generate a historical praxis from Derridean and postmodernist perspectives that are inherently inimical to it. These perspectives undermine possibilities for such a praxis in two ways. First, because they regard any intervention by the historian or interpreter in the past as inherently illegitimate, a kind of complicity, they fail to acknowledge the particular and specific means by which that scholar acquires knowledge of the past. Prakash objects to our giving some analytical categories privilege on the grounds that this 'occludes the histories that lie outside of the themes which are privileged in history'. But this suggests that the themes of history are or should be given in the material of history itself, exposed or not exposed by the historian, whose cognitive relation to them is passive. What this objection reflects is actually a rather old-fashioned, even positivistic assumption about the sources of historical knowledge, but one also which may not surprise us. For as Searle has argued, Derrida's own obsession with the non-problem of objectivity and his failure to recognize our subjective need for knowledge as primary and legitimate, leaves his concerns also laden with residues of positivism.[24] The objection entirely misses the fact that the past, including its historical subjects, comes to the historian through fragmentary and fractured empirical sources, which possess no inherent themes and express no unequivocal voices. In and of themselves, these sources and voices are just noise: 'other' histories uncovered do not speak for themselves any more than the 'facts' of history do. To state the obvious, the historian must undertake the prior, and in part subjective, tasks that only the historian can do: to turn the noise into coherent voices through which the past may speak to the present and to construct the questions to which the past may give the present intelligible answers. Prakash seems to refuse to acknowledge the inevitability (and the responsibility) of this task. Indeed, he offers us a methodology that would seem to rule out even the refusals of which he speaks. He enjoins us to refuse particular themes and categories, most notably those pertaining to the global transition to modern capitalism, lest simply by engaging with them we become implicated in and so reproduce the hegemonies which they represent. But how can we refuse certain themes if we do not know what they are and how can we know what they are if we are not permitted to engage and study them?

Second, and in common with others who have drawn on postmodernist perspectives, Prakash seems to think that it is not possible to recognise differences or resistance under the rubric of general or totalizing systems and theories of transition. There are fundamental misconceptions here. As Raymond Williams and Fredric Jameson have argued in their different ways, it is unclear why a system or process should by definition be incapable of generating difference or raising resistances. Capitalism as most contemporary Marxist historians see it indeed constitutes a system or process but one inherently conflictual and changeful, incapable of realizing or of stabilizing itself. It produces and operates through a wide variety of social relations of production and exploitation, which are themselves in constant transformation. Although its forces may shape forms of resistance, they do not predetermine its outcomes, for no hegemonic system can pervade and exhaust all social experience, least of all one which fails to meet so many human and social needs.[25] Indeed, it is only in the light of some conception of a dominant cultural logic or hegemonic system that resistance, emancipation or difference can be meaningfully identified or measured at all.[26] It is also difficult to take Prakash seriously when he recommends postmodernist perspectives on the grounds that they avoid totalizing forms of theory or explanation. As Jameson has also pointed out, postmodernist approaches are themselves built around a form of totalizing abstraction that distinguishes postmodern culture by its logic of difference and its sustained production of random and unrelated subsystems of all kinds.[27] In these ways, then, post-foundationalist history and the wider perspectives from which it derives seem to us to offer an uncertain and deeply inconsistent premise from which to conceive our relationship to the past.

Representation, Self-representation and Politics

If these practical examples of a post-foundationalist approach seem beset with problems, what of the theoretical arguments, the combination of cultural critiques, styled after Said, Foucauldian perspectives on power, engaged politics of difference, and aspects of postmodernist theory that Prakash sees as animating these new directions in history? The core of his argument is that these perspectives can be combined and employed both to emancipate other histories and to develop new approaches to the larger question of representation and its politics. But there are critical questions here too, in particular as these arguments relate to the wider issue of self-representation by minority and marginal groups themselves and in contexts involving the developed as well as undeveloped nations. As we shall argue, we need to look rather more carefully here at what we are emancipating ourselves into.

Prakash clearly wishes to retain some notion of an emancipatory politics for the dispossessed, as against, for example, an extreme Foucauldian view of the inescapability of relations of power and domination. If we do not wish to hold to some view of political struggle as potentially emancipatory, yet simultaneously refuse to define what the larger structures and trajectories of such struggle might be, on the grounds that this would constitute a totalizing form of analysis, we push the burden of representing such a politics and its trajectories on to those who are in struggle themselves. This is not just by default. The principle of self-representation is, as we shall see, enshrined and positively recommended in much explicit postmodernist theory as the very means to recovering suppressed histories and identities. The obvious problem here, though, is that self-representation, the idea that there can be unitary and centred subjects who are able to speak for themselves and present their experience in their own authentic voices, is precisely what postmodernist theory attacks in the Western humanist tradition.

A number of critics have tried to blur this problem by talking in terms of a kind of rainbow alliance shared among a range of oppositional voices. This may, indeed, be Prakash's attempted solution to this dilemma. He describes how 'the new post-Orientalist scholarship's attempt to release the third world from its marginal position forms a part of the movement that advocates the "politics of difference" – racial, class, gender, ethnic, national and so forth'.[28] This appears at first to resolve the difficulties in privileging self-representation, for what is offered instead is a common platform shared between a variety of dissenting groups, who can speak to and for others and for themselves. In some respects, resistances from the point of view of class, gender, ethnicity or third-world nationhood indeed share common ground; but assuming that these share the same agenda in some more general and positive way simplifies what are actually very complex and sometimes fiercely antagonistic positions.[29] It is also very difficult, from any set of Foucauldian perspectives at least, to generate a common platform or a fusion of struggle for these localized oppositional groups. Doing so means subordinating them to a transcendent or totalizing form of political logic. If it is hard to generate a common agenda for these oppositional groups, we are led back to some form of privileged self-representation. Very clearly, it is tremendously important to attend to the experiences and self-accounts of marginal groups; but this is very different from the nativist view, implicit here, that they have some kind of inherently superior validity. Prakash disassociates himself strongly from such a view, but it is hard to see how he can avoid it, given the contradictions described above.

This leads on to a further set of problems. We are invited to see these new critiques of Orientalist and other forms of privileged knowledge as contestatory acts, to commend their concern with relationships of domination and their efforts to unlock and release histories, cultures and identities frozen by the essentializations of the past. This implies not only that subjects can and do represent themselves on the basis of their experience; it suggests also that their resistances eventuate in forms of knowledge which are emancipatory, transcending relationships of domination, in some senses at least. The problem is that these assumptions are not consonant with the kind of Foucauldian perspective on power and identity that Prakash commends elsewhere. As a range of critics have pointed out, including Said himself, it is difficult to see how any concerted political engagement, let alone one with the processes of capitalist modernization, is possible on the basis of Foucault's deliberately amorphous and dispersed vision of power.[30] Such an engagement looks even less promising when we are told that post-foundationalism's major virtue is its intellectual refusal to accept the very analytical theme of capitalist modernity, lest we take on its ideologies by admitting to any of its realities. The principal casualty of this inadequacy must be politics, for what kind of resistance can be raised to capitalism's systemic coercions if that resistance apparently denies their existence?

Indeed, it is even less clear that one can generate what is ultimately a politics of emancipation from a set of Foucauldian assumptions about power and social relations. Prakash and many who share his approaches vigorously and virtuously assert the presence of struggle in all social relations while saying very little about the systematic political means by which emancipation is to be pursued or what indeed it might look like if it were ever achieved. According to this view, emancipation becomes a struggle purely internal to the consciousness of those who resist and only representable by them. The precise effect of this reading of emancipation back into Foucault is to return these areas of his argument to their sources in Nietzsche. Emancipation becomes a Nietzschean act of pure autonomous will. This might seem an ironic position for a theory concerning itself with the struggles of underclasses,[31] but as Prakash himself notes, this has been precisely the approach of the *Subaltern Studies* group, which he then commends to us for its creative appropriation of post-structuralist perspectives!

There are further difficulties concerning questions of subjectivity and hence of history and agency. Prakash draws on Foucault to argue that subalternity, indeed the multiplicity of changing positions within Indian society, are to be regarded as 'effects of power relations'. The subject-position of the subaltern likewise is an effect, contingent and unstable, which 'resides in difference'. Questions of subjectivity are discussed in terms of the discourses which construct it. Thus,

> the identification with the subordinated's subject-position, rather than national origin, has been the crucial element in formulating critical third-world perspectives. Of course, as subordinated subjects, Indian historians have obviously developed and embraced the victim's subject-position more readily. But because the experience and expression of subordination are discursively formulated, we are led back to the processes and forces that organise the subordinate's subject-position.[32]

The difficulty here is that it is hard to see how this approach can have room for any theory about experience as the medium through which resistances emerge and are crystallized or about the conditions under which the subordinate can become active agents of their own emancipation on the basis of this experience. Some conceptions of experience and agency are absolutely required by the dispossessed's call for a politics of contest, for it is not clear how a dispersed effect of power relations can at the same time be an agent whose experience and reflection form the basis of a striving for change. To argue that we need these categories in some form does not at all imply a return to the undifferentiated and static conceptions of nineteenth-century liberal humanism. Our present challenge lies precisely in understanding how the underclasses we wish to study are at once constructed in conflictual ways as subjects yet also find the means through struggle to realize themselves in coherent and subjectively centred ways as agents.[33]

The question of historical understanding is still more crucial. As Fredric Jameson and Andreas Huyssen have argued, and we have tried in a different way to suggest above, postmodernist approaches desperately lack a sense of history, a capacity for that labour of remembrance and understanding through which agents become able to experience history in an active way, to orient themselves individually and collectively in the present, and so to act. Indeed, this capacity must lie at the very centre of what Prakash and many others call for – in the recovery of frozen and silenced histories as part of a conscious political strategy designed to engage contemporary relations of domination, as these have affected third-world societies. The problem, though, is that it is extremely difficult to see how we can actually have a postmodern perspective which possesses any kind of strong historical sense. On present definitions, the two would seem to be a rather strong contradiction in terms. What distinguishes the former is precisely its sense of depthlessness, of the past's disassembly into a vast collection of images and fragments available in the present only for the purposes of nostalgia or pastiche.[34]

While acknowledging the extent to which he and others have drawn on these perspectives, Prakash certainly emphasizes the very significant differences in their approaches to issues of politics and power. The concerns of postmodernism have in the end been different in two ways. First, they have tended to take pleasure in a Bakhtinian proliferation of voices for its own sake and in a way more aesthetic than political. Second, their own efforts to fragment Western procedures of representation run the risk of using third-world voices and cultures merely as others. Yet Prakash does not really tell us how his more politically engaged stance is substantially different from the politics of postmodernism. In fact, it is striking how much the two have in common. Both are caught between the critique of objectivist forms of representation on the one hand and what becomes a slide towards self-representation on the other. Likewise, post-foundational history tries to dissolve the concepts of experience and identity and to question the use of any historical category 'which resists further decomposition into heterogeneity'. Like postmodern theory itself, this tends to inhibit rather than to promote an active politics.

Ironically, in fact, not all feminist and black criticism, which Prakash would draw into alliance, is actually so hostile to founding categories or concepts of experience, identity or political agency. Within feminist criticism there is, of course, an immensely wide range of positions and approaches; but as Denise Riley has argued, if feminism abandons the category of women and the proposition that they have a different history, it dissolves its own subject. Although feminists contend strongly among themselves as to whether the concept of woman constitutes a universal category, they must for some purposes and at some levels continue to act as if such a category indeed exists, precisely for the reason that the world continues to behave and treat women as though one does.[35] Not all feminists have foreclosed on questions of agency, experience and identity. Both feminism and postmodernism strive to reveal the implication of many forms of knowledge in power, but many feminists argue that they cannot limit themselves to dissection or to the fundamental cultural relativism that underlies postmodernism's refusal to do more than proliferate deconstructive questions. Showing how certain kinds of knowledge are privileged does not in itself change very much. Postmodernism itself cannot provide a theory for or make the move to agency, precisely because it regards all knowledge as tainted and complicit. Because its ultimate concern is with real social change feminism can and must make this move, which also keeps open the possibility that there may be some forms of knowledge which are emancipatory rather than tainted and complicit and which are measured against their usefulness for feminist purposes rather than against the inverted positivist standards of postmodernist epistemology. Likewise, questions of experience and identity remain open ones for many feminists. In the Western tradition, as Linda Hutcheon suggests, women have not been identified historically with origins, authority or ego. On the contrary, they envisage themselves as lacking these attributes already. Their task must be to reconstruct as well as question concepts of self and experience, for as emphasized above, political action becomes impossible if women as subjects see themselves and their experience only in terms of dispersal.[36]

If feminists have made these differences very clear, so too have at least some critics writing from other minority backgrounds, certainly some of those to which Prakash refers. In an article on these minority discourses in their relation to the Western intellectual tradition and its academic institutions, Abdul JanMohamed and David Lloyd do not hesitate to use privileged categories or totalizing forms of analysis. For them, the problems of minority intellectuals spring 'as inevitably from the modes of late capitalist society as do the systematic exploitation of the less privileged minority groups and the feminization of poverty'.[37] They are very clear, moreover, that for all the importance of changes at the level of discourse, emancipation depends ultimately on 'radical transformations of the material structures of exploitation'.[38] The question of identity also remains an open one, significant only in the end for issues of practice and struggle. Fragmented identity

> is for minorities a given of their social existence. But as such a given it is not yet by any means an index of liberation, not even of that formal and abstract liberation which is all that poststructuralism, in itself and disarticulated from any actual process of struggle, could offer. On the contrary, the non-identity of minorities remains the sign of material damage, to which the only coherent response is struggle, not ironic distanciation.[39]

Edward Said: Problems of a Paradigm

That Prakash's position should be so shot through with inconsistencies is in some senses understandable. He takes his definitions and many of his premises from Said, whose text also has many of these same contradictions. It is worth returning to these aspects of Said's work, because Prakash is only one of a great number of historians who seem to us to have based themselves on Said's positions without attending adequately to the problems in them.

It is well known that Said draws heavily on a range of Foucauldian perspectives, both for the analysis of Orientalism as a form of discourse and for his own repudiation of Europe's 'universalising historicism'. He brings these themes together to press home one of his central arguments: Orientalist constructions are not merely inaccurate, biased or in need of replacing with more adequate ones. Rather, Orientalism as a style of authoritative representation is itself the tainted product of an epistemology and an intellectual tradition in which 'the one human history uniting humanity either culminated in or was observed from the vantage point of Europe'.[40]

Said's continuing commitment at other levels both to conventional humanist techniques of representation and to an implicitly universalist discourse of freedom is often less well appreciated. Despite his criticism of Orientalism as a style of representation, he makes it clear that his concern is not to reject the possibility of any kind of objective representation. Knowledge for Said clearly is not just the endlessly self-referential product of all-pervasive power relations. On the contrary, his interest lies in developing forms of representation and knowledge which are emancipatory in their effects and which can serve as a basis for active political commitment and intervention. As he says, unless intellectuals are interested in changing political relations, in dismantling systems of domination as well as defining them, the critique of Orientalism is merely 'an ephemeral pastime'.[41] He sees any worthwhile cultural criticism as 'constitutionally opposed to every form of tyranny, domination, and abuse; its social goals are non-coercive knowledge produced in the interests of human freedom'.[42] This pursuit of criticism's active emancipatory potential is 'a fundamental human and intellectual obligation'.[43] He differs sharply here from Derrida and Foucault, whom he sees as having abandoned the critic's proper task of an engagement which is ultimately political in its nature with the dominant structures of contemporary culture. Derrida elected to illustrate what is undecidable within texts, rather than to investigate their worldly power; and Foucault forgot that ultimately 'the fascinated description of exercised power is never a substitute for trying to change power relations within society'.[44]

Said also reserves a place and a significance for individual agents and individual experience in the shaping of Orientalist discourse: 'Yet unlike Michel Foucault, to whose work I am greatly indebted, I do believe in the determining imprint of individual writers upon the otherwise anonymous collective body of texts constituting a discursive formation like Orientalism'.[45] This position is wildly at odds with Foucault's own unremitting attempts to fragment these categories on the grounds of their humanist and essentialist character. In contrast, Said refers to his own and similar projects as humanist in a broad sense and in an interview in 1986 referred very explicitly both to the contradictions in his own position and to his radical disagreement with Foucauldian perspectives on representation and power: 'Orientalism is theoretically inconsistent, and I designed it that way: I didn't want Foucault's method, or anybody's method, to override what I was trying to put forward. The notion of a non-coercive knowledge, which I come to at the end of the book, was deliberately anti-Foucault.'[46]

How, then, is the critic to go about the universal moral and political tasks which Said commends, without appearing to invoke the tainted authority of European or any other single and dominating intellectual tradition? He notes that a whole range of intellectual projects, just like his own, have already begun to break up old objects of knowledge ruled by Orientalism and to form new fields of investigation. These projects are local and self-convicted but form a common endeavour. Their methods deliberately avoid totalizing and systematizing: rather, they strive consciously to be secular, marginal, oppositional. They work out of a decentred consciousness, intending the end of dominating, coercive systems of knowledge; but they do not seek common unity by appeals to any kind of sovereign authority, methodological consistency, canonicity, science.[47]

The point about consistency is certainly true, for what comes out of all this is a very strained and contradictory position. Said recommends that we abandon totalization and systematization in favour of the off-centre and the marginal. But what view could have been more centrally focused and systematizing than that which he presented in *Orientalism*? What gave the latter its power was precisely its ability to reinterpret, within a single analytical framework, core elements in the European intellectual and political tradition for a very long period and, indeed, to reinterpret them in ways that obscured internal relations of contestation and resistance in Western cultures. If Said had followed his own injunctions, now echoed in Prakash, *Orientalism* would never have been written, with much loss to the whole scholarly community. Again, Said advocates humanist values and a set of universal moral imperatives regarding politics and human freedom, the fundamental obligations of intellectuals, the proper role of cultural criticism. But how are these strong and central normative themes reconciled with the secular and marginal position, the extreme relativist 'plurality of terrains, multiple experiences and different constituencies' which Said commends elsewhere?[48] Ambiguity also marks Said's position on representation. He repudiates the view that only women can write about women, blacks about blacks, that only criticism which treats them well is good criticism. But as he himself says, the kind of local and self-committed intellectual projects he commends are always in danger of slipping into a kind of 'possessive exclusivism', which holds that the only valid kind of representation is the self-representation of insiders.[49]

Of course, it is true that such contradictions can be very fruitful, particularly in hands as deft as Said's. But their fruitfulness lies surely in prompting us to recognize and go beyond them. Moreover, there do seem to be levels in Said's wider position at which creative tensions begin to look like submerged self-contradictions. This was perhaps most interestingly so, for our purposes, in what he said early in 1989 during the battles over Salman Rushdie's work. Rushdie's 'fundamental rights' should be protected, Said argued, because the contemporary world, for all its particularities, must be regarded as one world and human history as one history. (But not, to paraphrase his earlier remarks, a human history seen from Europe's vantage point.) This means that there was no pure unsullied essence to which Muslims or anyone else could return; this single world was irredeemably heterogeneous, and Rushdie's work was a part of that. At the same time, one feature of his work that made it legitimate was that 'Rushdie, from the community of Islam, has written for the West about Islam. *The Satanic Verses* is thus a self-representation.'[50] This brings Said very close to what he rejected earlier about self-representation: its tendency merely to invert the essential categories of Orientalism. It is simply very difficult to combine arguments concerning fundamental rights and possibilities for emancipation with a postmodernist refusal of any kind of unitary or systematizing perspective as to what these rights might be or what emancipation is from or into. Consequently, rights, dominance and emancipation are defined only from the extreme relativist perspective of the multifarious struggles of oppositional groups. And when one version of emancipation conflicts with another, the natural defence for both becomes the principle of self-representation as such.

Historicizing Postmodernism? Perspectives on a Liberal Culture

Why, then, have these perspectives achieved such widespread popularity in Western, particularly American, academic circles? There is now, of course, a large and influential body of postmodernist writing in history and anthropology, mostly published in the United States.[51] This writing does not just embrace postmodernist and post-structuralist strategies partially and contradictorily as Said and Prakash do but advocates them wholeheartedly as the very means to fashion new possibilities for writing and representation in a postcolonial world. There have been a range of prominent contributors here, but perhaps the most influential has been James Clifford, both in the collection edited with George Marcus in 1986, *Writing Culture*, and his own more recent volume of essays, *The Predicament of Culture*.[52] We would like to turn now to look at Clifford's more thoroughgoing recommendation of postmodernist perspectives, to discuss what we see to be its extremely conservative political implications, implications which Prakash cannot logically disassociate himself from.

Clifford himself notes that Said remains 'ambivalently enmeshed in the totalizing habits of Western humanism'.[53] For him, the relativist and post-structuralist features of Said's work make it important; its humanist and universalist elements are merely an unfortunate hang-over from an outmoded intellectual tradition:

> the privilege of standing above cultural particularism, of appealing to the universalist power that speaks for humanity, for universal experiences of love, work, death, etc., is a privilege invented by totalizing Western liberalism.[54]

Clifford's critique of Said flows out of a set of clear postmodernist and post-structuralist commitments. New possibilities for postcolonial ethnography are best opened up through a rejection of all universal forms of understanding culture or the past. Ethnography should focus instead on the ways in which cultures, as forms of 'collectively constituted difference', are in a constant process of local invention, carried out in relation to recent colonial histories and new national identities.[55] In this mobile postcolonial world, in which exotic others return the ethnographer's gaze, new ways must also be found of talking about relations between cultures which emphasize that these are relationships of power. This does not mean, however, that we can devise new theories about global homogenization or the transformation of postcolonial societies in the image of Europe. Certainly, Clifford concedes, there are increasingly pervasive processes of economic and cultural centralization at work. But these do not tell the whole or the only story. What emerges constantly at the level of local societies are new and inventive orders of cultural difference and of subversion, mockery, syncretism and revival, which challenge all efforts to construct any single master narrative of global historical change: 'Indeed, modern ethnographic histories are perhaps condemned to oscillate between two metanarratives: one of homogenization, the other of emergence; one of loss, the other of invention.'[56] Here, then, postmodernist hostility to any kind of universal history, and what is in effect a position of extreme cultural relativism, feed into and reinforce one another. From this perspective, one can see why Clifford is anxious to hold on to some concept of culture itself, for its 'differential and relativist' functions are precisely what is important.[57] What we therefore need, he argues, are new ways of constructing and authorizing knowledge about others. Instead of the ethnographer as the privileged purveyor of such knowledge, we must learn to envisage a world of generalized ethnography and texts which are frankly the product of many voices. This means going beyond methods which make the writer into an omniscient authority and spokesman, which screen off the whole business of research and writing, and which deal with abstract collectivities and typifying processes, such as 'the Nuer think . . .' It means having ethnographies which are open about their status as 'a constructive negotiation involving at least two, and usually more, conscious, politically significant subjects'.[58] These new dialogical approaches not only strive to create texts which are an open-ended interplay of many voices, along the lines that Mikhail Bakhtin envisaged. They also seek to return control over knowledge to its indigenous sources, to represent adequately the authority of informants, and to open real textual spaces for a multitude of indigenous voices whose perspectives and agendas are not imposed on them from outside: 'If accorded an autonomous textual space, transcribed at sufficient length, indigenous statements make sense in terms different from those of the arranging ethnographer. Ethnography is invaded by heteroglossia.'[59]

Although these aims are in some senses still utopian, Clifford points to a range of recent studies that have tried to accord to particularly knowledgeable or sophisticated informants the status not merely 'of independent enunciators, but of writers'.[60] Anthropologists writing from this perspective 'have described the indigenous "ethnographers" with whom they shared, to some degree, a distanced, analytic, even ironic view of custom. These individuals became valued informants because they understood, often with real subtlety, what an *ethnographic* attitude toward culture entailed.'[61] In this way, anthropology has been able not only to move towards a world of plural authorship but to recognize ethnography's participation in the actual invention of culture, as in the collectively produced study, *Piman Shamanism and Staying Sickness.* The ethnographer, Donald Bahr, appears on the title page with three other authors, who are Papago Indians. The book is intended 'to transfer to a shaman as many as possible of the functions normally associated with authorship'.[62] The shaman, Gregorio, is thus the main source for the 'theory of disease' described in the book. The audiences to which the book is addressed are also multiple. Gregorio's commentaries are in Piman, with translations made by the interpreter, David Lopez; and the linguist, Albert Alvarez; and accompanied by Bahr's own interpretations. Thus the book not only keeps distinct the contributions of each but provides material for qualified Papagos as well as for Western audiences. Indeed, Alvarez himself designed the translations so that the book could be used in language teaching, thus contributing to the development of Piman as a written language:

'Thus the book contributes to the Papagos' literary invention of their culture.'[63]

What, then, are the broader implications of this approach? Certainly, issues of power are taken to be central to the relation between ethnographer and writer-informant; and a very large effort is made to change the terms on which they conduct their exchanges. However, we need to look more closely at these terms of exchange and to ask how far they manage to avoid the problems identified earlier. We would like to argue not only that these problems are not avoided, but that there is actually another and much more disturbing political logic in these arguments as presented by Clifford.

Here certainly, the principle of self-representation is pushed to its logical conclusion, which is the self-representation of individuals. This is precisely what is implied in the new dialogical approach to ethnography that Clifford and others advocate as the means to supersede older styles of representation, with their questionable assumptions about authorship, their typifying procedures and their references to abstract collectivities. If we are not to employ the latter, indeed, it certainly is very difficult to see what other categories and accounts ethnographers could work with except for direct indigenous statements, quotations and translations, such as those of Gregorio the shaman, who have a sophisticated knowledge of the culture and an understanding of what a properly ethnographic attitude entails. But because it privileges only the voices of authoritative indigenous individuals, this approach presents a clear problem. It is hard to see how such an approach can recognize or give adequate place to conflict within social contexts thus examined or to those groups or communities who may dissent very strongly from these authoritative accounts. It is not clear how such relationships of power are discussed at all if the analytical means of abstraction and typification are eschewed in favour of a dialogue between individuals.

Indeed, the strategies proposed here look disturbingly similar to those of East Indian Company officials, who also thought of culture as 'collectively constituted difference' in early colonial India. When they wished to elucidate the major principles of what they assumed to be a composite Hindu culture, they turned to the Brahman pandits who were deemed to be experts and authorities in the matter. The result of this privileging of particular informants was the longer-term emergence of an all-India Hindu tradition very much in the image of Brahmanic religious values. These values, now embodied in written legal codes and disseminated in a wide range of social contexts, gradually eroded what had previously been a much more heterogeneous collection of local social and religious practices.[64] Given the great play that Clifford and others make with their vigorous repudiation of all legacies of colonialism, one would have thought that an especial target of their attack would have been precisely this sort of colonial effort to establish dominance through the textualization of cultures in collaboration with carefully chosen indigenous authorities. But this is just the kind of intervention that he seems to recommend in the example of the jointly produced book on Papago culture, in which the shaman Gregorio's translated accounts were designed in part to contribute to 'the Papagos' literary invention of their culture'.

Postmodernism supposedly distinguishes this kind of collaboration from colonial strategies, of course, with the argument that ethnographic consciousness is now no longer the monopoly of Western specialists but is shared with a whole range of indigenous audiences who will scrutinize ethnographic texts and decode them in their own ways. Indigenous as well as Western voices are now free to negotiate and contest such representations on what has become a worldwide cultural stage. Local cultures constantly reinvent themselves within and against these new circumstances of global relationality. Their stories are different. They continually undercut and forbid the construction of any single or totalizing narrative.

To question these basic suppositions is not to deny that indigenous audiences are sharply alive to the political consequences of novel cultural interpretations and interventions. The dissemination of Brahmanical religious values was consciously and bitterly contested in nineteenth-century India and continues to be fought by rather different groups at present. But it is quite a different thing to posit, as Clifford appears to here, a shared ethnographic consciousness, a common participation in the textualization of cultures and in what he calls the 'distanced, analytic, even ironic view of custom' that ethnographic consciousness entails.[65] Most obvious, it seems unlikely that those among indigenous audiences who are neither powerholders nor specialist purveyors of knowledge will be able to afford a detached or abstracted view of custom, particularly when its terms are being reinterpreted from outside as well as from above. Even within the terms of a dialogical approach, which focuses much more narrowly on exchanges between ethnographers and their selected writer-collaborators, it is hard to see how we can speak of a dialogue or negotiation which both share on near-equal terms. The issue is not simply the problem of a text's internal composition, which is the chief concern of dialogical approaches. It is also, as Bob Scholte has argued, that ethnographic texts are subject to external as well as to internal relations of production, which include a professional academic apparatus of seminars, lectures and conferences, funding bodies, research councils and committees of appointment.[66] It would be very difficult to deny that this intellectual and institutional apparatus helps set to a considerable extent the agendas and framing questions which ethnographers take with them into the field and that it also exerts a large control in shaping professional standards, styles of writing, and access to publication; in awarding recognition and conferring academic authority; and in approving and financing further research. Local writer-collaborators may indeed have long-lasting and intimate connections with individual ethnographers. It is much less clear what access and influence they, let alone wider and less privileged indigenous audiences, are able to command in these complex external contexts of a text's production.

This is an extraordinary blindness. As we have seen, postmodernist writing in this field repeatedly insists that its paramount concern is with relationships of power and the immersion of all knowledge within them. But this apparently applies to all knowledge and to all forms of historical and social belonging except the postmodern critic's own. In many ways, such a position is entirely consistent with postmodernism's broader premises, which deny possibilities for an active historical self-understanding and experience in favour of mythified and fabulized stories which melt our sense of the past's solidity. They refuse to equip themselves for any kind of wider historical or sociological vision, for to do so would need the range of analytical tools that both Clifford and Prakash ask us to eschew: privileged categories which 'occlude' other histories, abstract collectivities and typifying processes, totalizing and systematizing forms of understanding. What follows from this, in terms of postmodernism's refusal to examine its own historical provenance, may be consistent; but it is none the less disconcerting. It bears a strange resemblance to colonial strategies of knowledge, which notoriously regarded all indigenous identities and relations as proper objects for investigation (in consultation, of course, with proper indigenous authorities) while veiling its own history from scrutiny.

If, as Clifford sees it, indigenous writers now virtually define and represent themselves through ethnographic texts, so too do local cultures themselves in these new global relationships. In view of postmodernism's hostility to totalities, of course, it is somewhat difficult to hold on to any concept of a culture as such. The way around this, which Clifford takes, is to suggest that cultures may not actually be totalities at all but 'mobile ensembles' that constantly reinvent themselves, tell their own stories and create their own variants on global political relationships. We end up with still a totality but one conceived, like postcolonial subjects themselves, in extremely volatile and voluntaristic ways. Postcolonial societies are free, it would seem almost, to reinvent global political and economic relationships at will. There are forces through which the world is becoming increasingly homogeneous, but we cannot accept a unitary or systematic analysis of these changes. Our stories of homogenization are in the end no different from their stories of local and different self-invention.

What, then, are we to make of the apparent popularity of this combination of extreme cultural relativism with a liberal, almost individualist understanding of these postcolonial societies' ability to define and create themselves? For Prakash, as indeed for others who share his approaches, postmodernist perspectives help make possible a radical-sounding assault, issued along with a declamatory public commitment to the emancipation of marginalized cultures, on all existing frameworks of interpretation. For Clifford, just as for Prakash, modern capitalism's global spread can produce only homogenization, just as any history focusing on the theme of capitalist transition can recognize only homogeneity to the detriment of other and different histories. We see here the postmodernist misconception described above, that systems can only generate sameness. This makes it possible, within a culture deeply antagonistic to any kind of materialist historical explanation, to dismiss suggestions that the local differences we see emerging in postcolonial societies might have something at least to do with logics of differentiation intrinsic to modern capitalism, since it is against and in spite of such logics that these local cultures invent themselves. But the result brings us strangely close to the classic liberal view that culture represents some realm of freedom and choice. Although we can study larger forces of global economic centralization and the coercions they exert, cultural relativism means that this metanarrative can do no more than stand alongside its opposite, that of local cultures' self-creation. Further, these very public commitments to cultural emancipation seem to displace most of the intellectual risk on to writer-collaborators who authorize their own representations, indigenous audiences who decode texts in their own ways, and a range of national, ethnic and other marginalized people who are made responsible for their own self-representation, their own visions of emancipation and political struggles towards it.

Clifford Geertz has identified some of the logics underlying this position. All these approaches (he calls them pretensions) try to 'get round the un-get-roundable fact that all ethnographical descriptions are homemade, that they are the describer's descriptions, not those of the described'.[67] Although the business of representation has become infinitely more complex in recent years, although ethnographers and historians are more sharply aware than ever before of its acute moral and political difficulties, these cannot be shifted on to those whose control over the production of ethnographic texts is more apparent than real; nor can it be resolved through technique:

> The burden of authorship cannot be evaded, however heavy it may have grown; there is no possibility of displacing it onto 'method', 'language' or (an especially popular maneuver at the moment) 'the people themselves' redescribed ('appropriated' is probably the better term) as co-authors.[68]

We would go rather further than this. These postmodernist approaches, particularly Clifford's, actually offer us an epistemology that denies that its own history can be seriously investigated and an analytical preoccupation with a very narrowly defined set of individual relationships. Effectively depoliticized by being insulated from their material and institutional contexts, these relationships are presented as an arena in which indigenous collaborators and audiences are free, as it were, to invent and be themselves. Such efforts to sever off spheres of activity for free individuals or cultures are a very old device of liberal ideology. The British colonial record is full of them.

If all this looks more like a device for legitimation than any basis for an emancipatory form of knowledge, what is being legitimized? Said, Huyssen and others have made the point that French postmodernism and post-structuralism underwent a peculiar metamorphosis when they were domesticated within American liberal culture from the early 1960s. Their rapid growth in popularity reflected the degree to which they were eviscerated of their earlier and radical political content by literary and cultural critics, who converted them into forms of 'writerly connoisseurism and textual gentrification'.[69] We see these intellectual positions sustaining key aspects of contemporary political culture in the United States. The first concerns the way in which the advance of arguments about the self-representation of third-world peoples fits neatly into its self-consciously multi-minority academic culture. What marks debate here is, of course, a deep concern with multiple and conflictual identities. Yet what is striking about these debates, particularly those employing postmodernist perspectives, is how one particular identity, that of class or material relations, is so often downplayed or screened off. Not only do participants in these debates frequently ignore questions of class, but they see themselves also as having to challenge the larger intellectual tradition of historical materialism that establishes those questions as central, on the grounds that its universalist and objectivist pretensions are really no different to those of liberal modernization theory. One consequence of this is that self-defined minority or subaltern critics are saved from doing what they constantly demand of others, which is to historicize the conditions of their own emergence as authoritative voices – conditions which could hardly be described without reference of some kind to material or class relations.

At other levels, the exclusion of class and of the materialist critique of capitalism from the agenda of scholarship has implications that seem to us absolutely critical. What it means is that the true underclasses of the world are only permitted to present themselves as victims of the particularistic kinds of gender, racial and national oppression which they share with preponderantly middle-class American scholars and critics, who would speak with or in their voices. What such underclasses are denied is the ability to present themselves as classes: as victims of the universalistic, systemic and material deprivations of capitalism which clearly separate them off from their subaltern expositors. In sum, the deeply unfortunate result of these radical postmodernist approaches in the minorities debate is thus to reinforce and to give new credence to the well-known hostility of American political culture to any kind of materialist or class analysis.

These approaches also seem to us to have had important and wider implications in American political and academic culture. Another anthropologist who employs them, Paul Rabinow, tells us engagingly that he is 'temperamentally more comfortable in an oppositional stance'.[70] The same seems to be true of a wide range of current academic writing. There runs through it a desire to be seen on the side of the dispossessed against power, working with their strange voices and different stories, subverting dominant cultures and intellectual traditions 'from within the academy'. But in the case of postmodernist approaches, these commitments can be made with a lightened burden of authorship and a comforting sense that in this volatile new world of cultural self-invention, the critic's own history is at best a fable. What all this begins to look very like, in fact, is a new form of that key and enduring feature of Western capitalist and imperialist culture: the bad conscience of liberalism, still struggling with the continuing paradox between an ideology of liberty at home and the reality of profoundly exploitative political relations abroad, and now striving to salve and re-equip itself in a postcolonial world with new arguments and better camouflaged forms of moral authority. But the solutions it offers – methodological individualism, the depoliticizing insulation of social from material domains, a view of social relations that is in practice extremely voluntaristic, the refusal of any kind of programmatic politics – do not seem to us radical, subversive or emancipatory. They are on the contrary conservative and implicitly authoritarian, as they were indeed when recommended more overtly in the heyday of Britain's own imperial power.

Prakash himself does not push these perspectives to their most authoritarian conclusions and tries rightly to be critical of their depoliticizing effects. But since he shares many of their core assumptions, his efforts result in ambiguity and contradiction. His is basically an attempt, like that of Said and of many others who try to use his position as a point of departure, to ride two horses at once. But one of these may not be a horse that brooks inconstant riders, and Said himself does at least seem to know which of them in the end he would rather be on.

Acknowledgements

We would like to thank Ajay Skaria, Crispin Bates, Saurabh Dube, David Ludden, Fred Reid and Burt Stein for their reading and comments on this paper.

Notes

1. Gyan Prakash, 'Writing Post-Orientalist Histories of the Third World: Perspectives from Indian Historiography', in this volume, pp. 163–90.
2. Ibid., 169.
3. Ibid., 176–7.
4. Ibid., 178.
5. Ibid., 177.
6. Ibid., 180.
7. Ibid., 183.
8. Ibid., 185.
9. Ibid., 179.
10. Ibid., 183–4.
11. Ibid., 184.
12. John Searle, 'The Word Turned Upside Down', *New York Review of Books* (27 October 1983), 78. A good introduction to this debate is in Jürgen Habermas, *The Philosophical Discourse of Modernity* (Cambridge: Polity Press, 1990), 194–9. Ajay Skaria kindly provided this reference.
13. Prakash's notion of what constitutes Marxist history is problematic, for neither of the two examples which he provides fall easily into the category. The first, concerning Bengali histories of the Bengali renaissance, would seem most influenced by Bengali nationalist ideology, as it is not clear why Bengal's failure to generate a secular rationalist culture and a bourgeois social order prior to the development of industrial capitalism is a problem for Marxism. The second, concerning usage of Andre Gunder Frank's concept of underdevelopment, also ill fits the category, for the concept derives from neo-Smithian rather than Marxist economic theory: see R. Brenner, 'The Origins of Capitalist Development: A Critique of Neo-Smithian Marxism', *New Left Review*, 104:4 (1977), 25–92.
14. See, for example, T. H. Aston and C. H. E. Philpin, eds, *The Brenner Debate*

(Cambridge: Cambridge University Press, 1985); T. J. Byres and Harbans Mukhia, eds, 'Feudalism and Non-European Societies', *Journal of Peasant Studies* (Special Issue), 12:2, 3 (January, April 1985).

15. For these arguments in Bayly, see *The Local Roots of Indian Politics: Allahabad 1880–1920* (Oxford: Oxford University Press, 1975); *Rulers, Townsmen and Bazaars: North Indian Society in the Age of British Expansion* (Cambridge: Cambridge University Press, 1983) and *Indian Society and the Making of the British Empire* (Cambridge: Cambridge University Press, 1988). For a general guide to recent research in this field, see D. A. Washbrook, 'Progress and Problems: South Asian Economic and Social History c. 1720–1860', *Modern Asian Studies*, 22.1 (1988), 57–96.

16. These arguments are developed in C. A. Bayly, *Imperial Meridian: The British Empire and the World 1780–1830* (London: Longman, 1989).

17. Prakash, 'Writing Post-Orientalist Histories', 177.

18. Idem.

19. See, for example, Cohn's 'The Command of Language and the Language of Command', in R. Guha, ed., *Subaltern Studies IV* (Delhi: Oxford University Press, 1985), 279–80.

20. See especially Ashis Nandy, *The Intimate Enemy: Loss and Recovery of Self Under Colonialism* (Delhi: Oxford University Press, 1983).

21. Ranajit Guha, *Subaltern Studies I* (Delhi: Oxford University Press, 1982), 7.

22. Guha's latest contribution to *Subaltern Studies*, 'Dominance without Hegemony and Its Historiography', distinguishes between a British and a pre-colonial Indian form of political authority, the latter organized around principles of Brahmanic and kingly authority. He concludes by describing his argument as 'a critique of our *own* approach to the Indian past and our *own* performance in writing about it', designed to 'assist in the *self-criticism of our own historiography* – the historiography of a colonized people' (Guha's emphasis; *Subaltern Studies IV* [Delhi: Oxford University Press, 1989], 306–7).

23. In this case, the royal and dominant Kallar caste in Pudukottai. See Nicholas B. Dirks, *The Hollow Crown: Ethnohistory of an Indian Kingdom* (Cambridge: Cambridge University Press, 1987).

24. Searle, 'The World Turned Upside Down', 78–9.

25. Raymond Williams, *Marxism and Literature* (Oxford: Oxford University Press, 1977), 125; Fredric Jameson, 'Marxism and Postmodernism', *New Left Review*, no. 176 (1989), 34–9.

26. Fredric Jameson, 'Postmodernism, or the Cultural Logic of Late Capitalism', *New Left Review*. no. 146 (1984), 57.

27. Jameson, 'Marxism and Postmodernism'. 34.

28. Prakash, 'Writing Post-Orientalist Histories', 185.

29. On the issue of *sati* in India, for example, compare Ashis Nandy, *At the Edge of Psychology: Essays in Politics and Culture* (Delhi: Oxford University Press, 1980), 1–31, with Sharada Jain, Nirja Misra and Kavita Shrivastava, 'Deorala Episode: Women's Protest in Rajasthan', *Economic and Political Weekly*, nos. 7, 11 (1987), 1891–94. See also the very interesting discussion of Nandy's position on the Roop Kanwar case in Lata Mani, 'Multiple Mediations: Feminist Scholarship in the Age of Multinational Reception', *Inscriptions*, no. 5 (1989), 15–16.

30. Edward Said, *The World, the Text and the Critic* (London: Faber and Faber, 1984), 245.

31. The wider and deeply conservative implications of post-Nietzschean projects for emancipation outside any framework of instrumental reason are discussed in Jürgen Habermas's classic article, 'Modernity versus Postmodernity', *New German Critique*, 22 (Winter 1981).

32. Prakash, 'Writing Post-Orientalist Histories', 181–2.

33. This question of how we might conceptualize the presence of the subaltern is discussed further and with different emphases in R. O'Hanlon, 'Recovering the Subject: *Subaltern Studies* and Histories of Resistance in Colonial South Asia', in this volume.

34. For these arguments in Jameson and Huyssen, see Jameson, 'Postmodernism,

or the Cultural Logic of Late Capitalism', especially pp. 64–71; and Andreas Huyssen, *After the Great Divide: Modernism, Mass Culture and Postmodernism* (London: Macmillan, 1988).

35. Denise Riley, *Am I That Name? Feminism and the Category of 'Women' in History* (London: Macmillan, 1988), 112–14.

36. Linda Hutcheon, *The Politics of Postmodernism* (London: Routledge, 1989), 39 and 167–8.

37. Abdul R. JanMohamed and David Lloyd, 'Introduction: Minority Discourse – What is to Be Done?', *Cultural Critique*, Fall (1987), 12.

38. Ibid., 15.

39. Ibid., 16.

40. Edward Said, 'Orientalism Reconsidered', in Francis Barker *et al.*, eds, *Literature, Politics and Theory* (London: Methuen, 1986), 223.

41. Ibid., 229.

42. Said, *The World*, 29.

43. Ibid., 30.

44. Ibid., 222.

45. Said, *Orientalism* (London: Peregrine Books, 1985), 23.

46. See the interview with Said in Imre Salusinszky, *Criticism in Society* (London: Methuen, 1987), 137.

47. Said, 'Orientalism Reconsidered', 228.

48. Idem.

49. Ibid., 229.

50. This short article appeared in the *Observer* newspaper (26 February 1989), 14.

51. Useful introductions to this literature are Andreas Huyssen, *After the Great Divide: Modernism, Mass Culture and Postmodernism*; and D. Kellner, ed., *Postmodernism, Jameson, Critique* (Washington, D.C.; Maisonneuve Press, 1989).

52. James Clifford and George E. Marcus, eds, *Writing Culture: The Poetics and Politics of Ethnography* (Berkeley: University of California Press, 1986); James Clifford, *The Predicament of Culture: Twentieth-Century Ethnography, Literature and Art* (Cambridge, Mass.: Harvard University Press, 1988).

53. Clifford, *The Predicament of Culture*. 271.

54. Ibid., 263.

55. Ibid., 274. For a good summary of the arguments about culture as collectively constituted, see Roger M. Keesing, 'Anthropology as Interpretative Quest', *Current Anthropology*, 28:2 (April 1987).

56. Clifford, *The Predicament of Culture*, 17.

57. Ibid., 274.

58. Ibid., 41.

59. Ibid., 51.

60. Idem.

61. Ibid., 49.

62. Ibid., 51.

63. Ibid., 52.

64. Historians have documented this process across a range of fields. See, for example, L. Mani, 'Contentious Traditions: The Debate on Sati in Colonial India', *Cultural Critique*, Fall (1987); D. Washbrook, 'Law, State and Agrarian Society in Colonial India', *Modern Asian Studies*, 15:3 1981; R. O'Hanlon, 'Cultures of Rule, Communities of Resistance: Gender, Discourse and Tradition in Recent South Asian Historiographies', *Social Analysis*, no. 25 (September 1989); C. A. Bayly, *Indian Society and the Making of the British Empire*, 136–68; N. Dirks, 'The Invention of Caste: Civil Society in Colonial India', *Social Analysis*, no. 5 (September 1989); Lucy Carroll, 'Law, Custom and Statutary Social Reform: The Hindu Widow's Remarriage Act of 1856', *Indian Economic and Social History Review*, 20:4 (1983).

65. Clifford, *The Predicament of Culture*, 49.

66. Bob Scholte, 'The Literary Turn in Contemporary Anthropology', *Critique of Anthropology*, 7:1, 38.

67. Clifford Geertz, *Works and Lives: The Anthropologist as Author* (Cambridge: Polity Press, 1988), 144.

68. Ibid., 140.

69. Huyssen, *After the Great Divide*, 212; Said, *The World*, 3–5.

70. Paul Rabinow, 'Representations Are Social Facts: Modernity and Post-Modernity in Anthropology', in Clifford and Marcus, *Writing Culture*, 258.

10

Can the 'Subaltern' Ride? A Reply to O'Hanlon and Washbrook

Gyan Prakash

The problem with Prakash, O'Hanlon and Washbrook conclude, is that he tries to ride two horses at once – one Marxist, the other post-structuralist–deconstructionist.[1] 'But one of these may not be a horse that brooks inconstant riders . . .'. So, they say we must choose only one to ride on, not both, because the two, in their view, have opposing trajectories. One advances historical understanding and progressive change, the other denies history and perpetuates a retrogressive status quo. Posed in this manner, the choices involve more than a dispute over which paradigm provides a better understanding of the histories of the third world and India. At stake is the writing of history as politicial practice, and the only safe bet, from their point of view, is Marxism (of their kind), not the endless deferral and nihilism of deconstruction and postmodernism. Having set up this opposition, O'Hanlon and Washbrook's either/or logic has no place for the productive tension that the combination of Marxist and deconstructive approaches generates. They are uncomfortable with those recent writings that employ Marxist categories to analyse patterns of inequalities and exploitation while also using deconstructive approaches to contend that Marxism is part of the history that institutionalized capitalist dominance – approaches which argue that although Marxism can rightfully claim that it historicizes the emergence of capitalism as a world force, it cannot disavow its history as a nineteenth-century European discourse that universalized the mode-of-production narrative. Obviously, this is a strategy predicated on the understanding that historical processes and their critical analysis operate ambivalently; but because such a strategy cannot provide mastery, O'Hanlon and Washbrook resist the ambivalence involved in recognizing complicity in a history that the critic also seeks to unravel. Therefore, called upon to deconstruct structures and identities rendered foundational by history and faced with the admittedly difficult but enabling strategy of writing histories in terms other than in those they come to us, my critics present us with a stark dichotomy. We are offered the choice of either recognizing that history is structured by certain master narratives, the direction of responsible and critical thinking, or entertaining the illusion that there exist forces and processes other than those authorized by master categories – the road to irresponsible, endless deferral. By thus posing historical writing and deconstructive criticism as opposites, O'Hanlon and Washbrook overlook the possibility of exceeding the limits that history imposes on criticism – a possibility opened up when we recognize that criticism derives both its potential and its limits from its historicity. Turning away from the ambivalent criticism that such a perspective provides, O'Hanlon and Washbrook's desire for a pure, contradiction-free strategy reaches for horses to ride to mastery.

The use of the image of the rider is worth pursuing because it illustrates what is at issue in the desire for mastery over ambivalence. In nineteenth-century India, the British used, among other things, the inability of the Western-educated Indian (the Bengali *babu*) to ride horses to keep them out of the covenanted civil service. By pointing to a lack in the Indian, the polarity between the native and the Englishman was preserved, thus containing the threat that the equivocal figure of the English-speaking Indian posed to the binary structure of colonizer and the colonized. The British rulers' deceit in using the Indian's lack of horse-riding skills can be construed in the same way as Homi Bhabha reads the utilization of pseudo-scientific theories and the citation of spurious authorities in colonial discourses – that is, as an attempt to normalize the ambivalence produced in the contradictory enunciation of the colonial discourse. This ambivalence, he argues, arose in the colonial discourse from the 'tension between the synchronic panoptical vision of domination – the demand for identity, stasis – and the counter-pressure of the diachrony of history – change, difference'.[2] Under these opposing pressures, the colonial discourse was caught up in conflict, split between 'what is always "in place", already known, and something that must be anxiously repeated . . . as if the essential duplicity of the Asiatic or the bestial sexual license of the African that needs no proof, can never really, in discourse, be proved'.[3] If, on the one hand, the colonial discourse asserted that the colonizers and the colonized were fixed, unchanging identities, the repetition of this assertion, on the other hand, meant that discourse was forced constantly to reconstitute, refigure this fixity: consequently, the discourse was split between proclaiming the unchangeability of colonial subjects and acknowledging their changing character by having to re-form, reconstitute subjects. If it produced a dichotomy between the colonizer and the colonized that operated to secure domination in the Hegelian form of master–slave and self–other dialectic, then the discourse's operation also gave rise to figures and processes which could not be easily accommodated in the given structure of power relations.[4] Either way, such conflict caused the colonial discourse to serve domination equivocally. Bhabha traces an example of such an ambivalent functioning of discourse in the construction of the colonial stereotype of mimicmen imposed on English-speaking Indians. He argues that if the British portrayal of the resemblance of Anglicized Indians with Englishmen as mimicry was a 'strategy of reform, regulation, and discipline, which "appropriates" the Other', the stereotype of mimicry was also the mark of a recalcitrant difference, '*a difference that is almost the same, but not quite*'.[5] If the colonial discourse produced a reformed Other – the Anglicized Indian – the product only resembled, but did not replicate, the Self. Because the resemblance alluded not only to sameness but also to a recalcitrant difference – 'not white/not quite' – a conflictory economy, based on the simultaneous domestication and recognition of difference, was set into motion. In this economy, because sameness – 'English in taste, in opinions, in morals, and in intellect' – was embodied in the strange – 'Indian in blood and colour' – the self-sameness changed to grotesque difference. Mimicry returned as menacing mockery. An assertion of mastery countered the threat that the ambivalence of this mimicry posed to the binary opposition of the colonizer and the colonized by pointing either to a crucial lack (poor horse-riding skills) or a ludicrous excess (the 'Johnsonian English' of the Anglicized Indian).

O'Hanlon and Washbrook also counter the threat of equivocality ('riding two horses at once') that they see in my arguments for post-foundational histories with a discourse that longs for mastery and has the ability to survey the field from a panoptic position and speak in a singular voice. Deeply problematic for them are my arguments for historical writings that resist the urge to ground history in foundational themes and describe histories that both inhabited and exceeded different systems of power, culture, identity formation and subject position. From their point of view, anything less than a totalizing vision appears as inadequate, confused, not in control. Thus not only are my views characterized as 'deeply misconceived' (p. 196), I also become one of the many who do not really know what is going on (Prakash is 'only one of a great number of historians who seem . . . to have based themselves on Said's positions without attending adequately to the problems in them' [p. 204]). Joining the horde of post-structuralists and postmodernists (the two are the same in their opinion), my position becomes 'shot through with inconsistencies' (p. 204); and because I follow Jacques Derrida, Michel Foucault and postmodernists without knowing that they are 'inherently inimical' to historical praxis, I land inevitably in the camp of American political culture. What is worse, I cannot avoid views which, along with those of James Clifford, place me in a relation of 'strange resemblance to colonial strategies of knowledge' (p. 212). Other writers also receive a rough treatment, as they are grossly misread and summarily dismissed.[6]

The condescending and dismissive tone is not accidental; it flows out of their desire for mastery over ambivalence. The nature of their enterprise is to assert the supremacy of an either/or logic through hasty, simplistic and even ill-informed readings of my essay and of many others whose writings are faulted for one reason or another. I will confine my response to the five areas in which their desire for an unequivocal strategy leads them to serious misreadings: Derrida and the critique of foundations; deconstructive criticism and the possibility of historical writing; the theme of capitalist modernity and its relation to colonialism; Edward Said's *Orientalism* and its relation to liberal humanism; and postmodernism and the politics of differentiated subject positions.

Derrida and the Critique of Foundations

It is perhaps not surprising that Derrida, a philosopher who has striven the most in recent times to show the possibility and impossibility of master categories, is the biggest casualty of hasty and ill-advised reading. We are told that Derrida's critique of foundational thought 'can do little more than reveal, over and over again, the subjective and arbitrary nature of our categories and the uncertainty of knowledge derived from them' (p. 195); that 'preoccupied with the non-problem of objectivity', he can only lead us into an 'intellectual cul-de-sac' (p. 194). Strong words. But not one of Derrida's writings and interviews is cited as a basis for this reading. Instead, we are offered John Searle's review essay in the *New York Review of Books* as the authoritative word on Derrida. We are told, on Searle's authority, that, laden as he is with the 'residues of positivism', Derrida is hardly in a position to offer us a new method, let alone one with 'purposive adequacy' (p. 195). As this extraordinary misreading informs their views on my critique of foundational history, let us examine the prejudice that Derrida is a philosopher of scepticism and nihilistic demolition.

Deconstruction is emphatically not about showing the arbitrariness of our categories; rather, its purpose has been to show that structures of signification effect their closures through a strategy of opposition and hierarchization that edit, suppress and marginalize everything that upsets founding values. And yet the very staging of this strategy reveals what is repressed. Derrida explores the marks of such closures and disclosures in the odd turns of phrase, silences, unguarded details and contradictions in texts overlooked by traditional notions of meaning, identity, authorial intentions. In *Of Grammatology*, Derrida shows that Rousseau's conception of speech as the origin of language and writing as its degradation involves placing the latter as a supplement in order to establish the originality of speech. He then goes on to show that the logic of supplementarity renders problematic the idea of origin: 'Supplemantarity wrenches language from its condition of origin.'[7] Derrida concludes from this that the place of writing in Western metaphysics has been 'a debased, lateralized, repressed, displaced theme, yet exercising a permanent and obsessive pressure from the place it remains held in check'.[8] Referring to this powerful myth of presence, its effects, and how its repression of the Other is incomplete, Derrida writes:

> Metaphysics – the white mythology which reassembles and reflects the culture of the West: the white man takes his own mythology, Indo-European mythology, his own *logos*, that is, the *mythos* of his idiom, for the universal form that he must still wish to call Reason . . . White mythology – metaphysics has erased within itself the fabulous scene that has produced it, the scene that nevertheless remains active and stirring, inscribed in white ink, an invisible design covered over in the palimpsest.[9]

It would be a gross misreading to conclude from the above passage that its deconstruction of the founding myth of presence is directed just to show the non-objective character of our knowledge. On the contrary, the purpose of disclosing that origins operate by erasing the signs of their own production is to undo foundations, to open up the structure of *différance* for rearticulation. The purposive adequacy of this strategy, then, consists in revealing that the politics displacing other claims to the margins can be undone by rearticulating the structure of differences that existing foundations seek to suppress and that strategies for challenging the authority and power derived from various foundational myths (History as the March of Man, Reason, Civilization, Progress, Modes-of-Production) lie inside, not outside, the ambivalence that these myths seek to suppress. From this point of view, critical work seeks its basis not without but within the fissures of dominant structures. Or, as Gayatri Chakravorty Spivak puts it, the deconstructive philosophical position consists in saying an 'impossible "no" to a structure, which one critiques, yet inhabits intimately'.[10] *Inconstant rider?*

Deconstructive Criticism and Historical Writing

Because they disavow equivocality, O'Hanlon and Washbrook fail to see that deconstruction opens up productive ways of reading and reinscribing the structure of ambivalence closed by foundations in serving certain types of authority and power. Instead, they choose to read its critique of foundational thought as amounting to no more than a demonstration that our knowledge is subjective. Therefore, when my essay proposes that the thematization of modern history in terms of capitalist modernity fails to place that history in a critical light, they jump to the conclusion that I am saying nothing, except to repeat 'over and over again', that our knowledge is subjective. They follow this extraordinary conclusion with the assertion that the critique of foundations leads to the paralysis of the interpreter because deconstruction's alleged 'residual positivism' results in a failure to see that 'the past, including its historical subjects, comes to the historian through fragmentary and fractured empirical sources, which possess no inherent themes and express no unequivocal voices' (p. 198). Because the past comes as 'noise', they continue, it is the responsibility of the historian to give it voice – a responsibility that they think I duck because deconstruction and postmodernism regard any intervention by the historian/interpreter in the past as inherently illegitimate, a kind of complicity' (p. 198).

Let us attend to the noise first. Is it the case that the past comes to us through empirical sources with no inherent themes, as noise? Evoked here is a primeval scene, an original encounter before history when the historian faces fragmentary and fractured empirical sources and seeks to give it voice. This staging of interpretation as the first encounter between the all-powerful interpreter and the lifeless evidence is blind to the history of its own enactment. Hidden from its view are the stories told in the very presence of particular sources and in the processes by which the historian gets placed as a sovereign interpreter who turns noise into voice. Gone are the traces of the history of archives, the monumentalization of history in documents, and erased are the marks of the historian's conditioning in this dramatization of interpretation as the first discovery.

To illustrate the point that empirical sources do not enunciate noise but a structure of audible historical voices, let us take an example. Among the sources on modern India are archival documents dealing with the abolition of *sati*, or Hindu widow sacrifice in the early nineteenth century. These do not come as noise to us; we encounter them as voices speaking of other encounters between the British civilizing mission and Hindu heathenism, between modernity and tradition; and of previous readings about the beginning of the emancipation of Hindu women and about the birth of modern India. If we ignore the fact that these sources come with stories to tell, we run the risk of believing them uncritically and disregarding their history as archives of imperialism and patriarchy; for, as Lata Mani has shown,[11] the very existence of these documents has a history involving the fixing of women as the site for the colonial and the indigenous male elite's constructions of authoritative Hindu traditions. The accumulated sources on *sati* – whether or not the burning of widows was sanctioned by Hindu codes, did women go willingly or not to the funeral pyre, on what grounds could the immolation of women be abolished – come to us marked by early-nineteenth-century colonial and indigenous patriarchal discourses. And just as the early-nineteenth-century encounter between colonial and indigenous elites on the one hand, and textual sources on the other, was resonant not with noise but with colonial patriarchal voices, the historian's confrontation today with sources on *sati* cannot but escape the echo of that previous rendezvous. In repeating that encounter, how does the historian today *not replicate* the early-nineteenth-century staging of *sati* as a contest between tradition and modernity (or different visions of tradition), between the slavery of women and efforts towards their emancipation, between barbaric Hindu practices and the British civilizing mission? Lata Mani accomplishes this task brilliantly by showing that the opposing arguments were founded on the fabrication of the law-giving scriptural tradition as the origin of Hindu customs: both those who supported and those who opposed *sati* sought the authority of textual origins for their beliefs. During the debate, however, the whole history of the fabrication of origins was effaced, as was the collusion between indigenous patriarchy and colonial power in constructing the origins for and against *sati*. Consequently, as Spivak states starkly, the debate left no room for the woman's enunciatory position. Caught in the contest over whether traditions did or did not sanction *sati* and over whether the woman self-immolated willingly or not, the colonized subaltern woman disappeared: she was either literally extinguished for her dead husband in the indigenous patriarchal discourse or was offered the disfiguring liberation of the Western notion of sovereign, individual will.[12]

In other words, it is not as if the sources come with a noise in which the historian can decipher the woman's voice. Nor is the problem one of sources (the absence of woman's testimony), but that the very staging of the debate left no place for the widow's enunciatory position: she is left no position from which she can speak. Without doubt Spivak makes this silencing of the woman speak of the limits of historical knowledge, but the critic can do so because the colonial archive comes not with noise but with a pregnant silence.[13] Contrary to O'Hanlon and Washbrook's charge that deconstruction refuses to take responsibility for interpretation, Spivak very correctly marks the silencing of the subaltern woman as the point at which the interpreter must acknowledge the limits of historical understanding; for it is impossible to retrieve the woman's voice when she was not given a subject-position from which to speak. But this refusal to retrieve the woman's voice because it would involve the conceit that the interpreter speaks for her does not disable understanding; rather, Spivak manages to reinscribe the colonial and indigenous patriarchal archive when she shows that the tradition versus modernization story was told by obliterating the colonized women's subject-position. Here, the interpreter's recognition of the limit of historical knowledge does not disable criticism but enables the critic to mark the space of the silenced subaltern as *aporetic* that, by resisting a paternalist recovery of the subaltern's voice, frustrates our repetition of the imperialist attempt to speak for the colonized subaltern woman. *Basically, an attempt to ride two horses at once.*

The Relationship between Capitalism and History

Let us now move to O'Hanlon and Washbrook's objection to my argument that representing Indian history in terms of the theme of capitalist modernity cannot constitute critical writing because it does not displace the categories framed in and by that history. At issue here is the relationship between capitalism and difference. In my essay, I had stated that we cannot thematize Indian history in terms of the development of capitalism and yet also contest capitalism's homogenization of the contemporary world. Critical history cannot simply document the process by which capitalism becomes dominant, for that amounts to repeating the history we seek to displace; instead, criticism must reveal the difference that capitalism either represents as the particular form of its universal existence or sketches only in relation to itself. These two authors contend that my position not only commits me to viewing capitalism as a 'disposable fiction' (p. 196) but is also based on a simplistic understanding of the relationship between capitalism and heterogeneity (p. 196). Their alternative proposes that we recognize the structure of domination as a totality (capitalism) and that this conception alone provides the basis for understanding the sources of historical oppression and formulating critical emancipatory positions.

Does a refusal to thematize modern Indian history in terms of the development of capitalism amount to saying that capitalism is a disposable fiction and that class relations are illusory? Not at all. My point is that making capitalism the foundational theme amounts to homogenizing the histories that remain heterogeneous with it. As this formulation attracts the most vehement objection, let me elaborate it a bit further than I did in my essay. It is one thing to say that the establishment of capitalist relations has been one of the major features in India's recent history but quite another to regard it as the foundation of colonialism. It is one thing to say that class relations affected a range of power relations in India – involving the caste system, patriarchy, ethnic oppression, Hindu–Muslim conflicts – and quite another to oppose the latter as forms assumed by the former. The issue here is not that of one factor versus several; rather, it is that, as class is inevitably articulated with other determinations, power exists in a form of relationality in which the dominance of one is never complete. For example, although the colonial rule in India constructed the labour force according to the economy of the free–unfree opposition, this domestication of otherness (of Hindu and Islamic forms of slavery) as unfreedom also left, to use Derrida's evocative formulation, 'an invisible design covered over in the palimpsest'.[14] It is precisely by sketching the 'invisible design covered over in the palimpsest' that capitalism's attempts either to subsume different structures within itself or polarize them as its opposite can be shown as incompletely successful. This task cannot be accomplished by regarding history as a noise that we turn into a coherent voice, for that amounts to pretending that the investigator occupies a space outside history and that sources do not come to us already with some stories to tell. If, as I am suggesting, the investigator stands squarely in the middle of history, inhabiting a structure that seeks to place colonialism within a mode-of-production narrative, then the investigator's critical role is to examine the fault-lines of this discourse. Only then could the investigator deal responsibly with the historicity of his or her own position as an historical subject. Specifically, this means making visible the ambivalence and alterity present in the constitution of capitalism as a foundational theme. It means listening attentively when the culture and history that the critic inhabits make capitalism name and speak for histories that remained discrepant with it. To the extent that these discrepancies are made to speak in the language of capitalism – as pre-capitalist peasants, unfree labourers, irrational peasants – its foundational status is not a disposable fiction. But it is equally true that, in domesticating all the wholly other subject positions as self-consolidating otherness (*pre*-capitalist, *un*-free labourers, *ir*-rational peasants), capitalism is also caught in a structure of ambivalence it cannot master. This is why study after study shows that capitalism in the third world, not just in India, was crucially distorted, impure, mixed with pre-capitalist survivals. To think of the incompleteness and failures of capitalist modernity in the third world in critical terms, therefore, requires that we reinscribe the binary form in which capitalism's partial success is portrayed, that we render visible processes and forms that its oppositional logic can appropriate only violently and incompletely. Of course, historians cannot recover what was suppressed, but they can critically confront the effects of that silencing, capitalism's foundational status, by writing histories of irretrievable subject positions, by sketching the traces of figures that come to us only as disfigurations. Again, not to restore the original figures but to find the limit of foundations in shadows that the disfigurations themselves outline.

This strategy strikes O'Hanlon and Washbrook, who want to get on with the business of showing how the British conquest of India forms a part of the larger theme of the development of world capitalism, as nihilistic.[15] But if 'colonialism was the logical outcome of South Asia's own history of capitalist development', as Washbrook writes elsewhere,[16] one is entitled to ask: how did this logic make the English East India Company the ruler? If the configuration of class forces produced indigenous agents for India's colonization, why was it that these remained just that – collaborators? How did the universalistic logic of capital discriminate between turning power over to the English company and making the natives into the ruled? Washbrook can only offer specific histories of South Asia and Europe, making an unacknowledged gesture towards such particularistic sources as region, culture, race, nation . . . in other words, difference. So, it turns out that, in the very process of appropriating difference, the sovereign logic of capital gets compromised, its universality undone. Even the most insistent claim for the foundational status of capitalism cannot do without the supplementarity of the particularistic! Instead of pursuing the logic of supplementarity to split the originating presence of capitalism and rather than exploring the cohabitation of capital with race and culture, O'Hanlon and Washbrook wish to retain the pure presence of capital. How and why this logic of capital distinguishes between brown and white people in the latter's favour gets tucked away from our sight, and colonialism – the violent institution of a set of racial, political, epistemic and economic systems – becomes an unfortunate episode in the narrative of mode-of-production. The Cambridge School's long dormant historiography of India,[17] which sought in the 1970s to delegitimize nationalism's challenge to colonialism by portraying the former as nothing but an ideological cover for the elite's manipulations for power and profit, comes roaring back once again to salvage colonialism, this time by subordinating colonialism to the logic of unfolding capitalism. This is how history turns into a process of the self-realization of a Hegelian totality: the universalizing narrative of mode-of-production becomes the guise in which White mythology, as Derrida calls it, returns as History.[18]

The burden of Eurocentrism on the narrative of mode-of-production as History cannot be lightened by arguing, as O'Hanlon and Washbrook do, that one seeks to 'break down East–West dichotomies, by exploring the indigenous forms of capitalism . . .' (p. 196). Indigenous forms of a universal phenomenon? At issue here is an unexamined Eurocentric Marxism that they ask us to accept uncritically. I am not suggesting that acknowledging Marx's Eurocentrism requires abandoning Marxism altogether. But students of Indian history, who know only too well the Eurocentricity of Marx's memorable formulation that the British conquest introduced a history-less India to History, cannot now regard, as do O'Hanlon and Washbrook, the mode-of-production story as a normative universal. In fact, like many other nineteenth-century European ideas, the staging of the Eurocentric mode-of-production narrative as History should be seen as an analogue of the nineteenth-century territorial imperialism. From this point of view, Marx's ideas on changeless India – theorized, for example, in his concept of the 'Asiatic mode of production' – appear not so much as mistaken views but as evidence of the alterity that was suppressed in universalizing the story of Europe's transition from feudalism to capitalism. Such a historicization of the Eurocentrism in nineteenth-century Marxism enables us to understand the collusion of capitalism and colonialism and to undo the effect of that collusion's imperative to interpret third-world histories in terms of capital's logic. To suggest that we reinscribe the effects of capitalism's foundational status by writing about histories that remained heterogeneous with the logic of capital, therefore, is not to abandon Marxism but to extricate class analysis from its nineteenth-century heritage, acknowledging that Marxism's critique of capitalism was both enabled and disabled by its historicity as a European discourse.

O'Hanlon and Washbrook, on the other hand, operate with a

Eurocentric Marxism and invite us to see colonialism as reducible to the development of capitalism in Britain and in India. The conflation of the metropolitan proletariat with the colonized subaltern that this approach involves amounts to a homogenization of irreducible difference. My critics claim that capitalism, rather than homogenizing difference necessarily, is perfectly capable of utilizing and generating heterogeneity. But the notion that capitalism is a founding source responsible for originating and encompassing difference amounts to appropriating heterogeneity as a self-consolidating difference, that is, refracting 'what might have been the absolutely Other into a domesticated Other . . .'[19] This assimilation of difference into identity is characteristic not of all systems, as my critics allege I imply, but of totalizing systems. When capitalism is made to stand for History – so that the heterogeneity of histories of the colonized subaltern with those of the metropolitan proletariat is effaced – absolute otherness is appropriated into self-consolidating difference. We are thus invited to think once again of colonialism as part of the career of capitalism, demanding a single, undifferentiated strategy of resistance. *Just one horse.*

The Place for Ambivalence in Said's *Orientalism*

The consequence of O'Hanlon and Washbrook's commitment to totalizing analysis is a failure to appreciate that historical attempts at mastery were so riven by conflictory economies as to create possibilities for resistance in terms other than those determined by power. This failure is particularly evident in their reading of Edward Said's *Orientalism.*[20] Although Said's work has been justifiably regarded as a breakthrough, providing a basis for a number of deconstructive accounts, several critics have also pointed out that his analysis suffers from an unnecessary and untenable closure that dismisses conflicts and resistance inherent to the functioning of Orientalism as a system of power and knowledge. O'Hanlon and Washbrook, on the other hand, commend Said's neglect of 'internal relations of contestation and resistance in western cultures' because it enabled him to present 'within a single analytical framework, core elements in the European intellectual and political tradition for a very long period' (p. 206). They also applaud when Said parts company with Foucault and, using the liberal humanist notions of intentionality and individual subjects, reduces Orientalism to the Western will to power and places the burden of resistance on the humanist intellectual. This endorsement of Said's liberal humanism is 'wildly at odds' with O'Hanlon and

Washbrook's strident denunciation of the liberal tendencies of the postmodern culture, but it helps to explain why they think that Said knows which horse he would ultimately rather be on.

Said did suggest that Orientalism functioned as a discourse unified by the Western will to dominate. But, as Bhabha shows convincingly, it is also equally true that Said himself provides plenty of evidence for Orientalism's ambivalence when he describes it as a discourse not only of Western scholarship but also of Western fantasy, as a discipline for domination but also as a desire for the Other, as a manifest but also as a latent discourse.[21] Although he describes Orientalism as a 'static system of "synchronic essentialism"', Said also shows how this discourse of stable signifiers was threatened by its own 'diachronic forms of history and narrative, signs of instability'. But reluctant 'to engage with the alterity and ambivalence in the articulation of these two economies which threaten to split the very object of Orientalist discourse as a knowledge and the subject positioned therein', Said seeks to unify 'these two economies in Western intention'.[22] With the structure of ambivalence closed, the exercise of power and the mounting of resistance can be located, not in the history of Orientalism as textured and contradictory enunciations, but in the ahistorical, unified will of individual subjects. Here Said, who parts company with Foucault, invokes authorial intention and individual subjects, explaining Orientalism as the Western will to power and finding resistance in intellectuals who, as individuals endowed with critical consciousness and humanist values, stand outside totalizing systems of domination.[23] O'Hanlon and Washbrook note approvingly Said's move towards intentions and individual subjects, as also his criticism of Foucault and Derrida, and conclude that both *Orientalism*'s critical edge and Said's political commitment are advanced by his embrace of Western humanism (p. 205). In fact, such notions of intentionality and sovereign subjects end up supporting the Orientalist's claim, challenged throughout by Said's work, to be a detached observer; and, with historically enunciated ambivalence and alterity effaced by the ahistorical 'single analytical framework' of intentions, we are invited to think that the critic is not 'worlded' in power relations but stands 'outside', as a sovereign subject. Those inside the structure of Orientalist power are allowed little space for resistance when, in fact, there are plenty of examples to show that the conflictory economy of Orientalism itself provided the basis for challenging colonial power.[24] *Said at least seems to know which horse in the end he would rather be on.*

Postmodernism and the Politics of Difference

Acknowledging the potential for resistance within the structure of power, however, requires the recognition that the functioning of the structure makes equivocality, contingency and difference possible. O'Hanlon and Washbrook are indeed willing to consider difference, but only to the extent that it can accommodate a totality. Thus, they regard the contemporary fragmentation of identities and insistent heterogeneity as symptomatic of postmodernism. Like Fredric Jameson, they take this as the cultural logic of late capitalism;[25] but their understanding of the postmodern condition has an unacknowledged though important difference. For Jameson, the postmodern decentring is a new stage of cultural dominance, not a refiguration of the older liberal culture. Indeed, he develops the idea of the postmodern as a totality to such an extreme that it abolishes its binary opposite, the outside, from which the humanist critic of O'Hanlon and Washbrook speaks.[26] From this, Jameson draws the following conclusion:

> In place of the temptation either to denounce the complacency of postmodernism as some final symptom of decadence, or to salute the new forms as harbingers of a new technological and technocratic Utopia, it seems more appropriate to assess the new cultural production within the working hypothesis of a general modification of culture itself within the social restructuration of late capitalism as a system.[27]

Because Jameson's notion of postmodernism as the cultural logic of late capitalism includes global heterogeneity as its defining condition, the idea of disjunctions within the structure, disallowed by the idea of totality, returns curiously enough but in the domesticated form of 'cognitive mappings'. The responsibility is placed now on the (first-world?) intellectual critic to provide a cognitive map through which we can find our way out of the postmodern disorientation.

O'Hanlon and Washbrook, on the other hand, see postmodernism in terms of a text and context dichotomy; culture reflects the ideological imperatives of late capitalism. The insistence on difference, then, can be nothing other than the cultural form that the ideology of liberal individuality assumes in the late capitalist United States, and it must be opposed by a universalist class-based 'materialist conception of history'. But from whence do they speak? Having identified postmodernism and deconstruction as the expressive cultural ideological form of the totality of late capitalism in the United States, Britain becomes the unacknowledged privileged space from which universalism fixes its stern gaze across the Atlantic (the empire strikes back?).

To the eye of class universalism, heterogeneity appears problematic; it must be familiarized as the mere form in which class identity rests – just as, in commodity form, exchange value finds the concreteness of use value as the mere form of its universal existence. If not, difference creates a structure of equivocality that threatens to split apart the foundational status of class, placing it alongside different and incommensurable forms of difference. To prevent this eventuality, they argue that the decentring of foundations inevitably privileges the politics of self-representation which, given the 'well-known hostility of American political culture to any kind of materialist or class analysis' (p. 215), leads inevitably to liberal individuality – a position they now attack as politically conservative, contradicting their earlier endorsement of liberal humanism in Said as politically enabling.

Their deep discomfort with difference surfaces when they state that postmodernists and deconstructionists screen off 'universalistic, systemic and material deprivations of capitalism, which clearly separate them [the under-classes] from their "subaltern" expositors', so that the underclasses are permitted only to appear as 'victims of the particularistic kinds of gender, racial and national oppression which they share with predominantly middle-class American scholars and critics' (p. 215). Once again, they show an unwillingness to give up polarizing different systems of power into universalistic (class) versus particularistic (gender, race, nation). If we follow their prescription, class oppression in Britain will stand for colonial exploitation of India, gendered power in Britain will be commensurable with patriarchal oppression in India. It is just such a search for subject positions, valid for all times and places, that leads them to argue that we cannot give up the universal category of woman. Here, it is interesting to read what O'Hanlon has written elsewhere:

> What is interesting, indeed, is that just the same issue, of the attempt to reintroduce homogeneity and consensus within a redrawn idea of an essential collectivity, has arisen in the feminist debate. Toril Moi describes how minority feminist groups have forced white heterosexual feminists to 're-examine their own sometimes totalitarian conception of "woman" as a homogeneous category'. To maintain radical thrust of feminist criticism, she argues, these groups 'ought to prevent white middle-class First World feminists from defining their own preoccupations as *universal* female (or feminist) problems'.[28]

Contrary to the above passage, we are now asked to project the universal category of woman on to multiple and heterogeneous subject-positions, even if it is discontinuous with the colonial history wherein there was no subject-position for the subaltern woman. From their point of view, universal categories are apparently valuable in conceiving agency and active politics, whereas Foucauldian and postmodernist perspectives allegedly inhibit possibilities of resistance because they suggest dispersed rather than centred power and subjectivity.[29] There are two key assumptions here: first, that the historical enunciation of such 'universal' categories as woman, black, Asian and native carried out the intentions of the dominant successfully and unproblematically; and second, that just as power operates on the basis of a centred and homogeneous identity, so does resistance: agency can be conceived only when the agent experiences oppression as a woman or a native and mounts resistance based on the given and experienced identity. Both these assumptions are deeply problematic. It is one thing to recognize that certain systems of dominance operate by conferring and constituting identities such as the woman and man, colonizer and the colonized, and quite another to assume that such homogeneous identifications do not split and open themselves up to heterogeneous formations in historical articulation. A case in point is the breakdown of the colonizer–colonized dichotomy when faced with the ambivalent figure of the English-speaking Indian in British India. Similarly, it is one thing to acknowledge that political practice requires the notion of agency and quite another to assert that the space for agency must be defined in terms of centred, not dispersed, power relations. If agency and 'experience' are attributed to the centring and 'founding' force of power relations, then how can resistance be even conceived except in terms given them by the dominant? How can we envisage agency unless we see that the ambivalent, conflictory and dispersed operation of power relations enunciated subject-positions and discourses heterogeneous with and covered over by universal categories? O'Hanlon and Washbrook, however, think that we have no recourse other than to operate with homogeneous identities given us by dominant relations: because the world operates and behaves as though 'woman' was a universal category, we, too, must conceive resistance on this basis (p. 203). But a contestatory appropriation of the position woman can occur because the operation of power relations marks the term woman with heterogeneity (white/black/working class/native) and breaks down the patriarchal man–woman opposition; agency rests on the simultaneous possibility and impossibility of the category woman. O'Hanlon and Washbrook are averse to agency produced in such ambivalence; they prefer the homogeneous subject produced by 'foundational' and centred power relations, an agent who turns the 'experience' of oppression into the basis for resistance. This conception is dangerously close to the liberal vision of self-representing subject-agent they disparage. But no matter.

It has the secure and comforting either/or logic; either man or woman, either class or race and gender. *Once again, one horse.*

History and Marginalized Others

In asking us to attribute multiple and particularistic forms of oppression to the unitary and universalistic forces of capitalism, O'Hanlon and Washbrook, once again, express their desire to master those histories which remain heterogeneous with it. Nowhere is this more disabling than in understanding the dealing with the effects of colonialism. If the West sentenced the otherness of the conquered to History, to recognize that project now as the work of a universal logic which used and produced difference without compromising its sovereignty is to repeat that act of incarceration. This leaves no room for the otherness and resistance that was not determined by the Western conquest; it denies that anti-colonial nationalism and subaltern struggles, while being constituted by dominant structures, could slip beyond and come back to haunt the conditions of their own constitution. If the conflicts, contradictions and ambivalence in colonial history cannot be said to have upset their founding source in some universality, then the difference of postcoloniality, its critical edge, cannot even be postulated. This means that historians and critics, who have been constituted in the economic, political, epistemic transformations of colonial history and presently work in institutions and in disciplines dominated by Western thought, cannot hope to criticize structures that they inhabit. This is a deeply depressing and disabling prospect for critical historiography because it closes the possibility of reinscribing the assumptions and methodologies of historical writing. But, as we have seen, all totalizations reveal their impossibility in their use of supplements. This means that history becomes possible in the structure of marginalized others; Western discourses may have constituted and transformed colonial and postcolonial subjects, but they cannot determine the agency that these subjects find in the contradictions and equivocality set in motion in discursive fields. The assertion of this heterogeneity, the insistence that the histories of the metropolitan proletariat and the colonized worker are discrepant, even if both are exploited by capitalism, therefore, is to insist on difference as the condition of history's possibility, and to rearticulate it differently than White mythology. It neither implies the dismissal of foundations as disposable fictions, nor does it recommend nihilistic destruction. Rather, the purpose of underscoring difference is to argue that if historical effects were reduced to their founding origins – if the contradictions and ambivalence in colonial social, economic, cultural and epistemic productions were reduced to their origins in capitalism – history would only amount to a return to origins, the recovery of the original presence, the White mythology – not something O'Hanlon and Washbrook would want, even if their arguments lead them in that direction. As for me, I say, *let us hang on to two horses, inconstantly.*

Acknowledgements

I am grateful to the following who commented on previous drafts of this essay: Homi Bhabha, Natalie Z. Davis, Nick Dirks, Tony Grafton, Bill Jordan, Peter Mandler, Mark Mazower, Gayatri Chakravorty Spivak, Bob Tignor, Jyotsna Uppal and Dror Wahrman.

Notes

1. Rosalind O'Hanlon and David Washbrook, 'After Orientalism: Culture, Criticism and Politics in the Third World', in this volume, pp. 191–219. Page numbers for all subsequent references appear within parentheses in the text.
2. 'Of Mimicry and Man: The Ambivalence of Colonial Discourse', *October*, 34 (Fall 1985), 126.
3. Homi Bhabha, 'The Other Question . . .', *Screen* 24:6 (1983), 18.
4. Ibid., 23–5.
5. 'Of Mimicry and Man: The Ambivalence of Colonial Discourse'. 126.
6. An example of hasty reading of this sort occurs when they accuse Ranajit Guha of 'referring to the (undifferentiated) Indian nation as "us"' (p. 197). In fact, phrases such as 'our *own*' in the text refer to Indian historiography. See his 'Dominance without Hegemony and Its Historiography', *Subaltern Studies VI*, Ranajit Guha, ed. (Delhi: Oxford University Press, 1989). For examples: 'On our own part, we present our views on the structure of domination in colonial India and historiography's relation to it as a critique of our *own* approach to the Indian past and our *own* performance in writing about it not to an undifferentiated Indian nation' (p. 306); or 'This [Guha's essay], we hope, may assist in the *self-criticism of our own historiography* – the historiography of a colonized people' (p. 307). An 'undifferentiated nation'? Their reading that Ashis Nandy generalizes the experience of 'Bengali literati to that of the whole nation' (p. 147) is similarly hasty for Nandy is quite clear that he is speaking about intellectuals; he never claims that India as a whole experienced colonialism in the same way.
7. *Of Grammatology*, Gayatri Chakravorty Spivak, trans. (Baltimore: The Johns Hopkins University Press, 1976), 243. See also pages 216–45, 270–80.
8. Ibid., 270.
9. *Margins of Philosophy*, Alan Bass, trans. (Chicago: The University of Chicago Press, 1982), 213.
10. 'The Making of Americans, the Teaching of English, and the Future of Cultural Studies', *New Literary History*, 21:4 (1990), 28.
11. 'Contentious Traditions: The Debate on Sati in Colonial India', *Cultural Critique*, 7 (Fall 1987), 119–56.

12. Gayatri Chakravorty Spivak, 'Can the Subaltern Speak?' in *Marxism and Interpretation of Culture*, Cary Nelson and Lawrence Grossberg, eds (Urbana: University of Illinois Press, 1988), 271–313. See, in particular, pages 299–307.

13. For a similar argument about the colonized woman caught between indigenous patriarchy and the politics of archival production, see also Spivak's 'The Rani of Sirmur: An Essay in Reading the Archives', *History and Theory*, 24:3 (1985), 247–72.

14. For a study of the process of this covering over in the context of unfree labourers, see my *Bonded Histories: Genealogies of Labor Servitude in Colonial India* (Cambridge: Cambridge University Press, 1990). Nicholas Dirks's *The Hollow Crown: Ethnohistory of an Indian Kingdom* (Cambridge: Cambridge University Press, 1987), similarly, traces the marks of a relationship between caste and power in the process that hollowed out the political space in a south Indian kingdom and filled it with colonial power.

15. This view is elaborated by Washbrook in his 'Progress and Problems: South-Asian Economic and Social History c. 1720–1860', *Modern Asian Studies*, 22:1 (1988), 57–96.

16. Ibid., 76.

17. For examples of this historiography, see Anil Seal, *The Emergence of Indian Nationalism* (Cambridge: Cambridge University Press, 1968), and D. A. Washbrook, *The Emergence of Provincial Politics: The Madras Presidency 1870–1920* (Cambridge: Cambridge University Press, 1976). For a recent critique, see Guha, 'Dominance without Hegemony'.

18. On the Eurocentrism of History, see Robert Young, *White Mythologies: Writing History and the West* (London and New York: Routledge, 1990), particularly pp. 2–12.

19. Spivak, 'Three Women's Texts and a Critique of Imperialism', *Critical Inquiry*, 12:1 (1985), 253.

20. *Orientalism* (New York: Random House, 1978).

21. 'The Other Question', 23–6.

22. Ibid., 24.

23. See Robert Young, *White Mythologies*, 129–36.

24. For an argument demonstrating how nationalist thought in India shared the thematic of Orientalism, see Partha Chatterjee, *Nationalist Thought and the Colonial World – A Derivative Discourse?* (London: Zed Books, 1986).

25. 'Postmodernism, or the Cultural Logic of Late Capitalism', *New Left Review*, 146 (1984), 53–92. Following Jameson, O'Hanlon and Washbrook conflate postmodern culture and post-structuralist theory, unlike Andreas Huyssen to whom they also mistakenly attribute this conflation. See Huyssen, *After the Great Divide: Modernism, Mass Culture, Postmodernism* (Bloomington: Indiana University Press, 1986), 200–16.

26. 'The point is that we are *within* the culture of postmodernism to the point where its facile repudiation is as impossible as any equally facile celebration of it is complacent and corrupt' (*The Ideologies of Theory, Essays 1971–1986*, vol. 2, Minneapolis: University of Minnesota Press, 1980, 111).

27. Ibid.

28. 'Recovering the Subject: *Subaltern Studies* and Histories of Resistance in Colonial South Asia', *Modern Asian Studies*, 22:1 (1988), 212; reprinted in this volume. This essay makes a very different reading from the present O'Hanlon and Washbrook essay on virtually every issue.

29. This view runs right through their critique. See pp. 199–204, particularly, where they state that a Foucauldian perspective disallows the notion of agency.

11

Orientalism Revisited: Saidian Frameworks in the Writing of Modern Indian History

Sumit Sarkar

It has become obligatory in many intellectual circles to begin with a critique of Orientalism, of colonial discourse, if one wants to acquire or retain a radical reputation. A framework derived from Edward Said's *Orientalism* has performed a major unificatory function, linking up new kinds of literary or cultural studies with third-world feminism and what is considered increasingly to be avant-garde history writing. This has been achieved, furthermore, through what might appear at first sight to be a wholly welcome focus on power relations and, particularly, colonial domination, about which many of the previously unrelated disciplines had been notably reticent. Radical critics of the liberal-humanist English literature establishment, for instance, have welcomed Said with particular enthusiasm, for this has been an area from which the brutal facts of empire and racism had been largely excluded. As in 'reflexive' anthropology, the critique of colonial discourse involves a questioning of the power relations embedded in the location of the still predominantly Western, or Western-educated, and largely male academic investigator.

The appeal of such auto-critiques is obvious, particularly today in a political context constituted by the collapse of the second world, the consequent apparently total centrality of the North–South divide, and resurgent neo-colonialism and racism. Intellectually, too, the Saidian framework carries with it associations, powerful through their very vagueness, of being somehow a part of much wider 'postmodern' tendencies and moods. In the specific area of modern Indian history, for instance, the first entrance of postmodernistic language has been through the Saidian turn of a section of the Subaltern Studies group. What is involved is not any definite affiliation with Foucault, Derrida,

Lacan, or other acknowledged masters of postmodernism or post-structuralism, or even perhaps at times with Said himself, but a kind of academic 'common sense', if one is permitted to extend Gramsci's analysis from the plebeian or popular to the highbrow. The academic mood or common sense I am referring to certainly often partakes of some of the features emphasized by Gramsci.[1] It tends to be fragmentary and eclectic, yet powerful through its taken-for-granted qualities: a point I intend to substantiate through the specific texts I will take up later on in this essay. This common-sensical or even nebulous quality, incidentally, makes critique somewhat difficult: one has to keep using shorthand terms like 'framework' to describe what remains a notable kind of intellectual influence, and yet such words imply a definiteness and rigour that is not really present here. Finally, the Saidian ambience has been able to combine an attractive radicalism with remarkable success in the Western, particularly US, academic market, and this amid the wholesale collapse of radical hopes. An enviable combination, perhaps, but surely also a point where doubts should arise and questionings begin.

My questioning of what has really become a counter-orthodoxy will relate principally to recent trends in modern Indian historiography: the current dominant trajectory of Subaltern Studies, and some recent historical writing about colonial India by feminists and scholars of English literature. But first a few more general comments may be in order. Orientalism, for a start, seems to be a devil peculiarly difficult to exorcize. If Orientalism essentialized and homogenized the 'Oriental other', critics from James Clifford in 1980 down to Aijaz Ahmad in 1992 have regularly found Said guilty on an identical charge.[2] The critique of Orientalism and colonial power-knowledge does often use terms like 'Enlightenment rationality', 'colonial discourse', 'third-world culture', as well as of course 'Orientalism' itself, in the grossest of homogenizing ways. The pattern of rejections intermingled with complicities actually extends further, into many other varieties of postmodernisms too. Thus Toril Moi's generally sympathetic analysis of French feminist theory still makes the point that 'every time a Derridean idea is evoked, it is opposed and undercut by a vision of women's writing steeped in . . . the metaphysics of presence'. Similarly, Gerald Graff uses the phrase 'anti-essentialist essentialism' to describe much of New Historicism.[3]

The argument sometimes offered – that such complicity is bound to be there, as it is impossible today to go totally beyond post-Enlightenment discursive patterns – sounds suspiciously like an attempt to have the best of both worlds: critiquing others for essentialism, teleology and related sins, while claiming a special immunity from doing the same oneself. There is, it is true, a more sophisticated and convincing version of this defence, which can argue that one has to operate with concepts that tend to get congealed, essentialized, constructed into teleologies: deconstruction is helpful here in maintaining a critical stance. But then the repeated claims to total novelty or originality that are so often made nowadays need to be seriously qualified, for surely many earlier thinkers, too – Marx, to give an obvious, if now unfashionable, example – were quite aware of the fetishizing capacities of concepts.[4] In a notable article, Gayatri Spivak has drawn attention to the 'curious persistence of essentialism within the dialectic' in Marx as 'a profound and productive problem'.[5] But the question remains as to whether the bulk of today's critics of essentialism and teleology are sufficiently careful and self-critical about their own deployment of concepts. If, as seems fairly obvious, this is not happening, the real gains of the 'linguistic turn' – the thoroughgoing problematizations of language – are being lost, and there is a need to probe why this should be happening.

The homogenizations to which the Saidian framework seem particularly prone are related, I feel, to major problems in its conception of power. There is first the tendency, ultimately traceable to Foucault but expressed in a more unqualified manner in Said and his epigoni, to ascribe virtually unlimited domination to ruling forms of power knowledge. Such assumptions appeared from the late 1970s onwards in a large number of otherwise unrelated fields. Thus Robert Muchembled developed an 'acculturation thesis' stressing the conquest of once-autonomous popular culture in early modern France through the Counter-Reformation Church, absolutist state, and Enlightenment reason. Muchembled's book came out in 1978, the same year as Said's *Orientalism*.[6] Althusserian structuralist Marxism, to take a second example, was also becoming very influential, as indicated by E. P. Thompson's violent polemic against its alleged denial of human agency in *Poverty of Theory*.[7] This, too, came out in 1978. Said and Muchembled worked quite independently of each other and in unrelated fields, and both were innocent of the influence of Althusserian or any other variety of Marxism. What became often an obsessive focus on the totalizing nature of power relations probably had some connections, however, with changes in political atmosphere, as radical hopes in the transformative possibilities of popular action aroused by Vietnam and May 1968 ebbed away. It is not surprising that subsequent events, culminating in today's unipolar world, have strengthened such intellectual tendencies. An automatic extension of the assumption to all historical periods still seems curiously unhistorical and essentialist.

Assumptions of total domination foreclose investigation of elements of resistance or partial autonomy, and rob subordinate groups of agency. The colonial middle class, in particular, has been found capable of only 'derivative discourses' in one, extremely influential, version.[8] Such assumptions also tend grossly to simplify and homogenize power relationships. In the Saidian framework, for example, the focus remains relentlessly on colonial domination alone. The indigenous and pre-colonial roots of many forms of caste, gender or class domination are generally ignored, for the dominant assumption is of a kind of total rupture or tabula rasa, with colonialism completely remoulding such indigenous structures, making them dependent or derivative. The possibility of these helping to mediate colonial authority in vital ways, and even functioning autonomously at times – and there is ample evidence for both – is simply ignored.[9] A parallel homogenization occurs at the other end of the power equation. Colonial domination gets robbed of all complexities and variations, and so Macaulay's notorious Minute is thought to be a sufficient description of more than a century of British cultural policy in India.

In colonial discourse analysis and work on early modern European popular culture influenced by the acculturation thesis alike, the realm of freedom, if there is one at all, must lie in domains somehow untouched by post-Enlightenment rationalist power knowledge. Not much can be said with any certitude about such 'pre-modern', or 'precolonial', or 'popular' domains, since the sources (inevitably of elite, colonial or colonial middle-class origin) and the mind-sets of today's historians are bound to be tainted also by Englightenment rationality. This in practice at times allows space for romanticizations – for what in today's context can become dangerous forms of 'indigenism', in which an undifferentiated West is held responsible for all ills, and institutions and practices, however oppressive, get acquitted of blame if they appear untainted by 'alien' forms of power knowledge. We shall shortly encounter examples of even radical scholars coming perilously close to formulations like these.

Power, finally, tends to get curiously disembodied, for any effort to explore connections with socio-economic processes is thought to be tainted with the sins of reductionism and teleology. What began as a legitimate turning away from the crude determinisms of 'official' Marxism has degenerated in academic common sense into a suspicion-cum-contempt for anything 'economic' – as if reductionism cannot be 'cultural' or 'political', too. Thus Foucault's path-breaking analysis of the emergence of 'carceral' institutions – asylums, hospitals, modern armies, schools and prisons (and, just occasionally in *Discipline and Punish,* factories, too) invariably locates the vital shifts within a time-span that coincides with what historians have been accustomed to call the transition to industrial capitalist society. But Foucault himself carefully avoids such connections, and, significantly, does not discuss the modern business firm or multinational organizations which, one would have thought, provide excellent examples of his own model of disciplinary, as contrasted to spectacular, authority. But if Foucault remains impressive through his studies of the 'microphysics' of power as expressed in areas previously unexplored, the same, emphatically, cannot be said about the bulk of Saidian work, at least so far as South Asian history is concerned. This, it needs to be emphasized, is an area where the dominant paradigm has for long been nationalistic and critical of colonial rule, and the critique of colonial discourse, despite vast claims to total originality, quite often is no more than a restatement in new language of old nationalist positions – and fairly crude restatements, at that. The combination of radicalism with academic respectability also begins to make sense in this context, for a critique that targets Macaulay, and not Western monopoly over new communicational networks, as crucial expressions of Western power knowledge is unlikely to worry establishments overmuch.

But it is time to turn to specific examples.

More than ten years ago, Ashis Nandy had sketched out the principal parameters of today's counter-orthodoxy in his *The Intimate Enemy*, a work with little overt Saidian influence that sought to 'justify and defend the *innocence* [my italics] which confronted modern Western colonialism'.[10] The *locus classicus* for the entry of the Saidian framework into the historiography of modern India is still the turn within the Subaltern Studies inaugurated by Partha Chatterjee's *Nationalist Thought in the Colonial World.* The book has enjoyed remarkable success, particularly in the West where it is now a prescribed text in many university courses. It brought together previously separate strands of analysis (specifically, an early-1970s Calcutta-based critique of the myth of a Bengal Renaissance in the nineteenth century, and Ranajit Guha's exploration of peasant consciousness in colonial India through studies of moments of rebellion), and inserted them into an international academic discourse the parameters of which had been set by Said's *Orientalism.* Chatterjee's work did seem to fill a kind of void, for there had been little effort so long to theorize Indian nationalism. Like its counterparts the world over, conventional nationalistic historiography mythified its object as natural and immutable. Left-wing and radical history writing, in contrast, tended rather to evade the question: the focus on elements of autonomy in popular movements which remains the most significant and enduring contribution of Subaltern Studies in its early phase, for instance, had little to say about nationalism (or communalism) as ideologies.[11]

A further advantage of the book, one is tempted to add, lay in its basic simplicity of presentation. Nationalist thought was conveniently packaged for newcomers into a neat succession of just three figures, Bankimchandra, Gandhi and Nehru, allegedly signifying a succession of moments of departure, manoeuvre and arrival. Presentation even of these three is highly selective: thus Bankim's novels, for which he is principally remembered, are not taken up at all. Any argument, of course, necessarily selects and excludes, but the point here is that the principles of selection are never explicated. The instant success of such simplified exposition would seem to indicate that even the fairly small section of the Western intelligentsia interested in third-world history prefers its material conveniently packaged, without too much detail or complexities. Totally different standards would be expected in mainstream work on any branch, say, of European historiography. Only in third-world studies, for instance, can a historian get by without mastering the language of the country or region s/he is researching, as is still not entirely uncommon in South Asian scholarship in the West. Comparison with the work of generations of Indologists, from William Jones down to Max Muller and beyond – 'Orientalist' in the original meaning of that word – might arouse uncomfortable questions about where precisely 'Orientalism' – in the Saidian, pejorative, sense – ought to be located.

The basic structure of *Nationalist Thought* is woven around three premises. In a pattern that we shall see to be quite common in applications of Said, these begin as hypotheses but speedily become assumptions, even axioms. Colonial Indian middle-class thought, in the first place, is declared to be a 'derivative discourse', with Gandhi as the solitary exception. Its strivings for autonomous 'problematics' were invariably undercut by the essentialist 'thematic' derived from post-Enlightenment rationality (p. 38). The basic problem here is that the central polemical target, 'post-Enlightenment rationality', is never demarcated with any precision. Thus 'post-Enlightenment' might seem to hint at a Habermasian distinction between certain broader emancipatory possibilities of the initial Enlightenment project with its concomitant in the emergence of bourgeois public space, and later narrower, positivistic instrumental rationality. But the precise status of the Enlightenment proper is never made clear, and quite often much broader targets are implied. There is in fact a continual slippage between narrower and wider meanings, reminiscent of Said's own usage of 'Orientalism', and this makes the key argument about derived 'thematics' completely unverifiable.

In chapter III, on Bankimchandra, for instance, three quite distinct meanings are given to the alleged surrender to colonial discourse. On pages 61–4, this is associated with Bankim's acceptance of the political economy of free trade: a perfectly clear and precise meaning, but one that raises major problems about locating Naoroji and nationalist economic thought in general. Free trade arguments were far from universal in space and time even in nineteenth-century Europe. A much wider definition of what Bankim had surrendered to is implied, however, on page 58, where his 'method, concepts and modes of reasoning' are found to be 'completely contained within the forms of post-Enlightenment scientific thought. One major characteristic of this thought is its celebration of the principle of historicity as the essential procedure for acquiring '"objective" knowledge'. It says much for the conversion of diluted fragments of postmodernism into common sense that such a statement would probably be widely accepted today and even considered obvious. But geology, Darwin, Hegel and Marx apart, the bulk of that natural sciences, mathematics, neo-classical economics, social anthropology and, from the early twentieth century, much of social sciences after Saussure, Durkheim and Freud should then be excluded from the category of 'post-Enlightenment scientific thought', if the identification of the latter with the 'principle of historicity' is seriously meant. Finally, other passages seem to gesture towards even wider definitions of post-Enlightenment rationality, as virtually equivalent to what would today be commonsensically regarded as 'rational' or 'logical' argument. If these are to be confined to the modern West, we are back to really crude kinds of Eurocentrism, with only the values inverted – Macaulay, with the signs reversed.

The Gandhian 'moment of manoeuvre' is exempted by Chatterjee from the general charge of subordination to post-Enlightenment Western rationality, presumably because of Gandhi's 'indictment of modern civilization' and rejection of the 'very notions of modernity and progress' (p. 86). It is difficult, however, to get rid of a lurking suspicion that Gandhi, too, could have been incorporated within the capacious and ever-flexible boundaries of post-Enlightenment rationality, had not the structure of Chatterjee's argument dictated otherwise. From Rousseau and the Romantics onwards, there has certainly been no lack of not dissimilar critics of modernity and progress from within Western culture, some of whom are known to have considerably influenced Gandhi himself. If all of them have to be excluded, like

Gandhi, from Enlightenment traditions, doubts begin to arise as to how dominant these have been even in their countries of origin.

The moment of manoeuvre is followed by that of 'arrival', with the Nehruvian appropriation of Gandhian populism, which culminates in the fetishization of the modern nation-state. There is no doubt that this part of Chatterjee's exposition resonates powerfully with much present-day disquiet about centralized, bureaucratic and oppressive contemporary states, including to a considerable extent, the Indian. How analytically and politically effective such a critique can become, with its very general sweep and deliberate and total avoidance of categories of class and production relations, remains another matter. Sticking closer to Chatterjee's text, however, what does occasion some surprise is the extent of complicity with patterns of argument which are simultaneously being denounced. Thus Gramsci's 'passive revolution' is somehow quietly exempted from the overall rejection of Eurocentric models, and the whole book turns around a strictly linear, excessively neat, schema of (Hegelian?) moments. Interestingly, in one place this is posed as a problem: 'But is a theory of stages not one which assumes a certain linearity of evolution, a certain teleology? We need to face this question' (p. 43). No doubt, but the question is not faced, or raised again, in the rest of the book.

Critiques of modern Western power knowledge cast in the Saidian mould, I have argued, have often tended to evoke a romanticized 'pre-modern' or 'pre-colonial', and Chatterjee, too, often gestures vaguely towards 'community consciousness' as valorized counterpoint. The discussion of such consciousness, both here as well as in other writings of Chatterjee, is kept at a level abstract enough to avoid, on the whole, a slide towards overtly conservative conclusions. But that such a possibility remains in the structure of the argument is indicated by the following curious passage, in which Gandhi's standpoint, located 'outside the thematic of post-Enlightenment thought', is declared to be one 'which could have been adopted by any member of the traditional intelligentsia in India', and then is further described as having 'an inherently [sic] "peasant-communal" character' (p. 100). The differences between the 'traditional intelligentsia', overwhelmingly Brahman or at least upper-caste and male, and peasant-communal consciousness, are apparently of no importance whatsoever: caste and gender divides do not seem to matter. One or two of Chatterjee's colleagues in the Subaltern Studies group have gone very much further. Thus Gautam Bhadra, in an interview given to a Bengali journal in early 1991, came close to discovering in the Ramjanambhoomi movement a genuine, and therefore laudable, subaltern upsurge, as contrasted to allegedly elitist, alienated and state-sponsored secularists. The formidable organization, financial resources and media backup that have underpinned the Rashtriya Swayamsevak Sangh-Bharatiya Janata Party-Vishwa Hindu Parishad campaign to destroy the Babri Masjid and change the nature of the Indian polity, the predominantly high-caste composition of the leadership and even of a major part of the participants in this movement, and its consequences, already quite evident by early 1991, in terms of unprecedented communal carnage, have all disappeared from this analysis. In another Bengali article, Dipesh Chakrabarty has found an admittedly problem-ridden, yet basically valid, counterpoint to surrender to Western power knowledge in a cookery book written by a traditionalist Bengali housewife which extols the pleasure women get from preparing and serving food for their husbands.[12]

Movements by, or on behalf of, women and lower castes clearly raise severe problems for the application of the Saidian framework to the history of colonial India, for very often these did try to utilize Western ideologies and colonial law, justice and administration as major resources. If reforms like the banning of *sati*, the legalization of widow remarriage – measures brought about primarily through pressure from some Indians and usually after considerable official hesitation – are to be condemned as instances of surrender to Western values, we are really back to the crudest and most obscurantist forms of nationalism. Most surprisingly, a fair amount of recent feminist scholarship seems to be falling into this trap, and one hears about nineteenth-century efforts to educate women as being somehow retrogressive, and even the raising of the age of consent in 1891 from ten to twelve as a Victorian curtailment of feminine sexuality.

The two examples I am presenting here, however, are deliberately taken from much more cautious and nuanced writings. As with Partha Chatterjee, they indicate the implicit thrust of a flawed logical framework quite possibly working against the personal values and preference of the authors. Lata Mani's paper, 'Contentious Traditions: the Debate on Sati in Colonial India', is one of the more substantial and best known of specific studies built around the assumption of an overwhelmingly dominant 'colonial discourse'.[13] It provides an excellent instance, however, of the recurrent pattern through which even interesting hypotheses are being turned into restrictive assumptions or axioms through an uncritical devotion to Said. Mani's basic argument is that official, conservative and reformist discourses about *sati*, among the Indians as much as among Englishmen, had an underlying unifying structure derived from a totally new valorization of textual authority – from which followed the repeated appeals by all participants in the debate to ancient, 'classical' texts. Such textualism, further, was allegedly a unique product of post-Enlightenment colonial discourse. Even if we leave aside the innumerable examples of textual appeals in medieval European and pre-colonial Indian intellectual debates (the elaboration of alternative systems of philosophy through interpretations of the Vedanta-sutra, for instance), one would have thought that the hypothesis needed to be tested through a comparison with earlier discussions of *sati*. Lata Mani does briefly mention commentaries about the issue dating from the eleventh to the eighteenth centuries, criticizes others for ignoring them – then proceeds to do the same herself.[14]

It soon becomes clear that the real purpose of establishing such a unifying structure is to imply that the reformist advocates for the discouragement or banning of *sati* were not in any meaningful sense more progressive and humanistically inclined than their opponents. Improvement of the lot of women was no more than the means to the end of establishing the priority of classical texts. And so a late (1830) text of Ramchan, in which humanistic arguments do not appear (fairly obviously, because it was written as a rejoinder to a conservative plea for the withdrawal of Bentinck's ban which used legalistic, textual arguments alone) is chosen as a key sample of reformist literature, ignoring far more powerful earlier writings by Rammohan himself. But then humanistic pleas on behalf of suffering womankind *had* figured movingly and very prominently in these other tracts. Selective and partial quotations, torn out of their proper context of specific polemics, are hardly the best way of establishing what could have been an interesting hypothesis. Lata Mani does have a point when she argues that conservative and reformist discourses both denied agency to women, but somehow in that process the basic palpable horror of *sati* as 'one of the most violent of patriarchal practices' tends to get almost elided.[15]

My seconed example is Rosalind O'Hanlon's 'Issues of Widowhood'.[16] O'Hanlon is the author of a fine study of Phule's anti-caste movement and ideology in late-nineteenth-century Maharashtra. Her more recent article, too, contains a valuable account of a remarkable feministic tract by Tarabai Shinde written in 1882 in the context of an infanticide by a Brahman widow. At the beginning of 'Issues of Widowhood', O'Hanlon makes what I consider to be an entirely valid criticism of the valorization by some Subaltern Studies historians of community consciousness taken as a bloc: such an assumption, she points out, could be a hindrance in the analysis of gender and other kinds of tensions within the community. Yet O'Hanlon, too, eventually succumbs to the lure of the Saidian framework. She criticizes Tarabai for failing to see 'the essentialization of feminine nature in public debate – as a reproduction from the gendered idiom which colonial officials employed in the naturalization of their authority, reappearing – among Indian men themselves'. But 'Indian men' hardly required the help of British officials to essentialize feminine nature as dangerous unless kept under patriarchal control. They had two thousand years or more of indigenous, highly patriarchal and oppressive traditions and texts where, too, feminine nature had been essentialized. But in such analyses all agency is now confined to colonialists, due to a highly simplified and homogenized conception of domination. The possibility that colonial conceptions of gender could also have been moulded in part by inputs from high-caste Indian male assistants and subordinates on whom they often had to depend is not explored at all. British conceptions of gender, again, are implicitly taken as finished and unchanging: an assumption particularly absurd and unhistorical for the nineteenth century.[17]

Applications of the Saidian framework to India, then, have so far produced little more than reiterations of the already said. The centrality of colonial power and racism had been the staple of Indian nationalist polemics throughout its long history. No major sophisticated textual analysis has emerged as yet: Chatterjee's book, fundamentally, remains a fairly conventional history of ideas, conclusions and jargon apart. Nor has the influence of Foucault produced substantial work on the microphysics of colonial power as conveyed through the nitty-gritty of administration and disciplinary institutions.

In the principal area affected by colonial discourse analysis, studies of the nineteenth-century middle class, partial continuities emerge not only with earlier assaults on the once-dominant 'renaissance' model, but even, paradoxically, with features of that model itself.[18] That had been an impact–response schema, in which Western education was supposed to have brought about an 'awakening' into 'modernity'. The current critique inverts the value judgements, so that awakening becomes enslavement. But the constituent elements remain the same, as well as the assumption of a basically one-way flow of inspiration or power, and there is a similar, indeed often much enhanced denial of autonomy or agency to Indians. The focus remains, as before, on the well-known intellectuals, the 'high' literati – this is particularly noticeable, for instance, in Chatterjee's *Nationalist Thought*. A similar pattern is noticeable in critiques of the role of English education and literature as principal instruments of colonial hegemony. It is forgotten how marginal these things usually remained to the overall colonial enterprise – in financial terms, for instance.

Imperialist controls over the peasantry can hardly be explained by an educational system from the benefits or ills of which the vast majority of them were entirely excluded. As for the intelligentsia, the transformation in two generations of Macaulay's dream-child into Kipling's banderlog is sufficient indication that the earlier expectations had not been entirely realized. With the rise of nationalism, it became regular colonialist practice to brand the English-educated as an alienated elite, in contrast to the simple uneducated peasant who would trust his paternalist British overlord if not misguided by the babus.

The limits of the Saidian assumptions in the field of colonial cultural studies are perhaps most clearly revealed through Gauri Viswanathan's *Masks of Conquest*, precisely because this is a work with considerable insights and new data. Yet the mere historian cannot but be startled by the assertion, right at the beginning, that the problem is to understand why English education (or perhaps the teaching of English literature – the two are never clearly distinguished in the book) became the core of colonial hegemony, whereas 'the exercise of direct force [was] discarded as a means of maintaining social control'.[19] Again, Viswanathan does refer occasionally to the possibility of autonomous and multiple appropriations by Indians of the culture being imposed on them – only to declare promptly that how Indians may have 'manipulated . . . and selectively reinterpreted it for their own purposes [is] outside the scope of this book . . . in fact irrelevant to it'. The reason given for this self-denying act is that the work is restricted to 'literary textual analysis' (p. 11) – a curiously old-fashioned disjunction of 'literary' and non-literary, one would have thought. In effect, then, the seamless cultural hegemony of English education/literature can be assumed, since any testing out of this proposition through analysis of the impact on educated Indians has been ruled out of court.[20] But all that has been 'proved', really, is that the British often had hegemonic intentions when they introduced English education and English literature: which should hardly qualify as stop-press news.

It is interesting to consider also how 'elitist' historiography, much abused by early Subaltern Studies, has in effect returned under the same auspices in the wake of the Saidian entry. Such a pattern has not been an uncommon feature of the postmodernistic turn in other countries, too.[21] The framework, further, has become a positive barrier in the way of exploring new themes even in its preferred field of nineteenth-century middle-class studies. These could include, for instance, the implications of two developments, contemporaneous with Western education but very much less studied: the belated entries, under colonial auspices, of print culture and clock time. The first, through its concomitant in the rise of vernacular prose, vastly enlarged discursive possibilities, advantage of which could be taken also by some women and low-caste men. As for clock time, its disciplinary dimensions manifested themselves in colonial Bengal primarily through *chakri*, the clerical job in British-controlled administrative and mercantile offices. The colonial middle class did not consist only of successful intellectuals or professional people. It included a much larger number of humble, if still predominantly upper-caste, clerks who had been largely ignored both in 'renaissance' historiography and by its present-day critics.[22] And if the Saidian framework is unhelpful in such matters, it has had the further unfortunate consequence of leading many to disregard the very considerable work being done in areas of modern Indian history untouched by its influence. Thus there have been major advances in economic history, yet many young students and scholars who want to be 'in' with changes nowadays often develop a contempt for research considered, illogically, almost by definition 'reductionist' and philosophically naive.

The political implications of the Saidian framework deserve equal attention, for many of its adherents sincerely value it as a radical intervention. The problems here, as I have already indicated, have been highlighted in recent years by the congruence noticeable between some possible implications of this approach and the standpoint of the more sophisticated Hindutva intellectuals.[23] Certainly a total rejection of the modern, post-Enlightenment West as alien, colonial importation can lead to dangerous kinds of 'indigenist' obscurantism. Even the well-intentioned argument, elaborated by Gyan Pandey, for example, that communal divisions are Western colonial constructs, products of census categories, is at best double-edged:[24] caste (or, for that matter, class) divisions may be treated in similar manner as illegitimate importations of Western classificatory devices.[25]

Why, then, the undoubted popularity of this framework among so many subjectively radical intellectuals? Variations across disciplines could be one explanation – the colonial dimension, for instance, had been largely ignored earlier in literature studies, or for that matter in much first-world feminism. The expatriate status of many of the votaries of what today can be almost called a Said cult is also relevant. Racial discrimination and Western arrogance might well appear much more obvious from such a location, particularly today, than power structures and tensions within third-world countries – and too much talk about oppressive features of life there possibly even demeaning. Above all, intellectual tendencies embodied in Said and Foucault with their emphasis upon the all-pervading and irresistible nature of modern forms of power do appear for many to be responding to basic and characteristic features of the world we live in today. An additional factor has been the general disillusionment with earlier kinds of radical theory, most notably Marxism. Looking back upon the past from perspectives like these appears 'natural' enough, but then surely one of the real strengths of postmodernist tendencies has been their call to question all that seems 'natural'.

One can respond to vital and central issues, but in ways that are ultimately unhelpful and even counter-productive – and that, I have been arguing, is what fundamentally characterizes the Saidian framework, at least so far as my own discipline of history is concerned. The assumption that no other intellectual tradition or resource exists to confront the admittedly central issues highlighted by Said or Foucault is deeply self-limiting. The untimely death of E. P. Thompson forcibly brings to mind one such resource: the social history tradition of which he had been the pioneer and finest representative, rooted in a most creative kind of Marxism which is by no means dead, and indeed shows some signs of getting revived. Thompson in his last major historical work, *Customs in Common*, raised important questions about the assumption, so often made nowadays, that hegemony necessarily 'imposes an all-embracing domination upon the ruled'. His work on eighteenth-century England had revealed the many ways in which plebeian groups had been able to appropriate and use in their own, partly autonomous ways, gentry conceptions of order and deference: the 'moral economy of the poor' underpinning fixation of prices through crowd action being one notable example. A second limitation consisted in the many areas of eighteenth-century plebeian life largely untouched by ruling-class norms. Always acutely aware of the 'discipline of historical context', Thompson was quick to add 'This [all-embracing domination] may perhaps have happened here and there, but not in England, not in the eighteenth century.'[26] Surely extrapolating one reading of the totalizing nature of contemporary forms of power into earlier times, as axiom rather than hypothesis, is a foreclosure of possibilities through 'essentialization'. Was Thompson a better postmodernist than many of its votaries today? And, to return for a moment to nineteenth-century India, Thompson's two suggested limits to hegemony do seem worthy of exploration. The colonial educated middle class was able to appropriate elements from the culture being imposed on them to develop critiques of colonial power and exploitation, and some areas of indigenous life did remain relatively free of foreign penetration.[27]

A book written by a colleague of Thompson, Peter Linebaugh's *The London Hanged: Crime and Civil Society in Eighteenth-century England,* which I happened to read around the time of Thompson's death, provides heartening evidence of the continuing strengths of the social-historical tradition he had done so much to mould.[28] Linebaugh uses Tyburn records and a host of other documents to raise questions about the omnipotence of Foucault's 'carceral' society. More significantly, he has been able to relate the development of effective disciplinary power (including Bentham's Panopticon) to transformations in production relations in capitalistic ways: the whittling down, for instance, on grounds of efficiency and sanctity of capitalist private property of earlier customary rights and perquisites of specific groups of London artisans and casual labourers. And, unlike Thompson, he extends his narrative into a kind of analysis of the Atlantic economy from below, with women and black labourers figuring prominently as protagonists in a complex interweaving of class, race and gender. Reading Thompson's *Customs in Common*, or Linebaugh, reminds one of how much many of us are losing through confinement within what is currently trendy in Western 'third-world studies'.

But insights from social historians working in very different spatial fields can help only a small part of the way: what is crucial is the development of analytical tools appropriate for South Asian colonial contexts which will be able to handle more effectively the nuances, ambiguities and interrelationships of multiple kinds of power and oppression. It is unlikely that a single, fully satisfactory alternative to Saidian common sense is going to emerge, but germs of more complex understandings are already discernible: particularly perhaps in the two areas most difficult to accommodate within colonial discourse analysis, gender and caste.[29]

Notes

1. Antonio Gramsci, *Selections from the Prison Notebooks*, eds G. Hoare and G. N. Smith (New York: International Publishers, 1971), 323–8.

2. 'Said's work frequently relapses into the essentializing modes it attacks and is ambivalently enmeshed in the totalizing habits of Western humanism', James Clifford, 'Review Essay: *Orientalism*, by Edward Said', *History and Theory* 19 (1980); Aijaz Ahmad, *In Theory: Classes, Nations, Literatures* (London: Verso, 1992).

3. Toril Moi, *Sexual/Textual Politics* (London: Methuen, 1985), 110–19; Gerald Graff, 'Cooptation', in H. Aram Veeser, ed., *The New Historicism* (New York: Routledge, 1989), 174.

4. Thus the *Holy Family* warns of the dangers of making 'history . . . a person apart, a metaphysical subject of which real human individuals are but the bearers'. See also the attack on teleology in *German Ideology* – the temptation of making 'later history . . . the goal of earlier history', D. McLellan, ed., *Karl Marx: Selected Writings* (Oxford: Oxford University Press, 1977), 139; Marx–Engels, *Collected Works* (Moscow: Progress Publishers, 1976), V: 50.

5. Gayatri C. Spivak, 'Can the Subaltern Speak? Speculations on Widow Sacrifice', in *Marxism and the Interpretation of Culture*, eds Cary Nelson and Lawrence Grossberg (London: Macmillan, 1988), 271–313.

6. R. Muchembled, *Culture populaire et culture des élites dans la France moderne (XV–XVIII siècle)* (Paris, 1978).

7. E. P. Thompson, *The Poverty of Theory* (London: Merlin, 1978).

8. Partha Chatterjee, *Nationalist Thought in the Colonial World: A Derivative Discourse* (Delhi: Oxford University Press, 1986). Future page references are incorporated in the text.

9. For an effective critique of Saidian assumptions in the field of Hindu patriarchy and law, see Tanika Sarkar, 'Rhetoric against Age of Consent: Resisting Colonial Reason and the Death of a Child-Wife', *Economic and Political Weekly* 28: 36 (4 September 1993).

10. Ashis Nandy, *The Intimate Enemy* (Delhi: Oxford University Press, 1983), ix.

11. I now consider this to have been a major limitation also of my *Modern India 1855–1947* (Delhi: Macmillan, 1983).

12. Gautam Bhadra's interview is in *Nayya*, 2 (1991); for a rejoinder, written by Neeladri Bhattacharji, Sumit Sarkar and Tanika Sarkar, and Bhadra's reply to this criticism, see *Nayya*, 3 (1992). Dipesh Chakrabarty's article, 'Our History and His Master's Voice', is in *Baromas* (Autumn 1992). For a recent, more nuanced, but fundamentally similar article, see Dipesh Chakrabarty, 'The Difference/Deferral of a Colonial Modernity: Public Debates on Domesticity in British Bengal', *History Workshop Journal* 36 (1993).

13. Lata Mani, 'Contentious Traditions: the Debate on Sati in Colonial India', in Kumkum Sangari and Urvashi Vaid, *Recasting Women: Essays in Colonial History* (New Delhi: Kali for Women, 1989), 88–126.

14. Here Mani's article stands in marked contrast to the much more substantive discussion of pre-colonial and colonial discourses on *sati* in Spivak, 'Can the Subaltern Speak?'

15. In significant contrast, it is violence which is foregrounded in the essay (emphatically not written from Saidian premises) by Sudesh Vaid and Kumkum Sangari from which I have taken this quotation: 'Institutions, Beliefs, Ideologies: Widow Immolation in Contemporary Rajasthan', *Economic and Political Weekly*, 26: 17 (27 April 1991).

16. Rosalind O'Hanlon, 'Issues of Widowhood', in *Contesting Power*, eds Douglas Haynes and Gyan Prakash (Delhi: Oxford University Press, 1991).

17. For some exploration of this dialectic, see Tanika Sarkar, 'Rhetoric Against the Age of Consent'.

18. This is readily acknowledged; see, for instance, Partha Chatterji, 'Fruits of Macaulay's Poison Tree', in Asok Mitra, ed., *The Truth Unites* (Calcutta: Subarnarekha, 1985). Chatterji argues, quite rightly, that the newness of the 1980s writing is the extension of the earlier critique into a questioning or rejection of Enlightenment reason as a whole. To my mind, there, precisely, lies the problem.

19. Gauri Viswanathan, *Masks of Conquest: Literary Study and British Rule in India* (New York: Columbia University Press, 1989), 10. One had not realized before that direct force had ever been abandoned, with 1857, Jalianwalabagh, and 1942 as only the most obvious examples.

20. Actually a 'test' of a sort is carried out later in chapter V, through extracts of highly loyalist examination papers of Hindu College students taken from Parliamentary Papers. The near-contemporary proceedings of the Derozian Society for Acquisition of General Knowledge, which is easily available in reprint today, would considerably qualify this impression of unqualified loyalism.

21. The point has been made by several fairly sympathetic critics: see, for example, Raphael Samuel, 'Reading the Signs', *History Workshop Journal* 32–3 (Autumn 1991, Spring 1992); David Mayfield and Susan Thorne, 'Social History and Its Discontents', *Social History* 50 (May 1992).

22. For some attempts to explore problems of this sort, see my 'Calcutta in the "Bengal Renaissance"', in Sukanta Chaudhuri, *Calcutta the Living City*, vol. I (Delhi: Oxford University Press, 1990); 'Kaliyuga, Chakri, and Bhakti: Ramakrishna and His

Times', *Economic and Political Weekly* 27: 29 (18 July 1992); and Tanika Sarkar, 'A Book of Her Own, A Life of Her Own: Autobiography of A Nineteenth Century Woman', in *History Workshop* 36 (1993).

23. Hindutva intellectuals are defenders of Hindu-Right, Sangh Parivar, positions.

24. Gyanendra Pandey, *The Construction of Communalism in Colonial North India* (Delhi: Oxford University Press, 1990).

25. Thus it is not really surprising, or even entirely unfair, that the late Girilal Jain and Swapan Dasgupta have, in their journalistic essays, occasionally tried to appropriate Said, or Ronald Inden's *Imagining India* (Oxford: Blackwell, 1990).

26. E. P. Thompson, *Customs in Common* (Harmondsworth: Penguin, 1993), 87.

27. See, for instance, Tanika Sarkar's essays referred to above.

28. Peter Linebaugh, *The London Hanged: Crime and Civil Society in Eighteenth-century England* (Harmondsworth: Penguin, 1993).

29. I am thinking particularly of essays like Uma Chakravarti, 'Whatever Happened to the Vedic Dasi? Orientalism, Nationalism, and a Script for the Past', in Sangari and Vaid, eds, *Recasting Women*, 27–87, and Vaid and Sangari, 'Institutions, Beliefs, Ideologies . . .'; the works of Gail Omvedt and Rosalind O'Hanlon on Phule; and the ongoing research of scholars like M. Pandyan, Sekhar Bandopadyay or Swaraj Basu on lower-caste movements in south India and Bengal.

12

Radical Histories and Question of Enlightenment Rationalism: Some Recent Critiques of *Subaltern Studies*

Dipesh Chakrabarty

Yes, I know all that. I should be modern.
Marry again. See strippers at the Tease.
Touch Africa. Go to the movies.

Impale a six-inch spider
under a lens. Join the Test-
ban, or become The Outsider.

Or pay to shake my fist
(or whatever-you-call-it) at a psychoanalyst.
And when I burn

I should smile, dry-eyed,
and nurse martinis like the Marginal Man.
But, sorry, I cannot unlearn

conventions of despair.
They have their pride.
I must seek and will find

my particular hell only in my hindu mind:
must translate and turn
till I blister and roast . . .

Source: A. K. Ramanujan, 'Conventions of Despair', in *Selected Poems*, Delhi, 1976

Subaltern Studies, the Gramsci-inspired series on Indian history that became influential in the 1980s, has recently come in for a substantial amount of hostile criticism, particularly in India, on the ground that it has gone reactionary.[1] Why? Because, comes the answer, the Marxist critique of capitalism that informed the earlier volumes in the series has now been replaced – under the baleful influence of deconstructive, post-structuralist and postmodernist philosophy, it is said – by a critique of the rationalism that marked the European Enlightenment. Since Marxism is inconceivable except as a legatee of this rationalist tradition, a critique of this nature must be, at least implicitly, a critique of Marxism as well. And is not that dangerous, it is asked, in a situation in India where the rise of a 'religious' and aggressive Hindu right demands, if anything, an ever more vigilant attention to the secular goals of class struggle, democracy and socialism?

In a recent essay on the 'fascist' nature of the Hindu right, the eminent Indian left-wing historian, Sumit Sarkar, spells out why a critique of Enlightenment rationalism is dangerous in India today. His propositions could be arranged as follows: (1) 'Fascist ideology in Europe . . . owed something to a general turn-of-the-century move away from what were felt to be the sterile rigidities of Enlightenment rationalism'; (2) '[N]ot dissimilar ideas have become current intellectual coin in the West, and by extension they have started to influence Indian academic life'; (3) That these 'current academic fashions' (Sarkar mentions 'postmodernism') 'can reduce the resistance of intellectuals to the ideas of Hindutva [Hindu-ness] has already become evident'. Examples: 'The "critique of colonial discourse" . . . has stimulated forms of indigenism not easy to distinguish from the standard Sangh parivar argument . . . that Hindutva is superior to Islam and Christianity (and by extension to the creations of the modern west like science, democracy or marxism) because of its allegedly unique roots.' Sarkar warns that '[a]n uncritical cult of the "popular" or "subaltern", particularly when combined with the rejection of Enlightenment rationalism . . . can lead even radical historians down strange paths' that, for Sarkar, bear 'ominous' resemblance to Mussolini's condemnation of the 'teleological' idea of progress and to Hitler's exaltation of the German *volk* over hair-splitting intelligence (Sarkar 1993: 164–5). Gautum Bhadra and myself, identified by Sarkar as two 'members of the *Subaltern Studies* editorial team', are Sarkar's examples of historians who have been led down 'strange paths' by their 'uncritical' adulation of the subaltern and by their 'rejection of Enlightenment rationalism' (Sarkar 1993: 167). Sarkar stops short of calling us 'fascist' – we still qualify for the label 'radical' – but one can see that things may change.

Tom Brass, in a review article on Gyan Prakash (Prakash has since joined the *Subaltern Studies* collective), and the respected civil liberties activist K. Balagopal, in an essay on the dangers of neo-Hinduism, express similar misgivings. The charge appears in a summary form in Brass's piece: 'The real importance of postmodernism lies in its theoretical impact on political practice: it forbids socialism, encourages bourgeois democracy and allows fascism' (Brass 1993: 1165). Misquoting Gramsci (and thereby Romain Rolland), Brass accuses postmodernism (and his other phobias) of having distorted Gramsci:

> postmodernism, popular culture and resistance theory have all combined to invert/subvert the famous dictum of Gramsci [here Brass manages to get the quote wrong in spite of referring to the right pages in the *Prison Notebooks*] about the nature of political action: instead of pessimism of the spirit and optimism of the will, they now license optimism of the spirit and pessimism of the will'. (Brass 1993: 1165)

K. Balagopal blames postmodernists' and subalternists' alleged rejection of the possibility of 'objective' analysis for the inadequacies of left resistance to the fascistic Hindutva push:

> Having noted in more than sufficient detail [he writes] the sins committed by secularists, it is time now to look at matters objectively, however dubious that task may seem to the subaltern theorists and the postmodernists whose current preponderance among the progressive intelligentsia is one reason . . . for the latter's hopelessly inadequate response to the bulldozing of Hindutva. (Balagopal 1993: 790)

The agenda, according to him, is that of fighting for 'equality and justice at all levels' and 'to create a real unity of all oppressed people'. This is what he sees thwarted by both 'seemingly down-to-earth and untheoretical Gandhians' as well as the 'incomprehensible postmodernists' whose resulting attitude of 'theoretical and political flippancy is doing a lot of damage' (Balagopal 1993: 793).

The accusations are not unique to the Indian situation. Readers may be reminded of Christopher Norris's *The Truth of Postmodernism*, which argues that postmodernist critiques of 'universalism' and 'Enlightenment rationalism' preach in effect a form of cultural relativism which is at least politically irresponsible when it is not downwright dangerous (Norris 1993). Our critics are seldom as well read in poststructuralist philosophy as Norris, but the sentiment they express is the same. For a historian, the advantage in discussing the Indian or South Asianist critics is that their accusation is levelled against historians, thus allowing me an opportunity to discuss why maintaining a critical relationship to Enlightenment rationalism may be of value in developing a third-world historiography. So in the rest of this essay, I will engage these critics and their criticisms, focusing in particular on Sarkar, not only because his is the most elaborate of the three statements at hand but also because his criticisms repudiate his own earlier involvement with the project of *Subaltern Studies*. Sarkar, in other words, belongs to the same tradition of historiography from which *Subaltern Studies* has evolved, the tradition of Marxist history writing in the subcontinent. This conversation, in many ways, is with that tradition. But it also concerns a larger criticism now being made of post-structuralism generally.

As this essay itself will, I hope, make clear, maintaining a critical position with respect to the legacies of the European Enlightenment does not entail a wholesale rejection of the tradition of rational argumentation. My procedure here will be grounded in that tradition while being critical of it. My argument will be presented in three parts. In the first segment, I will seek to demonstrate how a certain form of hyper-rationalism characteristic of colonial modernity has impaired Indian Marxists' capacity to engage with 'religion' (something without which India cannot be imagined). The second section will argue how colonial histories are particularly useful in making visible what is sometimes called 'the unreasonable origins of reason'. And the final section will endeavour to show – without in any way attempting a general defence of post-structuralism – why post-structuralist and deconstructionist philosophies are useful in developing approaches suited to studying subaltern histories under conditions of colonial modernities.

Hyper-rationalism of Colonial Modern

My argument here is simple and I will basically use some material from Bengali history and historiography – traditions I share with Sarkar – to make my points. My contention is that scientific rationalism, or the spirit of scientific enquiry, was introduced into colonial India from the very beginning as an antidote to (Indian) religion, particularly Hinduism, which was seen, both by missionaries as well as by administrators – and in spite of the Orientalists – as a bundle of 'superstition' and 'magic'. Hinduism, wrote the Scottish missionary Alexander Duff in 1839, is 'a stupendous system of error' (Laird 1972: 207). Indeed, the paradox of early European-founded schools in Bengal being more 'liberal' and 'secular' in their curricula than their counterparts in England is resolved by the fact that the missionaries did not perceive much contradiction between 'rationalism' and the precepts of Christianity and assumed that an awakening to reason, rather than the more provocative strategy of direct conversion, would itself lead to the undermining of the superstitions that made up Hinduism. As Michael Laird writes of the period:

> Apart from a genuine desire to advance learning for its own sake, the missionaries also believed that western science would undermine belief in the Hindu scriptures; the new geography, for example, could hardly be reconciled with the *Puranas* . . . [They] thus acted as instigators of an intellectual awakening, or even revolution . . . [and their] schools were obvious agents of such a Christian Enlightenment. There is incidentally an instructive contrast with contemporary England, where the wide curriculum that was beginning to appear in Bengal was still very unusual in elementary schools. (Laird 1972: 86–7)

Even the very act of mastering English, wrote Alexander Duff, must make 'the student . . . *ten-fold less* the child of Pantheism, idolatry and superstition than before' (Laird 1972: 207–8).

It is this simultaneous coding of (Western) 'knowledge' itself as rational and Hinduism as something that was both a 'religion' as well as a bundle of superstitions, that launched the career of a certain kind of colonial hyper-rationalism among Indian intellectuals who self-consciously came to regard themselves as 'modern'. Of course, there have been important Indian intellectuals both before the British rule and after – the nineteenth-century reformers like Rammohan Roy and Swami Dayanand Saraswati or even the nationalist scientist J. C. Bose would fall in this category – who strove, not unlike many intellectuals in European history, to develop dialogues between the 'scientific-rational' and the 'religious-spiritual'.[2] But we are yet to work out how these heritages have influenced the nature of modern academic knowledge formations in India. In its self-image, modern Indian secular scholarship, particularly the strands that flowed into Marxist social history writing, not only partakes of the social sciences' view of the world as 'disenchanted', it even displays antipathy to anything that smacks of the 'religious'. A certain kind of intellectual bankruptcy, a paralysis of imagination, and a certain spell of reductionism have often attended attempts by Indian Marxist scholars to understand religious practices. The blight that this has produced in the intellectual landscape of a country whose people have never shown any sense of embarrassment about being able to imagine the 'supernatural' in a variety of forms, is only matched by the marginalization of the Marxist left in the struggles that constitute everyday lives in India.

To be sure, these developments in India shared something of the spirit of the eighteenth-century Enlightenment in Europe to the extent that the Enlightenment, for all its internal diversity, 'meant repudiation of the irrational and the superstitious' (Behrens 1985: 26). Or as a historian of the Enlightenment has put it:

> Insofar as it was concerned with social and political questions, the 18th century Enlightenment . . . produced a great variety of mutually

> incompatible ideas . . . For all this, nevertheless, there were points on which people with any claim to being enlightened were agreed in every country. Particularly, Enlightenment meant the repudiation of the irrational and the superstitious . . . To be superstitious was to believe in the supernatural. (Behrens 1985: 26)

Thus, while it is true that historians today are more sensitized to the diversity within the Enlightenment, what propagated itself among modern Indian intellectuals was something like – to take Preserved Smith's expression somewhat out of context – 'the propaganda of Reason' which equated, as indeed did Smith in his own book on the Enlightenment, 'modernity' with the possession of 'scientific outlook' and 'ignorance' with 'superstition' (Smith 1966: 117). The resulting predicament for the Hindu modern was two-fold: (1) the intellectual possessing a self-defined 'scientific rationality' never made a distinction – unlike, say, practising Indian scientists who have often, without any apparent difficulty, separated their own beliefs from the philosophical assumptions of their professional knowledge systems, so that it is possible for even a theoretical physicist to seek out as *guru* some 'miracle-making' holy man – between 'science as outlook' and 'science as a collection of so many efficacious techniques', while (2) at the same time it proved impossible, in spite of some notable attempts, to align Hindu practices, the mainstream pantheon of gods and goddesses, with Christian Enlightenment.[3] It, therefore, always remained possible, given the nature of the Hindu deities, to see them as so many manifestations of belief in the magical.

Why this came to be so is a long, involved, and on the whole an unresearched story. But that analytical frameworks derived from the legacies of the European modernity create a peculiar split in our self-recognition or self-representation, can be easily shown. Take, for instance, the model of the autonomous, individual subject without which the idea of individual rights cannot be thought. The idea and the language of 'rights' have been of undoubted utility in a multitude of struggles in India – so much so that it would be silly to regard them as in any sense foreign. Yet, what is their relationship to the ideals of the extended family or kinship which also mould us as subjects in India? (To avoid unnecessary argumentation, however, I should make it clear that I am not reproducing here an 'extended versus nuclear family' argument. On the ground, many extended families are as horrible as many nuclear families. Nor am I suggesting any essentialistic East/West distinctions, for quite a few of my 'Western' friends live in or practise versions of extended kinship.) The question usually goes unanswered in Indian history when it is not seen through some version of the sterile 'tradition/modernity' dichotomy. An instance of the historiographical silence that our frameworks produce could be the phenomenon of friendship. We have as yet no researched histories of modern friendships in India, but surely it would not be surprising if it turned out that kinship-derived models of personhood and sociality have been extremely influential in the formation of the affective bonds we now develop in European-derived public spaces and institutions such as the school, university and the office (not to speak of the political party).

A similar point can be made about the so-called religious as it comes into our lives and shapes the structures of our perception cognition and affect. A large range of our pleasures, desires, emotions and understanding of what constitutes the social (including the family) have the religious built into them at least as collectively practised rituals. How else could I – and here I deliberately speak autobiographically, as a male, Bengali, (Hindu) *middle-class* Marxist (of some kind!) – have emotional access to the human and other relations conjured up in (middle-class versions of) the *Ramayana* and the *Mahabharata* in 'medieval' Bengali literature about minor gods and goddesses, in Vaishnava stories and songs about Radha and Krishna, in the puranic legends about Durga and Kali, in the mystical songs of 'bauls' and 'fakirs'? What makes it possible for me (and many others) still to be moved by nationalist songs of Mukundadas, Tagore, D. L. Roy, Atulprasad Sen, Nazrul Islam that directly draw on 'dharma'/kinship to provide a sense of the nation/community? It is obviously because the process of becoming 'modern' in the Bengali context never left these things out so that my desires, emotions, aesthetics and even my sense of what it means to be a person were never trained simply in the light of a world view that was just liberal or 'secular' (in the sense of 'godlessness' in which this word is used in India).

The problem is not the so-called alienation of the secular intellectual in India from its 'religious' elements. The Hindu right often makes this criticism of the people on the left and Sarkar is quite right to reject it (Sarkar 1993). The problem is rather that we do not have analytical categories in academic discourse that do justice to the real, everyday and multiple 'connections' we have to what we, in becoming modern, have come to see as 'non-rational'. 'Tradition/modernity', 'rational/non-rational', 'intellectual/emotion' – these untenable and problematic binaries have haunted our self-representations in social science language since the nineteenth century. Andrew Sartori's work on the nineteenth-century Bengali Orientalist and Indologist Rajendralal Mitra has recently drawn our attention to this problem. As Sartori shows, the split between the analytic and the affective is something itself produced by the colonial discourse and marks for ever the speech of the colonial intellectual. Sartori has given us a telling example of this phenomenon from the last century. He quotes Rajendralal Mitra, writing, in the early 1870s, on the custom of 'blood sacrifice' in ancient India, a practice the Orientalist in him would no doubt have seen as barbaric and uncivilized. However, this 'ancient' practice was in no sense antiquated in Mitra's own times. As the following quotation shows, Mitra had had some personal exposure to it. Yet notice how he categorizes his own, lived connection to the ritual as part of his 'affective' rather than the 'rational' or 'reasoning' self. At the end of his essay discussing the custom, Mitra writes in a memorable passage:

> The offering of one's blood to the goddess [Kali] is a medieval and modern rite . . . The last time I saw the ceremony was six years ago [when?] when my late revered parent, tottering with age, made the offering for my recovery from a dangerous and long-protracted attack of pleurisy. Whatever may be thought of it by persons brought up under a creed different from that of the Indo-Aryans, I cannot recall to memory the fact *without feeling the deepest emotion for the boundless affection* which prompted it. (emphasis added)[4]

This strong opposition between the rational and the affective, or between reason and emotion, characteristic of our colonial hyper-rationalism, has generally afflicted Indian Marxist historians' attempt to understand the place of the 'religious' in Indian public and political life. Since my polemic at this point is especially directed to Sarkar's critique of *Subaltern Studies*, I will begin with him, with his own study of the Swadeshi [Swadeshi = one's own land] movement that broke out in Bengal around the year 1905 when the British, in an imperious and high-handed manner, decided to split Bengal into two halves and thus endanger the modern (Hindu) Bengali identity. Sarkar's book, *The Swadeshi Movement in Bengal*, a study of the nationalist resistance against this piece of British imperialism, is undoubtedly one of the most important monographs of modern Indian history. Erudite and enormously well documented as it is, this 'Marxist' piece of Indian history scrupulously steers clear of any formulaic approach. Yet there is a remarkable failure of the intellect in this book every time it is a question of interpreting or explaining the role 'religion' played in this political movement which did more than any other phase in modern Bengali history to bring to life and immortalize, for both Muslims and Hindus, the image of Bengal as a mother-goddess demanding love and sacrifice from her children.

This was a movement, as Sarkar himself so carefully documents, absolutely full of Hindu-religious sentiments and imagination. But notice how Sarkar, while he is willing to grant that a modern political movement may have to use 'religion' as a means to a political end (and particularly so in a peasant society), disapproves of moments when, for the historical actors involved, religion looked like becoming 'an end in itself'. He writes:

> what seems indisputable is that the other-worldly pull of religion tended to assert itself particularly at moments of strain and frustration. *Religion cultivated at first as a means to the end of mass contact and stimulation of morale, could all too easily become an end in itself.* The process of inversion is reflected clearly in Aurobindo's [a nationalist leader] famous Uttarpara speech . . . 'I spoke once before with this force in me and I said then that this movement is not a political movement and that nationalism is not politics but a religion, a creed, a faith. I say it again today, but I put it in another way. I say no longer that nationalism is a creed, a religion, a faith; I say that it is the Sanatan Dharma which for us is nationalism.' (Sarkar 1977: 316; emphasis added)

So religion as a 'means' is acceptable, but religion as 'an end in itself' is not. For Sarkar, the Marxist historian, the question never arises as to whether a 'religious sensibility' could also use a political structure and vocabulary as a means to a (religious) end (for that indeed is the burden of Aurobindo's speech from which Sarkar seems to have his ear turned away).

Why does this happen? Why does one of our most capable and knowledgeable historians fail to give us any insight into moments in the history of our political and public life when religious sentiments presented themselves as their own end and not as means to some end defined by a European political philosophy, however much some Indians may have made this philosophy their own? It is because history for Sarkar is a perpetual struggle between the forces of 'reason' and 'humanism' on the one side and those of 'emotion and faith' on the other, and we are left in no doubt as to which side Sarkar himself is on. Of the Swadeshi movement he writes in a manner that also discloses to us his view of this 'ideological battleground' on which he positions himself:

> [An] . . . important . . . theme [of the Swadeshi movement] is the ideological conflict between modernism and traditionalism – between an attitude which broadly speaking demands social reforms, tries to evaluate things and ideas by the criteria of reason and present-day utility, and bases itself on a humanism seeking to transcend limits of caste and religion; and a logically opposite trend which defends and justifies existing social mores in the name of immemorial tradition and the glorious past, and which tends to substitute emotion and faith for reason. (Sarkar 1977: 24)

What else is this but an unreflexive (re)statement of 'the struggle of the Enlightenment with Superstition'? 'Reason and truth' on the side of democracy and humanism, and 'faith' – a 'tissue of superstitions, prejudices and errors', as a famous philosopher of the Enlightenment put it – on the side of tyranny (Hegel 1977: 330). This conflict, for Sarkar, structures the whole narrative of Bengali modernity. He traces it 'right through the nineteenth century from the days of the Atmiya Sabha and the Dharma Sabha [1820s]' and sees it 'continu[ing] at the heart of the Swadeshi movement just as in the [Bengal] "renaissance" which had preceded and prepared the way for it'.

> Insofar as the swadeshi age saw a determined though not entirely successful effort to give the national movement a solid mass basis, the period can be regarded as a sort of test for the relevance of these opposed ideological trends in the work of national awakening. (Sarkar 1977: 34–5)

This is Enlightenment rationalism indeed, but now (re)visiting the history of the colonized as a modernist dogma and wreaking intellectual havoc in its trail. Sarkar's failure to give us any insights into the 'religious' that constantly erupts into the political in Indian modernity is not a personal failure. It is failure of hyper-rationalism, a failure that marks the intellect of the colonial modern. It occurs within a paradigm that sees 'science' and 'religion' as ultimately, and irrevocably, opposed to each other.

This dogmatism is an old and even respectable part of the history of Bengali 'secularism'. I will provide two examples to give the reader some idea of the intellectual tradition that Sarkar and I have both inherited and against which, in part, we have to struggle. In 1949, some leading Bengali academic intellectuals of left-liberal persuasion organized a series of lectures in Calcutta to discuss the question of Indian modernity. The lectures were published in 1950 by the Left Book Club as a book, *Modern Age and India.* Its essays, edited by A. N. Bose, reflected an implicit consensus among the contributors as to what 'modernity' was. They agreed, (1) modernity, apart from the differences imposed by different national histories, was universally the same all over the world (a view most powerfully expressed by Nirmal Bhattacharya, pp. 242–3); (2) that 'the Modern Age all over the world undeniably stem[med] from modern European history' (Triupurari Chakravarti, p. 13); (3) that '[t]he most glorious characteristic of the spirit of the modern age [was] its emancipation from dogmas ... [which] ha[d] marked the ceaseless pursuit of scientific knowledge in modern times' (these are the very opening sentences of the book written by Naresh Chandra Sen Gupta, p. 1); (4) that science itself was value-neutral, 'exemplifie[d] how man ha[d] tamed the forces of nature', and science '[was] obliged to oppose religion uncompromisingly' whenever religion '[spoke] about things of this earth' (Satyendranath Bose, pp. 144 and 148); and (5) that a central meaning of modernity lay in the theme of emancipation/freedom. To be fair, the celebration of science in this book was not totally devoid of any critical spirit. Writing in the shadows of the first atom bomb, several of our authors warned about the evil consequences that could follow from the 'unlimited nature' of the power that 'science' could offer humankind (see in particular the contributions by Satyendranath Bose and Nareshchandra Sen Gupta). They also made some pertinent criticisms of contemporary political leadership in India. But the faith in the capacity of 'scientific spirit' to deliver humankind from their problems runs intact through these essays. M. N. Roy, the communist-turned-radical-humanist, who also contributed to this volume, even argued that the tenets of 'modernity' were but theoretical expressions of what were 'natural instincts' in human beings anyway. Roy even extended part of the argument to animals![5]

Modern Age and India was the voice of a generation now mostly gone – optimistic, in love with the vision of a modernized, democratic India, and sure in its belief that what was opposed to scientific rationality could only be characterized as 'dogma'. Certain things had changed by the 1960s and the 1970s when Sarkar wrote *The Swadeshi Movement*. For Sarkar and his colleagues who were our intellectual mentors in a shared Calcutta, the optimism of the 1950s had been extinguished. Indian capitalism itself had put an end to that. But the colonial hyper-rationalism which opposed 'reason' to 'faith' remained. The 1970s Marxist critique of colonial India argued, as one respected historian put it, '[a]lien rule and modernity are never compatible', and deduced therefore that what India had received as a legacy of the colonial period could be characterized only as 'enclaves' of modernity:

> there were indeed variances in western European early modern developments ... on a comparative scale. Yet each particular pattern in western Europe was clearer and more spontaneous, and where foreign interference could be resisted, more *secular* and *rational* than conditions in the previous period ... What is normally described as modernity represents the superstructure of a given culture, whose economic base is the emergence of capitalism. It is unrealistic to define a superstructure without its base, to expect the fruits of modernity without the uneven development and hard-headed exploitative practices of a European modernity which often [in places like India] came to terms with feudal remnants ... and which took to colonialism for maintaining progress in its capitalist development. (De 1976: 123–4; emphasis added)

This reference to base and superstructure was representative of what would have passed for 'common sense' in Indian Marxist historiography of the 1970s. For the purpose of this discussion, however, I wish to highlight what this statement, admittedly short of the optimism of the 1950s, shares with the latter: a common understanding of what it meant to be modern. True, modernity born in Europe had been productive of colonialism in India, but it still had a discernible 'progressive content' which was 'diluted' in the colony because of underdevelopment (remember that this was the period also of 'dependency theory'). This 'progressive content' had in part to do with 'rational outlook', the 'spirit of science' and 'free enquiry', etc. '[I]t is possible', wrote Barun De in concluding his piece, 'that some future historians . . . might put the 19th and early 20th centuries at the end of a medieval period of uncertainty, instead of the beginning of the modern period, which still awaits us in the third world' (De 1976: 121–5).

'Modernity still awaits us' – this is the refrain of the hyper-rational colonial modern. Why would modernity still await us in India, more than 200 years after it was introduced by European imperialism? How long does it take for an Indian to become modern? A 'full-fledged modernity', as the idea is used in these texts, is by definition something good. It embodies the fullness of everything – of prosperity, of rationalism. It cannot ever be what we have got is all we have got. What we have is only a bad version of what is in itself good. We have not yet arrived. We look faulty though it is not our fault. The blame lies with colonialism. Colonialism stopped us from being fully modern. Scholars will repeat Barun De's lament: we are incompletely modern. Sumit Sarkar will open his book *Modern India*, published a decade after Barun De's essay, on this elegiac note: India's is a story of a 'bourgeois modernity' that is 'grievously incomplete'. The mourning will speak through Susie Tharu and K. Lalitha's impressive and sensitively edited collection *Women Writing in India: 600 BC to the Early 20th Century*:

> Scholars who have questioned . . . a linear or progressive understanding of history claim that the liberal ideals of reformers [of women's conditions] could not have been realised under the economic and political conditions of colonial rule, and warn against applying such simple, linear narratives of progress to the study of nineteenth century India. What appears as retrogressive in nationalism was not a conservative backlash, but the logical limits of reformist programmes in a colonial situation that would never, as Sumit Sarkar writes, allow more than a 'weak and distorted' caricature of 'full blooded' bourgeois modernity, either for women or for men. (Tharu and Lalitha 1991: 184)[6]

Does it now become clear as to why it might be useful for us, intellectuals of a colonial formation, to maintain a critical watch on the history of (European) reason? Why it might be helpful to see that the Enlightenment's story of the struggle of 'science-rationalism' versus 'faith-religion' can be repeated in India only as an example of bad translation? For both sides of the equation are violated in translating them across to our past and present practices. The history of our hyper-rationalism is not the same as that of Enlightenment rationalism, and the practices that we gather under the name 'religion' do not repeat the history of that European category of thought. I accept that in today's world such translations are unavoidable and often needed. But we need to recognize them for what are: they are mistranslations, no matter how much we need them in pursuing our multifarious conflicts of interests. It may precisely be an irony of our modernity that we are constantly called upon to believe in what only requires to be performed, to treat a bad translation as though it was a perfectly adequate one, that is to say, to *be* what we also *are not*. This is not a question of having to dissemble or simulate, it is rather a question of having to live poorly, in and as bad translations.

To move from the register of lament to that of irony: that is the shift produced by an attitude of incredulity towards the metanarratives of the European Enlightenment. But that is only the first step though it prepares us for opening up our histories to other possibilities, some of which I will consider in the final section of this essay.

Unreasonable Origins of Reason

Salman Rushdie's *Midnight's Children* contains a subplot which illustrates how the problem of 'force' or 'coercion' may arise in the conversation between the so-called 'modern' and the 'non-modern', and indeed how strategies of domination emerge as a necessary move to bring to a close an argument that cannot be settled through purely rational procedures. It is significant that the subaltern of this particular narrative of modernity should be a woman.

Adam Aziz, the Europe-returned medical doctor who is also the grandfather of the narrator Saleem Sinai, inaugurates a nationalist project in his domestic life when he marries Naseem Ghani. Aziz, as a modern person, knows that women in Islam/tradition have been confined/unfree. He instructs his wife 'to come out of purdah' and, as a demonstration of his will, burns her veils, saying: 'Forget about being a good Kashmiri girl. Start thinking about being a modern Indian woman' (Rushdie 1984: 34). Naseem, later the Reverend

Mother of Saleem Sinai's description, the daughter of a Muslim landlord, is from the beginning portrayed as tradition herself. Readers of the novel will recall that when Adam Aziz first encountered her as a patient in a conservative/traditional Muslim family, she could be examined only through a seven-inch hole in a bedsheet held over her body with only the relevant part of her body made visible. The doctor fell in love with this fragmented body and discovered only after their wedding the formidably 'traditional' heart that beat inside it. Their mutual incomprehension starts with their lovemaking when, on their second night, Aziz asks her 'to move a little':

> 'Move where?' she asked. 'Move how?' He became awkward and said, 'Only move. I mean, like a woman . . .' She shrieked in horror. 'My God what have I married? I know you European-returned men. You find terrible women and then you try to make us girls be like them! Listen Doctor Sahib, husband or no husband, I am not . . . any bad word woman'. (Rushdie 1984: 34)

The battle continues throughout their marriage, Aziz conducting it from the position of the knowing, willing and judging subject of modernity. His modernizing political will sometimes expresses itself in the form of physical force. He physically throws out of the house the Muslim maulvi the Reverend Mother had appointed for their children's religious education, the only element in the children's education that was of her choice. The reason he gives to his wife in defence of his action will probably warm the heart of every 'secular-rationalist' Indian: 'He was teaching them [the children] to hate, wife. He tells them to hate Hindus and Buddhists and Jains and Sikhs and who knows what other vegetarians.'

The Reverend Mother is in the position of the classic subaltern. The reasonableness of the doctor's position is never self-evident to her. And so the battle goes on in the lives of the Reverend Mother and her husband, a battle organized around mutual incomprehension (Rushdie 1984: 42–3). This mutual incomprehension is what, one could argue in Aziz's defence, drives both the good doctor and his wife to their respective desperate measures.

If I were to read this part of the novel as an allegory of the history of modernity, historians would object. It would be said that this allegory, powerful because it ran such a strong black-and-white binary of traditon/modernity right through the storyline, was not true to the complexities of 'real' history (which historians are fond of picturing in the colour grey). The narrative could have gone differently (as indeed we know from women's and subaltern histories) and might not have been structured by such a stong opposition between the modernizer and the yet-to-be-modernized. In such possible alternative accounts the Reverend Mother might have in fact needed Aziz's alliance against other patriarchal authorities, her father, or a possible mother-in-law, and could have been more amenable to his suggestions. Similarly, the peasants held down by tyrants might seek out the help of the modern in their own struggles. And what if the subaltern through their own agency discovered for themselves the pleasures of the modern: of the autonomous-self, of interiority, of science, of technology, of post-Enlightenment rationalism itself? The coming of Enlightenment rationalism, in such historical recall, would not be a story of domination. Have not the critics of the modern state had it said to them that the people actually want the state, or the critics of modern medicine that the people, once introduced to modern medicine, want it?

Granted, but then what is the relationship between Rushdie's story and the history of modernity? Rushdie's is an allegory of the *origins* of modernity. It tells us about the beginnings of the historical process through which women in the Aziz family became 'modern'. This process was not benign and that is not an unfamiliar tale to historians of modernity even in the homeland of the Enlightenment, western Europe. The door by which one enters citizenship or a nationality always has a *durwan* (gatekeeper) – himself usually only partially admitted to the rites of equality – posted outside: his job is to be mean, to abuse, bully, insult and exclude or to humiliate even when he lets you in. This is recognized by European historians and intellectuals. The violence of the discourse of public health in nineteenth-century England directed itself against the poor and the working classes (Stallybrass and White 1986). The process by which rural France is modernized in the nineteenth century is described by Eugen Weber as something akin to 'internal colonialism' (Weber 1976). Derrida discusses the same problem from within the experience of being French. 'As you know,' he writes,

> in many countries, in the past and in the present, one founding violence of the law or of the imposition of the state law has consisted in imposing a language on national or ethnic minorities regrouped by the state. This was the case in France on at least two occasions, first, when the Villers-Cotteret decree consolidated the unity of the monarchic state by imposing French as the juridico-administrative language and by forbidding . . . Latin . . . The second major moment of imposition was that of the French Revolution, when linguistic unification took the most repressive pedagogical turn. (Derrida 1992 :21)

Derrida distinguishes between 'two kinds of violence in law, in relation to law . . .: the founding violence, the one that institutes and positions law . . . and the violence that conserves, the one that maintains, confirms, insures the permanence and enforceability of law' (Derrida 1992: 31).

These are known facts and probably are features of the history of modernity anywhere. The question is, what is our relationship to these two kinds of violence in Indian modernity? It is easy to see that our attitude to the first kind of violence – the founding one – is determined largely by our relationship to the second. For Eugen Weber, for instance, the fact that something like an 'internal colonialism' was needed to make peasants into Frenchmen, arouses no ire for the end result has been good for everybody: 'the past was a time of misery and barbarism, the present a time of unexampled comfort and security, of machines and schooling and services, of all the wonders that are translated as civilisation' (Weber 1976: 478). Beginnings, however ugly, do not matter for Weber – they cannot act as a site from where to develop a critique of the present (as Foucault teaches us to do with his genealogical method) – for he tells, and believes in, a story of progress. His teleology saves him from having to be critical. The pain of the nineteenth-century French peasant is no longer his own. It is a wound over which time has formed a scab; it does not bleed any more.

Where can we, historians of a third-world country like India, where the distinction between the founding and the preservative modes of violence in the functioning of the law is hard to sustain, anchor such facile optimism?[7] The process of making 'peasants' or individuals into 'Indians' takes place every day before our eyes. It is not a process with a single or simple characteristic, nor is it without any material benefits to the people involved. But were we to convert particular benefits, which often do create problems in their turn, into some kind of a grand narrative of progress, it would leave us with a few important and nagging problems. If a certain kind of colonizing drive is inherent to the civilizing-modernizing project, and if one were, in one's point of view, to side uncritically with this project, how would one erect a critique of imperialism? Weber's solution to this problem does not solve anything: he says, in effect, maybe it's all right to practise colonialism on one's people. But that is getting the story back-to-front, for the assumed purpose of this colonialism, in Weber's schema, was to make real the category 'one's own people'! One cannot assume into existence at the beginning of a process what the process is meant to produce as its own outcome. If Weber's sentiment has any political validity in France today, it only means that the colonizing process succeeded in achieving this end, popularizing the story of progress (though that would be taking a rather Whiggish view of that history). Let me repeat my point once more: if it is true that Enlightenment rationalism requires as its vehicle the modern state and its accompanying institutions – the instruments of governmentality, in Foucault's terms – and if this entails a certain kind of colonizing violence anyway (however justifiable the violence might be from a retrospective point of view), then one cannot both uncritically welcome this violence and yet maintain a critique of European imperialism in India except on some kind of essentialistic and indigenist ground (e.g. only Indians have a right to colonize themselves in the interest of modernity). In the 1970s, Marxist historians in India and elsewhere – seeing themselves as inheritors of the European Enlightenment and yet wanting to distance themselves from the fact of European colonialism – tried out another solution. By fusing Marxism with dependency theory they sought to fetishize colonialism into a distinct socio-economic formation, inherently productive of underdevelopment. The demise of dependency theory has robbed us of that ground. Frankly, if Enlightenment rationalism is the only way human societies can humanize themselves, then we ought to be grateful that the Europeans set out to dominate the world and spread its message. Will our self-proclaimed 'rationalist' and 'secularist' historians say that?

History as Democratic Dialogue with Subaltern

I now come to what to me is the hardest part of my argument, not least because I myself have not practised what I am about to preach. I am trying to think my way towards a subaltern historiography that actually tries to learn from the subaltern. It is also an attempt to transcend the position that early *Subaltern Studies* took as its point of departure.

Let me go back to one of the fundamental premises of this essay. I do not deny the immense practical utility of left-liberal political philosophies. One cannot perform effectively in the context of modern bureaucracies – and therefore one cannot access the benefits these institutions are capable of delivering – if one is not able to mobilize one's own identity, personal or collective, through the languages, skills and practices these philosophies make possible. The very idea of distributive justice requires that these languages and competencies – of citizenship, of democracy, of welfare – be made available to all classes, particularly those subordinated and oppressed. It means that whenever we, members of the privileged classes, write subaltern histories – whether we write them as citizens (i.e. on behalf of the idea of democratic rights) or as socialists (desiring radical social change) – a certain pedagogic drive comes into play in our writing.

We write, ultimately, as part of a collective effort to help teach the oppressed of today how to be the democratic subject of tomorrow.

Since pedagogy is a dialogue, even if it is only the teacher's voice that is heard – as Barthes once said, 'when the teacher speaks to his audience, the Other is always there, *puncturing* his discourse' – the subaltern history produced in this manner, is dialogical (Barthes 1979: 95). But the dialogue, by its very structure, is not democratic (which is *not* to say that it is not of use to the subaltern). To be open-ended, I would argue, a dialogue has to be genuinely non-teleological, i.e. one must not presume, on any a priori basis, that whatever position our political ideology suggests as correct will be necessarily vindicated as a result of this dialogue. For a dialogue can be genuinely open only under one condition: that no party puts itself in a position where it can unilaterally decide the final outcomes of the conversation. This never happens between the 'modern' and the 'non-modern'. Because, however non-coercive the conversation between the Kantian subject (i.e. the transcendent academic observer, the knowing, judging and willing subject of modernity) and the subaltern who enters into a historical dialogue with the former from a non-Enlightenment position, this dialogue takes place within a field of possibilities that is already structured from the very beginning in favour of certain outcomes. To put this in terms of Gyan Prakash's book on *kamiauti* (bonded, in bad translation) labour in the Indian district of Bihar, if the peasant has until now understood the world of power in terms of ghosts and spirit cults, surely the intended result of this communication between the position of the modern subject and that of the peasant would be entirely predictable: that the peasant would learn to see his world structured by the (removable) inequalities of class, gender and ethnicity (Prakash 1990). The reverse, that the peasant might convince the modern, political 'commentator' of the existence of ghosts and spirits, would be an unimaginable (therefore disallowed) consequence of this process of communication. (In the limiting case of the problem, all peasants would be educated out of their peasantness.)

In pedagogic histories, it is the subaltern's relationship to the world that ultimately calls for improvement. *Subaltern Studies*, the series, was founded within this gesture. Guha's insurgent peasants, for instance, fall short in their understanding of what is required for a 'comprehensive' reversal of the relations of power in an exploitative society (Guha 1983). And this was exactly the position of the man who gave us the category 'subaltern'. For Antonio Gramsci, readers will recall, the subaltern named a political position that, by itself, was incapable of thinking the state; this was a thought to be brought to that position by the revolutionary intellectual. Once the subaltern could imagine/think the state, he transcended, theoretically speaking, the condition of subalternity. While it is true that Gramsci developed a dialogic Marxism which was meant to take seriously what went on inside the heads of the oppressed, he was clear on what the subaltern lacked and his words would bear repetition:

> The subaltern classes, by definition, are not united and cannot unite until they are able to become a 'State' . . . The history of subaltern social groups is necessarily fragmented and episodic. There undoubtedly does exist a tendency to (at least provisional stages of) unification in the historical activity of these groups, but this tendency is continually interrupted by the activity of the ruling groups . . . In reality, even when they appear triumphant, the subaltern groups are merely anxious to defend themselves. (Gramsci 1971: 52, 54–5)

As I have already indicated, histories written in this pedagogic-dialogic mode are not only welcome, this mode is in fact inescapable. We live in societies structured by the state and the oppressed need knowledge-forms that are tied to that reality. Indeed, this must remain one entirely legitimate mode of producing subaltern histories.

Yet the problem of undemocracy remains in the structure of this dialogue. Can we imagine another moment of subaltern history, where we stay – permanently, not simply as a matter of political tactics – with what is fragmentary and episodic, precisely because that which is fragmentary and episodic does not, cannot, dream of the whole called the state and therefore must be suggestive of knowledge-forms that are not tied to the will that produces the state? This is where we, the middle classes, children of the state, go to the subaltern in order to learn, learn to imagine what knowledge might look like if it were to serve histories that were fragmentary and episodic. What would Indian history be like if it were imagined as fragmentary? Not 'fragmentary' in the sense of fragments that refer to an implicit whole but fragments that challenge not only the idea of wholeness but the very idea of the 'fragment' itself (for if there were not to be any wholes what would be 'fragments' be 'fragments' of)? (Pandey 1992: 27–55; Chatterjee 1993).

I raise this question because to me it seems to be connected to the question of the limits to academic forms of knowledge of society. I am not, as I have said, sceptical of the practical utility of the language of left-liberal political philosophy, particularly in enabling the subaltern classes to enjoy the benefits that the institutions of modernity offer. But I am deeply sceptical of an intellectual assumption that runs through the writings of social scientists who think only through this language. This is the assumption that the diversity of cultures, the divergent ways of being human that culture is all about, could be rendered *fully* transparent to the gaze of any one particular political philosophy, no matter how different the circumstances within which the philosophy originated might be from the culture under study.

A certain kind of monomania often speaks through statements by liberal scholars, the idea, for instance, that it is intellectually possible to envision a good society for everybody on this earth even if we are ignorant of the circumstances and cultures of others. In this, all pedagogic histories, whether liberal or socialist, are one. There is always the assumption that while the world is plural, it could never be so plural as to be impossible of description in any one system of representation. For example, this passage occurs in an otherwise interesting book on Heidegger by an American philosopher, arguing against Heidegger's attachment to the ideal of 'enrootedness':

> The result, or one possible result, of this demythologising [of Heidegger] is a world that . . . Heidegger – the man – would abhor. It is a multilingual, multicultural, miscegenated, polymorphic, pluralist world without national-ethnic unity, without the unity of a single language or a deep monolinguistic tradition. It is a world of gay rights and feminists, of radically democratic, anti-hierarchical, anti-elitist structures, with a pragmatic view of truth and principles, and in which children would be educated not in a Classical Gymnasium but in free public institutions with schools in which Andy Warhol would get as big a hearing as Sophocles and Aeschylus, schools filled with computers and the latest technological advances, schools that make a particular effort to reach the disadvantaged. Heidegger would rather be dead. (Caputo 1993: 97)

Not only would a Heidegger die in such a world, the absence of a 'deep monolinguistic tradition' would kill a Tagore too! Our philosopher does not even recognize the profoundly parochial nature of his own favourite brand of North American campus radicalism that he prescribes for everybody.

To go to the subaltern in order to learn to be radically 'fragmentary' and 'episodic' is to move away from the monomania of the imagination that operates within the gesture that the knowing, judging, willing subject always already knows what is good for everybody, ahead of any investigation. The investigation, in turn, must be possessed of an openness so radical that I can only express it in Heideggerian terms: the capacity to hear that which one does not already understand.[8] In other words, to allow the subaltern position to challenge our own conceptions of what is universal, to be open to the possibility of a particular thought-world, however concerned it might be with the task grasping a totality, being rendered finite by the presence of the Other: such are the utopic horizons to which this other moment of *Subaltern Studies* calls us.[9] Knowledge-forms produced at this end will not be tied to the state or governmentality for they will not reflect a will to rule. The subaltern here is the ideal figure of he who survives actively, even joyously, on the assumption that the effective instruments of domination will always belong to somebody else and never aspires to them.

What will history produced in this mode look like? I cannot say, for one cannot write this history in a pure form. The languages of the state, of citizenship, of wholes and totalities, the legacy of Enlightenment rationalism (that is to say, the bad translations productive of hyper-rationalism) will always cut across it. At the same time this other history will present itself as that which disrupts these languages. To open ourselves to these histories would mean to listen carefully to the radical polysemy of our languages and practices, to admit to our consciousness the many possible worlds we inhabit, seriously to allow for the possibility that these worlds may be incommensurable with respect to each other, and hence to grant our social life a constant lack of transparency with regard to any one particular way of thinking about it. This is no ground for rejection of Enlightenment rationalism; it is, on the other hand, the ground on which I, an intellectual produced by a colonial formation, accept Enlightenment rationalism, secure in the knowledge that investigative procedure embodying this rationality only gives us a partial hold on our lives, and that too through necessary, much needed and yet inevitably poor translations.

Which means our lives are no longer adequately representable through the unitary language of a particular political philosophy, that is, through some kind of a Hegelian synthesis that can contain and subsume all our differences with others and those between ourselves. This is why we need to go to a Derrida, or a Lyotard or a Levinas, not because they have become 'fashions in the West' (that's raising the question at its most superficial level) but because they are the philosophers of 'difference' and 'non-commensurability' for our times.

Sarkar's fear that a critical understanding of our intellectual inheritances from the European Enlightenment would only help the 'fascistic' Hindus is based on some spurious assumptions. Granted that European fascism drew on a certain spirit of disenchantment with 'post-Enlightenment rationalism', but from this the reverse does not follow. One cannot argue on this basis that every critique of this 'post-Enlightenment rationalism' must end up being fascist. Or else, we would have to count some strange candidates among our list of 'reactionaries', and among them would be such different people as

Gandhi and Weber and, for our times, not only Michel Foucault but Jürgen Habermas as well. They remind us that to critique post-Enlightenment rationalism, or even modernity, is not to fall into some kind of 'irrationalism'. As Lydia Liu has recently remarked in her discussion of Chinese history, 'the critique of modernity has always been part of the Enlightenment legacy from the Romantics, Nietzsche, Marx, and Heidegger to Horkheimer, Adorno, Foucault, Derrida and even Habermas' (Liu 1993: 191). It is also true that the experience of fascism has left a certain trauma in leftist intellectuals in the West. They have ceded to the fascists all moments of poetry, mysticism and the religious and the mysterious in the construction of political sentiments and communities (however transient or inoperative). Romanticism now only reminds them of the Nazis. Ours are cultures rich in these elements. Gandhi, Tagore and a host of other nationalists have shown by their examples what tremendous creative energies these elements could unleash in us when mobilized for the purpose of fabricating new forms of life. It would be sad if we ceded this entire heritage to the Hindu extremists out of a fear that our romanticism must be the same as whatever the Europeans produced under that name in their histories, and that our present blunders, whatever these are, must be the same as theirs in the past. What, indeed, could be a greater instance of submission to a Eurocentric imagination than that fear?

Acknowledgements

I am grateful to audiences at the University of Melbourne and at the University of California campuses at Berkeley, Irvine and Riverside who heard and commented on an earlier version of this paper. Conversations with David Lloyd, Lisa Lowe, Naoki Sakai, Fiona Nicoll, Simon During, Christopher Healy, Robin Jeffrey, Jane Jacobs, Leela Gandhi, Lawrence Cohen, Gautam Bhadra, Sanjay Seth, Rajyashree Gokhale, Ranajit Guha and Gayatri Spivak have been extremely helpful.

Notes

1. The intensity of the hostility of these criticisms may be gauged from some of tactics employed in this debate. A historian of Sarkar's distinction, for instance, finds it necessary to suppress or ignore or omit facts pertinent to a discussion of the disagreements he has aired. In criticizing Bhadra, for example, he does not mention the debate he and others have already had with Gautam Bhadra in the pages of *Naiya* (the Bengali journal he mentions) where Bhadra's interview was first published and where Bhadra

has subsequently defended his position. I am equally surprised by his distorted reading of what I said. My Bengali essay does not, contrary to Sarkar's claim, equate Macaulay with Marx; in fact it does not even mention Marx. Nor does it, being concerned with discussing a cookbook written by a woman of an elite, *zamindar* family, have much to do with subalterns, uncritically or otherwise. And finally, it does not reject Enlightenment rationalism though it includes a critique of the Kantian and Hegelian ideas of 'universal history' – my position being, both in that essay and elsewhere, that academic critiques of Enlightenment rationalism can be produced only through a performative contradiction, i.e. by staying strictly within the procedures of such a rationalist tradition itself. Here is, in translation, what I wrote:

> The early vehicles for the spread of modernity throughout the world were European imperialisms and their various violent procedures. This has lodged a permanent contradiction at the very centre of the history of modernity. Martin Heidegger once said that, in any attempt to understand society, it was almost impossible to resist the temptations of European categories today since both 'man' and 'world' had become 'Europeanised'. One has to accept one's position within modernity – whatever this word means: scientific rationalism, the autonomous individual, economic development, the hungry society of consumerism, technical, governmental and bureaucratic rationality, civic/democratic rights, public health (and one has to add to this, population increase [explosion], mass poverty, and large-scale ethnic conflict or racism) – and write history [from that position]. What Gandhi once called 'English rule without the Englishmen' has some kind of truth today. It is no longer possible therefore to build individual or collective lives ignoring the demands of the thoughts already entailed in [concepts] such as 'democracy', 'individual freedom and autonomy', the 'nation-state', 'nationality', etc. These are the contributions that European civilization has made to our society and many desirable changes have been achieved with their help. ('Amader itihas o his masters voice' ['Our History and His Master's Voice'], *Baromas*, p. 72)

2. It is a well-worn point of European history than the idea of an irrevocable opposition between 'science/rationalism' and 'religion' goes against all available evidence. For a recent collection of careful discussions, see David C. Lindberg and Ronald I. Numbers (eds), *God and Nature: Historical Essays on the Encounter between Christianity and Science* (Berkeley, 1986).

3. See the interesting discussion in A. K. Ramanujan, 'Is There an Indian Way of Thinking? An Informal Essay', in McKim Marriott (ed.) *India through Hindu Categories* (New Delhi, 1990), pp. 41–58. Ramanujan discusses the case of his own scientist father who was both an astronomer and 'an expert astrologer'. Ramanujan writes, 'I had just been converted by Russell to the "scientific attitude" . . . I looked for consistency in him, a consistency he did not seem to care about or even think about' (pp. 42–3).

4. Rajendralal Mitra, *Indo-Aryans*, vol 2, pp. 111–12, cited in Andrew Sartori's master's thesis (Melbourne University, 1993), p. 60. The thoughts expressed here owe much to Sartori's analysis of this passage.

5. See M. N. Roy, 'Cultural Requisites of Freedom', in A. N. Bose, (ed.), *Modern Age and India*, p. 181: 'Mankind has pursued the ideal of freedom from time immemorial. Because the struggle for freedom . . . i.e. to experience the unfoldment of human potentialities, is a biological urge in every human being.' And on p. 183: 'It is one thing to feel the urge for freedom, as all animals do' (Roy then proceeds to distinguish humans from animals).

6. The reference is to Sumit Sarkar's *A Critique of Colonial India*, pp. 1–17, 71–6.

7. See the Amnesty International's report on India in 1992 where the majority of illegal torture is documented to have been inflicted by the law-enforcing arm of the state machinery, the police.

8. Heidegger speaks about ridding 'ourselves of the habit of always hearing only what we already understand'. See Martin Heidegger, 'The Nature of Language' in his *On the Way to Language*, p. 58. Should Heidegger's name raise politically correct hackles because of his Nazi past, let us remember that the Nazis sometimes mounted the same

objection against his thoughts as those raised by the old left against post-structuralism: 'in his last rector's speech [said a Nazi evaluation of Heidegger] philosophy tends in practice to ... dissolve into an aporetic of endless questioning ... In any case, one ought not to be silent about certain themes of the philosophy of "care" [*Sorge*] which, like anguish, could lead to truly paralysing effects' (Victor Farias, *Heidegger and Nazism*, p. 165).

9. My debt to Levinas and Derrida and their numerous commentators will be obvious at this point.

References

Balagopal, K. (1993): 'Why Did December 6, 1992 Happen?', *Economic and Political Weekly*, Vol. 28, No. 17, April 24.

Barthes, Roland (1979): *Image-Music-Text* (translated by Stephen Heath), Glasgow.

Behrens, C. B. A. (1985): *Society, Government and the Enlightenment: The Experiences of Eighteenth Century France and Prussia*, Thames and Hudson.

Bose, A. N. (ed.) (1950): *Modern Age and India*, Left Book Club, Calcutta.

Brass, Tom (1993): 'A-away with Their Wor(l)ds: Rural Labourers through the Postmodern Prism', *Economic and Political Weekly*, 5 June.

Caputo, John D. (1993): *Demythologising Heidegger*, Bloomington.

Chakrabarty, Dipesh (1992): 'Amader Itihas on His Master's Voice', *Baromas*, Annual Number 1992.

Chatterjee, Partha (1993): *The Nation and Its Fragments*, New Jersey.

De, Barun (1976): 'The Colonial Context of the Bengal Renaissance', in C. H. Phillips and Mary Doreen Wainwright (eds), *Indian Society and the Beginnings of Modernisation, 1830–1850*, London.

Derrida, Jacques (1992): 'Force of Law: The "Mystical Foundation of Authority"', in Drucilla Cornell *et al.* (eds), *Deconstruction and the Possibility of Justice*, New York.

Farias, Victor (1989): *Heidegger and Nazism* (translated by Paul Burrelli), Philadelphia.

Gay, P. (1971); *The Party of Humanity: Essays in the French Enlightenment*, New York.

———(1977): *The Enlightenment: An Interpretation*, New York.

Gramsci, Antonio (1971): *Selections from the Prison Notebooks of Antonio Gramsci*, Quintin Hoare and Geoffrey Nowell Smith (eds), New York.

Guha, Ranajit (1983): *Elementary Aspects of Peasant Insurgency in Colonial India*, Delhi.

Hegel, G. W. F. (1977): *Phenomenology of Spirit* (translated by A. V. Miller), Oxford.

Heidegger, M. (1982): *On the Way to Language* (translated by Peter D. Hertz), New York.

Laird, M. A. (1972): *Missionaries and Education in Bengal 1793–1837*, Oxford.

Lindberg, David C. and Ronald L. Numbers (eds) (1986): *God and Native: Historical Essays on the Encounter between Christianity and Science*, Berkeley.

Liu, Lydia H. (1993): 'Translingual Practice: The Discourse of Individualism between China and the West', *Positions: East Asia Cultures Critique*. Vol. 1, No. 1, Spring.

Norris, Christopher (1993): *The Truth of Postmodernism*. Oxford.

Pandey, Gyanendra (1992): 'In Defence of the Fragment: Writing about Hindu–Muslim Riots in India Today', *Representations*, Winter.

Prakash, Gyan (1990): *Bonded Histories: Genealogies of Labour Servitude in Colonial India*, Cambridge.

Ramanujan, A. K. (1990): 'Is There an Indian Way of Thinking? An Informal Essay', Mckim Marriott (ed.), *India through Hindu Categories*, New Delhi.

Rushdie, Salman (1984): *Midnight's Children*, London.

Sarkar, Sumit (1977): *The Swadeshi Movement in Bengal 1903–1908*, Delhi.

———(1985): *A Critique of Colonial India*, Calcutta.

———(1993): 'The Fascism of the Sangha Parivar', *Economic and Political Weekly*, Vol. 27, No. 5, January 20.

Smith, Preserved (1966): *The Enlightenment 1687–1776*, New York.

Stallybrass, Peter and Allon White (1986): *The Politics and Poetics of Transgression*, London.
Tharu, Susie and K. Lalitha (eds) (1991): *Women Writing in India: 600 BC to the Present, I*, Delhi.
Weber, Eugen (1976): *Peasants into Frenchmen: The Modernisation of Rural France, 1870–1914*, Stanford.

13

Voices from the Edge: The Struggle to Write Subaltern Histories

Gyanendra Pandey

'Voices from the edge', 'writings at the margin' and 'fragmentary statements' have been the subject of animated debate for some time now in circles concerned with the production of academic histories. There has been much contentious argument about the status of such 'trivia' (as some have characterized them) and their uses for historical writing: that is to say, their validity as evidence, perspective or representation. Arguments of this kind have added a new dimension to debates that were initiated long ago by the efforts of radical historians to write 'history from below' and of followers of the *Annales* school to move towards 'total history'. To the question of 'history from whose point of view' and 'history with what left out' have been added questions about the status of the historical narrative itself and how we might try to narrate alternative histories.

As the debate has gone on, more than one senior scholar has wondered about the difference, if any, between the 'fragment' and the 'microcosm', pointing out that historians have always relied on a study of the latter for a close understanding of social, cultural and political formations and change. This objection regarding the overlap or distance between fragments and microcosms may appear to be superficial and scarcely worthy of attention, but the concern that lies behind it needs to be understood.

One aspect of this concern is an understandable commitment to received unities – to established societies and communities, the modern nation-state and, more broadly still, to a vision of progress. There is also, without doubt, a deeper, philosophical question at stake here. 'Fragment' of what? it is implicitly asked. Is not a 'fragment' always part of something larger? Is there not a need then to try and understand that larger something, the 'totality': and is this not a charge especially upon the historian? It is to these questions that I return in the following reflections on historical evidence and the unity of historians' history.

Historical Evidence

We begin with an apparent paradox. What the historian trades in, we are told, is facts. What s/he inherits and collects and explores are narratives.[1] 'Facts' or, more broadly, 'evidence' comes to the historian in the form of narratives and narrative fragments: the narratives, one might say (with only a little exaggeration), of the ruling classes, and the 'fragments' of the subordinated.

The Italian Marxist Antonio Gramsci put the point well in his 'Notes on Italian History':

> The history of subaltern groups is necessarily fragmented and episodic . . . Every trace of independent initiative on the part of subaltern groups should therefore be of incalculable value for the integral historian . . . this kind of history can only be dealt with monographically, and each monograph requires an immense quantity of material which is often hard to collect. (Gramsci 1971: 54–5)

What the historian of subaltern groups has to work with, then, are precisely, 'fragments', 'traces' (in Gramsci's phrase) that survive in available narratives to tell of other suppressed narratives and perspectives.

The narratives preserved by the state in archives and other public institutions – that is, the narratives most commonly used by historians – belong overwhelmingly to the ruling classes, and owe their existence largely to a ruling class's need for security and control. Lodged in the records found in these institutions, however, are fragments (traces) of many lost (and usually irrecoverable) narratives, prised out by a predatory official or observer from earlier (often unknown) contexts and situated in others: the statement of a 'mute' subject under trial; rumours heard in the bazaar; slogans shouted by rebels or rioters; the Ashokan pillars in Ferozeshah Kotla (Delhi), and on the ridge near Delhi University; and the Lodi tombs in the Lady Willingdon Park in New Delhi (which continues to be known by the more appropriate name of Lodi Gardens) – testimony not only to the power of British rule and its appropriation of the treasures of layer upon layer of history, but to other presences and other pasts.

There are fragments of a similar kind found in unofficial records, too. Such, for instance, is the evidence of two Muslim women being transported to Pakistan in the course of the abducted persons' recovery programme after Partition, who told an Indian social worker when they were 'recaptured' after running away from a transit camp *en route*, that all they had wanted was 'to see, for one last time the respective [Hindu or Sikh, "Indian"] fathers of the children they were carrying [in their wombs] before being taken away forever' (Das 1995: 79).

Or, to take an example from my own research on Partition, here is the testimony of a middle-class Hindu woman writer, a male Sikh mechanic and a poor male *dhobi* (washerman), whose narratives about 1947 were constructed in the course of interviews I had with them but whose answers still appeared like fragments on my tape when I asked the question, 'What were you doing on 15 August 1947?' 'My son was unwell, I could do nothing but sit with him the whole day,' responded the writer. 'What were we doing? What do you think?' asked the Sikh mechanic somewhat angrily. Part of a refugee family from West Pakistan, living in Delhi since 1947, he went on to explain: 'We didn't know where we'd be from one day to the next . . . would we be able to stay on, even here? . . . Worrying about this, that's what we were doing.' While the old washerman looked at me in some surprise and said: 'What would I be doing? I was doing my work [washing clothes] . . .'

These are fragments that come to the historian as parts of 'alien', aggrandizing narratives – court records, newspaper accounts, civil servants' letters and reports, a social worker's memoirs, a (nationalist) researcher's interviews. Clearly, these are not the only sites that they might inhabit: and they constitute, as I have already said, at least potentially a 'disturbance', a fracture in the narrative, which might enable us to prise it open and read it differently from the judge, the journalist, the bureaucrat, the social worker and the nationalist historian.

Some examples from a recent paper by Ranajit Guha will help to clarify the point. In 'The Small Voice of History' Guha focuses attention, *inter alia*, upon the 'small voices' of the sick in nineteenth-century rural Bengal – voices that historians have consistently failed to hear although they are present in the official records so widely used by all of us in the profession. The subaltern historian quotes from various petitions submitted to those in positions of authority by the poor and sick to make the point that, to them, 'absolution was . . . as important as cure'. Abhoy Mandal of Momrejpur, deemed 'polluted' by the asthmatic attacks suffered by his mother-in-law, submitted himself for expiation to the local council of priests: 'I am utterly destitute; would the revered gentlemen be kind enough to issue a prescription that is commensurate to my misery?' Panchanan Manna, suffering from anal cancer, pleaded before the parallel authority in his home village of Chhotobainan: 'I am very poor; I shall submit myself to the purificatory rites of course; please prescribe something suitable for a pauper' (Guha 1996).

'Are we to allow these plaintive voices to be drowned in the din of a statist historiography?' the historian asks. 'What kind of a history of our people would that make' (ibid.) which turns a deaf ear to these cries for absolution, and concentrates – as historians' history has usually done in such instances – solely on the fact of educational or economic deprivation? Who is it who nominates an event or a deed, or statements, that speaks of these events or deeds, as 'historical' in the first place?, Guha asks in the same paper. 'It should be obvious,' he says, 'that in most cases the nominating authority is none other than an ideology for which the life of the state is all there is to history.' 'The right to speak', Veena Das writes in another context, 'has been appropriated by the state.' This has not been accomplished by coercive, police action alone, she points out: the same tendency has been promoted in the course of the state's exercise of a paternalist, benevolent function (Das 1995: 177).

The privileged discourse of modern times has been the discourse of the expert – the social worker, the judge, the medical scientist, the historian. Their authority and the province of their expertise has expanded over the last two centuries, at the cost of other voices and other 'truths' that might once have been heard. In regard to the question of writing subaltern histories, there is a need, however, to say something more about the popular 'archive' which is obviously present in all societies. In addition to the narratives of state officials, of newspaper editors, and those to be found in institutional collections of 'private papers', historians have available to them the narratives of storytellers, and balladeers, and folk memories available in oral accounts (which are, at points, taped and/or written down as well). And there is the whole corpus of religious life, rituals, beliefs and prayers – the 'oldest of archives' (Guha 1985: 1) and (one might add) among the most neglected in many parts of the world.

These 'folk' archives and narratives are, however, notoriously difficult to date and to use. Contrary to common-sense belief, they do not give us any simple, direct access to the 'authentic' voice and history of subaltern groups. They are in this respect no different from other 'sources' for the historian: they too need to be 'read'. For they too are shot through with contradictory, naturalizing features: the constructions of the dominant and the privileged – 'classical' Hinduism and Islam, the 'Great Tradition', the language of the upper classes mingled with folk forms and lower-class motifs. Guha makes the point very well indeed in his comment on the tribal rites, usages and myths that D. D. Kosambi used and enjoined us to use: 'the pull of "parallel traditions" and the pressure of upper-caste, especially Brahmanical, culture tend to assimilate and thereby transform them [these rites, myths and usages] to such an extent that they show up as little more than archaic traces within an established Hindu idiom' (ibid.: 2).

This is not a plea to abandon the search for, or use of, unofficial, 'popular' sources; on the contrary, as the paper from which the above quotation is taken, on the Dom reconstruction of the Rahu myth, shows so well. It is rather a cautionary note against treating them as unmediated carriers of transparent truths,[2] an appeal for a different kind of historical practice to recover the possibility of another kind of history.

The 'traces', 'fragments', 'voices from the edge' to which we have referred, should not be thought of as nuggets, buried beneath layers of predatory meaning construction that can be prised out by the more diligent (or lucky) among us to reveal their worth and meaning automatically. What is in question here, as I have already said, is the ability to 'hear', especially to hear that which we have not heard before, and to transgress in situating the text or the 'fragment' differently. For as we all recognize now, dialogue, speech and, by extension, the 'fragmentary' perspective is situational. The 'text' has no intrinsic or fixed meaning: rather, it is surrounded, infused and positioned (as in the case of acting) by the speaker's experience, gestures, mode, as also by the audience's placement and participation. We do not conform action simply to text or merely confirm the text by action: texts, or 'source materials', are inevitably shaped by the experience of the reader/actor.

Historians today can and do use their 'sources' in two very different ways: as repositories of the 'truth' ('reality'), or as sites of contending histories and contending politics, aiming to establish the ascendancy of particular points of view.[3] The early writings in *Subaltern Studies*, for example, retained a belief in some kind of ultimate truth which the historian could uncover by peeling back the layers of elitist historiography and interpretation, and delving deep into the historical records. More recent studies in this vein have been a great deal more reflexive, recognizing at once the extraordinary difficulty of recovering and representing the 'authentic' voice.

Subaltern narratives will not find a place in the institutionalized public archive and the history it authorizes, Gramsci argues, until the subaltern groups have been unified in the form of a state (Gramsci 1971: 53, 55). 'The subaltern cannot speak,' writes Gayatri Spivak, making, I suggest, much the same point (Spivak 1988). All that we have in the record is the trace of suppressed voices and unfinished contests. It is a charting of such a field of contest that Ranajit Guha engages in, in his documentation of the successive stages of the Dom ('untouchable') reconstruction and inversion of the Rahu myth, or his close reading of the Bagdi women's fragmentary statements in the court records about the choices and compulsions they faced and the deliberations and demonstration of fellow-feeling that preceded 'Chandra's Death' (Guha 1985, 1987). Veena Das carries the exercise further, or at any rate in a different direction, in her sustained attention to the language of the body of women who have suffered from violence. 'The ideology of the female body among Punjabi families emphasizes the interior orientation of the body!' she writes: 'A woman hides the faults of her husband inside her womb.' 'In the case of the partition [of India in 1947], women had to hide not only the aggression of men defined as enemies but also the betrayal of their own men. However, the suppression of speech sometimes led the body to form its own speech. This could be observed at several levels' (Das 1991, 1996).

As in the instance of lower-caste/class legends mediated by a Brahmanical culture, what all these examples do is to remind us that it is within clearly marked fields of power, and identifiable cultural limits, that narrative – any narrative – is constructed. Narratives (including our own historical ones) are necessarily 'interested', conditioned by power equations and varied expectations, bound by different kinds of narrative conventions, productive of different kinds of truth-effects. Anyone who has gone out to the field, notebook or tape-recorder in hand, to collect oral evidence, knows this only too well (cf. Pandey 1992). But let me illustrate the point by reference to some of my own experiences while interviewing people about the Partition of 1947.

There have been numerous occasions when I have been met with suspicion: although I was myself not always aware of this, my bona fides and the 'real' reason for my unexpected visit have been in doubt. Mistaken for some kind of intelligence agent in one instance, I was invited back several days later by a highly articulate homoeopathic medical practitioner with whom I had had a long (and, as it seemed to me, remarkably 'open') interview. I was told then that he had mistaken my purpose at first, and was treated to a somewhat different rendering of the story that I had heard on that earlier occasion – with the same basic chronological sequence of events, but different nuances, subtle enough to challenge the official nationalist version of the history of those times in various ways, without contradicting the doctor's own previous 'nationalist' account. I was also presented with a bundle of political propagandist pamphlets and leaflets of right-wing inclination.

At another place, a businessman in his forties expressed anger at the fact that his eighty-year-old mother was being repeatedly interviewed. 'Why do you all come here? What will you do with this?' he asked. 'What will we get out of it?' 'Others have been and interviewed her before, and made big promises about writing up this history. I don't believe any of you will publish our account.'

Again, to take a final example, a person whom I had been asked to meet by several people from his village because of his unusual personal history, refused in the course of our entire conversation to acknowledge that history. Now the owner of a fleet of taxis, a local Congress leader and a municipal corporator in a town not far from this village, he did not say even once that he had been a Muslim, who was converted to Sikhism in the 'dreadful' days of 1946–47 (as he himself described them) and who had – unlike many others – stayed on with the new religious affiliation even when circumstances improved. In the course of our interview I scribbled in my notepad: 'This is just like rape.' How does the rapist, or the raped, talk about the experience of rape? And how does the interviewer ask about it?

One other point may be made in connection with the examples cited above. None of the people I have referred to here would be described as 'poor', at any rate in their present situation, or as socially or culturally down-and-out. Yet they are all Partition 'sufferers', in their own reckoning and in the accounts that others give of them. It will perhaps help us to maintain our sense of the always ambiguous and contextual character of the category of the subordinated and disprivileged if we recognize that the accounts of Partition provided by these men and women share more than a little with the accounts of other subordinated and disprivileged groups in our societies. It may be worthwhile also to reflect for a moment on the specificities of the construction of the subaltern voice – the voices of slaves and untouchables, of workers and women, of Partition sufferers and other marginalized groups – in the narratives available to the historian.

Let me try to do this by means of a quotation from the African-American writer, William Du Bois, which points in my view to one of the conditions making for the specific 'subalternity' of the subaltern voice. Du Bois wrote of the question that he was repeatedly *not* asked in the United States, that is to say, a question that was on the lips of many people he met, but one that was rarely enunciated: 'How does it feel to be a problem?' (Du Bois 1969: 43). The African-American in the USA was 'a problem' almost by definition. 'Untouchables' in

India are 'a problem'. So is the girl-child (in large parts of the society). So were the raped and abducted women of Partition. We must bear in mind that upper- and middle-class, upper-caste Hindu boys and men in India, and White Anglo-Saxon Protestant males in the USA are never thought of as being 'a problem' in this generalized way.[4]

One consequence of living life as 'a problem', Du Bois suggested, was that one lived with a 'double consciousness' – 'two souls in one dark body'.[5] This is an important insight. Anyone who has had the privilege, and time, to collect subaltern testimony, or to 'work' on subaltern testimony collected by other privileged individuals or institutions, will have been struck by the truncated, fragmentary and often self-contradictory character of so many subaltern accounts. The memories of people (and especially of women) who lived through the Partition of India, relating to the history of rape and abduction, murder and looting, to the recovery of abducted persons and the resettlement of the uprooted, provide an exceptionally telling example of this. What these are, are fitfully told stories, or stories that cannot be told: of coping with minimal resources in impossible conditions, of wishing to die but wanting to live, of surviving – and trying to put together a new life – through multiple subject-positions and multiple narratives, many of which are scarcely scripted by themselves.

It may be objected that this is, in some senses, the universal human condition, especially amid the rapid changes of modern times. Nevertheless, there is a specificity here which derives from the different access that different groups, classes, genders have to the texts, and to the economic, political and cultural power that they need, to build their lives and tell their stories: and in this respect, the subordinated and disprivileged *are* subordinated and disprivileged. This necessarily conditions the construction of their lives and of their narratives. It is often a choice between 'living life somehow, anyhow' or 'dying in accordance with the rules of honour laid out by male society', as Veena Das puts it in a remark about the 'truth of womanhood' in Partition and post-Partition India (Das 1991: 69); or of dying rather than accepting the 'living death' of *bhek* that was the lot of innumerable widows in nineteenth-century Bengal, as Ranajit Guha points out in 'Chandra's Death' (Guha 1987).[6]

It is this, I suggest, that is reflected in the fragmentary, broken, self-contradictory character of subaltern existence, consciousness, struggles, voices. 'Why did God make me an outcast and a stranger in mine own house?': Du Bois asks the question on behalf of African-Americans (Du Bois 1969: 45). It is a question that so many abducted and recovered women in India (and Pakistan) might have asked literally in the years after Partition. It is also a question that many women in Indian society – and not only in Indian society – are perhaps forced to ask even in what are construed as 'normal' times.

'Partition sufferers', African-Americans, slaves, untouchables and women, like other subordinated groups and classes, have lived in such circumstances through multiple scripts and multiple narratives – 'two souls in one dark body'. Certainty of knowledge, the clarity of History, and the consistency of ideological 'truth' are sometimes costly luxuries in conditions like these. The well-ordered, disciplined, unified script (or voice) can be a foolish ambition, if not an impossibility. Yet these are conditions that make for the possibility (indeed, the necessity) of historical narratives very different from the historians' history that we have come to privilege over the last two hundred years. Let me turn to an examination of this privilege and this possibility.

Historians' History

For the modern, 'scientific' historian, 'history' is unified, uni-directional, and fully interconnected (albeit in complex ways, not always fathomed by the individual historian). The overarching categories, the wider questions, the 'big *why* questions' of this history are given: they are fundamental and unalterable. They have had to do, in the writing of modern history, with Progress, with the spread of Science, Rationality and Enlightenment, and in the political sphere, the victory of concepts like nations and nationalism, development and modernization, equity and justice. Moreover, although ideas like nationhood and modernization have been considerably refined and modified in the course of the present century, and notions of equity and justice are increasingly fraught, all such concepts appear (in the general run of academic history writing) to be absolute and fixed in their meanings. In that sense, they have no history and themselves require little investigation.

One result of the jealous preservation of these preconstituted objects of enquiry is the persistence of some major historical blind spots. With nationalism and history having been as closely allied as they are, this is particularly well reflected in the historiography of nationalism. I shall take the sophisticated Indian historiography of Indian nationalism, which I know better than other cases, as my central example for the rest of this article. This is a long-established and powerful tradition of history writing which has both contributed to and acknowledged those theoretical advances of the last decade and more that have brought into question any notion of a 'natural', predestined, inevitable nation.

There is by now a widespread scholarly consensus in India, as elsewhere, that nations are not given from seed, but are constituted in self-contradictory struggles, and in struggles that are prolonged and in some senses endless. The Indian nation, too, it is conceded, even argued, was constituted in this way. However, even as this point is made, the notion of the 'natural' persists in the actual writing of the history of British colonialism and Indian nationalism.

How else do we frame the struggle between different kinds of nationalism? it is asked. How else do we tell 'good' nationalism from 'bad', the nationalism that was relevant to this age from that that was not? Received Indian historiography makes a sharp distinction between the two sets – the 'good' and the 'bad', the 'progressive' and the 'reactionary', the 'relevant' and the 'irrelevant' – and proceeds to give (or to take over from the 'high' nationalism of the 1930s) a distinct name for the latter. That name is 'communalism': what one might have otherwise described as an aggressive kind of nationalism based on putative religious community, becomes in this account the other of 'real' nationalism – divisive, reactionary and, in the words of nationalist thinkers and writers of that earlier period, 'against the trend of world history' (Nehru 1936; Vidyarthi 1978).

Historical writing on 'communalism' in India, and more especially on the Partition of the subcontinent into two (now three) independent nation-states in 1947, underlines the point. It works with the same vision of the natural and the proper – that which was supposed to be. There is, in India, only one 'big *why* question' regarding Partition. What went wrong? What were the causes of this deviation from the natural course of Indian history? Who was responsible? In Pakistan, of whose intellectual climate and debates I know comparatively little, the question would, I think, be reversed: 1947 is Independence, not Partition; it is nationalism, not communalism. What, the historian will ask, were the struggles and sacrifices that were needed to realize this 'natural' course of history?

What we tend to get, in both cases, is a refurbished narrative of Indian or Pakistani nationalism,[7] in which the historian's chief contribution is a detailing of the economic, social and cultural preconditions, and the political moves or miscalculations that allowed for this noble victory or tragic loss. The 'loss' or 'victory', 'Partition' or 'Partition/Independence', must remain largely unproblematized.

The question of problematizing Partition, Independence, nationalism, democracy and other well-worn common-sense concepts allows us to take the argument about received historical limits a little further. One may take heart from the considerable new work on Partition that is being undertaken in the subcontinent, to suggest that it is precisely the meaning and resonance of Partition (or Partition/Independence) that one needs to constitute as the object of investigation – an investigation that might allow us the possibility of writing a different kind of history. What, the Indian historian would have to ask, was this 'Partition' and this 'Independence'? What were the meanings that people attached to these terms – if they used these terms at all?[8] What were the narratives built around these events – the narratives that, in fact, constituted 'Partition' and 'Independence'? When, one might further ask, did these events occur (in the sense that they came to be recognized as 'historical' events and acquired the meanings that are now commonly assigned to them)? When did attackers, victims, onlookers, people at the edge, come to realize that something of enormous consequence had happened, and that there was from that point on no going back? Not only *what*, but *when* was Partition?

It may be helpful to dwell a moment longer on some of the concerns articulated by recent research on this theme. Perhaps the most obvious sign of the Partition of India in 1947 was the massive violence that (as we are told) 'surrounded', 'accompanied' or (as we might put it) constituted it. It is estimated that some 600,000 people were killed in the Partition 'disturbances'. Another 14 million were uprooted and became refugees for long years to come. An uncounted number were raped and abducted. A few months after coming to power, the governments of the two new Dominions entered into an inter-Dominion agreement to rescue and rehabilitate abducted persons left on the wrong side of the new international border, and this programme of compulsory recovery and repatriation – which entailed considerable coercion and physical violence – was continued officially for the better part of a decade.

How are we to write the history of this moment? Is it possible to suggest, as some of us have done (Bhasin and Menon 1993; Butalia 1993; Pandey 1994; Das 1995, ch. 3), that the history of Partition is the history of rape and abduction and killing, and of the state-sponsored drive that followed to evict 'aliens' and recover 'nationals' (especially abducted women and children), irrespective of their personal wishes? For the meaning of Partition is disturbingly captured in these acts. Or must we always face the objection, as we embark on these studies, that talk of rape and abduction and murder is all very well but it misses the main point – which, we are glibly told, is that the cause of all this was 'Partition'. The *real* historical task, we are reminded, is to investigate the *causes* of Partition. It is to ask the question: what led to this tragedy, this departure from the normal, assigned course of Indian history?

A slightly different kind of illustration, taken again from India, will help to round off this part of my argument. If we turn aside for a moment from the urgency and emotionalism of the nationalist enterprise as reflected in the historiography of 'liberation struggles', we will find that the same underlying assumptions – and indeed some of the same emotionalism – informs much of the historical work on earlier periods in the history of the world. 'India' is, in much the same way as the 'Indian nation', the obvious, natural site of Indian history, it is suggested. This is as true for the earlier periods of Indian history as it is for the later. (What could be more self-evident than that, after all?) So historians proceed to write about 'medieval India' and 'ancient India' much as they write about 'modern India' – and search in pre-colonial, pre-capitalist times for the same kind of homogeneity and uniformity, the same kind of 'centre', and the same kind of all-India history, as they construct and present for the 'modern' period.

I am not referring here to the problem of periodization found in the notion of an 'ancient', a 'medieval' and a 'modern' India – which has been most usefully opened up by a number of leading scholars in India (among them R. S. Sharma, Romila Thapar and B. D. Chattopadhyaya). I am pointing rather to the assumed unities and uniformities lodged in the notions of 'medieval Indian history' and 'ancient Indian history'. It has been rare for writers to ask how this 'medieval India' and 'ancient India' came to be constituted, by whom, in what context, with what results, and to investigate the connections between different aspects of human life – 'economic', 'political', 'cultural', 'religious' – different discourses, different histories, not only between regions but also in any one region, of 'ancient' or 'medieval India'. Rather, the connection between these different aspects and discourses is assumed, as if they are always connected (part of a larger whole) and always connected in the same way – that is, in the way in which they have come to be connected, more and more, in the age of capital. That this transcendental understanding of 'unity' and 'connectedness' is fundamentally ahistorical does not seem to have bothered the historian.

It is a difficult and, perhaps, an unsettling question to ask how we might try to construct differently the history of 'India' in pre-colonial (i.e. pre-capitalist) times, 'medieval' or 'ancient'. What would an 'Indian history' of the last 3,000 (or 5,000) years look like if seen from the deep south of present-day India, or from its north-eastern extremities, or from the perspectives of *dalits* ('untouchables') or of women or of religious preachers (Brahmans, *bhikkus*, *sanyasis*, Sufis), in one area or another? But it is a question that needs to be asked.

In a word, I would argue, the 'natural unities', the 'overarching categories', and the 'wider questions' of history have been taken for granted for far too long – in India as elsewhere – as has the ('natural') mode of presentation of this history. The debate on these questions, such as it is, has also laboured long under the weight of a demand for 'political correctness', a demand that has contributed to the suppression of many alternative voices and interesting questions, but also one that tends to become less and less enlightening as it becomes more and more strident.

The point perhaps needs to be spelt out just a little. Let me try to do this by taking a closer look at a debate that has raged among historians of Indian nationalism over the last few years. It is well known that a distinct and powerful Indian historiography, of the modern, 'scientific' kind, emerged in India out of the struggle against British imperialism and colonial domination in the subcontinent. Debates and writings in Indian history still necessarily carry the marks of that birth.

Of the many formulations that follow from this, one of the more potent in recent years has been a division of Indian historians into the 'nationalist' (and thereby, it is often implied, modernist, progressive and secular in outlook) and the 'antinational(ist)', into those who emphasize unifying trends in Indian history and those who highlight the opposite, those who would write the history of the 'Indian nation' and of the struggles to carry it forward, as against those who would – by their attention to the particular, the local, the contradictory and the tangential – contribute, as it is suggested, to its fragmentation.

A statement published a few years ago by a prominent Delhi historian, Professor K. N. Panikkar, illustrates the point very well indeed. In a condemnation of what he calls 'neo-colonial' historiography, which he seems to equate with 'postmodernism' and with 'micro-history' as practised in India, this historian charges the new 'micro-historians' of 'fracturing . . . [the] overarching categories' of Indian history and protests against what he sees as progressive shifts away from the appropriate locus of its study: 'the province instead of nation, locality instead of province, and family instead of locality'.

The critic of recent historiographical trends in India quotes Eric Hobsbawm's defence of established historical procedures, published in 1980 – 'There is nothing new in choosing to see the world via a microscope rather than a telescope, so long as we accept that we are studying that same cosmos' – and goes on to say:

> Implying an integral connection between the micro[cosm], and the macro[cosm], Hobsbawm suggested that the former is not an end in itself but a means for illuminating wider questions, which goes far beyond a particular event, story or character. It is the pursuit of this connection which in a way enabled the 'big *why* questions'. In contrast, the tendency of neo-colonial history is to isolate the micro from the macro and to imbue the former with independence both from its origin and context. (Panikkar 1994)

Before I take up the propositions contained in this passage, let me put by its side another astonishing statement, from a far more powerful historian, doyen of medieval Indian history and an important commentator on the colonial and postcolonial experience in India, Professor Irfan Habib. In several recent statements on *Subaltern Studies*, Irfan Habib has seconded the argument summarized in the last two paragraphs. I cite the concluding lines of only one recent lecture:

> The 'Subaltern' historians . . . seldom touch upon the aggregates in statistics, e.g., those of national income and exports, the drain of wealth, taxation (indicating the exploitation of the Indian peasantry by indirect taxation), etc. . . . But if we want to know what was happening to India, we must keep the national level statistics in mind. Let us see what the Indian people in their majority were passing through and then find out what colonialism meant and what the Indian national movement was about.

All that I have said about continuing assumptions regarding the 'naturalness' of the nation is amply illustrated here. However, there are a number of other issues at stake as well. By way of explicating his position, Habib raises the question:

> Are we going to have a modern nation, a nation with social equity, for which the national movement fought [*sic*]? Or are we going to have a divided country, living in a manufactured, imagined past of the most parochial kind and, therefore, leading ourselves towards disaster. I am sure that duty calls to all of us whether [as] historians or as citizens, who want to defend the Indian nation to close ranks in the battle of ideas that is now taking place. (Habib 1994)

One response would be to point out that the battle of ideas can never be won, or for that matter much advanced, through 'closed ranks' alone: what is required, at least as much, is open minds, and persistent enquiry and questioning. There is also the question, 'closing ranks' around what? – which cannot easily be set aside today, when the unified revolutionary subject is so much less self-evident than it appeared to be a century ago. There is surely a need to investigate how the closing of ranks occurred in the first place, how the national movement was consolidated, how the idea of a nation arose, was modified and contested – and not just once. It is for this reason that the search for dissonant voices and fragmentary perspectives, for elements that question the self-evidence of received 'totalities', becomes especially important.

Irfan Habib is appealing in the passages quoted above for the kind of history of India that A. R. Desai wrote forty-five years ago and R. P. Dutt wrote ten years earlier (Desai 1948; Dutt 1940) – for 'social background' and the 'gross' facts of economic life, from which implicitly the rest of history follows. It is as if E. P. Thompson's *Making of the English Working Class* (1963) and all the work that followed in its wake, plus the critical intervention of feminist critiques of mainstream historiography, not to mention minor ventures like *Subaltern Studies*, had disappeared altogether. Whatever else its achievements or failures, one thing that this body of work should have done is to make it plain to all students of history that neither the existence of particular social and political structures, nor the institution of new forms of production relations and extraction of surplus, automatically produces working-class consciousness, or peasant struggles, or nationalism. Even economic history cannot be written today as it was in the 1950s; there have been too many important new debates, and new questions asked about the 'Indian economy', e.g., what it means to speak of an 'Indian economy', how it was constituted, what was and is its relation to 'regional' economies (and cultures). The appeal to return to history in the 1950s mould is, to say the least, puzzling in this context.

But Habib and Panikkar are hardly alone in their objection to the 'fragmentation' of the object of historical investigation. It was Lawrence Stone who coined the phrase the 'big why questions', and restated the need for continued attention to them in an essay entitled 'The Revival of Narrative: Reflections on a New Old History' (Stone 1979); and Hobsbawm in his comment on this essay scarcely understated the demand to investigate the larger questions, although he disagreed with much else that Stone had to say on the subject of recent historical writings (Hobsbawm 1980). In *The Past is a Foreign Country* (1985), David Lowenthal made the same kind of point against recent trends, citing Stone (with approval) in his footnote. He noted how the 'once-popular broad sweep over entire cultures or nations' was now 'condemned as egregiously simplistic', and that many historians went on to 'scrutinise particular institutions and arenas circumscribed in time and space'. Unfortunately, he added 'the focus is sometimes so narrow that "case studies" seem eccentric rather than characteristic; failing to relate the lives and events they treat to larger trends, they further fragment knowledge of the past' (Lowenthal 1985: 223–4).

There is more than the fear of the break-up of recognized nation-states, or societies, or cultures, that makes for this criticism (not to say denunciation) of new kinds of investigation by so many established historians. There is also the fear of fracturing the certainty of knowledge as it has been produced and accepted for a long time now. Joan Scott made the point not long ago that history departments in the USA 'regularly' refused to consider for positions in general American history 'scholars who write on women or African Americans (or homosexuals, or other particular groups), arguing that they are not generalists, unlike those who are no less specialists but have written about national elections or politicians' lives – subjects that are taken to stand for what the whole discipline is about' (Scott 1992: 71).

I suggest that the same kind of assumptions regarding 'what the whole discipline is about' lie behind the objections of Habib, Panikkar, Stone and others. What inspires their defence of 'old history' is the comforting familiarity of fixed objects of investigation, established methods of research and writing, and known courses of history, all underwritten by the liberal assumption of an inexorable, linear progress towards nationhood and modernity. By contrast with this condensed, or elaborated, study of the already-constituted object of enquiry – through a microscope or a telescope – the study of the fragment, or the voice from the edge, aims to uncover alternative viewpoints, other perspectives and other ways of writing, to try and capture other perspectives. The 'fragment' in this usage is not just a 'bit' – the dictionary's 'piece broken off' – of a preconstituted whole. Rather, it is a disturbing element, a 'disturbance', a contradiction shall we say, in the self-representation of that particular totality and those who uncritically uphold it.

The fragment is, in this sense, an appeal to an alternative perspective, or at least the possibility of another perspective. It is a call to try and analyse the historical construction of the totalities we work with, the contradictions that survive within them, the possibilities they appear to fulfil, the dreams and possibilities apparently suppressed: in a word, the fragility and instability of the 'givens' (the 'meaningful totalities') of history.

The colonizing discourse of a triumphant modernist rationality and male order often sniffs at such fragmentation. It is similarly impatient with the 'inconsistency' of subaltern narratives and statements. We are uncomfortable with truncated narratives and undisciplined fragments, and can scarcely make them our own. We seek, rather, to appropriate and unify them in fully connected, neatly fashioned historical accounts, without any jagged edges if possible.

In the monopolizing authority we claim for these 'scientific' accounts, however, we tend only to perpetuate the standpoint and privilege of that colonizing discourse.[9] Instead, what we could perhaps learn from those who are disprivileged (and this should ideally include ourselves) is that our strengths and what is most human about our work, lie in responding to our inadequacies – or, as one might say, in the struggle itself – and not in the making of perfection.[10]

Notes

1. It should be unnecessary here to dwell on the status of 'facts'. But historians as a tribe perhaps need periodic reminders that there are no pre-conceptual, pre-linguistic facts. Cf. Macintyre:

> Facts, like telescopes and wigs for gentlemen, were a 17th century invention. In the 16th century and earlier 'fact' in English was usually a rendering of the Latin 'factum', a deed, and action, and sometimes in scholastic Latin an event or an occasion . . . It is of course . . . harmless, philosophically and otherwise, to use the word 'fact' of what a judgement states. What is . . . not harmless, but highly misleading, was to conceive a realm of facts independent of judgement or of any other form of linguistic expression. (1988: 357–67)

2. Cf. Joan W. Scott (1991) where she argues against taking the category of experience for granted in its 'immediacy and entirety', as some kind of pre-discursive reality. 'Talking about experience in these ways leads us to take the existence of individuals for granted (experience is something people have) rather than to ask how conceptions of selves (of subjects and their identities) are produced' (1991: 782, 786).

3. Cf. Foucault's distinction between 'exhaustiveness' and 'intelligibility' as alternative ideals in dealing with historical evidence. What follows from that, I suggest, is the possibility of two kinds of history: one that looks for evidence of 'all that happened' in the past or in a designated part of the past; as against one that examines evidence of how a particular discourse or field came to be constituted, became possible.

4. There was extensive discussion of the 'untouchable problem' and the 'women's problem' in the course of the Indian nationalist struggle for liberation from colonial rule, never of course of a 'men's problem' or the 'upper-caste problem'.

5. Du Bois writes,

> It is a peculiar sensation, this double-consciousness, this sense of always looking at one's self through the eyes of others, of measuring one's soul by the tape of a world that looks on in amused contempt and pity. One ever feels (one's) twoness – an American, a Negro; two souls, two thoughts, two unreconciled strivings; two warring ideals in one dark body, whose dogged strength alone keeps it from being torn asunder. (Du Bois 1969: 45)

6. 'Chandra's Death', *passim*. 'To wear a Boishnob habit, that is, to adopt the dress, ornaments and body markings which make up the semiotic ensemble called *bhek*, is to move out of caste,' writes Guha. Over time, *bhek* came to signify loss of caste by 'expulsion' rather than by 'abdication'. Some observers spoke of the *akhras*, where such outcaste women were frequently confined, as 'abortion centres', others of how religion was being used to 'corrupt' women – ignoring their own complicity in this exploitation of harassed women. Guha notes that the largest group of female outcastes placed in

this situation was made up of 'Hindu widows ostracized for defying the controls exercised on their sexuality by the local patriarchies' (Guha 1987: 156–9).

7. In Bangladesh, nationalist historiography has had a more chequered career, with the Partition of 1947 now being seen as the 'first stage' in a struggle for liberation that was fulfilled finally only in 1971. One should note that the reassuring belief in the natural course of history, paradoxically, detracts from the need for struggle to produce the particular results and directions in history that nationalism, above all, has fought for.

8. The number of different local terms available as a description of the partition of 1946–47 is very large: 'migration', '*maashalla*' (martial law), '*mian mari*', '*raula*', '*gadbad*' is a small sample. One may note in this context the common description of 1971 in Bangladesh not only by the 'correct' term, *swadhintar bachar* (the year of independence), but also by the informal *gondogoler bachar* (the year of the troubles).

9. Lest this appear a purely rhetorical or bombastic statement, let me try to clarify what I mean here. My feeling is that after all our objections have been made to totalizing narratives, neatly fashioned histories and claims to omniscience, we are under pressure (not excluding our own) to produce these again. It may be that, in our present political and intellectual circumstances, we are fated to continue to write statist and nationalist histories for some time to come: and perhaps the best we can do is to try to problematize these histories even as we produce them.

10. I owe this particular formulation to Arthur Kleinman. I am grateful to him and to Veena Das, Pamela Reynolds, Ulf Hannerz and other participants in the Vega Symposium on 'Voice and Culture in Anthropology' (Stockholm, 24 April, 1995) for their comments on an earlier draft of this paper which was presented there.

At the end here, perhaps there is the need to say one word more about a question that frequently follows the kind of statement I have tried to make above. What happens, then, it will be asked, to the authority of the historian? Or is it our suggestion that all historical interpretations are equally valid, that one history is as good as any other? My answer to this question is clear. The authority of the historian derives from the privilege of the historian – to do research, read, reflect, organize and present authoritative historical accounts. It is a privilege – and an authority – granted by the community, academic and non-academic, and at the same time taken and maintained by the historian through a process of claim (assertion, proposition) and dialogue in which s/he needs continuously to persuade the community (primarily academic but, to a certain extent and at certain times, non-academic too) of her/his authority and expertise. The assent of the reader is a crucial part of the authority of a text.

References and Further Reading

Bhasin, Kamla and Ritu Menon (1993) Recovery, Rupture, Resistance: Indian State and Recovery of Women during Partition. In 'Review of Women's Studies', *Economic and Political Weekly*, XXVIII, 7 (April).

Butalia, Urvashi (1993) Community, State and Gender: On Women's Agency during Partition. In 'Review of Women's Studies', *Economic and Political Weekly*, XXVIII, 7 (April).

Das, Veena (1991) Composition of the Personal Voice: Violence and Migration. *Studies in History*, n.s. 7(1).

———(1995) *Critical Events: An Anthropological Perspective on Contemporary India.* Delhi: Oxford University Press.

———(1996) Language and Body: Transactions in the Construction of Pain, *Daedalus*, 125, 1 (Winter).

Desai, A. R. (1948) *Social Background of Indian Nationalism.* Bombay: University of Bombay.

Du Bois, W. E. B. (1969) *The Souls of Black Folk.* New York: Signet.

Dutt, R. P. (1949), *India Today*, London: Victor Gollancz.

Gramsci, Antonio (1971) Notes in Italian History. In *Selections from the Prison Notebooks of Antonio Gramsci*, edited by Q. Hoare and G. N. Smith. New York: International Publishers.

Guha, Ranajit (1985) The Career of an Anti-God in Heaven and on Earth. In *The Truth Unites: Essays in Tribute to Samar Sen*, edited by A. Mitra. Calcutta: Subarnarekha.

———(ed.) (1987) Chandra's Death. In *Subaltern Studies: Writings on South Asian Society and History*, vol. V. Delhi: Oxford University Press.

———(1996) The Small Voice of History. In *Subaltern Studies*, vol. IX, ed. Shahid Amin and Dipesh Chakrabarty. Delhi: Oxford University Press.

Habib, Irfan (1994) *Reason and History* (Zakir Husain Memorial Lecture). Delhi: Zakir Husain College.

Hobsbawm, E. J. (1980) The Revival of Narrative: Some Comments. *Past and Present*, 86 (February).

Lowenthal, David (1985) *The Past is a Foreign Country*. Cambridge: Cambridge University Press.

Macintyre, Alasdaire (1988) *Whose Justice? What Rationality?* London: Gerald Duckworth & Co.

Nehru, Jawaharlal (1936) *An Autobiography*. London: Victor Gollancz.

Pandey, Gyanendra (1992) In Defence of the Fragment: Writing on Hindu–Muslim Riots in India Today. *Representations* (Winter).

———1994. The Prose of Otherness. *Subaltern Studies*, vol. VIII, edited by D. Arnold and D. Hardiman. Delhi: Oxford University Press.

Panikkar, K. N. (1994) In Defence of Old History. *Economic and Political Weekly*, XXIX, 40 (October).

Scott, Joan W. (1991) The Evidence of Experience. *Critical Inquiry* (Summer).

——— 1992. The Campaign Against PC: What's Really at Stake. *Radical History Review*, 54.

Spivak, Gayatri C. (1988) Can the Subaltern Speak? Speculations on Widow Sacrifice. In *Marxism and the Interpretation of Culture*, edited by L. Grossberg and C. Nelson. New York: Macmillan.

Stone, Lawrence (1979) The Revival of Narrative: Reflections on a New Old History. *Past and Present*, 85.

Vidyarthi, Ganesh Shankar (1978) *Kranti ka Ughhosh: Ganesh Shankar Vidyarthi ki Kalam se*, edited by R. Awasthi. Kanpur: Pratap Press.

14

The Decline of the Subaltern in *Subaltern Studies*

Sumit Sarkar

My title may sound provocative, but at one level it is no more than description, with no necessarily pejorative implications. A quick count indicates that all fourteen essays in *Subaltern Studies I* and *II* had been about underprivileged groups in Indian society – peasants, tribals and in one instance workers. The corresponding figure for Volumes *VII* and *VIII* is, at most, four out of twelve.[1] Guha's preface and introductory essay in the first volume had been full of references to 'subaltern classes', evocations of Gramsci, and the use of much Marxian terminology. Today, the dominant thrust within the project – or at least the one that gets most attention – is focused on critiques of Western-colonial power-knowledge, with non-Western 'community consciousness' as its valorized alternative. Also emerging is a tendency to define such communities principally in terms of religious identities.

Change within a project which is now well over a decade old is entirely understandable and even welcome, though one could have hoped for some internal analysis of the shifting meanings of the core term 'subaltern' and why it has been thought necessary to retain it despite a very different discursive context. What makes the shifts within *Subaltern Studies* worthy of close attention are their association with changes in academic (and political) moods that have had a virtually global range.

Subaltern Studies emerged in the early 1980s in a dissident-left milieu, where sharp criticism of orthodox Marxist practice and theory was still combined with the retention of a broad socialist and Marxian horizon. There were obvious affinities with the radical-populist moods of the 1960s and 1970s, and specifically with efforts to write 'histories from below'. The common ground lay in a combination of enthusiastic response to popular, usually peasant, rebellions, with growing disillusionment about organized left parties, received versions of orthodox

Marxist ideology and the bureaucratic state structures of 'actually existing socialism'. In India, specifically, there were the embers of abortive Maoist armed struggle in the countryside, the spectacle of one of the two major communist parties supporting an authoritarian regime that was close to the Soviet Union, and then the hopes briefly aroused by the post-Emergency electoral rout of Indira Gandhi. Among historiographical influences, that of British Marxian social history was probably the most significant. Hill, Hobsbawm and Thompson were much admired by the younger scholars, and Thompson in particular had a significant impact when he visited India in the winter of 1976–77 and addressed a session of the Indian History Congress.[2] Ranajit Guha seems to have often used 'subaltern' somewhat in the way Thompson deployed the term 'plebeian' in his writings on eighteenth-century England. In the largely pre-capitalist conditions of colonial India, class formation was likely to have remained ichoate. 'Subaltern' would be of help in avoiding the pitfalls of economic reductionism, while at the same time retaining a necessary emphasis on domination and exploitation.[3] The radical, Thompsonian, social history of the 1970s, despite assertions to the contrary which are made sometimes nowadays for polemical purposes, never really became respectable in the eyes of Western academic establishments. It is not surprising, therefore, that the early *Subaltern Studies* volumes, along with Guha's *Elementary Aspects of Peasant Insurgency in Colonial India* (1983), were largely ignored in the West, while they attracted widespread interest and debate in left-leaning intellectual circles in India.[4]

Things have changed much since then, and today a transformed *Subaltern Studies* owes much of its prestige to the acclaim it is receiving from that part of the Western academic postmodernistic counter-establishment which is interested in colonial and postcolonial matters. Its success is fairly obviously related to an ability to move with the times. With the withering of hopes of radical transformation through popular initiative, conceptions of seamless, all-pervasive, virtually irresistible power-knowledge have tended to displace the evocation of moments of resistance central to the histories from below of the 1960s and 1970s. Domination is conceptualized overwhelmingly in cultural, discursive terms, as the power-knowledge of the post-Enlightenment West. If at all seen as embodied concretely in institutions, it tends to get identified uniquely with the modern bureaucratic nation-state: further search for specific socio-economic interconnections is felt to be unnecessarily economistic, redolent of traces of a now finally defeated Marxism, and hence disreputable. 'Enlightenment rationalism' thus becomes the central polemical target, and Marxism stands condemned as one more variety of Eurocentrism. Radical, left-wing social history, in other words, has been collapsed into cultural studies and critiques of colonial discourse, and we have moved from Thompson to Foucault and, even more, Said.

The evolution has been recently summed up by Dipesh Chakrabarty as a shift from the attempt 'to write "better" Marxist histories' to an understanding that 'a critique of this nature could hardly afford to ignore the problem of universalism/Eurocentrism that was inherent in Marxist (or for that matter liberal) thought itself'. His article goes on to explain the changes within *Subaltern Studies* primarily in terms of 'the interest that Gayatri Spivak and, following her, Edward Said and others took in the project'.[5] Going against the views of my ex-colleagues in the *Subaltern Studies* editorial team, I intend to argue that the trajectory that has been outlined with considerable precision and frankness by Chakrabarty has been debilitating in both academic and political terms. Explanations in terms of adaptations to changed circumstances or outside intellectual influences alone are, however, never fully adequate. I would like to attempt a less 'external' reading, through a focus on certain conceptual ambiguities and implicit tensions within the project from the beginning.

The achievements of the early years of *Subaltern Studies* in terms of widening horizons and concrete historical research need to be rescued, perhaps, from the enormous condescension of recent adherents like Gyan Prakash, who dismisses such work as 'the familiar "history from below" approach'.[6] (It is difficult to resist at this point the retort that postmodernistic moods are today not only 'familiar' but academically respectable and advantageous in ways that would have been inconceivable for radical social historians in the 1970s.) The early essays of Ranajit Guha in *Subaltern Studies* located the origins of the new initiative in an effort to 'rectify the elitist bias', often accompanied by economistic assumptions, common to much colonialist, 'bourgeois-nationalist' and conventional-Marxist readings of modern Indian history.[7] Thus it was argued with considerable justice by Guha and other contributors that anti-colonial movements had been explained far too often in terms of a combination of economic pressures and mobilization from the top by leaders portrayed as manipulative in colonial, and as idealistic or charismatic in nationalist, historiography. Studies of peasant and labour movements, similarly, had concentrated on economic conditions and left organizational and ideological lineages. The new trend would seek to explore the neglected dimension of popular or subaltern autonomy in action, consciousness and culture.

Subaltern Studies, from its beginnings, was felt by many, with some justice, to be somewhat too dismissive about predecessors and contemporaries working on not entirely dissimilar lines,[8] and the claims of setting up a new 'paradigm' were certainly over-flamboyant. Yet a new theoretical – or at least polemical – clarity was added to ongoing efforts at exploring histories from below, along with much empirical work at once solid and exciting. Thus Ranajit Guha's analysis of specific themes and movements – the role of rumour, the interrelationships and distinctions between crime and insurgency, or aspects of the Santal rebellion and the 1857 upheaval, to cite a few stray examples – were appreciated by many who could not accept the overall framework of *Elementary Aspects*. The publications of the *Subaltern Studies* group, within, outside, and in some cases before the constitution of the project, helped to modify significantly the historiography of anti-colonial nationalism through a common initial emphasis on 'pressures from below'. One thinks, for instance, of David Hardiman's pioneering exploration of the peasant nationalists of Gujarat through his meticulous collection of village-level data, Gyanendra Pandey's argument about an inverse relationship between the strength of local Congress organization and peasant militancy in Uttar Pradesh, and Shahid Amin's analysis of rumours concerning Gandhi's miracle-working powers as an entry point into the processes of an autonomous popular appropriation of messages from nationalist leaders.[9] Reinterpretations of mainstream nationalism apart, there were also important studies of tribal movements and cults, Dipesh Chakrabarty's stimulating, if controversial, essays on Bengal labour history, and efforts to enter areas more 'difficult' for radical historians such as mass communalism, or peasant submissiveness to landlords.[10]

Once the initial excitement had worn away, however, work of this kind could seem repetitive, conveying an impression of a purely empiricist adding of details to confirm the fairly simple initial hypothesis about subaltern autonomy in one area or form after another. The attraction felt for the alternative, apparently more theoretical, thrust also present within *Subaltern Studies* from its beginnings is therefore understandable. This had its origins in Guha's attempt to use some of the language and methods of Lévi-Straussian structuralism to unravel what *Elementary Aspects* claimed was an underlying structure of peasant insurgent consciousness, extending across more than a century of colonial rule and over considerable variations of physical and social space. Guha still confined his generalizations to Indian peasants under colonialism, and sought to preserve some linkages with patterns of state-landlord-moneylender exploitation. Partha Chatterjee's first two essays in *Subaltern Studies* introduced a much more general category of 'peasant communal consciousness', inaugurating thereby what has subsequently become a crucial shift from 'subaltern' through 'peasant' to 'community'. The essays simultaneously expanded the notion of 'autonomy' into a categorical disjunction between two 'domains' of politics and 'power' – elite and subaltern. Chatterjee claimed that 'when a community acts collectively the fundamental political characteristics are the same everywhere', and achieved an equally breathtaking, unmediated leap from some very general comments in Marx's *Grundrisse* about community in pre-capitalist social formations to Bengal peasant life in the 1920s.[11]

In the name of theory, then, a tendency emerged towards essentializing the categories of 'subaltern' and 'autonomy' in the sense of assigning to them more or less absolute, fixed, decontextualized meanings and qualities. That there had been such elements of 'essentialism', 'teleology' and epistemological naivete in the quest for the subaltern subject has naturally not escaped the notice of recent postmodernistically inclined admirers. They tend, however, to blame such aberrations on Marxist residues which now, happily, have been largely overcome.[12] What is conveniently forgotten is that the problems do not disappear through a simple substitution of 'class' by 'subaltern' or 'community'. Reifying tendencies can be actually strengthened by the associated detachment from socio-economic contexts and determinants out of a mortal fear of economic reductionism. The handling of the new concepts, further, may remain equally naive. The intervention of Gayatri Chakravorty Spivak,[13] we shall see, has not changed things much in this respect for the bulk of later *Subaltern Studies* work, except in purely verbal terms.

The more essentialist aspects of the early *Subaltern Studies* actually indicated moves away from the Marxian worlds of Thompson and Gramsci. Reification of a subaltern or community identity is open to precisely the kind of objections that Thompson had levelled in the famous opening pages of his *Making of the English Working Class* against much conventional Marxist handling of class: objections that paradoxically contributed to the initial *Subaltern Studies* rejection of the rigidities of economistic class analysis. It is true that Thompson's own handling of the notion of community has been critiqued at times for being insufficiently attentive to 'internal' variations:[14] the contrast in this respect with the ultimate trajectory of *Subaltern Studies* still seems undeniable. Through deliberately paradoxical formulations like 'class struggle without class', Thompson had sought to combine the continued quest for collectivities of protest and transformation with a rejection of fixed, reified identities.[15] He refused to surrender totally the ground of class, and so the rejection of the base–superstructure analogy did not lead him to any 'culturalism'. Thompson, it needs to be emphasized, never gave up the attempt to situate plebeian culture 'within a particular equilibrium of social relations, a working environment of exploitation and resistance to exploitation – its proper material mode'.[16] What he possessed in abundant measure was an uncanny ability to hold together in creative, dialectical tension dimensions that have often flowed apart elsewhere.

It would be relevant in this context to look also at Gramsci's six-point 'methodological criteria' for the 'history of the subaltern classes', referred to by Guha with much admiration in the very first page of *Subaltern Studies I* as a model unattainable but worth striving for:

> 1. the objective formation of the subaltern social groups, by the developments and transformations occurring in the sphere of economic production ... 2. their active or passive affiliation to the dominant political formations, their attempts to influence the programmes of these formations in order to press claims of their own ... 3. the birth of new parties of the dominant groups, intended to conserve the assent of the subaltern groups and to maintain control over them; 4. the formations which the subaltern groups themselves produce, in order to press claims of a limited and partial character; 5. those new formations which assert the autonomy of the subaltern groups, but within the old framework; 6. those formations which assert the integral autonomy ... etc.[17]

Subaltern 'social groups' are emphatically not unrelated to 'the sphere of economic production', it will be noticed – and the indication is clear even in such a brief outline of an enormous range of possible meanings of 'autonomy'. Above all, the emphasis, throughout, is not on distinct domains of politics, but interpenetration, mutual (though obviously unequal) conditioning and, implicitly, common roots in a specific social formation. Otherwise the subaltern would logically always remain subaltern, except in the unlikely event of a literal inversion which, too, would not really transform society: perspectives that Gramsci the revolutionary could hardly be expected to endorse.

Chatterjee's terminology of distinct elite and subaltern domains was initially felt by many in the *Subaltern Studies* group to be little more than a strong way of asserting the basic need to search for traces of subaltern autonomy. (I notice, for instance, that I had quite inconsistently slipped into the same language even while arguing in my *Subaltern Studies III* essay against over-rigid application of binary categories.)[18] The logical, if at first perhaps unnoticed and unintended, consequences have been really far-reaching. The separation of domination and autonomy tended to make absolute and homogenize both within their separate domains, and represented a crucial move away from efforts to develop immanent critiques of structures that have been the strength of Marxian dialectical approaches.[19] Domination construed as irresistible could render autonomy illusory. Alternatively, the latter had to be located in pre-colonial or pre-modern spaces untouched by power, or sought for in fleeting, fragmentary moments alone. Late *Subaltern Studies* in practice has oscillated around precisely these three positions, of 'derivative discourse', indigenous 'community' and 'fragments'.

A bifurcation of the worlds of domination and autonomy, I have argued elsewhere, became characteristic of several otherwise unconnected spheres of intellectual enquiry in the political conjuncture of the late 1970s and 1980s: the 'acculturation thesis' about early modern French popular culture, Foucault's studies of modern power-knowledge, Said's critique of Orientalism.[20] Not surprisingly, the similar disjunction that was occasionally made in early *Subaltern Studies*[21] provided the initial point of insertion of Said, through an article, and then a very influential book, by Partha Chatterjee.[22] Said's views regarding the overwhelming nature of post-Enlightenment colonial power-knowledge was applied to the colonized intelligentsia, who were thus virtually robbed of agency and held to have been capable of only 'derivative discourses'. Beyond it lay the domain of community consciousness, still associated, though rather vaguely now, with the peasantry, but embodied somehow in the figure of Gandhi, who was declared to have been uniquely free of the taint of Enlightenment rationalism prior to his partial appropriation by the Nehruvian 'moment of arrival'. Both poles of the power relationship tend to get homogenized in this argument, which has become extremely influential. Colonial cultural domination, stripped of all complexities and variations, faces an indigenous domain eroded of internal tensions and conflicts.[23] The possibility of pre-colonial forms of domination, however modified, persisting through colonialism, helping to mediate colonial authority in vital ways, maybe even functioning autonomously at times – for all of which there is ample evidence – is simply ignored.[24] Colonial rule is assumed to have brought about an absolute rupture: the colonized subject is taken to have been literally constituted by colonialism alone.[25] And so Gandhi's assumed location 'outside the thematic of post-Enlightenment thought' can be described as one 'which could have been adopted by any member of the traditional intelligentsia in India', and then simultaneously identified as having 'an inherently [*sic*] "peasant-communal" character'. The differences between the 'traditional intelligentsia', overwhelmingly upper-caste (or elite Muslim) and male, and bound up with structures of landlord and bureaucratic domination, and peasant-communal consciousness, are apparently of no importance whatsoever: caste, class and gender divides have ceased to matter.[26]

There are elements of a rich paradox in this shift of binaries from elite/subaltern to colonial/indigenous community or Western/third-world cultural nationalist. A project that had started with a trenchant attack on elite nationalist historiography had now chosen as its hero the principal iconic figure of official Indian nationalism, and its most influential text after *Elementary Aspects* was built entirely around the (partial) study of just three indisputably elite figures, Bankimchandra, Gandhi and Nehru. The passage to near-nationalist positions may have been facilitated, incidentally, by an unnoticed drift implicit even in Guha's initial formulation of the project in *Subaltern Studies I*. The 'historiography of colonial India' somehow slides quickly into that of Indian nationalism: the fundamental lacuna is described as the failure 'to acknowledge the contribution made by the people *on their own* to the making and development of this nationalism', and the central problematic ultimately becomes '*the historic failure of the nation to come into its own*'.[27]

With *Nationalist Thought*, followed in 1987 by the publication in the United States of *Selected Subaltern Studies*, with a foreword by Edward Said and an editorial note by Gayatri Chakravorty Spivak, subaltern historiography was launched on a successful international, and more specifically metropolitan and US-academic, career. The intellectual formation of which its currently most prominent practitioners are now part, Aijaz Ahmad argues, has gone through two phases: third-world cultural nationalism, followed by postmodernistic valorizations of 'fragments'.[28] For *Subaltern Studies*, however, located by its subject matter in a country that has been a postcolonial nation-state for more than four decades, an oppositional stance towards existing forms of nationalism has been felt to be necessary from the beginning. The situation was rather different from that facing a member of a Palestinian diaspora still in quest of independent nationhood. This opposition was reconciled with the Saidian framework through the assumption that the postcolonial nation-state was no more than a continuation of the original, Western, Enlightenment project imposed through colonial discourse. The mark of late *Subaltern Studies*, therefore, became not a succession of phases, but the counterposing of reified notions of 'community' or 'fragment', alternatively or sometimes in unison, against this highly generalized category of the 'modern' nation-state as the embodiment of Western cultural domination. The original separation of the domains of power and autonomy culminates here in an oscillation between the 'rhetorical absolutism' of structure and the 'fragmented fetishism' of the subject – to apply to it the perceptive comments of Perry Anderson, a decade ago, about the consequences of uncritically applying the linguistic model to historiography.[29]

It might be interesting to take a glance at this point at the glimmerings of an alternative approach that had appeared briefly within *Subaltern Studies* but was soon virtually forgotten. I am thinking, particularly, of Ranajit Guha's seldom-referred-to article 'Chandra's Death' – along with, perhaps, an essay of mine about a very unusual village scandal and Gyanendra Pandey's exploration of local memory through a small-town gentry chronicle and a diary kept by a weaver.[30] 'Fragment' and 'community' were important for these essays, but in ways utterly different from what has now become the dominant mode within *Subaltern Studies.* Hindsight indicates some affinities, rather, with the kind of micro-history analysed recently by Carlo Ginzburg, marked by an 'insistence on context, exactly the opposite of the isolated contemplation of the fragmentary', advocated by postmodernism. This is a micro-history which has become anti-positivistic in its awareness of the constructed nature of all evidence and categories, but which nevertheless does not plunge into complete scepticism and relativism. 'Chandra's Death' and 'Kalki-Avatar' tried to explore general connections – of caste, patriarchy, class, colonial rule – through 'the small drama and fine detail of social existence' and sought to avoid the appearance of impersonality and abstraction often conveyed by pure macro-history. Their starting-point was what Italian historians nowadays call the 'exceptional-normal',[31] a local event that had interrupted the everyday only for a brief moment, but which had been unusual enough to leave some traces. And the 'community' that was unravelled, particularly through Guha's moving study of the death (through enforced abortion after an illicit affair) of a low-caste woman, was one of conflict and brutal exploitation, of power relations 'sited at a depth within the indigenous society, well beyond the reach of the disciplinary arm of the colonial state'. These are dimensions that have often been concealed, Guha noted, through a blending of 'indigenous feudal ideology . . . with colonial anthropology'.[32] Not just colonial anthropology but Guha's own brainchild, one is tempted to add, sometimes carries on that good work nowadays: with the result that essays in late *Subaltern Studies* which implicitly take a different stance tend to get relatively little attention.[33]

But there was no theorization on the basis of such micro-study, nothing of the kind being attempted nowadays by some Italian and German scholars to develop micro-history into a cogent methodological alternative to both positivism and postmodernism. And there was the further fact that this was emphatically not the kind of South Asian history that could win easy acclaim in the West, for its reading demanded, if not prior knowledge, at least the readiness to try to grasp unfamiliar and dense material, thick descriptions which were not at the same time exotic. One does get the strong impression that the majority among even the fairly small section of the Western intelligentsia interested in the third world prefers its material conveniently packaged nowadays, without too much detail or complexity. (Totally different standards would be expected in mainstream work on any branch, say, of European history.) Packaged, moreover, in a particular way, fitted into the slots of anti-Western cultural nationalism (one recalls Fredric Jameson's assertion that 'all third world texts are necessarily – *national allegories*')[34] and/or post-structuralist play with fragments. The West, it seems, to borrow from Said, is still engaged in producing its Orient through selective appropriation and essentialist stereotyping: Orientalism flourishes at the heart of today's anti-Orientalist tirade.

Partha Chatterjee's *The Nation and Its Fragments* epitomizes the latest phase of *Subaltern Studies* at its most lucid and comprehensive.[35] A new binary has been introduced, 'material'/'spiritual' (or 'world'/ 'home'),[36] probably to take care of the criticism that the earlier 'derivative discourse' thesis had deprived the colonized subject of all autonomy or agency. Through such a bifurcation, we are told, nationalists kept or created as their own an autonomous world of literature, art, education, domesticity and, above all it appears, religion. They were surrendering in effect to the West, meanwhile, on the 'material' plane: for the efforts to eradicate 'colonial difference' (e.g. unequal treatment of Indians in law courts, with respect to civil rights, and in politics generally) actually meant progressive absorption into the Western colonial project of building the modern nation-state – a project inevitably left incomplete by colonialism, but realized by Indian nationalists. Here is paradox indeed, for all commonsensically promising or effective ways of fighting colonial domination (mass political struggle, for instance, or even economic self-help) have become signs of surrender.

Further implications of this suspicion about indigenous ventures into the 'external' or 'material' domain become evident in the principles of selection followed in the chapters about the nation and 'its' women and subordinate castes. For Chatterjee, women's initiative or autonomy in the nationalist era apparently found expression only inside the home, or at best in autobiographies, while evidence for lower-caste protest against Brahmanical hegemony is located solely in the interesting, but extremely marginal, world of heterodox religious sects. He remains silent about the active role of women in virtually every kind of politics, as well as in specific women's associations, from at least the 1920s. Within the home, Chatterjee focuses much more closely on how women preserved pre-colonial modes of being and resistance, echoing standard nationalist concerns. There is not much interest in how women struggled with a patriarchal domination that was, after all, overwhelmingly indigenous in its structures. Even more surprisingly, the book tells the reader nothing about the powerful anti-caste movements associated with Phule, Periyar or Ambedkar. No book can be expected to cover everything, but silences of this magnitude are dangerous in a work that appears on the surface comprehensive enough to serve as a standard introduction to colonial India for non-specialists and newcomers, particularly abroad.

The new binary elaborated in *The Nation* is not just a description of nationalist ideology, in which case it could have had a certain, though much exaggerated, relevance. The pattern of stresses and silences indicates a high degree of authorial acceptance. And yet the material/spiritual, West/East divide is of course almost classically Orientalist, much loved in particular by the most conservative elements in Indian society in both colonial and postcolonial times.[37] Chatterjee remains vague about 'the new idea of womanhood in the era of nationalism', the 'battle' for which, he tells us, 'unlike the women's movements in nineteenth- and twentieth-century Europe and America', 'was waged in the home . . . outside the arena of political agitation'.[38] His editorial colleague Dipesh Chakrabarty has recently been much more explicit. Chakrabarty has discovered in nineteenth-century Bengali valorizations of *kula* and *grihalaksmi* (roughly, extended lineage and bounteous wife) 'an irreducible category of "beauty" . . . ways of talking about formations of pleasure, emotions and ideas of good life that associated themselves with models of non-autonomous, non-bourgeois, and non-secular personhood'. All this, despite the admitted 'cruelties of the patriarchal order' entailed by such terms, 'their undeniable phallocentrism'.[39] Beauty, pleasure, the good life . . . *for whom*, it is surely legitimate to ask.

Chatterjee's new book ends on the metahistorical note of a 'struggle between community and capital'. His notion of community, as earlier, is bound up somehow with peasant consciousness, which, we are told, is 'at the opposite pole to a bourgeois consciousness'. (Significantly, this work on what, after all, is now a fairly developed capitalist country by third-world standards, has no space at all for the nation and its capitalists, or workers.) A pattern similar to that just noticed with respect to gender now manifests itself. The Indian peasant community, Chatterjee admits, was never egalitarian, for 'a fifth or more of the population, belonging to the lowest castes, have never had any recognized rights in land'. No matter, however: this profoundly inegalitarian community can still be valorized, for its 'unity . . . nevertheless established by recognizing the rights of subsistence of all sections of the population, albeit a differential right entailing differential duties and privileges'. One is almost tempted to recall the standard idealizations of caste as harmonious, even if hierarchical. The Narodniks had tried to read back into the *mir* their own indisputably egalitarian and socialist ideals: Chatterjee's rejection of such 'populist idealization of the peasantry' has led him back to a Slavophile position.[40]

Late *Subaltern Studies* here comes close to positions of neo-traditionalist anti-modernism, notably advocated with great clarity and vigour for a number of years by Ashis Nandy.[41] A significant section of the intelligentsia has been attracted by such appeals to an earlier, precolonial or pre-modern catholicity of inchoate, pluralistic traditions, particularly in the context of the rise in India today of powerful religious-chauvinist forces claiming to represent definitively organized communities with fixed boundaries – trends that culminated in the destruction of the Babri Masjid and the communal carnage of 1992–93. Right-wing Hindutva can then be condemned precisely for being 'modern', a construct of late- and postcolonial times, the product of Western, colonial power-knowledge and its classificatory strategies like census enumeration.[42] It may be denounced even for being, in some paradoxical way, 'secular', and the entire argument then gets bound up with condemnations of secular rationalism as the ultimate villain. Secularism, inexorably associated with the interventionist modern state, is inherently intolerant, argued Nandy in 1990. To him, it is as unacceptable as Hindutva, a movement which typifies 'religion-as-ideology', imbricated in 'non-religious, usually political or socio-economic, interests'. Toleration, conversely, has to be 'anti-secular', and must seek to ground itself on pre-modern 'religion-as-faith' . . . which Nandy defines as 'definitionally non-monolithic and operationally plural'.[43]

What regularly happens in such arguments is a simultaneous narrowing and widening of the term secularism, its deliberate use as a wildly free-floating signifier. It becomes a polemical target which is both single and conveniently multivalent. Secularism, in the first place, gets equated with aggressive anti-religious scepticism, virtually atheism, through a unique identification with the Enlightenment (itself vastly simplified and homogenized). Yet in twentieth-century India systematic anti-religious polemic, far less activity, has been extremely rare, even on the part of dedicated leftists and other nonbelievers. Being secular in the Indian context has meant, primarily and quite often solely, being non- or anti-communal – which is why Mahatma Gandhi had no particular problem with it. 'The Indian version of secularism', Rajeev Bhargava has recently reminded us, 'was consolidated in the aftermath of Partition, where Hindu–Muslim sectarian violence killed off over half a million people': sad and strange, really, that such reminders have become necessary.[44] Even in Europe, the roots of secularism go back some 200 years beyond the Enlightenment, for elements of it emerged in the wake of another epoch of 'communal' violence, the religious wars of the Reformation era. The earliest advocates of a 'secular' separation of church from state were not rationalist freethinkers but sixteenth-century Anabaptists passionately devoted to their own brand of Christianity who believed any kind of compulsory state religion to be contrary to true faith.

The anti-secular position can retain its plausibility only through an enormous widening of the term's meaning, so that secularism can be made to bear the burden of guilt for all the manifold and indisputable misdeeds and crimes of the 'modern nation-state': 'the new forms of man-made violence unleashed by post-seventeenth-century Europe in the name of Enlightenment values . . . the Third Reich, the Gulag, the two World Wars, and the threat of nuclear annihilation'.[45] The logical leap here is really quite startling: Hitler and Stalin were no doubt secular, but was secularism, *per se*, the ground for Nazi or Stalinist terror, considering that so many of their victims (notably, in both cases, the communists) were also atheists? Must secularism be held responsible every time a murder is committed by an unbeliever?

A recent article by Partha Chatterjee reiterates Nandy's position, with one very significant difference.[46] The essay is a reminder of the almost inevitably slippery nature of the category of community. Sought to be applied to an immediate, contemporary context, romanticizations of pre-modern 'fuzzy' identities seem to be in some danger of getting displaced by an even more troubling 'realistic' reconciliation or accommodation with the present.[47] Community, in this article, becomes an 'it', with firm boundaries and putative representative structures: most startlingly, only communities determined by religion appear now to be worthy of consideration. Realism for Chatterjee now suggests that religious toleration and state non-interference should be allowed to expand into legislative autonomy for distinct religious communities:

> Toleration here would require one to accept that there will be political contexts where a group could insist on its right not to give reasons for doing things differently provided it explains itself adequately in its own

> chosen forum ... What this will mean in institutional terms are processes through which each religious group will publicly seek and obtain from its members consent for its practices insofar as those practices have regulative power over the members.[48]

This, to be sure, is in the specific context of the current motivated and majoritarian BJP campaign for imposing a uniform civil code through a unilateral abrogation of Muslim personal law. Chatterjee's argument has a certain superficial similarity with many other positions which express concern today over any imposed uniformity. It remains a world removed, however, from the proposals being put forward by some women's organizations and secular groups for mobilizing initially around demands for specific reforms in distinct personal laws. Such mobilization is definitely not intended to remain confined within discrete community walls, but seeks to highlight unjust gender inequalities within all communities. The Hindutva campaign demanding uniformity in the name of national integration, it has been argued, 'deliberately ignores the crucial aspect of "uniformity" within communities, i.e. between men and women'.[49] Chatterjee's logic, in contrast, unfortunately seems broad enough to be eminently appropriable, say, by the VHP claiming to speak on behalf of all 'Hindus', or fundamentalists in Bangladesh persecuting a dissenter like Taslima Nasreen. For at its heart lies the assumption that all really dangerous or meaningful forms of power are located uniquely in the modern state, whereas power within communities matters very much less. Despite the deployment of Foucauldian 'governmentality' in the article, this is a position that I find irreconcilable with the major thrust of Foucault's arguments, which have been original and disturbing precisely through their search for multiple locations of power and their insistence that forms of resistance also normally develop into alternative sites of domination.

These, however, cannot but be uncomfortable positions for intellectuals who remain deeply anti-communal and in some sense radical. Subaltern historiography in general has faced considerable difficulties in tackling this phenomenon of a communal violence that is both popular and impossible to endorse. There is the further problem that the Hindu right often attacks the secular, liberal nation-state as a Western importation, precisely the burden of much late-Subaltern argument: suggesting affinities that are, hopefully, still distasteful, yet difficult to repudiate within the parameters of an anti-Enlightenment discourse grounded in notions of community.[50] In two recent articles by Gyanendra Pandey, communal violence consequently becomes the appropriate site for the unfolding of that other pole of late-Subaltern thinking, built around the notion of the 'fragment', and seeking to valorize it against epistemologically uncertain and politically oppressive 'grand narratives'.[51] Epistemological uncertainty becomes the ground for rejecting all efforts at causal explanation, or even contextual analysis. (Such uncertainties, it may be noticed, have never been allowed to obstruct sweeping generalizations about Enlightenment rationalism, derivative discourses or community consciousness.) The polemical thrust can then be directed once again principally against secular intellectuals who have tried to relate communal riots to socio-economic and political contexts. Such efforts, invariably branded as economistic, allegedly leave 'little room for the emotions of people, for feelings and perceptions' through their emphasis upon 'land and property'.[52] That people can never get emotional about 'land and property' is surely a startling discovery. Even a distinction, drawn in the context of the terrifying riots of 1946–47 and simplistically represented by Pandey as one made between 'good' and 'bad' subaltern violence, is apparently unacceptable.[53] Pandey cannot stop here, for he remains an anti-communal intellectual: but the framework he has adopted leaves space for nothing more than agonized contemplation of 'violence' and 'pain' as 'fragments', perception of which is implicitly assumed to be direct and certain. But 'fragment', etymologically, is either part of a bigger whole or a whole by itself: one cannot avoid the dangers of homogenization that easily. It remains unnoticed, further, that valorization of the certainty of knowledge of particulars has been a classically positivistic position, well expounded many years ago, for instance, by Karl Popper in his *Poverty of Historicism.*[54]

But violence and pain, detached from specificities of context, become in effect abstract universals, 'violence' in general. The essays end with rhetorical questions about how historians can represent pain, how difficult or impossible it is to do so. One is irresistibly reminded of Thompson's devastating comment in his last book about the fatuity of many statements about 'the human condition', which take us 'only a little way, and a great deal less far than is sometimes knowingly implied. For "the human condition", unless further qualified and disclosed, is nothing but a kind of metaphysical full stop' – or: 'worse – a bundle of solecisms about mortality and defeated aspiration'.[55]

Let me try to sum up my disagreements with late *Subaltern Studies*, which flow from a compound of academic and political misgivings.

Two sets of misrecognitions have obscured the presence in *Subaltern Studies* of a high degree of redundancy, the tendency to reiterate the already said. Both follow from a novelty of situation: *Subaltern Studies* does happen to be the first Indian historiographical school whose reputation has come to be evaluated primarily in terms of audience response in the West. For many Indian readers, particularly those getting interested in postmodernist trends for the first time, the sense of being 'with it' strongly conveyed by *Subaltern Studies* appears far more important than any possible insubstantiality of empirical content. Yet some eclectic borrowings or verbal similarities apart, the claim (or ascription) of being postmodern is largely spurious, in whichever sense we might want to deploy that ambiguous and self-consciously polysemic term. Texts are still being read here in a flat and obvious manner, as straightforward indicators of authorial intention. There have been few attempts to juxtapose representations of diverse kinds in unexpected ways, or self-conscious efforts to think out or experiment with new forms of narrativization. Partha Chatterjee's *Nationalist Thought*, to cite one notable instance, reads very much like a conventional history of ideas, based on a succession of great thinkers. One of the thinkers, Bankimchandra, happens to have been the first major Bengali novelist: his imaginative prose, inexplicably, is totally ignored. Again, much of the potential richness of the *Ramakrishna-Kathamrita* explored as a text gets lost, I feel, if it is virtually reduced to a 'source of new strategies of survival and resistance' of a colonized middle class assumed to be living in extreme dread of its foreign rulers – a class moreover conceptualized in excessively homogenized terms.[56] Problems like these are not basically products of lack of authorial competence or quality. They emerge from restrictive analytical frameworks, as *Subaltern Studies* swings from a rather simple emphasis on subaltern autonomy to an even more simplistic thesis of Western colonial cultural domination.[57]

A reiteration of the already said: for it needs to be emphasized that the bulk of the history written by modern Indian historians has been nationalist and anti-colonial in content, at times obsessively so. Criticism of Western cultural domination is likewise nothing particularly novel. The empirical underpinning for the bulk of *Subaltern* cultural criticism has come in fact from work done in Calcutta some twenty years back, which had effectively demolished the excessive adulation of nineteenth-century English-educated intellectuals and reformers through an emphasis upon the limits imposed on them by their colonial context.[58]

Here the second kind of misrecognition comes in, for in the Western context there is a certain, though much exaggerated, novelty and radicalism in the Saidian exposure of the colonial complicity of much European scholarship and literature. Such blindness has been most obvious in the discipline of literary studies, in the West as well as in the ex-colonial world, and it is not surprising that radically inclined intellectuals working in this area have been particularly enthusiastic in their response to late *Subaltern Studies*. There had been some real absences, too, even in the best of Western Marxist or radical historiography, inadequacies that came to be felt more deeply in the new era of vastly intensified globalization, socialist collapse, resurgent neo-colonialism and racism, and the rise to unprecedented prominence of expatriate third-world intellectuals located, or seeking location in, Western universities. Hobsbawm apart, the great masters of British Marxist historiography have admittedly written little on Empire, and the charge of Eurocentrism could appear particularly damaging for a social history the foundation-text of which had deliberately confined itself to the making of the 'English' working class.

Yet the exposure of one instance after another of collusion with colonial power-knowledge can soon become predictable and tedious. Thompson has a quiet but telling aside about this in his *Alien Homage*,[59] while his posthumous book on Blake should induce some rethinking about uncritical denunciations of the Enlightenment as a bloc that have been so much in vogue in recent years. With its superb combination of textual close reading and historical analysis, *Witness Against the Beast* reminds us of the need for socially nuanced and differentiated conceptions of Enlightenment and 'counter-Enlightenment' that go far beyond homogenized praise or rejection. And meanwhile very interesting new work is emerging. Peter Linebaugh, for instance, has recently explored ways of integrating global, colonial dimensions and themes of Foucauldian power-knowledge within a framework that is clearly Thompsonian-Marxian in inspiration, and yet goes considerably beyond the parameters of the social history of the 1960s and 1970s.[60]

In South Asian historiography, however, the inflated reputation of late *Subaltern Studies* has encouraged a virtual folding back of all history into the single problematic of Western colonial cultural domination. This imposes a series of closures and silences, and threatens simultaneously to feed into shallow forms of retrogressive indigenism. An impression has spread among interested non-specialists that there is little worth reading in modern Indian history prior to *Subaltern Studies*, or outside it, today. Not that very considerable and significant new work is not going on along other lines: but this tends to get less attention than it deserves. One could cite major advances in economic history and pioneering work in environmental studies, for instance, as well as research on law and penal administration that is creatively aware of Foucault but tends to ignore, or go beyond, strict Saidian–Subaltern parameters. Such work does not usually begin with assuming a total or uniform pre-colonial/colonial disjunction.[61] Another example would be the shift in the dominant tone of feminist history. There had been interesting developments in the new field of gender studies in the 1970s and early 1980s, posing important questions about women and nationalism and relating gender to shifting material conditions. The colonial discourse framework threatens to marginalize much of this earlier work. A simple binary of Westernized surrender/indigenist resistance will necessarily have major difficulties in finding space for sensitive studies of movements for women's rights, or of lower-caste protest: for quite often such initiatives did try to utilize aspects of colonial administration and ideas as resources.

And finally there are the political implications. The spread of assumptions and values associated with late *Subaltern Studies* can have certain disabling consequences for sections of intellectuals still subjectively radical. This is so particularly because India – unlike many parts of the West, perhaps – is still a country where major political battles are engaged in by large numbers of people; where, in other words, depoliticization has not yet given a certain limited relevance to theories of sporadic initiative by individuals or small groups glorying in their imposed marginality. The organized, Marxist left in India remains one of the biggest existing anywhere in the world today, while very recently the forces of predominantly high-caste Hindutva have been halted in some areas by a lower-caste upthrust drawing on earlier traditions of anti-hierarchical protest. *Subaltern Studies*, symptomatically, has ignored histories of the left and of organized anti-caste movements throughout, and the line between past and present-day neglect can be fairly porous. Movements of a more innovatory kind have also emerged in recent years: organizations to defend civil and democratic rights, numerous feminist groups, massive ecological protests like the Narmada Bachao Andolan, and very new and imaginative forms of trade-union activity (the Chattisgarh Mukti Morcha arising out of a miners' union, one or two efforts at co-operative workers' control in the context of recession and structural readjustment). A 'social reform' issue like child marriage had been the preserve of highly educated, 'Westernized', upper-caste male reformers in the nineteenth century: today Bhanwari, a woman of low-caste origin in an obscure Rajasthan village, has been campaigning against that practice in Rajput households, in face of rape, ostracism and a gross miscarriage of justice. Any meaningful understanding of or identification with such developments is undercut by two kinds of emphasis quite central to late *Subaltern Studies*. Culturalism rejects the importance of class and class struggle, while notions of civil, democratic, feminist and liberal individual rights – many of them indubitably derived from certain Enlightenment traditions – get delegitimized by a repudiation of the Enlightenment as a bloc.

All such efforts need, and have often obtained, significant inputs from an intelligentsia which still includes many people with radical interests and commitments. This intelligentsia, however, is one constituent of a wider middle-class formation, upwardly mobile sections of which today are being sucked into globalizing processes that promise material consumerist dividends at the price of dependency. A binary combination of 'material' advancement and 'spiritual' autonomy through surrogate forms of cultural or religious nationalism is not at all uncommon for such groups. Hindutva, with its notable appeal in recent years among metropolitan elites and non-resident Indians, embodies this combination at its most aggressive. The political inclinations of the *Subaltern* scholars and the bulk of their readership are certainly very different, but some of their work nowadays seems to be unwittingly feeding into softer versions of not entirely dissimilar moods. Words like 'secular', 'rational' and 'progressive' have become terms of ridicule, and if 'resistance' (of whatever undifferentiative kind) can still be valorized, movements seeking transformation get suspected of teleology.[62] The decisive shift in critical registers from capitalist and colonial exploitation to Enlightenment rationality, from multinationals to Macaulay, has opened the way for a vague nostalgia that identifies the authentic with the indigenous, and locates both in the pasts of an ever-receding community, or a present than can consist of fragments alone. Through an enshrinement of sentimentality,[63] a subcontinent with its manifold, concrete contradictions and problems becomes a kind of dream of childhood, of a *grihalakshmi* presiding over a home happy and beautiful, by some alchemy, in the midst of all its patriarchy.

Let me end with a last, specific example. There is one chapter in Chatterjee's *Nation* which, for once, deals with an economic theme. This is a critique of the bureaucratic rationalism of Nehruvian planning: not unjustified in parts, though there has been no lack of such critiques, many of them much better informed and more effective. What is significant, however, is Chatterjee's total silence on the wholesale abandonment of that strategy in recent years under Western pressure. There is not a word, in a book published in 1993, about that other rationality of the 'free' market, derived at least as much from the Enlightenment as its socialistic alternatives, which is being imposed worldwide today by the World Bank, the IMF and multinational firms. The claim, elsewhere in the book, to an 'adversarial' relationship 'to the dominant structures of scholarship and politics' resounds oddly in the midst of this silence.[64]

Acknowledgements

I have benefited greatly from the comments and criticisms of Aijaz Ahmad, Pradip Kumar Datta, Mahmood Mamdani and Tanika Sarkar.

Notes

1. I am excluding from my count the two chapters in volume *VIII* about Ranajit Guha and his writings. Out of the four, one is by Terence Ranger about Africa, a second (Saurabh Dube) from outside the editorial group – which leaves us with David Hardiman on the Dangs and Ranajit Guha himself on nationalist mobilization/ disciplining of subaltern strata through 'social boycott'.

2. The paper he presented at that session was published by the journal of the Indian Council of Historical Research: 'Folklore, Anthropology, and Social History', *Indian Historical Review* (1977).

3. Guha's *Elementary Aspects of Peasant Insurgency in Colonial India* (Delhi, 1983) frequently cited Thompson with approval, and the references, significantly, were to *Whigs and Hunters* and the essay in *Albion's Fatal Tree.* In 1985 a defence by Dipesh Chakrabarty of the project against criticism in *Social Scientist,* some of it from orthodox Marxist standpoints, pleaded for greater openness to 'alternative varieties of Marxism' and rejected the base–superstructure metaphor in terms reminiscent of Thompson. 'Invitation to a Dialogue', in Guha (ed.), *Subaltern Studies IV* (Delhi, 1985), pp. 369, 373. See also Partha Chatterjee, 'Modes of Power: Some Clarifications', in *Social Scientist* 141, February 1985.

4. Thus the October 1984 issue of *Social Scientist,* a journal with CPI(M) affiliations, published a collective review essay on *Subaltern Studies II* written by a group of young scholars of Delhi University. A similar review of volumes *III* and *IV* came out in the same journal in March 1988. Guha and his colleagues, in significant contrast, were ignored by *Modern Asian Studies* till Rosalind O'Hanlon's 'Recovering the Subject: Subaltern Studies and Histories of Resistance in Colonial South Asia' (22, i, 1988), and the footnotes in this article clearly demonstrate that the initial debate around the project had been entirely within South Asia. Western discussion and acclaim has proliferated since then: within India, in contrast, there has been a largely derivative adulation, but nothing remotely resembling the critical engagement of the early years.

5. Dipesh Chakrabarty, 'Marx after Marxism: Subaltern Histories and the Question of Difference', in *Polygraph* 6/7, 1993.

6. Gyan Prakash, 'Writing Post-Orientalist Histories of the Third World: Perspectives from Indian Historiography', *Comparative Studies in Society and History,* 32, 1990.

7. Ranajit Guha, 'Preface', and 'On Some Aspects of the Historiography of Colonial India', in Guha (ed.), *Subaltern Studies I* (Delhi, 1982). The quoted phrases are from pp. vii and 1. A more explicit critique of orthodox Marxist historiography was made by Guha in the second volume (Delhi, 1983), in his 'The Prose of Counterinsurgency'.

8. One could think, for instance, of some of the essays in Ravinder Kumar's *Essays on Gandhian Politics* (Oxford, 1971) influenced by Rudé, or Majid Siddiqi's *Agrarian Unrest in North India: The United Provinces 1918–22* (New Delhi, 1978). In my *Popular Movements and Middle-Class Leadership in Late Colonial India: Problems and Perspectives of a 'History from Below'* (Calcutta, 1983), drafted before the publication of the first volume of *Subaltern Studies,* I attempted a catalogue of available research material relevant for such studies (fn. 3, p. 74). And the critique, central to much early *Subaltern Studies,* of nationalist leaders and organizations often restraining militant mass initiatives, had been quite common in some kinds of Marxist writing, most notably in R. P. Dutt's *India Today* (Bombay, 1947).

9. David Hardiman, *Peasant Nationalists of Gujarat: Kheda District, 1917–34* (Delhi, 1981); Gyanendra Pandey, *Ascendancy of the Congress in Uttar Pradesh 1926–34* (Delhi, 1978); Shahid Amin, 'Gandhi as Mahatma: Gorakhpur District Eastern UP, 1921–2', *Subaltern Studies III* (Delhi, 1984). My *Modern India, 1885–1947* (Delhi, 1983), written before I joined the *Subaltern Studies* group, tried to introduce a 'history from below' perspective while attempting an overall survey.

10. David Arnold, 'Rebellious Hillmen: The Gudem-Rampa Risings, 1839–1924', *Subaltern Studies I* (Delhi, 1982); David Hardiman, 'Adivasi Assertion in South Gujarat: The Devi Movement of 1922–3', *Subaltern Studies III* (Delhi, 1984), subsequently enlarged into his fascinating *The Coming of the Devi* (Delhi, 1987); Tanika Sarkar, 'Jitu Santal's Movement in Malda, 1924–32: A Study in Tribal Protest', *Subaltern Studies IV* (Delhi, 1985); Dipesh Chakrabarty, 'Conditions for Knowledge of Working-Class Conditions: Employers, Government and the Jute-Workers of Calcutta, 1890–1940', *Subaltern Studies II* (Delhi, 1983) and 'Trade Unions in a Hierarchical Culture: The Jute Workers of Calcutta, 1920–50', *Subaltern Studies III*; Gyanendra Pandey, 'Rallying Round the Cow: Sectarian Strife in the Bhojpur Region *c* 1888–1917', *Subaltern Studies II*; Gautam Bhadra, 'The Mentality of Subalternity: Kantanama or Rajdharma', *Subaltern Studies VI* (Delhi, 1989).

11. Partha Chatterjee, 'Agrarian Relations and Communalism in Bengal, 1926–35' and 'More on Modes of Power and the Peasantry', *Subaltern Studies I, II.* My quotation is from the first essay, p. 35.

12. See, particularly, Gyan Prakash, as well as a more nuanced and less dogmatically certain review article by Rosalind O'Hanlon, 'Recovering the Subject: Subaltern Studies and Histories of Resistance in Colonial South Asia', *Modern Asian Studies*, 22, i, 1988.

13. 'Subaltern Studies: Deconstructing Historiography', *Subaltern Studies IV* (Delhi, 1985).

14. See, for instance, Suzanne Desan, 'Crowds, Community and Ritual in the Work of E. P. Thompson and Natalie Davis', in Lynn Hunt (ed.), *The New Cultural History* (California, 1989). I owe this reference to Dr Hans Medick.

15. E. P. Thompson, 'Eighteenth-Century English Society: Class-Struggle without Class?', *Social History*, III, 2, May 1978.

16. E. P. Thompson, *Customs in Common* (London, 1993), p. 7. It is this methodological imperative to contextualize within specific social relations and material modes that has been progressively eliminated, we shall see, from the dominant strand within late *Subaltern Studies.*

17. Antonio Gramsci, 'Notes on Italian History', in Hoare and Smith (eds), *Selections from Prison Notebooks* (New York, 1971), p. 52.

18. 'The Conditions and Nature of Subaltern Militancy: Bengal from Swadeshi to Non-Cooperation, *c.* 1905–22', in Guha (ed.), *Subaltern Studies III* (Delhi, 1984), pp. 273–6.

19. For a powerful, if also highly 'revisionistic', exposition of the strength of Marxism as immanent critique, see Moishe Postone, *Time, Labor, and Social Domination: A Reinterpretation of Marx's Critical Theory* (Cambridge, 1993, 1995). The effort, on the other hand, to make resistance totally external to power can attain really curious levels, at times. See, for instance, Gyan Prakash's assertion that 'we cannot thematise Indian history in terms of the development of capitalism and simultaneously contest capitalism's homogenization of the contemporary world' ('Postcolonial Criticism and Indian Historiography', *Social Text* 31/32, 1992). How does one contest something, I wonder, without talking about it? The best critique of such positions that I have seen is Arif Dirlik, 'The Postcolonial Aura', *Critical Inquiry*, 20, ii, Winter 1994.

20. In studies of early modern French popular culture, notably, much early-1970s *Annales* scholarship assumed an autonomous popular level manifested in distinct texts, forms and practices. With the growing influence of Foucault, and Robert Muchembled's *Culture populaire et culture des elites dans la France moderne* (Paris, 1978), published, significantly perhaps, in the same year as Said, *Orientalism*, there was a shift towards frameworks of successful conquest of once-uncontaminated popular culture through the cumulative impact of Counter-Reformation Church, absolute monarchy and

Enlightenment rationalism. The more fruitful historical works, however, have on the whole operated with a model of multiple appropriations rather than distinct levels: see particularly Roger Chartier's critique of Muchembled's acculturation thesis in his *Cultural Uses of Print in Early Modern France* (Princeton, 1987), Introduction. I have elaborated these points in my 'Popular Culture, Community, Power: Three Studies of Modern Indian Social History', *Studies in History*, 8, ii, n.s., 1992, pp. 311–13, and 'Orientalism Revisited: Saidian Frameworks in the Writing of Modern Indian History', *Oxford Literary Review*, XVI, 1–2, 1994; reprinted in this volume.

21. Ranajit Guha's programmatic essay in *Subaltern Studies I* had also described '*the politics of the people*' as 'parallel to the domain of elite politics – an *autonomous* domain, for it neither originated from elite politics nor did its existence depend on the latter' (p. 4).

22. 'Gandhi and the Critique of Civil Society', *Subaltern Studies III* (Delhi, 1984), followed by *Nationalist Thought in the Colonial World: A Derivative Discourse?* (Delhi, 1986).

23. For a more detailed critique of Chatterjee's *Nationalist Thought*, see my 'Orientalism Revisited'.

24. For a more extensive discussion, see chapter 1 of Sumit Sarkar, *Writing Social History* (Delhi, 1996).

25. For an effective critique of this *tabula rasa* approach, see Aijaz Ahmad, *In Theory: Classes, Nations, Literatures* (London, 1992; Delhi, 1993), chapters III, V.

26. *Nationalist Thought*, p. 100; see also *Subaltern Studies III*, p. 176.

27. Ranajit Guha, 'On Some Aspects of the Historiography of Colonial India', *Subaltern Studies I*, pp. 2–3, 7.

28. Aijaz Ahmad, chapter V, and *passim*.

29. Perry Anderson, *In the Tracks of Historical Materialism* (London, 1983), p. 55. Very relevant also are his comments about the general trajectory from structuralism to post-structuralism: 'a total initial determinism ends in the reinstatement of absolute final contingency, in mimicry of the duality of *langue* and *parole*'.

30. Ranajit Guha, 'Chandra's Death', *Subaltern Studies V* (Delhi, 1987); Sumit Sarkar, 'The Kalki-Avatar of Bikrampur: A Village Scandal in Early Twentieth Century Bengal', *Subaltern Studies VI* (Delhi, 1989); Gyanendra Pandey, '"Encounters and Calamities": The History of a North Indian Qasba in the Nineteenth Century', *Subaltern Studies III* (Delhi, 1984). 'Chandra's Death' has been warmly praised by Aijaz Ahmad in *In Theory*, but this is unlikely to enhance its reputation with the bulk of present-day admirers of *Subaltern Studies*.

31. Carlo Ginzburg, 'Microhistory: Two or Three Things That I Know about It', *Critical Inquiry*, 29, August 1993. I have benefited also from Hans Medick's unpublished paper on a similar theme: 'Weaving and Surviving at Laichingen 1650–1900: Micro-History as History and as Research Experience'. I am grateful to Professor Ginzburg and Professor Medick for sending me copies of their papers.

32. The quotations from 'Chandra's Death' are from *Subaltern Studies V*, pp. 138, 144, 155.

33. I am thinking particularly about the very substantial and impressive ongoing work of David Hardiman, of which the latest example is *Feeding the Baniya: Peasants and Usurers in Western India* (Delhi, 1996), which seldom gets due recognition. But even Ranajit Guha's 'Discipline and Mobilize', in Chatterjee and Pandey (eds), *Subaltern Studies VII* (Delhi, 1992), far more critical of Gandhian nationalism than usual nowadays, based on a premise of 'indigenous' as well as 'alien' moments of dominance in colonial India, and emphasizing 'the power exercised by the indigenous elite over the subaltern amongst the subject population itself' – seems to have attracted little attention.

34. Fredric Jameson, 'Third World Literature in the Era of Multi-national Capital', *Social Text*, Fall 1986. For a powerful critique, see Aijaz Ahmad, *In Theory*, chapter III.

35. Partha Chatterjee, *The Nation and Its Fragments: Colonial and Postcolonial Histories* (Princeton, 1993; Delhi, 1994).

36. I have no space here to comment on this curious equation of the 'spiritual' with

home, domesticity and femininity. How, one wonders, did highly patriarchal religious traditions like Hinduism and Islam manage such an identification?

37. For some data about a near-perfect fit between early-twentieth-century cultural nationalism in Bengal and the current argument, see chapter 1 of Sarkar, *Writing Social History*.

38. Chatterjee, *The Nation*, p. 133.

39. Dipesh Chakrabarty, 'The Difference-Deferral of a Colonial Modernity: Public Debates on Domesticity in British Bengal', in *Subaltern Studies VIII* (Delhi, 1994), pp. 83–5.

40. Ibid., pp. 166–7, 238.

41. See, for instance, the declaration of intent at the beginning of Nandy's *The Intimate Enemy* (Delhi, 1983) 'to justify and defend the *innocence* [my italics] which confronted Western colonialism' (p. ix).

42. Gyanendra Pandey attempted to apply this Saidian framework to the study of early-twentieth-century communalism in his *The Construction of Communalism in Colonial North India* (Delhi, 1990).

43. Ashis Nandy, 'The Politics of Secularism and the Recovery of Religious Tolerance', in Veena Das (ed.), *Mirrors of Violence: Communities, Riots and Survivors in South Asia* (Delhi, 1990).

44. Rajeev Bhargava, 'Giving Secularism Its Due', *Economic and Political Weekly*, 9 July 1994.

45. Nandy, 'The Politics of Secularism', in Das, p. 90.

46. Partha Chatterjee, 'Secularism and Toleration', *Economic and Political Weekly*, 9 July 1994. For a more detailed discussion of both Nandy (1990) and Chatterjee (1994), see my 'The Anti-Secularist Critique of Hindutva: Problem of a Shared Discursive Space', *Germinal*/Journal of Department of Germanic and Romance Studies (Delhi University, 1994), vol. I.

47. Chatterjee takes over Nandy's secularism/toleration disjunction, but gives it a very 'presentist' twist, explicitly stating in a footnote that he is drawing out the implications of this position in terms of 'political possibilities within the domain of the modern state institutions as they now exist in India'. Ibid., fn. 2, pp. 1776–7.

48. Ibid., p. 1775.

49. Resolution entitled 'Equal Rights, Equal Laws', adopted by a national convention organized by the All India Democratic Women's Association (New Delhi, 9–10 December 1995).

50. In May 1994, for instance, the RSS ideologue S. Gurumurti described the Ayodhya movement as 'perhaps the first major sympton of social assertion over a Westernized and alienated state apparatus' that has imposed secularism and other 'foreign ideologies on the country, provoking a growing feeling of nativeness'. 'State and Society', in *Seminar 417* (May 1994). An article by Uma Bharati in the same issue entitled 'Social Justice' condemned any labelling of 'Hindutva [as] a Brahmanical and exploitative order' as 'the distorted view that followers of Macaulay hold'.

51. Gyanendra Pandey, 'In Defence of the Fragment: Writing about Hindu–Muslim Riots in India Today', *Economic and Political Weekly*, Annual Number, 1991, and 'The Prose of Otherness', *Subaltern Studies VIII*.

52. 'In Defence of the Fragment', p. 566.

53. 'The Prose of Otherness', *Subaltern Studies VIII*, referring to an old article of mine entitled 'Popular Movements, National Leadership, and the Coming of Freedom with Partition', in D. N. Panigrahi (ed.), *Economy, Society and Politics in Modern India* (New Delhi, 1985).

54. Relevant here would be Fredric Jameson's recent caustic comments about 'the latter-day transmogrification of these – quite unphilosophical empirical and anti-systemic positivist attitudes and opinions into heroic forms of resistance to metaphysics and Utopian tyrrany'. 'Actually Existing Marxism', *Polygraph 6/7*, p. 184.

55. E. P. Thompson, *Witness Against the Beast: William Blake and the Moral Law* (Cambridge, 1993), p. 188.

56. Partha Chatterjee, 'A Religion of Urban Domesticity: Sri Ramakrishna and the

Calcutta Middle Class', in Chatterjee and Pandey (eds), *Subaltern Studies VII* (Delhi, 1992), and Chatterjee, *The Nation*, Chapter III. The clerical ambience of Ramakrishna's early audience and often of his conversations with them, for instance, has been totally missed. For another kind of effort to explore the *Kathamrita* – one which in its author's opinion tries to go much beyond the mere 'biographical question of Ramakrishna in relation to the middle class of Bengal' (*The Nation*, p. 36), see my 'Kaliyuga, Chakri, and Bhakti: Ramakrishna and His Times', *Economic and Political Weekly*, 18 July 1992.

57. Shahid Amin's finely crafted *Event, Metaphor, Memory: Chauri Chaura 1922–92* (Delhi, 1995) might be taken to constitute a partial exception, within a basically early-*Subaltern* framework. But the latter often seems too narrow adequately to comprehend the richness of material, while far more has been achieved elsewhere in the innovative handling of representations: as stray examples, one could mention Stephen Greenblatt, *Renaissance Self-Fashioning: From More to Shakespeare* (Chicago, 1980); Marina Warner, *Joan of Arc* (London, 1981); and Sarah Maza, *Private Lives and Public Affairs: The Causes Célèbres of Pre-Revolutionary France* (Calcutta, 1993).

58. Partha Chatterjee fully acknowledged this debt in his 'The Fruits of Macaulay's Poison-Tree', in Ashok Mitra (ed.), *The Truth Unites* (Calcutta, 1985). For a sampling of the early-1970s critique of the Bengal Renaissance, see the essays of Asok Sen, Barun De and Sumit Sarkar in V. C. Joshi (ed.), *Rammohan Roy and the Process of Modernization in India* (Delhi, 1975); Asok Sen, *Iswarchandra Vidyasagar and His Elusive Milestones* (Calcutta, 1977); and Sumit Sarkar, 'The Complexities of Young Bengal', a 1973 essay, reprinted in my *Critique of Colonial India* (Calcutta, 1985).

59. Commenting on William Radice's statement that the elder Thompson had been 'limited by his missionary and British imperial background', E. P. Thompson comments: 'These stereotypes are limiting also, and are calculated to elicit predictable responses from a public as confined within the preconceptions of the "contemporary" as that of the 1920s . . . The limits must be noted . . . but what may merit our attention more may be what lies outside those limits or confounds those expectations.' *Alien Homage: Edward Thompson and Rabindranath Tagore* (Delhi, 1993), pp. 2–3.

60. Peter Linebaugh, *The London Hanged: Crime and Civil Society in the Eighteenth Century* (Harmondsworth: Penguin, 1991, 1993). For an elaboration of my argument with respect to such possibilities, see my 'A Marxian Social History Beyond the Foucaultian Turn: Peter Linebaugh's "The London Hanged"', *Economic and Political Weekly*, XXX, 30, 29 July 1995.

61. I am thinking particularly of the ongoing work of Sumit Guha on the Maharashtrian *longue durée*, and of Radhika Singha's *Despotism of Law* (Delhi, 1998), on legal practices in early-colonial India.

62. I am indebted for this resistance/transformation contrast to an illuminating oral presentation in Delhi recently by Madhavan Palat on the relevance of Marxist historiography today. He used these terms to indicate a vital contrast between Marxian and other strands of social history.

63. I owe this phrase to Pradip Kumar Datta. Such a shift in registers, it needs to be added, has become a cardinal feature of much postcolonial theory. See Arif Dirlik's pertinent comments on the dangers of reducing anti-colonial criticism to the elimination of its 'ideological and cultural legacy' alone; 'by fixing its gaze on the past it in fact avoids confronting the present'. Dirlik, p. 343.

64. *The Nation and Its Fragments*, chapter 10 and p. 156.

15

The New Subaltern: A Silent Interview

Gayatri Chakravorty Spivak

How do you define contemporary Subaltern Studies in relationship to Marxism and feminism, speaking theoretically and politically, even when considering the enormous diversity concealed by these general labels?

Subaltern Studies considers the bottom layer of society, not necessarily put together by capital logic alone. This is its theoretical difference from Marxism. Its theoretical relationship to feminism is that the subaltern is gendered, and hence needs to be studied with the help of feminist theory.

The imprisoned Antonio Gramsci used the word to stand in for 'proletarian', to escape the prison censors. But the word soon cleared a space, as words will, and took on the task of analysing what 'proletarian', produced by capital logic, could not cover. Gramsci's politics were to situate Marxism upon his contemporary Italian scene, divided by what would come to be called 'internal colonization'. Marx's comments about Germany and Britain in the Postface to the second edition of *Capital* I make this consonant with the politics of Marxian theory. Gramsci was not attempting to define 'subaltern'. Although he insisted on the fragmentary nature of subaltern history in a well-known passage, in his own writings, based on fascist Italy, the line between subaltern and dominant is more retrievable than in the work of subcontinental Subaltern Studies. Gramsci's project is not specifically gender-sensitive in its detail but can be made so. In his *Prison Notebooks* he lays out that future programme in a passage, quaintly but conscientiously phrased in a 'male'-marked idiom, fully visible under his neat erasure: 'until woman has truly attained independence in relation to man, the sexual question will be full of morbid characteristics and one must exercise caution in dealing with it and in drawing legislative conclusions'.[1]

Partha Chatterjee shows that Gramsci understood his own project as flexible when it came to the Indian colonial context.[2] For the historians of South Asia who took the word from Gramsci, 'subaltern' came to mean persons and groups cut off from upward – and, in a sense, 'outward' – social mobility. This also meant that these persons and groups were cut off from the cultural lines that produced the colonial subject.[3] If one follows the Gramscian line, this makes Subaltern Studies a more dynamic use of Marxian theory than the forced application of Marxian terminology upon the colonial scene. Marx's own remarks, not so much in the famously Eurocentric journalism, but in the few comments on 'foreign trade' in *Capital* III also imply that Marxist theory should be accommodated to the analysis of colonial history.[4]

The value-form makes things commensurable. A mode of production is, strictly speaking, a mode of production of value. The colonial subject could be measured by colonial standards in his very subjectivity. To change Marx slightly, 'he carried the subject of colonialism'. Since 'subaltern' in the subcontinental use defines those who were cut off from the lines that produced the colonial mindset, s/he did not emerge in the colonial cultural value-form. Thus, considerations of cultural problematics in Subaltern Studies are not a substitute for, but a supplement to, Marxist theory.

Except in the work of Susie Tharu, a relatively new member of the collective, Subaltern Studies is not informed by feminist theory as such. 'Chandra's Death', an exquisite piece by Ranajit Guha, still resonates with patriarchal benevolence and critique.[5] Chatterjee's scrupulous consideration of gender as one of the nation's fragments reads women's testimony as evidence at face value.[6] Thus Subaltern Studies, though not inimical to a feminist politics, is not immediately useful for it.

The general political importance of Subaltern Studies is in the production of knowledge, to quote a Marxian phrase, in 'educating the educators' (Third Thesis on Feuerbach). Disciplinary inclusion – it is now a paper for the Master's degree in history at Delhi University, and perhaps at other Indian institutions – is a pyrrhic victory, of course. The subalternist politics of the production of knowledge was to undermine the monopoly credit rating of the progressive bourgeoisie and rethink the 'political' so that subaltern insurgency is not seen as invariably 'pre-political'. Further, the cultural space of subalternity, although cut off from the lines of mobility producing the class- and gender-differentiated colonial subject, was not seen as stagnant by the subcontinental subalternists. How religion (culture) is transformed into militancy, and thus produces tangents for the subaltern sphere, is one of the most interesting aspects of subalternist analysis in its subcontinental phase.

With the rise of Hindu-dominant nationalism in the Indian polity, however, Marxist secularists have suspected a sympathy for the religious in Subaltern Studies that may be counter-productive in the context of today's India. On the other hand, education in postcolonial India has not become more democratic. Hence, to ignore the increasing class difference between the urban and rural poor – the word 'subaltern' loses theoretical force here – and further, to ignore the potential of the history of, first, conflictual coexistence among subordinate groups and, second, of alternative movements of subaltern theology, is to make subaltern participation in secularism a matter of law enforcement rather than agency, in the active voice. The work of Shail Mayaram and Shahid Amin is particularly noteworthy here although, as is usual with most work involving the production of knowledge anywhere, the line that goes from case study to public policy is not, perhaps cannot be, drawn by the scholar as scholar.

Today the 'subaltern' must be rethought. S/he is no longer cut off from lines of access to the centre. The centre, as represented by the Bretton Woods agencies and the World Trade Organization, is altogether interested in the rural and indigenous subaltern as source of trade-related intellectual property or TRIPs. Many ways are being found to generate a subaltern subject asking to be used thus.[7] Marxist theory best describes the manner in which such 'intellectual property' is made the basis of exploitation in the arenas of biopiracy and human genome engineering. (In so far as the remote origin of subalternist theory was Ranajit Guha's *A Rule of Property for Bengal*, the wheel may be said to have come full circle.) But 'the agent of production' here is no longer the working class as produced by industrial or post-industrial capitalism.

This new location of subalternity is being covered over by the sanctioned ignorance of elite theory. Recently, Foucault's 'bio-power' has been brought up for revision. Paul Rabinow, the eminent Foucauldian, comments on genome engineering as a move from *zoë* to *bios* and commends Iceland – 'the oldest democracy in Europe' – for having a citizenry that voluntarily allows its DNA to be mapped.[8] Giorgio Agamben, referring to bio-power, uses the *zoë–bios* argument and cites Rabinow, although in the last sentence of his *Homo Sacer* he does announce a disciplinary catastrophe as a result of 'a being that is only its own bare existence ... seiz[ing] hold of the very *haplos* [bottom line] that constitutes both the task and the enigma of Western metaphysics'.[9] One cannot quarrel with this general pronouncement. But in a more particular sphere, voluntary acceptance of the transformation of *zoë* to *bios* does not seem to us to be the last instance. The issue is the difference between dieting and starving, when the dieters' episteme is produced by a system that produces the starvers' starvation. In other words, although the 'agent of production' is not the working class, we must still heed the social relations of production of value. The issue is that some own others' *bios*-beings – human, animal or natural (the impossibility of listing them together must be postponed for the moment, since they can be owned in their data-being by similar patents) – and secure ownership by patenting, often fining and punishing those others for not having followed patenting laws in their subaltern past and thus having put up 'illegal trade barriers'. The issue, in other words, is one of property – and the subaltern body as *bios* or subaltern knowledge as (agri-) or (herbi-) culture is its appropriative object. Not only property, but Trade Related Intellectual Property.[10]

This new location of subalternity also requires a revision of feminist theory. The *genetically* reproductive body as the site of production questions feminist theories based only on the ownership of the phenomenal body as means of reproduction, and feminist psychological theories reactive to reproductive genital penetration as normality.[11]

Politically, this new understanding of subalternity leads to global social movements supported by a Marxist analysis of exploitation, calling for an undoing of the systemic–antisystemic binary opposition. In the domain of a specifically feminist politics, such Subaltern Studies would require an engagement with global feminism. The subcontinental Subaltern Studies collective, of which I am a sometime member, does not necessarily endorse this understanding of the new subalternity. I am therefore taking the liberty of writing according to my own stereotype of 'myself' here, rather than describing Subaltern Studies as it is commonly understood.

The word 'woman' has been taken for granted by the United Nations ever since the beginning of the large-scale women's conferences. In the domain of gendered intervention, today's United Nations is indeed international. Within a certain broadly defined group of the world's women, with a certain degree of flexibility in class and politics, the assumptions of a sex-gender system, an unacknowledged biological determination of behaviour, and an object-choice scenario defining female life (children or public life?; population control or 'development'?), are shared at least as common currency. I begin to think it is a discursive formation, and oppositions can be generated within it.

Although the subaltern is outside of this commonality there has been an attempt to access her within it by defining, not her way of acting, but her ways of suffering others' action. Its most overt tabulation was the six-point Platform of Action of the Fourth World Women's Conference in Beijing. There was something grand in the effort to bring the world's women under one rule of law, one civil society, administered by the women of the internationally divided dominant.

Even as we understand the Encyclopedist grandeur of this design, we must also see that it is the exact impersonal structural replica of the grand design to bring the world's rural poor under one rule of finance, one global capital, again run by the internationally divided dominant. To use a technique from Michel Foucault, let us say this is the most 'rarefied' definition of globalization that we can grasp.

If the dominant is represented by the centreless centre of electronic finance capital, the subaltern woman is the target of credit-baiting without infrastructural involvement, thus opening a huge untapped market to the international commercial sector. Here a genuinely feminist politics would be a monitoring one, that forbids the ideological appropriation of much older self-employed women's undertakings and, further, requires and implements infrastructural change rather than practise cultural coercion in the name of feminism. Farida Akhter's intercession with Grameen Bank to cancel its agreement with Monsanto is a case in point.[12] This is not the place to go into the connection between rural women as growers and managers of diversified seed and as chosen recipients of rural credit. I will expand upon the latter in my conclusion. This all too schematic answer is, I hope, flexible enough to suit the diversity of Marxisms and feminisms.

(One rider: With the break-up of the welfare state, the earlier definition of the subaltern as one cut off from lines of social mobility increasingly applies to the metropolitan homeless, although the cultural argument is subsumed under a class argument there.)

If Subaltern Studies can be identified with what Derrida calls 'a certain spirit of Marx', are there plausible Marxist and feminist rejoinders to the concepts of nation, class, caste, that is, political community, emerging within the work of those identified with Subaltern Studies?

Subaltern Studies has been more dynamically Marxist in its detail and in its presuppositions from its inception, than an 'identification with a certain spirit of Marx' would suggest, although, as I have suggested above, it has its differences from a more orthodox Marxist historiography. Derrida's *Specters of Marx*, from which your passage is taken, was originally published in 1993, after world-historical circumstances – not Derrida's words – obliged him to 're-read' Marx. When in the early 1980s, I connected the method of Subaltern Studies to 'deconstructing historiography', I was not engaging with the group's relationship to Marxism, but rather to the question of subalternity and subaltern consciousness. Thus I cannot grant the condition governing the question. I am hampered also by not being a scholar of subalternist work, but rather a sort of subalternist on the fringe of the main movement.

That said, here is an account of the possible implications of subalternist work for the concepts listed.

The notion of 'nation', as back-formation from the western European nationalisms that were at the helm of capitalist imperialism, informed and displaced the prevailing discourses of dominant protogovernmentalities – the Mughals, the Marathas – already in existence in 'India', as well as the emergent ground of colonial subject-formation – most especially the *bhadralok* society of Bengal. Chatterjee has prospectively narrativized the latter as departure-manoeuvre-arrival, giving it an exceptionalist Indian scope, locating each stage by one prominent individual – only the first of *bhadralok* origin. He has further suggested that the exceptionalist narrative is an uneasy collection of fragments in its Bengali context.[13] It can certainly be concluded from his work that the notion of an Indian nation as a miraculating ground of identity, thought and action, leading to a political community, was not discursively available to the larger proportion of the immensely diverse inhabitants of the subcontinent. To consider this in an evolutionist way is to consider European enrichment as nothing but a result of the survival of the fittest. K. N. Chaudhuri is not an avowed subalternist, but his *Asia Before Europe* is a good corrective for methods of analysis based on such a view.[14]

The concept of nation is the fuzzy partner to the more abstract 'state'. (I am borrowing the word 'fuzzy' from the 'fuzzy set' theory of Lotfi Zadeh, 'sets that', in the words of Daniel McNeill and Paul Freiberger, 'calibrate vagueness'.)[15]

Since 1989, the state has withered away some, since barriers removed between national economies and the functioning of global capital curtail redistribution and constitutional redress. (Marx had quietly moved from 'national economy' – *Economic and Philosophical*

Manuscripts – to 'political economy' – *Capital* I – a fact obliterated by English translations.) And the globalizing agencies directly confront those to whom nation-think was not accessible – thus the subaltern – during the colonial era. The work of the non-Eurocentric 'social movements', seeking to turn globalization persistently towards that subaltern front (no longer merely an arithmetical sum of 'local' movements), away from capital-ist ends, provides, however haphazardly, the goal of a loosely based 'regional' political agenda that must remain, as I have already suggested, Marxist in its analysis of exploitation. The Gramscian 'war of manoeuvre' – non-teleological and innovative – was unaware of broader consequences in the Italy of the beginning of the century. With full-scale globalized capitalism, this by-now subalternist alternative describes the most viable way of constructive resistance. (Paul Virilio's binarization of 'the cut [*coupure*] between developed and underdeveloped countries [as] . . . *absolute* [and] *relative*' is therefore not sufficiently nuanced.)[16] The 'regional' focus is perhaps less strong in the feminist aspects of these movements – reactive as they are to population control by pharmaceutical dumping, to the undermining of women's relationship to seed development and storage through biopiracy and monoculture, and to credit-baiting. The 'rejoinder' to the state offered by 'the international civil society' of powerful non-governmental organizations studies the subaltern in the interest of global capital, and cannot be called subalternist, although it is, to a very large extent, feminist in its professed interest in gender.[17]

Although the terrain of the colonial subaltern cannot be explained by capital logic alone, this cannot mean jettisoning the concept of class formation as a descriptive and analytical category. The new subaltern is produced by the logic of a global capital that forms classes only instrumentally, in a separate urban sphere, because commercial and finance capital cannot function without an industrial component. Post-Fordism had taken away the organizational stability of the factory floor and thus taken away the possibility of class consciousness, however imperfect. International labour is racist and thus has no class solidarity as such. The union movement in the United States is severely restricted and politically effective only in so far as it serves managerial interests. This is not the moment to find a 'rejoinder' to class – even as it must be recognized that not much can be done in its name, that it cannot produce an account of subalternity. I have written elsewhere about the 'exceptionalist' class mobility among aboriginal subalterns.

Is caste a 'political community' today? The transmogrification of caste outlines in Hindu-majority nationalism is a subject beyond my scope, and perhaps beyond the scope of this discussion.

How do you define Subaltern Studies in the wider field of postcolonial studies? Is it simply an Indian-national sector in this wider field or is it a cluster of distinct theoretical positions in this wider field?

Subaltern Studies did not relate to identity politics at its inception. In the introduction to the first edition of *A Rule of Property*, Guha makes some allusion to his origins. But that was twenty years before the collective came into being. Their goal was to set the record straight, to revise historiography, and thus discover the nineteenth-century subaltern, largely from the text of the elite. Postcolonial criticism, in so far as it takes its inspiration from Fanon and Said, sees itself as *engagé*, on behalf of the colonized. Even in its metropolitan hybridist form, its challenge to the purity of origins relates, however implicitly, to its own diasporic location. The Subaltern Studies collective is certainly related to South Asian history, as Gramsci was related to Italy. Its theoretical position, of studying how the continuity of supposedly pre-political insurgency brings culture to crisis and confronts power would make postcolonial studies more conventionally political. One major difference is that the disciplinary connection of postcolonial studies is to literary criticism rather than history and the social sciences. Subaltern Studies has not pursued oral history as unmediated narrative, and its investigations of testimony have generally confined themselves to legal utterance. I shall expand upon this in my conclusion.

Is there a political-theoretical horizon beyond the existing discourse of postcoloniality?

The discourse of postcoloniality developed rather haphazardly in response to a felt need among minority groups. Its focus is, in its grounding presuppositions, metropolitan. Its language skills are rudimentary, though full of subcultural affect. (The often excellent language resources within US Area Studies, by contrast, are good towards social-scientific fieldwork whose grounding presuppositions were Title 6 of the National Defense Education Act of 1958.)

Postcolonial discourse should thus be 'situated' as much as any style of analysis. And any situation limits itself in terms, necessarily, of what is beyond itself. It is possible to situate, in turn, the versions of the 'beyond' that are chosen as its negation, its condition, its effect. Otherwise historiography would end. In conclusion, then, I choose my own version of the beyond of postcolonial discourse: the question of subaltern consciousness. But I choose it with the deconstructive caution; it is a step beyond in the French mode: *un pas au-delà*. In French, *pas* is both step and the enclitic adverb that most often completes the negative. Colloquially, it is a negation that can also be a prohibition – the step beyond (can be also) a restriction within. It is one of those happy idiomatic accidents, like *Aufhebung*, which conveniently means both to keep intact and destroy.

Opening the question of subaltern consciousness is my *pas au-delà* of postcolonial discourse.

In 'Deconstructing Historiography' I had suggested that the Subaltern Studies collective assumed a subaltern consciousness, however 'negative', by a 'strategic use of essentialism'. Subaltern Studies had no need of such apologetics. But the theoretically inclined metropolitan identitarians did. In the name of their own groups, they argued identity, claimed strategy, and sometimes gave me credit. No one particularly noticed what I have already mentioned, that Subaltern Studies never presupposed a consciousness for 'their own group', but rather for their object of investigation, and for the sake of the investigation.

In the context of the emergence of the new subaltern, the question of subaltern consciousness has once again become important, now displaced to the global political sphere, so that a) knowledge can be made data, and b) a subaltern will for globalization can be put together as justification for policy. By contrast, the current writings of the collective no longer ponder that challenge.

It is around the issues of democratization and gender-and-development that the question of subaltern consciousness most urgently arises. This is because it is precisely those who were denied access to the lines leading to the European civil society mindset and to bourgeois-model female emancipation who must first be diagnosed today as culturally incapable of democracy and feminism, in the interest of the smooth global functioning of these issues. Thus 'democratization' – code name for the political restructuring entailed by the transformation of (efficient through inefficient to wild) state capitalisms and their colonies to tributary economies of rationalized global financialization – carries with it the aura of the civilizing mission accompanying transformative projects from imperialism to development. This aura carries over to the question of minority rights within developed civil societies, where it engages postcolonial radicalism of a more political sort. 'Consciousness' here does not engage subject-theory, deconstructive, psychoanalytic, or otherwise. We are here on the level of social agency – institutionally validated action. The institutions concerned are democracy and development – politics and economics.

Opposition to parliamentary democracy in the name of cultural origin (as advanced by Lee Kuan Yew, Senior Minister of Singapore, or, at the other end of the spectrum and in speech after speech, by Farid Zakaria, the editor of the influential conservative journal *Foreign Affairs*) is an obviously meretricious position. Opposition to female emancipation in the name of cultural sanctions is as onerous. But to produce a subject for democracy and development, must we then rely on crash courses in 'gender training' and 'election training' offered by the international civil society?[18]

As an alternative I offer that double-edged *pas*. It is a narrative concerning a tiny group of one kind of subaltern. I have got to know them well in the last ten years, after I gave up my apologetic formula for Subaltern Studies (which the collective did not need anyway): strategic use of essentialism. I found instead a different one emerging from my own subaltern study: learning to learn from below. This one will have had few takers.

Let me first present a context that is remote from the new subalternity, for 'reasons' that are too complex for this broad-stroke silent interview. It is the context of the smallest groups among Indian Aboriginals, at last count roughly ninety million as a whole. I use 'Aboriginal' just this once for the general readership. Neither 'Aboriginal' nor 'tribal' fits the Indian case, because historically – and this invocation of history is to beg the question – there is apparently no certainty about the authenticity of the Aryan settler/original inhabitants story.[19] I will therefore use 'ST', short for 'Scheduled Tribe', as laid down in the Indian Constitution, and regularly used by the state and activists alike.

This much is provisionally noticeable in the history of the present. These are people occupying remnants of varieties of oral culture permeated by dominant Sanskritized literate cultures without benefit of literacy. This last not because of widely disseminated anthropological piety, but because these people are among the increasing numbers of the Indian poor. Upward class mobility is harder for these people because of long-standing patterns of prejudice and therefore low-level graft works even better upon this terrain, destroying the possibility or attractiveness of real education for the intelligent child, the prospective leader or, of course, the ordinary child, the backbone of the functioning future electorate. Votes are bought and sold here, *en bloc* and individually. The prevailing system of education is to memorize answers to antiquated questions relating to set books. The occasional human-interest story – of villagers establishing their own schools or NGOs joining a UN drive for schools must, first, be evaluated against this grid – if indeed it penetrates to the bottom layers of the diversified life of the Indian scheduled tribes.

There is something like an opening into 'women's history', even here. The sharp young girls, wading up through the muddy sluggish currents of gendered rural politics, can aim for the reserved seats on the various organs of state government, generally to become pawns in the hands of veteran mainstream players. When they enter UN statistics as 'women entering politics' (see the Declaration of Mexico, 1975), the aporia of exemplarity is rather brutally crossed.[20] The single female out of the Lodha tribe who made it into university – studying, heartbreakingly, anthropology – hanged herself under mysterious circumstances some years ago. Various rumours about illicit love affairs circulate even as self-styled subalterns and oral history investigators assure each other in print that the subaltern can, indeed, speak.

I am not a historian. Here I am moving in an area – the task of writing the history of the Indian STs – which baffles the historian. I move upon this landscape in an attempt to learn to learn from below. I enter into yearly increasing intimacies with female and male children and adults. I bear witness to the storying of the vanishing present, the piecing together of characters (I might as well beg the question and call them 'historical agents') so that a detailed sequence may seem to pre-exist. At the same time, I try to disengage from the children and the teachers some pedagogic principles for teaching democratic habits. An electoral democracy is historical.

Are men and women different here? Only in so far as some indefinite thing called tribal 'culture' has started to resemble the class mobility patterns of the non-tribal poorer classes. The men get a greater opportunity to travel out and up through governmental and non-governmental possibilities, though they too are used. Our usual sex-gender system clichés work fine here.

But what about writing their history in the usual way? I see no difference between men and women for that project. Anti-colonial tribal insurgencies have occasionally been recorded. A handful of tribals get pensions as fighters for independence. Tribals emerge into history in the perspective of the drama of colonialism.

I should at once say that the ST communities in India are not everywhere equally deprived. Making allowances for very much larger numbers, a different position upon the grid of the global economic system, the relatively autonomous difference in its geopolitical standing, and its different place in the cultural politics of the dominant historical mythology of the so-called civilized world, the story of the *exceptional* ST has broad-stroke similarities to, say, the Aboriginal story in Japan – another non-European pre-colonial settler colony – the distance marked, let us say, between the stories recounted in Kayano Shigeru, *Our Land Was a Forest: An Ainu Memoir* at one end, and Richard Siddle's *Race, Resistance and the Ainu of Japan,* at the other – often a way for the exceptional Aboriginal(s) to reach the United Nations.[21] The altogether exceptional Rigoberta Menchù, the Nobel Prize-winning Aboriginal woman from Guatemala, distances herself from the common woman in her testimony. My point is that we are not yet ready to grasp the challenge of gender upon this terrain. Gender consciousness here is in the detail of unglamorous teaching, by patiently learning *from* below, not in directly confronting the challenge of history by impatient 'gender training' from above. It remains to me interesting that the vanguard of the Japanese Ainu have looked to European settler colonies – Native American and Australian – for forming a collectivity. In this they may have duplicated the continental isolationism of their dominant culture.

I will now give the bare bones of a narrative.[22] Activists from the institutionally educated classes of the general national culture have recently won a state-level legal victory against police brutality over the most deprived ST groups. They are trying to transform this into a national-level legal awareness campaign. (Like the United States, India has to be thought of, of course, in terms of national, state-level and local *politics.* On the other hand, like Japan, India represents itself as culturally homogeneous.)

In spite of the group's legal victory against the state, the ruling party, which notionally does not approve of police brutality, supports them on the state level. Nationally, since a different party is in power, the question is too complex to be discussed here. The ruling party on the local level, on the other hand, is trying to take its revenge against the group's victory over the police by taking advantage of three factors, one positive, two negative.

First, the relatively homogeneous dominant Hindu culture at the village level keeps the ST materially isolated through prejudice. Second, as a result of this material isolation, women's independence among the STs, in their daily in-house behaviour ('ontic idom') has remained intact. It has not been infected by the tradition of women's oppression within the general culture. Third, politically ('pre-politically?'), the general, supposedly homogeneous rural culture and the

ST culture are united in their lack of democratic training. This is a result of poverty and class prejudice existing nationally. Therefore, as I have said above, votes can be bought and sold here as normal practice; and electoral conflict is treated by rural society in general like a competitive sport where violence is legitimate.

Locally, since the legal victory of the metropolitan activists against the police, the ruling party has taken advantage of these three things by rewriting women's conflict as party politics. An incidental quarrel among ST women has been used by the police to divide the ST community against itself. One side has been encouraged to press charges against the other. The defending faction has been wooed and won by the opposition party. In the absence of education in the principles of democracy (not merely training in election control, which is also lacking) and *in the presence of women's power, however circumscribed*, police terror has been accepted as part of the party spirit by the ST community. This is a direct consequence of the educated activists' 'from above' effort at constitutional redress. If there should be a person holding the views that I am describing in this essay within this activist group – organized now as a tax-sheltered non-profit organization – who thinks, in other words, that the real effort should be to connect and activate the tribals' indigenous 'democratic' structures to *parliamentary* democracy by patient and sustained efforts to learn to learn from below, s/he would thus be both impractical and a consensus breaker. The consensually united vanguard is never patient. In my view, agency within rule-governed behaviour, a definition even more 'upstream' than Ronald Dworkin's 'democracy for hedgehogs', must be persistently reined in by engaging with the subject.[23]

Given that it is woman power separated from the dominant culture that is being used here, and given that the ST community is *generally* separated from access to disciplinary history, to focus on gendered history as a less class-conscious feminist theory is liable to do, is irrelevant and counter-productive here.[24]

The earliest work of the Subaltern Studies collective had met the general challenge of nationalist history by trying to deduce subaltern consciousness from the texts of the elite. Legal proceedings, where the subaltern gives witness or testimony, had been particularly productive for them. Are my interventions in subaltern education part of the documentation of Subaltern Studies? As resident teacher-trainer, I get into the grain of their lives. Yet is that a requirement for good history writing, after all? Could it not stand in the way?

Julia Kristeva quotes the eighteenth-century French thinker Montesquieu to steer a clear evolutionary path from family consciousness to state consciousness. In her forthcoming book *Speaking through the*

Mask, Norma Claire Moruzzi shows that such a story leaves out the postcolonial migrant, whose historical sequence and scenario are rather different. When we come to subaltern groups such as ST minorities within the postcolonial state, however, the lines become impossibly confused.

So far we have spoken only of society, of the outside world. If we come to the subaltern ST women's inner world – given our class, cultural and, yes, 'historical' difference – although I am so close to them, I can only dimly imagine the enormity of assuming that I could enter a continuity with their specific pattern of working with the mind, body divide, which is my understanding of an inner world. ('Inner' and 'outer' here are shorthand terms appropriate to the readership of this anthology.) A disciplinary anthropologist computes this from the outside, to make it understandable to other anthropologists. And yet I keep hoping that, while I work at my teacher training, understanding will perhaps have come to me in the way of fiction, a compromised way that history cannot challenge. I therefore think it is important that women of the international mainstream, such as we are, define and accept the challenge of women's history, again and again, in order to correct and deflect male domination. But where I am with the subaltern I cannot get a grip on it.

I must rather keep working at training half-educated rural teachers for the remote achievement of a living democratic culture in the classroom of subaltern children, protecting the girls by improvised tactics. This is to break subalternity not into hegemony but into a citizenship *without history*. If someone in my position and with my interests accepts the challenge of women's history as a goal, the specific kind of historylessness of the Aboriginal falls into an evolutionist primitivism that I will not accept.

No, I must keep imagining and presuming a challenge *to* history. Training in disciplinary literary criticism will come to my help. I must, however provisionally, keep the binarity between history and fiction alive. Ever since 'Deconstructing Historiography' I have tried to undo it and historians have advised against it. I now see their point, partly and as follows: mainstream 'Indian' culture is as distant from the Aboriginal subaltern in India as is Aristotle. Echoing Aristotle, then, I must keep telling myself that history tells us what happened and fiction what may have happened and indeed may happen. The uneven entry of my pre-adult students' future children into the historical record will be along paths that I cannot make myself imagine. I have lost track here, in the interest of learning rather than knowing, using rather than remaining within the comfort of describing with coherence for disciplinary access alone. Paradoxically, a classroom where you teach the reading of fiction as such – learning from the singular and the unverifiable – is a training ground for this. Here, too, of course, the scholar cannot draw the direct line to social action as public policy.

Hopeless? Perhaps. But without this nothing can undo the divisions put in place in the colonies by the Enlightenment and still conserve the best legacy of the subaltern. The 'encounter with apartheid' made Mahmood Mamdani ask 'How to transcend the urban–rural divide' – but he wrote a book about it.[25] That divide is the gap we live in, a gap which keeps apart the production of definitive and elite knowledge on the one hand and any hope of educating the subaltern educators on the other. To look into the gap is as hopeful as it is hopeless, at least. *Un pas au-delà.*

Acknowledgements

I thank Partha Chatterjee for a perceptive first reading of the essay. I thank Jamel Brinkley for research assistance.

Notes

1. Antonio Gramsci, *Prison Notebooks*, tr. Joseph A. Buttigieg and Antonio Callari (New York: Columbia University Press, 1975), vol. 1, p. 171.

2. Partha Chatterjee, *Nationalist Thought and the Colonial World: A Derivative Discourse* (Minneapolis: University of Minnesota Press, 1993), pp. 50–51.

3. The pertinent passage is Ranajit Guha, 'On Some Aspects of Historiography of Colonial India', in Ranajit Guha, ed., *Subaltern Studies I: Writings on South Asian History and Society* (Delhi: Oxford University Press, 1982), p. 8. In his most recent publication to date, Guha distinguishes subcontinental subalternist work from Gramsci's by referring to the concept of hegemony: 'As used in this work, *hegemony stands for a condition of Dominance (D), Persuasion (P) outweighs Coercion (C).* Defined in these terms . . . it avoids the Gramscian juxtaposition of domination and hegemony . . . as antinomies. This has, also, provided far too often a theoretical pretext for the fabrication of a liberal absurdity – the absurdity of the idea of an uncoercive state – in spite of the basic drive of Gramsci's own work to the contrary', Guha, *Dominance without Hegemony: History and Power in Colonial India* (Cambridge: Harvard University Press, 1997), p. 23.

4. Karl Marx, *Capital*, tr. David Fernbach (New York: Viking, 1981), vol. III, pp. 344–7.

5. Ranajit Guha, 'Chandra's Death', in Ranajit Guha (ed.), *Subaltern Studies V: Writings on South Asian History and Society* (Delhi: Oxford University Press, 1987), pp. 135–65.

6. Partha Chatterjee, *The Nation and Its Fragments: Colonial and Postcolonial Histories* (Princeton: Princeton University Press, 1993), pp. 135–57.

7. See the difference in tone between the meetings to grab Alaskan Inuit schoolchildren and similar disenfranchised groups on the one hand, and the in-house meetings where agencies and telecommunication giants discuss economic policy on the other, at, for one example among many, the Global Knowledge 1997 conference in

Toronto. In the name of 'Veeramma', a subaltern who 'wants modern science', a young Indian sociologist excoriated an older Indian activist scientist at a New York conference last week. My earlier criticism, in 'Can the Subaltern Speak?' (Lawrence Grossberg and Gary Nelson [eds], *Marxism and the Interpretation of Culture*, Urbana: University of Illinois Press, 1988), pp. 271–313, that while British colonial authorities and benevolent *Bhadraloks* can impose a discursively inaccessible will on the burning widow, when a woman acts without such authority to spell resistance by bodily practice, the women in her own family ignore this in the space of two generations, related to this particular social tendency. I will speak of 'credit baiting' later. This has been theorized as the subaltern being made to unspeak herself in Leerom Medlovoi *et al.*, 'Can the Subaltern Vote?', *Socialist Review* XX.3 (July–September, 1990), pp. 133–49.

8. Professor Rabinow read a chapter from his forthcoming *French DNA* at Columbia University on 28 October 1998. The string of adjectives for Iceland as a representative of the European Enlightenment was rather more fulsome.

9. Giorgio Agamben, *Homo Sacer: Sovereign Power and Bare Life*, tr. Daniel Heller-Roazen (Stanford: Stanford University Press, 1998), p. 188.

10. From the disciplinary perspective, this might perhaps be seen as a displacement from the anthropological 'research object' (Christine Nicholls, *Nicknaming and Graffiti – Writing Practices at Lajmanu, N.T.: A Post-Ethnographic Sociological Fiction*, Sociology dissertation, Macquarrie University, Sydney, 1998, p. 362) to development economics.

11. I have discussed the former in 'Diasporas Old and New: Women in a Transnational World', *Textual Practices* X.ii (1996), pp. 264–6, n. 8. The latter is too pervasive to tabulate.

12. Farida Akhter, 'Monsanto-r Biruddhe Bikkhobh o Protibad: BRAC o CARE-er Biruddhe Hu.ñshiari', *Chinta* VII.13 (15 September, 1998), pp. 36–9. Let me also quote two passages from mainstream US journalism to make the connection with intellectual property. (It is not that these things are unknown. It is just that the connection between Eurocentric discussions of biopower on the one hand and the emergence of the new subaltern as intellectual property on the other remains unmade.)

> I untied the purple mesh bag of seed potatoes that Monsanto had sent and opened up the Grower Guide tied around its neck . . . The guide put me in mind not so much of planting potatoes as booting up a new software release [*bios* into data]. [T]he potatoes I will harvest come August are mine to eat or sell, but their genes remain the intellectual property of Monsanto, protected under numerous United States patents, including Nos. 5,196,525, 5,164,316, 5,322,938 and 5,352,605. Were I to save even one of them to plant next year – something I've routinely done with potatoes in the past – I would be breaking Federal law. The small print in the Grower Guide also brought the news that my potato plants were themselves a pesticide, registered with the Environmental Protection Agency . . . A Monsanto agent can perform a simple test in my garden and prove that my plants are the company's intellectual property. The contract farmers sign with Monsanto allows company representatives to perform such tests in their fields at will. According to *Progressive Farmer*, a trade journal, Monsanto is using informants and hiring Pinkertons to enforce its patent rights; it has already brought legal action against hundreds of farmers for patent infringement. (Michael Pollan, 'Playing God in the Garden', *The New York Times Magazine*, 25 October 1998

Now transfer the scene of ownership and legal action from the USA (or Iceland) to subaltern space. One hopes that a book such as Mae-Wen Ho, *Genetic Engineering – Dream or Nightmare?: The Brave New World of Bad Science and Big Business* (Bath: Gateway, 1998), written by an interventionist scientist, will not be dismissed by the Eurocentric social philosophers for using a pre-critical epistemic vocabulary: 'the genetic determinist mindset that misinforms both practitioners and the public takes hold of people's unconscious, making them act involuntarily, unquestioningly, to shape the world to the detriment of human beings and all other inhabitants' (p. 1).

13. That is the logic of his *Nation and Its Fragments.*

14. K. N. Chaudhuri, *Asia Before Europe: Economy and Civilization of the Indian Ocean from the Rise of Islam to 1750* (Cambridge: Cambridge University Press, 1990).

15. Daniel McNeill, Paul Freiberger, *Fuzzy Logic* (New York: Simon & Schuster, 1993).

16. Paul Virilio, *Open Sky*, tr. Julie Rose (New York: Verso, 1997), p. 71 (translation modified).

17. It is this basically post-state situation, ravaged by the 'passionate intensity' in the underbelly of nation-thinking, that calls up other kinds of 'rejoinders': NATO stepping in to preserve 'Western values', as debated in October 1998, with reference to the situation where the Albanians in Kosovo are being 'ethnically cleansed' by the Serbs. By contrast, Subaltern Studies cautions against vanguardist rationalist solutions imposed from above, right or left.

18. Election training is pretty standard. Gender training by Oxfam is organized at the University of Sussex.

19. I wrote the last sentence in the wake of a conference on tribal culture and history (Bhasha Research Centre, Vadodara, India, 27–30 August 1998), where Professor Romila Thapar made this statement.

20. *The United Nations and the Advancement of Women (1945–1995)* (New York: United Nations, 1995), pp. 177–201.

21. Kayano Shigeru, *Our Land Was a Forest: An Ainu Memoir*, tr. Kyoko and Lili Selden (Boulder, Colorado: Westview Press, 1994); Richard Siddle, *Race, Resistance and the Ainu of Japan* (New York: Routledge, 1996).

22. I suppress names to protect confidentiality. This is an aporetic situation, where state and national-level resistance cannot stop because of the rupture with subalternity.

23. I have written at greater length on the imbrication of subject and agent in Spivak, 'A Dialogue on Democracy', David Trend, ed., *Radical Democracy: Identity, Citizenship, and the State* (New York: Routledge, 1995), p. 209–22.

24. Kamala Visweswaran, *Fictions of Feminist Ethnography* (Delhi: Oxford University Press, 1996) is a thoughtful study of related problems.

25. Mahmood Mamdani, *Citizen and Subject: Contemporary Africa and the Legacy of Late Colonialism* (Princeton: Princeton University Press, 1996), p. ix.

Appendix: Select Bibliography

I

Ranajit Guha, ed., *Subaltern Studies I: Writings on South Asian History and Society* (Delhi: Oxford University Press, 1982).

———, ed., *Subaltern Studies II: Writings on South Asian History and Society* (Delhi: Oxford University Press, 1983).

———*Elementary Aspects of Peasant Insurgency in Colonial India* (Delhi: Oxford University Press, 1983; reprint Durham: Duke University Press, 1999).

———, ed., *Subaltern Studies III: Writings on South Asian History and Society* (Delhi: Oxford University Press, 1984).

———, ed., *Subaltern Studies IV: Writings on South Asian History and Society* (Delhi: Oxford University Press, 1985).

———, ed., *Subaltern Studies V: Writings on South Asian History and Society* (Delhi: Oxford University Press, 1987).

Ranajit Guha and Gayatri Chakravorty Spivak, eds, *Selected Subaltern Studies* (New York: Oxford University Press, 1988).

Ranajit Guha, ed., *Subaltern Studies VI: Writings on South Asian History and Society* (Delhi: Oxford University Press, 1989).

Partha Chatterjee and Gyanendra Pandey, eds, *Subaltern Studies VII: Writings on South Asian History and Society* (Delhi: Oxford University Press, 1992).

David Arnold and David Hardiman, eds, *Subaltern Studies VIII: Essays in Honour of Ranajit Guha* (Delhi: Oxford University Press, 1994).

Shahid Amin and Dipesh Chakrabarty, eds, *Subaltern Studies IX: Writings on South Asian History and Society* (Delhi: Oxford University Press, 1996).

Ranajit Guha, ed., *A Subaltern Studies Reader 1986–1995* (Minneapolis: Minnesota University Press, 1997).

———*Dominance without Hegemony: History and Power in Colonial India* (Cambridge: Harvard University Press, 1997).

Gautam Bhadra, Gyan Prakash and Susie Tharu, eds, *Subaltern Studies*

X: Writings on South Asian History and Society (Delhi: Oxford University Press, 1999).

II

Advani, Rukun, *Indian History from Above and Below: Two Academic Parodies* (Delhi: Don't Press, 1990).

Ahmad, Aijaz, 'Between Orientalism and Historicism: Anthropological Knowledge of India', *Studies in History* 7, 1, n.s. (1991), pp. 135–63.

———'The Politics of Literary Postcoloniality', *Race & Class*, 36, 3 (1995), pp. 1–20.

———'Fascism and National Culture: Reading Gramsci in the Days of Hindutva', in *Lineages of the Present. Political Essays* (New Delhi: Tulika, 1996), pp. 221–66.

Alam, Javeed, 'Peasantry Politics and Historiography: Critique of New Trend in Relation to Marxism', *Social Scientist*, 11, 2 (1983), pp. 43–54.

Alam, S. M. Shamsul, 'When Will the Subaltern Speak?: Central Issues in Historical Sociology of South Asia', *Asian Profile*, 21, 5 (1993), pp. 431–47.

Apffel-Marglin, Frederique and Mishra, Purna Chandra, 'Gender and the Unitary Self: Looking for the Subaltern in Coastal Orissa', *South Asia Research*, 15, 1 (1995), pp. 78–130.

Arnold, J. H., 'The Historian as Inquisitor – The Ethics of Interrogating Subaltern Voices', *Rethinking History*, 2, 3 (1998), pp. 379–86.

Bagchi, Alakananda, 'Conflicting Nationalisms: The Voice of the Subaltern in Mahasweta Devi's Bashai Tudu', *Tulsa Studies in Women's Literature*, 15, 1 (1996), pp. 41–50.

Bahl, Vinay, 'Class Consciousness and Primordial Values in the Shaping of the Indian Working Class', *South Asia Bulletin*, 13, 1–2 (1993), pp. 152–72.

———'Relevance (or Irrelevance) of Subaltern Studies', *Economic and Political Weekly*, 32, 23 (1997), pp. 1333–44.

Banerjee, Prathama, 'The Subaltern-Effect: Negation to Deconstruction Hybridity?', *Biblio* (May–June 1999), pp. 17–18.

Barkan, Elazar, 'Post-anti-colonial Histories: Representing the Other in Imperial Britain', *Journal of British Studies*, 33, 2 (1994), pp. 180–204.

Baxi, Upendra, '"The State's Emmisary": The Place of Law in Subaltern Studies', in Partha Chatterjee and Gyanendra Pandey, eds, *Subaltern Studies VII* (Delhi: Oxford University Press, 1992), pp. 247–64.

Beverley, John, *Subalternity and Representation: Arguments in Cultural Theory* (Durham: Duke University Press, forthcoming).

Bhabha, Homi K., 'The Postcolonial and Postmodern: The Question of Agency', in *The Location of Culture* (London: Routledge, 1994), pp. 171–97.

———'The Voice of the Dom', *The Times Literary Supplement*, No. 4923 (August 8, 1997), pp. 14–15.

Bhattacharya, Nandini, 'Behind the Veil: The Many Masks of Subaltern Sexuality', *Women's Studies International Forum*, 19 (May/June 1996), pp. 277–92.

Bose, Brinda, 'Contemporary Problems Routed through History', *The Book Review*, 21, 6 (1997), pp. 5–7.

———'The Death of History? Historical Consciousness and the Culture of Late Capitalism', *Public Culture*, 4, 2 (1992), pp. 47–66.

Brass, Tom, *Peasants, Populism and Postmodernism: The Return of the Agrarian Myth* (London: Frank Cass, 2000).

Chakrabarty, Dipesh, 'Invitation to a Dialogue', in Ranajit Guha, ed., *Subaltern Studies IV* (Delhi: Oxford University Press, 1985), pp. 364–76.

———'History as Critique and Critique(s) of History', *Economic and Political Weekly*, 26, 37 (1991), pp. 2162–6.

———'Trafficking in History and Theory: Subaltern Studies', in K. K. Ruthven, ed., *Beyond the Disciplines: The New Humanities*, Occasional Paper No. 13, Papers from the Australian Academy of the Humanities Symposium (1991), pp. 101–8.

———'Postcoloniality and the Artifice of History: Who Speaks for "Indian" Pasts?', *Representations*, 37 (1992), pp. 1–26.

———'Marx after Marxism: A Subaltern Historian's Perspective', *Economic and Political Weekly*, 28, 22 (1993), pp. 1094–6. Additional versions published in *Meanjin* 52 (1993), pp. 421–34; *Polygraph* 6/7 (1993), pp. 10–16; *Positions*, 2, 2 (1994), pp. 446–63.

———'Minority Histories, Subaltern Pasts', *Economic and Political Weekly*, 33, 9 (1998), pp. 473–9.

———'Reconstructing Liberalism? Notes toward a Conversation between Area Studies and Diasporic Studies', *Public Culture*, 10, 3 (Spring 1998), pp. 457–81.

Chakravarty, Anita, 'Writing History', *Economic and Political Weekly*, 30, 51 (1995), p. 3320.

Chatterjee, Partha, 'Peasants, Politics and Historiography: A Response', *Social Scientist*, 11, 5 (1983), pp. 58–65.

———'Modes of Power: Some Clarifications', *Social Scientist*, 13, 2 (1985), pp. 53–60.

———'For an Indian History of Peasant Struggle', *Social Scientist*, 16, 11 (1988), pp. 3–17.

———'Secularism and Toleration', *Economic and Political Weekly*, 29, 28 (1994), pp. 1768–77.

———'Was There a Hegemonic Project of the Colonial State?' in Dagmar Engels and Shula Marks, eds, *Contesting Colonial Hegemony: State & Society in Africa and India* (London: British Academic Press, 1994), pp. 79–84.

———'History and the Nationalization of Hinduism', in Vasuda Dalmia and H. von Stietencron, eds, *Representing Hinduism* (New Delhi: Sage Publications, 1995), pp. 103–28.

———'In Conversation with Anuradha Dingwaney Needham', *Interventions*, 1, 3 (1999), pp. 413–25.

Chaudhury, Ajit K., 'In Search of a Subaltern Lenin', in Ranajit Guha, ed., *Subaltern Studies V* (Delhi: Oxford University Press, 1987), pp. 236–51.

Chaudhury, Binay Bhushan, 'Subaltern Autonomy and the National Movement', *Indian Historical Review*, 12, 1–2 (July 1985–January 1986), pp. 391–9.

Cherniavsky, E., 'Subaltern Studies in a United States Frame', *boundary 2*, 23, 2 (1996), pp. 85–110.

Chopra, Suneet, 'Missing Correct Perspective', *Social Scientist*, 10, 8 (1982), pp. 55–63.

Cooper, Frederick, 'Conflict and Connection: Rethinking African History', *American Historical Review*, 99, 5 (1994), pp. 1516–45.

Copland, Ian, 'Subalternative History: Reflections on the Conference on the Subaltern in South Asian History and Society, Canberra, 26–28 November 1982', *ASAA Review* (Canberra), 6, 3 (1983), pp. 10–17.

Coronil, Fernando, 'Listening to the Subaltern. The Poetics of Neocolonial States', *Poetics Today*, 15, 4 (1994), pp. 642–58.

Currie, K., 'The Challenge to Orientalist, Elitist, Western Historiography – Notes on Subaltern Project 1982–1989', *Dialectical Anthropology* (August 1995), 20, 2, pp. 219–46.

Das, Veena, 'Subaltern as Perspective', in Ranajit Guha, ed., *Subaltern Studies VI* (Delhi: Oxford University Press, 1989), pp. 310–24.

Das Gupta, Ranajit, 'Significance of Non-subaltern Mediation', *Indian Historical Review*, 12, 1–2 (July 1985–January 1986), pp. 383–90.

———'Indian Working Classs and Some Recent Historiographical Issues', *Economic and Political Weekly*, 31, 8 (1996), pp. L27–L31.

Dhanagare, D. N., 'Subaltern Consciousness and Populism: Two Approaches in the Study of Social Movements', *Social Scientist*, 16, 11 (1988), pp. 18–35.

Dhar, Hiranmay and Verma, Roop Rekha, 'Fractured Societies, Fractured Histories', *Economic and Political Weekly*, 34, 19 (1999), pp. 1094–7.

Dienst, Richard, 'Imperialism, Subalternity, Autonomy: Modes of Third World Historiography', *Polygraph* 1 (1987), pp. 68–80.

Dirlik, Arif, 'The Postcolonial Aura: Third World Criticism in the Age of Global Capitalism', *Critical Inquiry*, 20 (Winter 1994), pp. 328–56.

Dunne, T., 'Subaltern Voices? Poetry in Irish, Popular Insurgency and the 1798 Rebellion', *Eighteenth Century Life*, 22, 3 (1998), pp. 31–44.

Gavaskar, Mahesh, 'Subaltern Identities and Struggles – Agenda for Transformation', *Economic and Political Weekly*, 30, 7–8 (1995), pp. 363–5.

Guha Ramchandra, 'Subaltern and Bhadralok Studies', *Economic and Political Weekly*, 33, 33 (1995), pp. 2056–8.

———'Beyond Bhadralok and Bankim Studies', *Economic and Political Weekly*, 30, 8 (1996), pp. 495–6.

Gupta, Dipankar, 'On Alter Ego in Peasant History: Paradoxes of the Ethnic Option', *Peasant Studies*, 13, 1 (1985), pp. 5–24.

Gupta, Narayani, 'History for the Subalterns', *Economic and Political Weekly*, 25, 13 (1990), p. 663.

Hardiman, David, 'The Indian "Faction": A Political Theory Examined', in Ranajit Guha, ed., *Subaltern Sudies I: Writings on South Asian History and Society* (Delhi: Oxford University Press, 1982), pp. 364–76.

———'"Subaltern Studies" at Crossroads', *Economic and Political Weekly*, 21, 7 (1986), pp. 288–90.

Inden, Ronald, 'Forward to the Past', *Economy and Society*, 25, 2 (1966), pp. 290–98.

Ingram, P., 'Can the Settler Speak? Appropriating Subaltern Silence in Janet Frame's "The Carpathians"', *Cultural Critique*, 41 (Winter 1999), pp. 79–107.

Jackson, C., 'Women in Critical Realist Environmentalism: Subaltern to the Species?', *Economy and Society*, 26, 1 (1997), pp. 62–80.

Jalal, Ayesha, 'Secularists, Subalterns and the Stigma of "Communalism": Partition Historiography Revisited', *The Indian Economic and Social History Review*, 33, 1 (1996), pp. 93–103. Also published in *Modern Asian Studies*, 30, 3 (July 1996), pp. 681–9.

Kaviraj, Sudipta, 'On the Construction of Colonial Power: Structure, Discourse, Hegemony', in Dagmar Engels and Shula Marks, eds, *Contesting Colonial Hegemony: State & Society in Africa and India* (London: British Academic Press, 1994), pp. 19–54.

Kumar, Kapil, *et al.*, 'Subaltern Studies III & IV: A Review Article', *Social Scientist*, 16, 3 (1988), pp. 3–40.

Larson, P. M., 'Capacities and Modes of Thinking: Intellectual Engagements and Subaltern Hegemony in the Early History of Malagasy Christianity', *American Historical Review*, 102, 4 (1997), pp. 969–1002.

Latin American Subaltern Studies Group, 'Founding Statement', *boundary 2*, 20:3, 1993, pp. 110–21.

Little, Daniel, 'Subaltern Studies and the Peasant World: The Case of China', http://www.facstaff.bucknell.edu/dlittle/subalt2.htm

Lloyd, David, 'Outside History: Irish New Histories and the "Subalternity Effect"', in Shahid Amin and Dipesh Chakrabarty, eds, *Subaltern Studies IX* (Delhi: Oxford University Press, 1996), pp. 261–77.

Lochan, Rajiv, 'A Medley for Subalterns – Review Article', *Contributions to Indian Sociology*, 21, 1 (1997), pp. 225–37.

Loomba, A., 'Dead Women Tell No Tales. Issues of Female Subjectivity, Subaltern Agency and Tradition in Colonial and Post-Colonial Writings on Widow Immolation in India', *History Workshop Journal*, N.23 (1996), pp. 209–27.

Ludden, David, ed., *Reading Subaltern Studies: Perspectives on History, Society and Culture in South Asia* (Delhi: Oxford University Press, forthcoming).

Mallon, Florencia, 'The Promise and Dilemmas of Subaltern Studies: Perspectives from Latin American History', *American Historical Review*, 99, 5 (1994), pp. 1491–515.

Masselos, Jim, 'The Dis/Appearance of Subalterns: A Reading of a Decade of Subaltern Studies', *South Asia* (New Series), 15, 1 (June 1992), pp. 105–25.

Mathew, T. J., 'Subalterns and Subalterness', *Economic and Political Weekly*, 31, 26 (1996), pp. 1694–5.

McGuire, John, 'The Making of a New History for India: Subaltern Studies', *ASAA Review*, 10, 1 (1986), pp. 115–22.

Moore, D. S., 'Subaltern Struggles and the Politics of Place: Remapping Resistance in Zimbabwe's Eastern Highlands', *Cultural Anthropology*, 13, 3 (1998), pp. 344–81.

Mukherjee, Mridula, 'Peasant Resistance and Peasant Consciousness in Colonial India: "Subalterns" and Beyond', *Economic and Political Weekly*, 23, 41 (1988), pp. 2109–20; and *Economic and Political Weekly*, 23, 42 (1988), pp. 2174–85.

Mukund, Kanakalatha, 'Elites vs. Subalterns or Ideology vs. Methodology?', *Economic and Political Weekly*, 31, 28 (1996), p. 1881.

Nag, Sajal, 'Peasant and the Raj: Study of a Subaltern Movement in Assam (1893–1894)', *North-East Quarterly*, 2, 1 (1984), pp. 24–36.

Nelson, D. M., 'Crucifixion Stories, the 1869 Caste War of Chiapas, and Negative Consciousness: A Disruptive Subaltern Study', *American Ethnologist*, 24, 2 (1977), pp. 331–54.

Nugent, D., 'The Morality of Modernity and the Travails of Tradition.

Nationhood and the Subaltern in Northern Peru', *Critique of Anthropology*, 18, 1 (1998), pp. 7–33.

O'Hanlon, Rosalind, 'Cultures of Rule, Communities of Resistance: Gender, Discourse and Tradition in Recent South Asian Historiographies', *Social Analysis*, 25 (1989), pp. 94–115.

Ortner, Sherry, 'Resistance and the Problem of Ethnographic Refusal', *Comparative Studies in Society and History*, 37, 1 (1995), pp. 173–93.

Palaversich, D., 'Postmodernism, Postcolonialism and the Recuperation of the Subaltern History', *Chasqui – Revista de Literatura Latinoamericana*, 24, 1 (1995), pp. 3–15.

Pandey, Gyanendra, 'In Defense of the Fragment: Writing About Hindu–Muslim Riots in India Today', *Economic and Political Weekly*, 26, 11–12 (1991), pp. 559–72. Also published in *Representations*, 37 (1992), pp. 27–55.

——— 'Modes of History Writing: New Hindu History of Ayodhya', *Economic and Political Weekly*, 29, 25 (1994), pp. 1523–8.

——— 'The Appeal of Hindu History', in Vasuda Dalmia and H. von Stietencron, eds, *Representing Hinduism* (New Delhi: Sage Publications, 1995), pp. 369–88.

Pandian, M. S. S., 'Culture and Subaltern Consciousness – An Aspect of MGR Phenomenon', *Economic and Political Weekly*, 24, 30 (1989), pp. PE62–PE68.

——— 'Beyond Colonial Crumbs: Cambridge School, Identity Politics and Dravidian Movement(s)', *Economic and Political Weekly*, 30, 7–8 (1995), pp. 385–91.

——— 'Kumbakonam Encounters Subaltern Studies', *Economic and Political Weekly*, 32, 8 (1997), pp. 398–9.

Patnaik, Arun K., 'Gramsci's Concept of Common Sense: Towards a Theory of Subaltern Consciousness in Hegemony Processes', *Economic and Political Weekly*, 23, 5 (1988), pp. PE2–PE10.

Perusek, Darshan, 'Subaltern Consciousness and the Historiography of the Indian Rebellion of 1857', *Novel*, 25, 3 (1992), pp. 286–301. Also published in *Economic and Political Weekly*, 28, 37 (1993), pp. 1931–6.

Pinch, William R., 'Same Difference in India and Europe', *History & Theory*, 38, 3 (1999), pp. 389–407.

Pocock, J. G. A., 'The Politics of History: The Subaltern and the Subversive', *Journal of Political Philosophy*, 6, 3 (1998), pp. 219–34.

Prakash, Gyan, 'Postcolonial Criticism and Indian Historiography', *Social Text*, 31/32 (1992), pp. 8–19.

——— 'Subaltern Studies as Postcolonial Criticism', *American Historical Review*, 99, 5 (1994), pp. 1475–90.

———'Who's Afraid of Postcoloniality?', *Social Text* 49, 14, 4 (1996), pp. 187–203.

Rabasa, José, 'Of Zapatismo: Reflections on the Folkloric and the Impossible in a Subaltern Insurrection', in Lisa Lowe and David Lloyd, eds, *The Politics of Culture in the Shadow of Capital* (Durham: Duke University Press, 1997), pp. 399–431.

———'Historical and Epistemological Limits in Subaltern Studies', *Interventions*, 1, 2 (1999), pp. 255–64.

Rabasa, José, Sanjines, J. and Carr, R., eds, 'Subaltern Studies in the Americas', *dispositio/n*, 19, 46 (1994).

Ranger, Terence, 'Subaltern Studies and "Social History"', *South African Review of Books* (February/May 1990), pp. 8–10.

Rappaport, Joanne, 'Fictive Foundations: National Romances and Subaltern Ethnicity in Latin America', *History Workshop Journal*, 34 (1992), pp. 119–31.

Sarkar, Sumit, 'The Fascism of the Sangha Parivar', *Economic and Political Weekly*, 27, 5 (1993), pp. 163–7.

Satyamurthy, T. V., 'Indian Peasant Historiography: A Critical Perspective on Ranajit Guha's Work', *Journal of Peasant Studies*, 18, 1 (1990), pp. 93–141.

Schwarz, Henry, 'Subaltern Studies: Radical History in the Metaphoric Mode', in *Writing Cultural History in Colonial and Postcolonial India* (Philadelphia: University of Pennsylvania Press, 1997), pp. 128–61.

Sen, Ashok, 'Subaltern Studies: Capital, Class and Community', in Ranajit Guha, ed., *Subaltern Studies V* (Delhi: Oxford University Press, 1987), pp. 203–35.

Singh, Lata, 'Subaltern Historiographic Critique of Colonialist and Nationalist Discourses', *Indian Historical Review*, 21, 1–2 (July 1994–January 1995), pp. 99–112.

Singh, Sangeeta, *et al.*, 'Subaltern Studies II: A Review Article', *Social Scientist*, 12, 8 (1984), pp. 3–41.

Sivaramakrishnan, K., 'Situating the Subaltern: History and Anthropology in the Subaltern Studies Project', *Journal of Historical Sociology*, 8, 4 (December 1995), pp. 395–429.

Spivak, Gayatri Chakravorty, 'Can the Subaltern Speak? Speculations on Widow Sacrifice', *Wedge*, 7/8 (Winter/Spring 1985), pp. 120–30. Also published in Gary Nelson and Lawrence Grossberg, eds, *Marxism and the Interpretation of Culture* (Urbana: University of Illinois Press, 1988), pp. 271–313; and, Patrick Williams and Laura Chrisman, eds, *Colonial Discourse and Post-Colonial Theory: A Reader* (New York: Harvester/Wheatsheaf, 1994), pp. 66–111.

———'Subaltern Studies: Deconstructing Historiography', in Ranajit Guha, ed., *Subaltern Studies IV* (Delhi: Oxford University Press 1985), pp. 330–63. Also published in *Selected Subaltern Studies* (New York: Oxford University Press, 1988), pp. 3–32.

———'Subaltern Talk: Interview with the Editors', in Donna Landry and Gerald MacLean, eds, *The Spivak Reader* (London and New York: Routledge, 1996), pp. 287–308.

Stein, Burton, 'A Decade of Historical Efflorescence', *South Asia Research*, 10, 2 (1990), pp. 125–38.

Subramanyam, R., 'Class, Caste, and Performance in Subaltern Feminist Film Theory and Praxis – An Analysis of "Rudaali"', *Cinema Journal*, 35, 3 (1996), pp. 34–51.

Thomas, Brook, 'Parts Related to Wholes and the Nature of Subaltern Opposition', *Modern Language Quarterly*, 55 (1994), pp. 77–106.

Wald, A., 'The Subaltern Speaks', *Monthly Review*, 43, 11 (April 1992), pp. 17–29.

Washbrook, David, 'Orients and Occidents: Colonial Discourse Theory and the Historiography of the British Empire', in Robin Winks, ed., *Oxford History of the British Empire, Volume V: Historiography* (Oxford: Oxford University Press, 1999).

Winant, Howard, 'Gayatri Spivak on the Politics of the Subaltern', *Socialist Review*, 20, 3 (1990), pp. 81–97.

Yadav, Yogendra, 'Whither Subaltern Studies?', *New Quest*, 76 (1989), pp. 245–50.

Acknowledgements

I thank Vinita Chaturvedi, Tom Mertes and Ayanna Yonemura for their research assistance. I have also benefited from the resources of *Subaltern Studies – A Bibliography*

(http://www.lib.virginia.edu/area-studies/South Asia/Ideas/subalternBib.html).

Note

The 'Select Bibliography' is divided into two sections. The first includes bibliographic references which are organized chronologically from *Subaltern Studies* and selected volumes associated with the series. A comprehensive listing of monographs by members of the Subaltern collective is provided in *Subaltern Studies – A Bibliography* [see above acknowledgement for citation]. The second section includes a list of criticism, essays, and discussions around the Subaltern Studies project between 1982 and 1999, as well as a selection of references on 'subalternity' in a global and comparative framework.

Acknowledgements

'On Some Aspects of the Historiography of Colonial India', by Ranajit Guha, was first published in *Subaltern Studies I: Writings on South Asian History and Society* (Delhi: Oxford University Press, 1982), pp. 1–8.

'The Nation and Its Peasants', by Partha Chatterjee, was first published as chapter 8 of *The National and Its Fragments: Colonial and Postcolonial Histories* (Princeton: Princeton University Press, 1993), pp. 158–72.

'Gramsci and Peasant Subalternity in India', by David Arnold, was first published in *The Journal of Peasant Studies*, vol. 11, no. 4 (July 1984), pp. 155–77.

'"The Making of the Working Class": E. P. Thompson and Indian History', by Rajnarayan Chandavarkar, was first published in *History Workshop Journal*, issue 42 (1997), pp. 177–96.

'Recovering the Subject: *Subaltern Studies* and Histories of Resistance in Colonial South Asia', by Rosalind O'Hanlon, was first published in *Modern Asian Studies*, vol. 22, no. 1 (1988), pp. 189–224.

'Rallying Around the Subaltern', by C. A. Bayly, was first published in *The Journal of Peasant Studies*, vol. 16, no. 1 (1988), pp. 110–20.

'Moral Economists, Subalterns, New Social Movements, and the (Re-) Emergence of a (Post-) Modernized (Middle) Peasant', by Tom Brass, was first published in *The Journal of Peasant Studies*, vol. 18, no. 2 (1991), pp. 173–205.

'Writing Post-Orientalist Histories of the Third World: Perspectives from Indian Historiography', by Gyan Prakash, was first published in *Comparative Studies in Society and History*, vol. 32, no. 2 (April 1990), pp. 383–408.

'After Orientalism: Culture, Criticism and Politics in the Third World', by Rosalind O'Hanlon and David Washbrook, was first published in *Comparative Studies in Society and History*, vol. 32, no. 1 (January 1992), pp. 141–67.

'Can the "Subaltern" Ride? A Reply to O'Hanlon and Washbrook', by Gyan Prakash, was first published in *Comparative Studies in Society and History*, vol. 34, no. 1 (January 1992), pp. 168–84.

'Orientalism Revisited: Saidian Frameworks in the Writing of Modern Indian History', by Sumit Sarkar, was first published in *Oxford Literary Review*, vol. 16, nos. 1–2 (1994), pp. 205–24.

'Radical Histories and Question of Enlightenment Rationalism: Some Recent Critiques of *Subaltern Studies*', by Dipesh Chakrabarty, was first published in *Economic and Political Weekly*, vol. 30, no. 14 (8 April 1995), pp. 751–59.

'Voices from the Edge: The Struggle to Write Subaltern Histories', by Gyanendra Pandey, was published in *Ethnos*, vol. 60, nos. 3–4 (1995), pp. 224–42.

'The Decline of the Subaltern in *Subaltern Studies*', by Sumit Sarkar, was first published as chapter 3 of *Writing Social History* (Delhi: Oxford University Press, 1996), pp. 82–108.

The editor and publisher gratefully acknowledge permission to reproduce the essays in this volume.

Index